WYOMING

A 20th Century History of its Citizens, Businesses & Institutions

BY VICTORIA MURPHY

Author and Photo Editor: Victoria Murphy

Publisher: C.E. Parks

Editor-in-Chief: Lori M. Parks

VP/National Sales Manager: Ray Spagnuolo

VP/Corporate Development: Bart Barica

Development Director: Chuck Stubbs

CFO: Randall Peterson

Production Manager: Deborah Sherwood

Managing Editor: Betsy Baxter Blondin

Project Editor: Renee Kim

Coordinating Editors: Betsy Lelja, Elizabeth Lex,

Sara Rufner, Adriane Wessels, John Woodward

Profile Writers: Suzanne B. Bopp, John Clayton,

Sue Collier, Julianne Couch, Jeni Dalen, Jay Davis,

Dugan, Carole Eklund, Larry Haise, Geraldine Minick,

Allison Rainey, David Robatcek, Samara Sramek, Sonia Weiss

Art Director: Gina Mancini

Project Designer: Susie Passons

Production Staff: Jason Atzert, Jeff Caton, Sean Gates,

Andrea Giorgio, Brad Hartman, Dave Hermstead, Jay Kennedy,

John Leyva, Barry Miller, Norm Pruitt, Chris Rivera, Steve Trainor

Project Coordinators: Jan Warriner, Conley Stroud

Administration Manager: Ellen Ruby

Administration Staff: Juan Diaz, Emily Knopp, Mayka Penner,

Scott Reid, Patrick Rucker, Cory Sottek

Published by

Heritage Media Corp.

6354 Corte del Abeto, Suite B

Carlsbad, California 92009

www.heritagemedia.com

Produced in cooperation with the Wyoming Citizen of the Century Program

and sponsored by the American Heritage Center, University of Wyoming.

Printed by Heritage Media Corp. in the United States of America

Cover, endsheet and front matter photos courtesy of AHC Collection.

Contents

Table of

Acknowledgments
Page 8

Foreword
Page 10

Chapter One
AGRICULTURE
Page 12

Chapter Two
BUSINESS
Page 22

Chapter Three
EDUCATION
Page 32

Chapter Four
FINE & PERFORMING ARTS
Page 48

Chapter Five
GOVERNMENT & COMMUNITY SERVICE
Page 64

Chapter Six
HEALTHCARE, SCIENCE & TECHNOLOGY
Page 94

Chapter Seven
MILITARY
Page 112

Chapter Eight
MINERALS, OIL & GAS
Page 128

Chapter Nine
RELIGION
Page 140

Chapter Ten
SPORTS
Page 152

Chapter Eleven
PARTNERS IN WYOMING
Page 166

Bibliography
Page 294

Acknowledgments

The Wyoming Citizen of the Century Program would like to acknowledge the following individuals who helped to make this publication possible:

Win Hickey, our Citizen Council Chair. The Citizen program was Win's idea and since the beginning she has worked to see the project through to completion. Thanks to her persuasive efforts we received the support we needed to continue our program. Honorary Co-Chair, Governor Jim Geringer, who provided such generous financial support. Honorary Co-Chair Senator Al Simpson, who lent his name to our efforts. The former and present members of the Citizen Council, Reverend Carl Beavers, Marlene Brodrick, Judy Catchpole, Bill Dubois, Martin Greller, Don Hunton, Lisa Kinney, Gordon Mickelson, John & Mary Ostlund, Paul Roach, Terry Roark, Phil Roberts, Peg Shreve, Tom Stroock, Jane Sullivan, Lili Turnell and Charles Wing.

All of the volunteer members of the selection committees. The Associates Board of the American Heritage Center, for sponsoring the program. The President of the University of Wyoming, for his generous support. The members of Phi Alpha Theta who volunteered for the fact-checking project, Richard George, Deirdre E. Hoffer, Susan G. Horan, Kelly A. Jacobson, Benjamin S. Kirven, Clark Miller, Edourd D. Richard, Jurgita Saltanaviciute, Frank Van Nuys, Maria C. Vita and Deanna Williams. The staff of the Wyoming State Archives, for their assistance in locating information and photographs. Paul Jacques of Jacques Photography, for allowing us to reproduce his work. All of the individuals, too numerous to list, who submitted nominations and assisted in locating biographical data and photographs.

The author would like to thank the Staff of the American Heritage Center for their patience and support. Mike Devine, Director of the AHC, and Rick Ewig, Acting Director in his absence, were instrumental in bringing this publication to completion. Sally Sutherland, Executive Staff Assistant, has been especially generous with her time. The staff of the Reading Room, particularly Carol Bowers, worked above and beyond the call of duty in tracking down information. Daniel M. Davis, Photo Archivist, and Rick Walters, Photographic Technician, deserve special recognition for their work in locating and reproducing the photographs which appear in this book.

Finally, the author would like to thank the people of Wyoming, past and present, whose dedication to their state and preserving its history helped to make this project a reality.

Laramie, Wyoming
April, 1999

Foreword

The Citizen of the Century Program has given all of us an opportunity to learn about many people who have made significant contributions to Wyoming during the 20th century. This book contains more than 100 biographies of such individuals who have suffered hardships and enjoyed Wyoming's many benefits. By reading about their lives and understanding what they accomplished, we gain a clearer vision of what Wyoming has been, what it is today, and perhaps even a glimpse of where we might be heading in the years to come. The Citizen of the Century Program also prompts us to reflect on those less known individuals, perhaps our neighbors and friends, who have contributed to Wyoming and its way of life.

When I travel around the state I often see old, deserted cabins. I wonder who settled on that land, why they chose that location, if their story was one of success or tragedy, if the family is still in the state or had to leave. The 1890 federal census concluded that the frontier was closed, that there was nowhere else to homestead in the country. We in Wyoming know that was not true. The Big Horn Basin was still to be settled, as were other parts of the state. In fact, many people homesteaded in Wyoming during the 1920s, only to face persistent droughts and other formidable obstacles. By remembering these hearty souls and their efforts we acknowledge their many contributions.

The Citizen of the Century Program has recognized many individuals in the areas of religion, government service and community activism, sports, fine and performing arts, the military, minerals industry, healthcare, business and education. I hope you will enjoy reading about the many who were nominated, but I trust you also realize it is inevitable that such a program and book cannot include all the people who are worthy of recognition. So, as you read this book also think about the coal miners in Rock Springs, Kemmerer, and the Powder River Basin and what they have meant to Wyoming, the teachers who taught your children and grandchildren, the railroad workers and highway engineers who assisted with the state's transportation needs, the journalists who kept us informed about important issues, the many ranchers and farmers who persevered, those who volunteered their time to the many boards necessary for the running of all of our communities, and those who preserved our history so that future generations will appreciate where Wyoming has been during the past 100 years.

It is my hope that the Citizen of the Century Program and this book will not only provide information about our past to our children, but that it will provide them with inspiration to help them deal with the future challenges which will face Wyoming during the 21st century.

Rick Ewig
American Heritage Center
University of Wyoming

CHAPTER ONE AGRICULTURE

Manville Kendrick

Ken Kirkbride

Lester W. Maxfield

James Mickelson

Dean T. Prosser Jr.

Jack T. Turnell

(Top left) *Courtesy of Wyoming State Archives.*
(Top right) Photo by Charles Belden, Shoshone Dam, c. 1900 *Courtesy of AHC Collection.*
(Bottom left) Photo by Charles Belden, Pitchfork Ranch, c. 1920 *Courtesy of AHC Collection.*
(Bottom right) Photo by Charles Belden, Pitchfork Ranch, c. 1920 *Courtesy of AHC Collection.*

INTRODUCTION

Since railroads brought the first settlers to Wyoming, agriculture, both ranching and farming, has played a significant role in the state's development. Cattle rose to prominence first, but sheep were not far behind. Well represented by the powerful and influential Wyoming Stock Growers Association (WSGA), by the end of the 19th century grazing agriculture was established as a primary segment of Wyoming's economy.

At the dawn of the 20th century men like Stephen Covey came to Wyoming, attracted by the promise of extensive grazing lands. Covey and his brother, Almon, acquired several properties near Cokeville in Lincoln County. The Coveys built a successful ranching operation with 60,000 sheep, registered Hereford cattle and horses and they raised their own grain and hay.

Remaining true to Wyoming's title of the Equality State, it was not only men but also women who played a part in ranching. Susan Jane Quealy operated a cattle and sheep ranch in Shirley Basin. Quealy was a member of the Wyoming Wool Growers Association. She became the first women elected to the Wyoming Stock Growers Association and was the only women to serve on the Executive Committee.

Agriculture in Wyoming was originally seen as an adjunct to the livestock industry, supplying necessary hay and feed. But traditional crop cultivation, spurred on by the promises of irrigation and advances in dry farming, soon earned a place in the state's economy. In the early part of the 20th century a conscious effort was made to increase the role of farming in the agricultural economy, and by 1910 the number of farm and ranch units had nearly doubled.

Throughout the state's history, both farmers and ranchers have had to contend with one commodity that is always in short supply, water. The state has needed both irrigation and reclamation projects to ensure the survival of farmers and ranchers. During the 20th century, developments in both of these areas have made the continued success of Wyoming's agricultural economy possible.

Wyoming's farmers and ranchers met the challenges necessitated by the onset of both world wars, increasing their production to meet the nation's wartime needs. Since the 1940s, agriculture and livestock have remained among the state's foremost industries. The hard work of people like Annie Hines and Katherine Edwards has played a vital role in maintaining our state's agrarian traditions. Annie Hines established a sheep ranch near Gillette with her husband, John Dwight Hines. After his death she continued to operate the ranch and eventually passed it on to her children. Katherine Edwards worked for many years as an Agricultural Extension Agent in Big Horn and Sheridan Counties, and preserved the homestead established by her grandfather near Centennial.

Today, ranching and farming remain a mainstay of Wyoming's economy. This has been made possible by the work of men like Dave True. True's innovative approach to ranching was the key to his success. He acquired extensive ranch lands, farm and feeding pens and eventually feed lots. To support this growth, True eventually branched out into farming, producing crops to feed his cattle.

Today Wyoming's agrarian traditions contribute not only to the state's economy but also provide something more intangible. The lifestyle that Wyomingites enjoy — one of open spaces and western flavor — as well as the state's cowboy image — can all be attributed to the agricultural legacy.

MANVILLE KENDRICK
1900-1992

Manville Kendrick was born on July 20, 1900, in Sheridan, Wyoming. He was the only child of Senator John Benjamin Kendrick and Eula Wulfjen Kendrick and heir to the Kendrick Cattle Company. Kendrick's early years were spent on the family-owned OW Ranch, where he was educated by his mother. In 1909, his family moved to Sheridan and Kendrick began attending public schools.

The family moved to Cheyenne in 1914, when the elder Kendrick was elected governor. In the fall of 1915, Manville Kendrick began attending the Philips-Exeter Academy in New Hampshire, graduating in 1918 and enrolling in Harvard. During World War I he served in the Army Cadet Corps. Kendrick received a bachelor's degree from Harvard in government in 1922. He later attended Ames Agricultural College in Iowa.

During his visits to Washington D.C., where his father was serving as a senator, Kendrick made the acquaintance of one the capital's most eligible debutantes, the daughter of the surgeon general. Manville Kendrick married Clara Diana Cumming in 1929 in the Bethlehem Chapel of the Cathedral of St. Peter and Paul. Their wedding was considered the

social event of the year. In attendance at the reception at the Washington Club were First Lady Grace Coolidge, presidential cabinet members, numerous congressmen and senators and representatives of many foreign governments.

After a honeymoon cruise through the Panama Canal, the couple moved to the Kendrick family home, Trail End, in Sheridan. They lived in the guest wing until 1960, when they moved into a home of their own. The Kendricks had two sons, John Benjamin Kendrick II and Hugh Smith Cumming Kendrick, who died tragically at the age of 18 after suffering a pulmonary embolism.

After graduating from Harvard, Kendrick began working for the Kendrick Cattle Company, taking over as manager in 1937. Kendrick became an advocate for the cattle industry, dedicating his time not only to his own interests but also to organizations aimed at promoting the livestock business. He was elected president of the Wyoming-Montana Livestock Protective Association in 1940. Kendrick was later elected president of the Wyoming Stockgrowers Association and served on the executive committee of the American National Cattleman's Association.

Kendrick was active in business and the community. He was a director of a Sheridan bank and the Federal Reserve Bank in Oklahoma, in addition to serving as an officer of several Sheridan businesses. Kendrick was a founding member of the National Cowboy Hall of Fame and during the 1970s he served as member of the board of trustees. Kendrick was also appointed to the Wyoming Natural Resources Board. He was a member of the Elks Lodge and the American Legion and was a congregate at St. Peter's Episcopal Church in Sheridan. He remained as president of the Kendrick Cattle Company until the late 1980s, when the ranches were sold.

Manville Kendrick died in September of 1992, at the age of 92. During his lifetime Kendrick had seen displacement of cattle barons by cattle corporations. For some people, his death signified the passing of the era of the great western cattle empires. Admired by all who knew him for his gentlemanly ways, Kendrick represented the ideal of the Wyoming cattleman.

KEN KIRKBRIDE
1920-

Returning to Wyoming in 1945, Kirkbride joined the Harding and Kirkbride (H & K) Livestock Company. Formed in 1924, today the H & K has holdings in Laramie, Goshen, Albany, Platte and Carbon counties, with more than 5,000 head of cattle.

Kirkbride, an active participant in the ranching community, served the Wyoming Stockgrowers Association (WSGA) as a member of the executive committee from 1967-1979 and was president from 1981-1983. In his role as a member of the Executive Committee of the WSGA and the Wyoming Livestock Board (1973-1985), he supported the development of a statewide program to protect Wyoming cattle from scabies. During Kirkbride's term on the Wyoming Livestock Board, the practice of issuing custom range permits, which provides ranchers the ability to graze cattle between different Wyoming counties without brand inspection, was begun. Kirkbride was also a board member of the National Cattlemen's Association (NCA) from 1979 to 1985. During his tenure with the NCA, Kirkbride supported the development of the NCA Beef Check Off Program, in which members pay a charge for each head of cattle sold to provide revenue for beef advertising programs.

Kirkbride married Shirley Beeson in 1942. The couple has three sons, all of whom are involved in the family ranching business. The Kirkbrides have lived in Cheyenne since 1972 and are active community members, serving as the honorary chairs of the 1994 United Medical Center Foundation Campaign, "Denim & Diamonds V." Mr. Kirkbride is also a past president of the Cheyenne Rotary Club and the Laramie County School District. Kirkbride was a founder of Security First Bank and now serves as a director.

Ken Kirkbride's career represents the continuation of the state's ranching tradition into the 20th century. Courtesy of Kirkbride Family Collection.

Ken Kirkbride, a third generation rancher, was born in Cheyenne on November 18, 1920, the only child of Dan and Peggy Harding Kirkbride. Kirkbride attended high school in Laramie and Cheyenne, graduating from Cheyenne's Central High School. He attended the University of Wyoming and received a bachelor's degree in agriculture in 1942. Kirkbride was a member of the United States Army during World War II. He served in Australia and New Guinea as an officer in the 522 Engineer Boat and Shore Company, and commanded the company in the Philippines and Korea.

LESTER W. MAXFIELD
1912-1993

Lester W. Maxfield was born near Cimarron, Kansas, on July 2, 1912. His parents were Charles and Daisy Bahling Maxfield. He was raised on his family's small farming/ranching operation in southwest Kansas. Growing up, he attended local schools in Cimarron and Garden City, and learned first hand about the uncertainties, such as weather and market conditions, that all farmers and ranchers face on a daily basis. Maxfield and his family worked hard to make their operation a success, but ultimately the combined forces of the Depression and the Great Dust Bowl caused them to lose their home.

Maxfield was able to attend to University of Kansas, graduating with a degree in accounting. His first job, as an auditor and assistant general manager with a telephone company based in Newton, Iowa, resulted in his transfer to Scottsbluff, Nebraska. It was there that he met, courted and married Jean Halley, daughter of T.C. Halley, a local sheep farmer, despite stiff competition from other suitors. In 1941, Maxfield, who often said he'd "rather own and operate a peanut stand than work

for someone else," left his job and secured a loan to buy the Union Livestock Commission Company, one of two livestock salebarns in Scottsbluff, Nebraska.

In 1949, Maxfield parlayed his investment in Scottsbluff to secure the necessary funds to purchase the Torrington Livestock Commission Company and moved his family to eastern Wyoming. When Maxfield first purchased the Torrington Company, total annual sales were between 25,000 and 35,000 head of cattle. Under his management, the Torrington Livestock Commission Company, with annual sales in excess of 300,000 head, leapt to among the top five cattle auction markets in the United States and became the second largest employer in Goshen County. Whereas Wyoming had previously ranked in the bottom half of the states among number of cattle, this newly created market meant better prices for cattle producers, not only within the state, but also throughout the region. By 1970, Maxfield's firm was handling 13 percent of the total Wyoming cattle crop on an annual basis.

Maxfield maintained an interest in several other businesses, including the Dalhart Livestock Commission Company, which included a ranching and feeding operation. He was also a partner in Scottsbluff Ice and Storage. Maxfield was president of the American Cattle Company in Torrington, the Wyoming Land and Cattle Company and the Maxfield Ranching Company, which operated farm and ranching enterprises throughout Goshen County. He also owned an interest in the Spring Creek Ranch and was a partner in the Wheatland Cattle Company. Maxfield was a director of the Stockgrowers Bank in Wheatland, Wyoming, and served as chairman of the board of the Western Reserve Life Insurance Company, based in Casper, Wyoming.

A farmer and rancher in his own right, Maxfield also partnered with ranchers throughout the country. He was able to build his business by virtue of his personal experience with ranchers and ranching. Maxfield traveled an average of 60,000 miles every year, visiting ranchers and buying calves. He took great pride in the claim that he had visited every ranch in the state of Wyoming and knew, and counted among his friends, most of the ranchers in his generation. Maxfield was known as a man of his word, who dealt fairly with ranchers. He operated his business by handshake.

Maxfield was an active participant in his community, and for many years he sponsored 4-H and youth athletic activities within Goshen County. He was a long-time member of the Wyoming Stockgrowers Association and served on the Wyoming Highway Commission. A supporter of the University of Wyoming, Maxfield sponsored several scholarships and was a member of the Dean's Club. Maxfield was honored as an Outstanding Friend of the Wyoming Cowbelles in 1985 and the following year he was selected as Agri-Businessman of the Year by the Wyoming Chamber of Commerce.

Maxfield retired from the Torrington Livestock Commission in 1989. Before his retirement he oversaw the creation of an umbrella corporation, Torrington Livestock Market, Inc., under which the Torrington Livestock Commission and the Stockman's Livestock Auction merged. Maxfield saw the merger as good business deal, which would allow for better coverage and lower overhead costs.

During his four decades in the cattle auction business, Maxfield witnessed many changes. When he first started most cattle were shipped to major markets, such as Omaha, by train. In order for his business to prosper, he had to persuade ranchers to sell their cattle locally. This in turn caused the moving of major locations for meat packing plants and commercial feeding areas to the western states of Wyoming, Colorado and Utah. Maxfield was an instrumental figure in the reconfiguration of Wyoming's cattle market. Lester Maxfield died in Torrington on June 6, 1993. He is survived by five sons and 20 grandchildren.

JAMES MICKELSON
1903-1990

James Mickelson was born August 20, 1903, in Salt Lake City, Utah, to James and Mildred Avery Mickelson. James Mickelson, Sr. immigrated to the United States from Denmark and was instrumental in the development of Wyoming's Big Piney community. He established the Circle C Ranch, commonly known as the Leifer Ranch. James Mickelson was raised on the family ranch in Big Piney. Mickelson attended school in Sublette County through the 11th grade. He also attended business college in St. Joseph, Missouri, for one year. But the most important education he received was from his father, who taught him to carry on the family's ranching tradition.

After his father's death in 1921, Mickelson managed the family ranch, with the help of his partner, James Jensen. In 1928, Mickelson purchased the 5,000-acre 67 Ranch from A.W. Swan, including water and mineral rights, as well as the "67" brand. As he expanded his ranching operations, his holdings eventually covered lands in Middle Piney, North Piney and Cottonwood and Horse creeks.

James Mickelson was active in both the public service and business arenas. Mickelson served as a Sublette County Commissioner for 12 years and he was also a member and chairman of the Big Piney School Board for eight years. He was a trustee for the Congregational Community Church for 25 years. Mickelson served as a state representative for Sublette County from 1949-1950, in addition to his tenure on the Taylor Grazing Board and the State Bureau of Land Management Board. An active Mason and member of the Korean Temple and Sublette Royal Arch and Commandery, Mickelson was a 50-year member of the Big Piney Lodge #47, the Wyoming Consistory and the Big Piney Chapter #42 Order of the Eastern Star. He also donated the present building which houses the Masonic Organizations of Big Piney. Mickelson was president and chairman of the board of Big Piney State Bank for more than 50 years, and served as a director of the First National Bank of Kemmerer.

James Mickelson married Mae Elizabeth Stewart in Salt Lake City on June 24, 1922. The couple eventually had four children, three of whom survived their father. Mickelson and his family moved to the 67 Ranch in 1928 and he lived there until his death on December 22, 1990. Mickelson is remembered as a kind and giving man, who cherished his family above all. Mickelson lived according to the ideal that the most important things were the life a man led and the example he set. Through his work, as a cattleman and member of his community, Mickelson left a legacy that illustrates two of Wyoming's defining characteristics, the belief in hard work and individual responsibility.

DEAN T. PROSSER JR.
1917-

Dean T. Prosser Jr., a third generation Wyomingite, was born in Cheyenne, Wyoming, on May 10, 1917. An only child, his parents were Dean T. Prosser Sr. and Dorothy Riner Prosser, who owned a Hereford ranch in Albany County, where Prosser spent his childhood. Prosser's early education took place at the Pumpkin Vine School in Tie Siding, Wyoming. After completing the sixth grade there, he attended the Prep School at the University of Wyoming for the next two years. In 1929, his family purchased Chalk Bluffs Ranch near Cheyenne, where Prosser attended school, graduating from Cheyenne High School in 1934. Prosser continued his education at Colorado University in Boulder, earning a degree in business administration in 1939.

Prosser married Harriot Ann McSween in 1940. The couple eventually had two sons and one daughter. They settled on the family ranch, where Prosser assisted in his father's cattle operation, taking over management after his father's death in 1958.

In 1963, Prosser accepted the position of executive secretary of the Wyoming Stock Growers Association (WSGA,) which he held for more than 20 years. As executive secretary, and later as executive vice president, he worked with the American National Cattlemen's Association to change cattle import legislation to provide for quotas. In addition, he was in charge of Wyoming's brand inspection system, coordinating with over 150 brand inspectors in seven districts.

While working for the Stock Growers Association, Prosser ran for the Wyoming State Legislature and was elected on the Republican ticket in 1970. During his time in the legislature, he served as majority whip and on numerous committees, including Agriculture, Public Lands and Water Resources, and Mines and Minerals. The Department of Environmental Quality was established during his term as chairman of the Mines and Minerals Committee, and the Wyoming Mined Land Reclamation Act and the Wyoming Plant Siting Act became law.

Prosser also worked on issues relating to ranching while in the legislature. He sponsored the Wyoming Beef Council Act, which established a check-off system to collect money from ranchers to promote the sale of beef. He was instrumental in the legislature's decision to remove the ad valorem tax on livestock, saving ranchers up to $10 a year per head on livestock. Prosser also worked to improve brand inspection laws, helping to create a system that served as a model for other states. After being elected to six consecutive terms, Prosser retired from the legislature in 1983 and the following year he also left the WSGA. Prosser and his second wife, Gloria, whom he married after the death of his first wife, eventually moved to Green Valley, Arizona.

Prosser was honored in 1983 as a Northern International Livestock Exposition Hall of Fame member for his many contributions to agriculture. During his lifetime, Prosser saw ranching change from a strictly man-and-horse operation to mechanization, complete with semi-trucks to move cattle. He was quick to see that these developments meant changes for the industry's market, and was an early advocate for promotion. Prosser has also long supported a pro-active approach toward legislation affecting ranching, believing that the agricultural industry "can only survive by organizing and standing as one important voice." Having once said he knows and understands cattle, and loves to work with them, Prosser has taken his knowledge and applied it on a larger scale. By working to ensure the cattle industry meets the challenges of the 20th century, Prosser, a self described "cow-man," has helped to keep Wyoming's ranching tradition viable.

Dean T. Prosser Jr., through his work with WSGA, helped to modernize Wyoming's cattle industry.
Courtesy of Prosser Family Collection.

JACK TRACY TURNELL
1945-

Jack Tracy Turnell was born in Riverton, Wyoming, on November 13, 1945. Turnell attended local schools, graduating from Meeteetse High School. In 1965, Turnell married Frances Lili Turnell and the couple eventually had three daughters. After a stint in the oil fields, Turnell continued his education, attending Northwest Community College and later the University of Wyoming.

Turnell graduated in 1970 with a bachelor of science degree in Agricultural Education. In 1971, Turnell became general manager and president of the historic Pitchfork Ranch, working with his wife, Lili, to continue her family's heritage at the ranch. During his tenure at the 120,000-acre ranch, Turnell managed a successful business enterprise while remaining sensitive to environmental issues.

In 1987, Turnell was given the Chevron Conservation Award in recognition of his work as caretaker for a colony of black-footed ferrets. The ferrets, once believed to be extinct, were discovered on Turnell's Pitchfork Ranch in the early 1980s. In 1981, Turnell became a member of the newly created Wyoming State Black Footed Ferret Advisory Team. He modified ranching and oil exploration and drilling activities in the ferret study area, and also allowed scientists and other interested parties access to the area where the ferrets are located. As part-owner of Polecat Productions, which specializes in wildlife documentary films, Turnell produced "The Mysterious Black Footed Ferret," a public television documentary on the ferrets aimed at promoting understanding of the importance of the animals and their rediscovery.

The discovery of the black-footed ferrets on the Pitchfork Ranch gave Turnell an enhanced appreciation for the possibilities of combining successful ranching with environmental awareness. He replaced his traditional Hereford cattle with Salers, a breed of cattle from south central France because the French breed causes less damage to riparian areas. By developing more water resources, Turnell was able not only to ease the pressure on existing streams, but also actually saw an improvement in meat production as a result of the lusher grasses. Between 1980 and 1991, beef production on the Pitchfork ranch grew by 300,000 pounds, demonstrating that ranching using sound environmental principles can increase profits.

Turnell is a promoter of ranching and participates in many organizations dedicated to promoting the industry. A past president of the Meeteetse Livestock Association, he is a long-time member of the Wyoming Stock Growers Association. Turnell also belongs to the National Cattleman's Association, is a past officer of the American Salers Association, and is a past member of the International Salers Federation Board of Directors.

Living with the heritage of the Pitchfork Ranch has given Turnell a keen interest in Wyoming history. In 1978, he co-authored *Brand of a Legend* with Bob Edgar. The following year, the collaboration was repeated with *Lady of A Legend*. Both of Turnell's books received the recognition of the Wyoming Historical Society as outstanding publications.

Turnell is in demand as a speaker to interested groups throughout the region by virtue of his reputation as a proponent of environmentally sound agricultural practices. A founding member of the Western States Riparian Association, he was president of the Wyoming Riparian Council from 1989 to 1991. Turnell serves on the Wyoming State Coordinated Resource Management Executive Committee, has been a member of the Wyoming Wise Use Council since 1990 and has served on the Board of Directors of the Institute for Environmental and Natural Resource Research and Policy since 1994. Turnell is past officer of the Wyoming Public Lands Council and he also served as director of the National Public Lands Council.

Turnell's efforts to promote eco-friendly ranching were recognized by the National Cattleman's Association with one of its first Environmental Stewardship Awards. In 1992, Turnell was the recipient of the Wyoming Stockgrowers Guardian of the Grasslands Award. He has also been honored for his work by the National Soil and Water Society, the Society for Range Management, the Bureau of Land Management and the United States Forest Service. Turnell's many awards stem from his work as a practitioner of Wyoming's agricultural tradition and his efforts as a pioneer in the field of environmental stewardship. In both respects he exemplifies the best of Wyoming's past and its future.

CHAPTER TWO BUSINESS

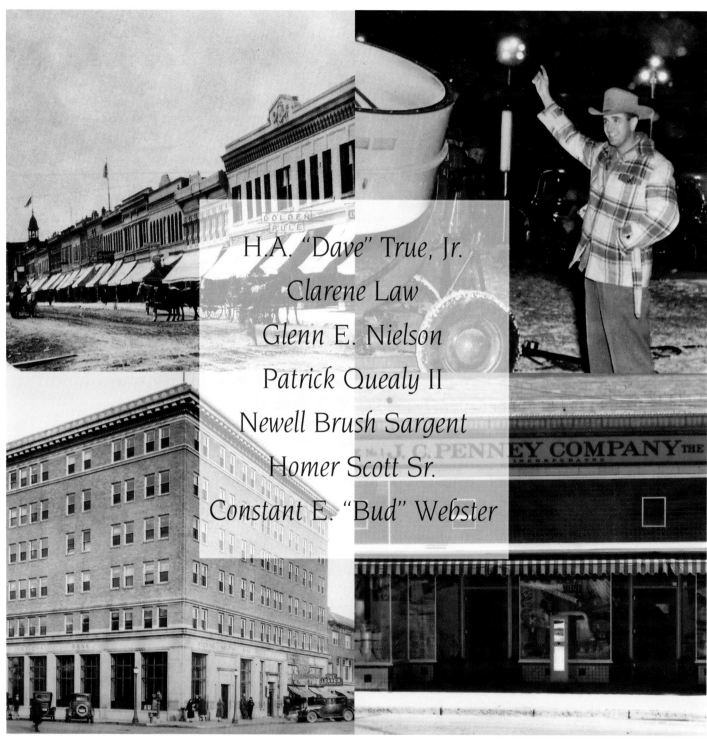

H.A. "Dave" True, Jr.

Clarene Law

Glenn E. Nielson

Patrick Quealy II

Newell Brush Sargent

Homer Scott Sr.

Constant E. "Bud" Webster

(Top left) Sheridan, c. 1900 *Courtesy of AHC Collection.*
(Top right) Bud Webster *Courtesy of Webster Family Collection.*
(Bottom left) Wyoming National Bank, Casper, c. 1920 *Courtesy of AHC Collection.*
(Bottom right) J.C. Penney Store, Green River, c. 1940 *Courtesy of Green River Historical Museum.*

INTRODUCTION

Business enterprises have played a vital role in Wyoming since the construction of the Union Pacific railroad led to the formation of the Wyoming Territory. Ambitious young men like F.E. Warren, who started as a clerk in another man's store and went on to become one of the richest men on the state, established Wyoming's reputation as a land of opportunity. James Cash Penny's introduction of chain store merchandising, in Kemmerer in 1902, carried this tradition into the 20th century.

Wyoming's abundant natural resources created different types of business opportunities on the eve of World War I. Fred Goodstein built a scrap metal business into a multifaceted business conglomerate including oil exploration operations and construction ventures. After World War II, development of resources played a vital role, attracting entrepreneurs to the state. Tom Stroock began his career as a businessman in the oil industry and went on to become president of his own oil and gas properties firm in Wyoming.

Wyoming also offered unique opportunities for women, as in the case of Clara Toppan. She graduated from the University of Wyoming in 1931 with a degree in accounting. After passing the CPA exam, becoming the first woman in Wyoming to become certified, Toppan established her own accounting firm in Jackson.

As the century progressed, Wyoming's economy, like the rest of the nation's, expanded to include new types of businesses. Visitors had always been attracted to Wyoming's natural beauty and many saw expanding tourism an as an opportunity for continued economic development. Frank Norris, who was appointed director of the Wyoming Travel Commission in 1963, accepted that challenge. Under his leadership the Wyoming Travel Commission achieved a national reputation for its creative promotions.

The history of business in Wyoming includes retail, service, and manufacturing operations, agricultural enterprises, oil and minerals industries, and tourism. All have played roles in the state's development. As the year 2000 approaches, each of these components continues to play a vital role in helping Wyoming meet the challenges of a new century.

H.A. "DAVE" TRUE, JR.
1915-1994

Dave True built a multifaceted business empire in Wyoming. Courtesy of True Family Collection.

Henry Alfonso "H.A." True, Jr. was born in Cheyenne, Wyoming, on June 12, 1915. His parents were Henry A. True, Sr., a civil engineer, and Anna Barbara Diemer True. He acquired his nickname, when at the age of four, inspired by the bible story of David and Goliath, he announced that in the future he would answer to "Dave." His family remained in Cheyenne until 1927 when they moved, briefly, to Florida and later to Colorado. In 1930, the family settled in Billings, Montana, where True graduated from high school.

True enrolled in the Civil Engineering School at Montana State College in Bozeman and received a degree in Industrial Engineering in 1937. The following

year, True married Jean Durland. The couple eventually had one daughter and three sons. After graduation, True had accepted a position with the Texas Oil Company (later Texaco), as oil field roustabout making less than $100 a month. True remained with Texaco for the next 11 years, learning the oil and gas business, and eventually rising to the position of superintendent of drilling and production in Wyoming.

In 1948, True accepted an offer to manage and become part owner in a one rig oil well drilling contractor business, Reserve Drilling Company, in Casper, Wyoming. True's new venture was not immediately successful, before he made his first strike he drilled nearly 100 dry holes. He persevered and by 1951 the company had increased its number of rigs to five. True, in partnership with Douglas S. Brown, eventually bought out the company and formed True and Brown Oil Producers and True and Brown Drilling Contractors.

In 1956, in a deal that marked his first major oil find, True drilled at Donkey Creek, in the previously unexplored Newcastle area of the Powder River Basin, and brought in the first significant Minnelusa discovery in Wyoming. True bought out his partner Brown in 1954 and began True Oil, True Drilling and True Service Company. In 1957, he formed the Belle Fourche Pipeline Company, which built the first pipeline out of the central Powder River Basin area. In 1964, True organized Black Hills Oil Marketers, which became a major marketer of crude oil in the Rocky Mountain region.

True continued to expand his business interests throughout the next three decades. In the 1970s, he consolidated his various trucking operations and formed Black Hills Trucking, which became one of the largest rig moving contractors in the Rocky Mountain region. In 1977, he purchased the stock of the Hilltop National Bank in Casper. In 1992, True formed True Environmental Remediation Company, which has successfully cleaned up several sites throughout the state.

True was an active participant in numerous educational, philanthropic and business organizations. Known for his commitment to education, True gave many scholarships to the University of Wyoming and Casper College. He served 12 years on the Board of Trustees of the University of Wyoming, and was that body's president from 1971 to 1973. True devoted many hours to the Cowboy Hall of Fame and served on the Board of Trustees of the Buffalo Bill Historical Center. He was a long time member of the National Cattleman's Association and the Wyoming Stockgrowers Association and served as president of the Independent Petroleum Association of America and chairman of the National Petroleum Council.

True received many honors throughout his career. In 1959, the Casper Chamber of Commerce recognized him as the Wyoming Oil Man of the Year. In 1967, the National Small Business Council chose him as the Outstanding Small Businessman for Small Business Management. In 1975, he was honored for his work with the Southwestern Legal Foundation and the Independent Petroleum Association of America. He was awarded an honorary law degree from the University of Wyoming in 1988 and received an honorary doctorate in engineering from Montana State University. In 1989, the Casper Centennial Corporation named him Oil Man of the Century.

True continued to manage all of his business interest until his death, maintaining his practice of arriving at the office at 6 am and working until 9 pm. As a result of his commitment to the state of Wyoming, his companies' headquarters remain in Casper. The True Companies employs more than 600 people throughout the state. True died in Casper, Wyoming, on June 4, 1994.

CLARENE LAW
1933-

Clarene Law was born Clarene Webb in Thornton, Idaho, on July 22, 1933. Her parents were Clarence Riley and Alta Simmons Webb. Law grew up in Idaho and graduated from Twin Falls High School, eventually completing two years of college course work. In 1951, she began working for the *Times News* in Twin Falls. After her 1953 marriage to Franklin Meadows she relocated, first to Cedar City and later to Moab, Utah, working as a newspaper reporter and court clerk.

In 1959, Law moved to Jackson, Wyoming, and for the next two years worked as the auditor of the historic Wort Hotel. In 1962, she became involved in the operation of Elk Country Motels, Inc. and the Old West Corporation. She now serves as chairman of the board and chief operating officer.

Clarene Law has an interest in several businesses. Along with her family, she owns and operates five lodging properties in Jackson Hole, ranging in size from the Alpine Motel, with 18 units, to the 143 unit 49'er Inn and Suites. She also operates a number of commercial rental properties including the Teton Steakhouse, Mama Inez's, the Ranger Trailer Park and the Snow King Trailer Park. She has extensive real estate holdings, including 3,000 acres of crop land in Idaho, used to raise wheat and barley. Law has investments in properties in Sheridan and Dubois, as well as the Lander Inn and Jackson's Snow King Resort.

Law is active in the Wyoming business community. A member of the Wyoming Lodging and Restaurant Association, she is a past president and chairman of the board. Law also serves on the boards of the Jackson State Bank, International Leisure Hosts and the Jackson Hole Resort Association. She is a past board member of the Jackson Hole Chamber of Commerce.

Law is also involved in community and political affairs. She has served on the Board of the Grand Teton Music Festival and as president of the Jackson Hole Fine Arts Foundation. An active member of Teton County's Republican Women, she was elected to the Wyoming House of Representatives in 1990. Law currently chairs the Travel, Recreation, Wildlife and Cultural Resources Committee. She was recently appointed by Governor Jim Geringer to serve on the newly created Business Council.

Law has received many awards in recognition for her work, among them the Chamber of Commerce Citizen of the Year Award (1976) and the State of Wyoming Business Person of the Year Award (1977). Law continues to reside in the Jackson area with her second husband, Creed Law, whom she married in 1973. She is the mother of two daughters and one son and has seven stepchildren. She lists her hobbies as "grandkids, old cars, horses, and work."

GLENN E. NIELSON
1903-1998

Glenn Nielson was born at Aetna, Alberta, on May 26, 1903. Nielson was raised in the Mormon faith, and after spending a year in England on a church mission, returned to Canada to run his family's 1,000-acre ranch. In 1928, he married Olive Wood, his childhood sweetheart. The couple eventually had two sons and three daughters. In 1933, Nielson completed his education by earning a degree in agriculture from the University of Alberta.

Nielson's eventual move from sheep farming into the oil business was the result of unforeseen circumstances. In 1935, unable to make a living in Canada because of poor economic conditions, he moved his family to Browning, Montana. A subsequent outbreak of hoof-and-mouth disease, in combination with a freak snowstorm that killed most of his flock, ended Nielson's days in the sheep business. Nielson then entered into a new field of endeavor, the oil business. He began by selling gasoline and diesel fuel for a small refinery in Cut Bank, Montana, to local farmers.

In 1937, Nielson, by now a U.S. citizen, moved his family to Cody and the following year acquired the Park Refining Company, later known as Husky Oil. Nielson was able to arrange the deal with the help of two partners both of whom put up $100,000. Under Nielson's leadership, Husky Oil flourished. Husky was known for specializing in asphalt and Nielson eventually became known as "Mr. Asphalt" in both the United States and Canada. Husky expanded into the service station business in 1939 and in 1943 won a contract to build a fuel oil refinery for the United States Navy.

An offer by a large oil company to buy Husky Oil for $1.3 million, nearly three times the original selling price, nearly put Nielson out of the oil business. Nielson's partners wanted to accept the offer and when Nielson refused, the farmers' cooperative exercised the terms of the buy-sell agreement, giving Nielson 60 days to buy out his partners or be forced to sell. It was the people of Cody, among them such prominent citizens as Milward Simpson, who helped Nielson raise the money he needed to hold onto Husky Oil. Nielson repaid those people's faith in him by continuing to successfully manage his company. Those who bought notes received an average profit of almost 40 percent, while those who opted to acquire Husky stock were eventually traded common stock for their preferred stock.

By the 1950s, Husky had expanded its operations to Canada and six western states. It was during this decade that the company bought Gates City Steel, began international exploration, and established its truck stop chain. In the 1960s the company built three pipelines for the heavy oil project in Lloydminster, Alberta, and acquired more than one million acres of heavy oil leases in Alberta. Husky Oil acquired Frontier Refining Company in 1968 and the company continued to expand its operations throughout the next decade, branching out into offshore exploration and natural gas production.

After a hostile takeover of Husky in 1978, Nielson retired from the company and eventually sold his holdings for an amount purported to be in excess of $100 million. After his retirement Nielson devoted his time to his community, serving as member of the Administrative Board of Utah University Hospital, a Trustee of the Buffalo Bill Historical Center in Cody, and a leader in the Mormon Church. Nielson died in at his home on October 19, 1998.

Glenn Nielson built Husky Oil into a company valued at more than $100 million. *Courtesy of Nielson Family Collection.*

PATRICK QUEALY II
1912-1997

Patrick John Quealy II was born in Kemmerer, Wyoming, on August 19, 1912. His parents, Patrick J. Quealy and Susan Quealy, were pioneers in Wyoming's early years, his father having been a coal developer and co-founder of the town of Kemmerer and his mother having been active in civic affairs. Upon graduation from Kemmerer High School in 1929, Mr. Quealy enrolled at the University of Wyoming, where he received a Bachelor of Arts degree in 1933. While at the University, he was member of Sigma Nu Fraternity. He continued his education at the University of Michigan where he was a member the Michigan Law Review, earning a law degree in 1937.

Quealy returned to Kemmerer and began managing various family business interests in the area in 1941. He participated in the development of oil and gas resources in the LaBarge area, which lead to the incorporation of Western Oil Refining Company, where he served as president for more than 50 years. Quealy served as president of five other smaller oil companies, and was a partner in the Carl-Pat Company, which promoted oil and gas development in southwestern Wyoming.

Quealy's varied business enterprises helped to develop the Kemmerer area. He was involved in the banking industry for over 40 years, serving as a director and chairman of the board of First Wyoming Bank of Kemmerer and as a director of Wyoming Bancorporation. Quealy was a founder and president of the Tip Top Finance Company, which filled the small loan company niche in the Kemmerer community. He participated in the formation of the local cable television company, KEM-TEV, in the 1950s. During the following decade he was responsible for many of the housing developments which were built in and around Kemmerer. During the late 1970s, Quealy became a partner in R & O Motors. Quealy served as a director for the San Francisco Chemical Company and was a member of the advisory board for the Wyoming Division of Mountain Bell.

Quealy was also active in civic affairs. He served as mayor of Kemmerer from 1952 to 1962 and was president of the Wyoming Association of Municipalities for the first three years of that organization's existence. He was director of the Wyoming Taxpayer's Association and served nine consecutive terms as president. He was on the Board of Trustees of the University of Wyoming for 18 years and was a member of the University of Wyoming Foundation. From 1971 to 1974 Quealy was director of the Cowboy Hall of Fame. In recognition of all he gave to his community and state, Quealy received several awards, including the Casper Kiwanis Distinguished Service Award (1968), the University of Wyoming Distinguished Alumni Award (1981), and the Medallion Service Award (1989).

Patrick Quealy II died in Pinedale, Wyoming, in 1997. A lifetime resident of the state, whose advice was sought by leaders across Wyoming for more than 50 years, his death marked the passing of a man who "showed his love for the state by giving of himself for the benefit of the people of Kemmerer and Wyoming."

NEWELL BRUSH SARGENT
1905-

Between 1961 and 1971, the company acquired several new franchises, including the 7UP and Dr Pepper franchises in Thermopolis and Casper, as well as the Pepsi franchise for Casper and the Pepsi and 7UP franchises in Cheyenne.

In 1970, Sargent's company was instrumental in the building of a cooperative canning plant in Worland, participating with bottlers throughout Wyoming, Montana and South Dakota in the establishment of what eventually became known as the Admiral Beverage Corporation (ABC). The impact of this plant on the area economy has been significant. As a result of the demand for cans at the ABC facility, the Crown Cork and Seal company built a plant in Worland. ABC and Crown Cork and Seal provide a significant number of jobs to the residents of Worland.

A longtime member of the Worland City Council (1959-1970), Sargent also served as a member of the Wyoming House of Representatives. He has been active in the Wyoming Waterfowl Trust. Sargent has followed a philosophy of ensuring that the money he has made in Wyoming is used to benefit the citizens of this state. Sargent has provided a scholarship endowment to the University of Wyoming School of Nursing.

Sargent has given generously, not only financially, but also of his time, in a variety of areas and to numerous charities. Sargent was a founding board member of the Wyoming Community Foundation. He supported the development of Pioneer Square in downtown Worland. He has been a contributor to the Cathedral Home for Children, donating a residence cottage. An active supporter of the Washakie County Museum, he and Vera Sargent donated a bronze sculpture of Chief Washakie to the museum.

Sargent married Mabel Alsworth in 1938 in Denver Colorado. After her death in 1960, he married Vera Hansen in January, 1962, in Meeteetse, Wyoming. Sargent and his family continue to reside in Wyoming.

Newell Sargent and his wife, Vera, donated a bronze sculpture of Chief Washakie to the Washakie County Museum. *Courtesy of Sargent Family Collection.*

Newell Brush Sargent was born in Fort Morgan, Colorado, on July 30, 1905. He is the only child of Fannie F. Brush and Frank Sargent. Sargent grew up in Denver, Colorado, graduating from East Denver High and attending the University of Denver.

Sargent moved to Worland, Wyoming, in the spring of 1947 and purchased the Pepsi and Nesbitts Orange franchises for the Big Horn Basin area. He eventually acquired the Schlitz Brewing distributorship for the area. In 1960, the business was incorporated as Fremont Beverage and has continued to expand.

HOMER SCOTT SR.
1904-1993

Homer Scott expanded his banking interests across Wyoming and Montana. Pictured here is the Wyoming National Bank in Casper, c. 1920. *Courtesy of AHC Collection.*

Homer Scott Sr. was born in Lincoln, Nebraska, on February 16, 1904. His parents were Homer M. and Carrie Koontz Scott. Scott attended local schools and worked on his parents' truck farm outside of Lincoln, milking cows and making deliveries. Although Scott showed promise as a heavyweight prize fighter (he won a three-state competition for a place in the Olympics), he decided to pursue his education instead. He earned a degree in civil engineering in 1927. After graduating, Scott traveled around the country, holding construction jobs in Ohio, New York and Alabama. The following year he married Mildred "Pill" Sandall of York, Nebraska. The couple eventually had four sons and a daughter.

In 1930, Scott was hired as a laborer by the general contracting firm of Peter Kiewit Sons Company, earning 55 cents an hour. Six years later, he moved to Sheridan, Wyoming, and opened the first Kiewit office outside of Omaha. He eventually assumed the position of district manager and vice president of Kiewit, covering an area including Wyoming, Montana, Idaho, North Dakota and South Dakota. When Kiewit entered into the mining industry with the purchase of the Big Horn Coal Company Mine in 1943, Scott assumed responsibility for those operations.

That same year Scott also entered the ranching business for himself, with the purchase of the Padlock Ranch. Situated in a fertile, irrigated valley near Dayton, Wyoming, Scott expanded the ranch and built a successful commercial cattle operation. The Padlock, known for its high-grade Hereford cattle, operated under the Padlock, 2 Open A Bar, Flying V and 7 Quarter Circle brands.

In 1960, Scott was chosen as deputy director of the Federal Reserve Bank of Kansas City and the following year he assumed the position of chairman, which he held until 1966. He then became a director of the Bank of Commerce, purchasing a controlling interest in 1968 and serving as chairman for the next eight years. With the acquisition of the Security Trust and Savings Bank in Billings in 1970, Scott expanded his banking interest into Montana. Three years later he acquired Big Horn County State Bank in Hardin.

Scott subsequently initiated new bank charters for Colstrip, West Billings, Billings Heights, Buffalo and Sheridan, demonstrating his commitment to serving the communities of this region. His interest in banking eventually evolved into the 34-office First Interstate Bank Organization, serving Wyoming and Montana. Scott's efforts in the business arena were recognized in 1963, when he was awarded the Wyoming Department of Commerce and Industry's Distinguished Businessman Award.

Scott played an active role in civic life, establishing the Scott Family Foundation which supports numerous charities, particularly those dedicated to serving the needs of young people. Scott organized the first YMCA board in Sheridan and served as president for five years, securing the original funding for the Sheridan YMCA. He served as a trustee for the Gottsche Foundation of Wyoming and was active in the campaign to fund the purchase of property for the Sheridan Children's facility. Homer Scott died in August, 1993, at the age of 89.

CONSTANT E. "BUD" WEBSTER
1912-

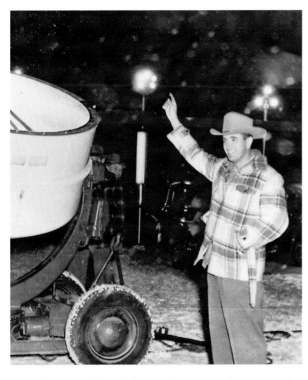

Constant E. "Bud" Webster was born on the Webster Ranch on the Greybull River near Meeteetse, Wyoming, in 1912, the oldest of three children. His parents were Clyde Charles Webster and Vivian McGee. Bud Webster grew up on his family's historic Webster Ranch, and attended the Webster School for three years, until it was consolidated with the Meeteetse School. He graduated in 1931, second in his class of two, and enrolled in the University of Wyoming. He earned an accounting degree in 1935.

In 1937, Webster and his brother Owen purchased the old Yellowstone garage in Cody and signed a contract to represent the Chevrolet Automobile Company. Noting that the Cody Enterprise's announcement regarding his business venture "didn't give us much space," Webster recalls that at the time, "the turnover of dealerships was tremendous so it was sort of ho-hum." The local press had no way of knowing that Webster would buck that trend. The following year he married his former classmate, Lucille Moncure, and the couple eventually had two sons and one daughter.

Webster, whose slogan was "You Can Do Better with Webster," devoted himself to building his business. In 1948, he purchased the Chevrolet Dealership in

Powell, which he named Eddie Chevrolet, after his four-year-old son, and opened his main car lot at the main intersection of Cody. In 1958, he was appointed as the Buick Motor Division's Cody dealer and, according to a newspaper account published at the time, the newly named Webster Chevrolet Buick Co. celebrated the occasion by displaying several new 1959 Buicks.

Webster served as president of the Wyoming Automobile Dealers Association and was a member of the Board of Directors of the National Automobile Dealers Association. He continued to expand his dealership, acquiring an entire block of downtown Cody for his operations by 1983. Three years later he began construction on the facilities where his dealership is currently housed. In 1989, he was the recipient of the *Time* magazine's "Quality Dealer Award." In 1997, Webster completed his 60th year as the Chevrolet Dealer in Cody. The occasion was marked by officials of Chevrolet honoring Webster for the distinction of having the longest operating Chevrolet dealership in the nation.

In addition to his achievements as an automobile dealer, Webster successfully pursued other business interests. He owned and operated the Big Horn Coca-Cola Bottling Company, with more than 1,000 outlets covering northwestern Wyoming for 36 years. In 1946, he began a 40-year term on the Board of Directors of Shoshone First National Bank in Cody; his initial investment in that institution "multiplied 61 times" during his tenure.

In 1963, Wesbster was appointed by Governor Cliff Hansen to serve on the Wyoming Highway Commission. During his six-year tenure, he spearheaded the completion of the Chief Joseph Scenic Highway, over the protest of environmentalists. Webster himself has described the completion of this 31-year project as "my greatest accomplishment."

Webster has received many honors in recognition of his successful career. He was named a Distinguished Alumnus of the University of Wyoming in 1971 and the College of Business selected him as Businessman of the Year in 1987. At the age of 87, Webster continues working six days a week, operating "the Webster Chevrolet Buick after 61 years and enjoying every minute of it."

Bud Webster at the 1948 opening of his new dealership in Cody. The beam from the light at the dealership can be seen for 100 miles. Webster still uses it on special occasions. *Courtesy of Webster Family Collection.*

CHAPTER THREE EDUCATION

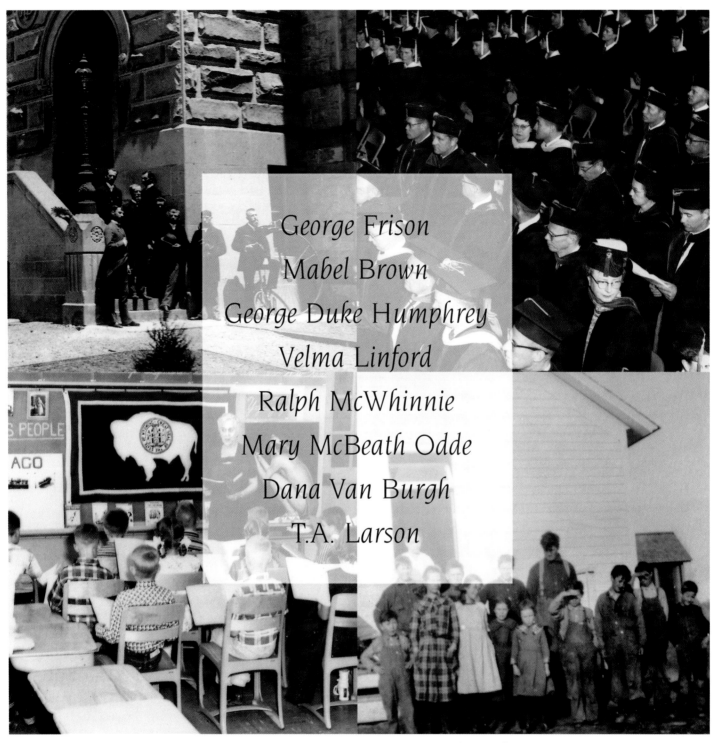

George Frison

Mabel Brown

George Duke Humphrey

Velma Linford

Ralph McWhinnie

Mary McBeath Odde

Dana Van Burgh

T.A. Larson

(Top left) University of Wyoming Faculty, c. 1891 *Courtesy of AHC Collection.*
(Top right) UW Commencement, c. 1960 *Courtesy of AHC Collection.*
(Bottom left) UW Prep School, c. 1957 *Courtesy of AHC Collection.*
(Bottom right) Webster School, c. 1920 *Courtesy of Webster Family Collection.*

INTRODUCTION

Wyoming has a proud tradition of providing educational opportunities. The land grant University of Wyoming, located in Laramie, was founded when Wyoming was still a territory. Many of the early faculty at the University of Wyoming achieved lasting reputations. Grace Raymond Hebard and Laura White, longtime members of the History Department, assumed leadership roles at the institution.

When statehood was granted in 1890, the new constitution specifically provided for "a free and adequate" public education for all children between the ages of six and 21. Throughout the 20th century, Wyomingites have continued to support and improve the state's educational system. Provisions were made for free textbooks in 1901. Subsequently, a state board of education was established and teacher certification was implemented. In 1919, the state began providing financial support to the public schools, with the distribution of income from public lands.

In the field of education, Wyoming continued to provide new opportunities for women. Verda James is only one example. James moved to Wyoming in 1935 and taught at Natrona County High School. As assistant superintendent of schools in Casper, James found her "most gratifying" work with disabled children. She was instrumental in organizing the School for the Deaf in Casper and served as director of Special Education and deputy state superintendent with the Wyoming State Department of Education for 12 years.

For the first half of the century, the University of Wyoming remained the state's only institution of higher learning. But the end of World War II and the passage of the GI Bill created an increased demand for educational opportunities. The state responded, not only by greatly expanding the University, but also with the creation of a statewide system of community colleges.

The first of these community colleges, Casper College, was established in 1945. Other colleges within the system include Central Wyoming College in Riverton, Eastern Wyoming College in Torrington, Laramie County Community College in Cheyenne, Sheridan College, Northwest College in Powell and Western Wyoming College in Rock Springs.

Throughout the latter part of the century, Wyoming's teachers have remained dedicated to providing educational opportunities. As the 21st century approaches, Wyoming's schools, colleges and the University are rising to meet new challenges. Providing students with the skills necessary to meet the demands of the information age, along with preserving the state's history and traditions, are of equal concern to Wyoming's educators.

GEORGE FRISON
1924-

George Frison was born in Worland, Wyoming, on November 11, 1924. His father, George S. Frison, died before he was born and he was raised by his grandparents on the family ranch, near Ten Sleep, at the base of the Big Horn Mountains. As a boy, Frison developed an interest in archaeology from his explorations of the area's abundance of fossils and other remains. When he was 10 years old, an encounter with a paleontologist from New York who was digging for dinosaur remains on Shell Creek further fueled his interest.

Frison attended local schools and enrolled at the University of Wyoming on a scholarship after his graduation from high school in 1942. After only one semester, Frison's studies were interrupted by World War II, when he left school to serve in the Navy's amphibious forces. Frison returned to his family's ranch after his discharge in 1946. The following year he married June Glanville and the couple eventually had one daughter. Frison spent the next 16 years working as a rancher and professional guide, while continuing to pursue his interest in archaeology.

In 1953, Frison discovered a cave in Spring Creek Canyon, near Ten Sleep, and decided to utilize excavating methods he had learned from archaeological books and journals. After he began to find rare perishable materials, Frison consulted with Dr. William Mulloy of the Anthropology Department of the University of Wyoming. Mulloy was impressed with Frison's abilities and, as word of the Spring Creek Canyon find spread, Frison made other contacts in the scientific world. Frison spent his spare time over the next several years studying and evaluating the material from Spring Creek Canyon. In 1959, he found another site, which he named the Wedding of the Waters Cave, that contained several levels of habitation dating back 4,000 years. Again Frison devoted his free time to examining his find, but eventually, no longer content to be just an amateur, he decided to become a professional archaeologist.

In 1962, Frison returned to the University of Wyoming to pursue a degree in archaeology. As Frison recalled, the transition from self-employed rancher to college freshman was not an easy one. He often found the curriculum, such as writing letters of application for an English course, did not apply to a man of his experience. He remembers "It took about six months to convince me that they couldn't make over the requirements just for me." After completing his bachelor's degree in two years, he went on to the University of Michigan, where he earned a master's degree and a doctorate in anthropology in three years. Frison's doctoral thesis dealt with the Crow Indians in northern prehistory, and was noted for its unique viewpoint in its study of buffalo hunts, with Frison drawing on his knowledge as an archaeologist and a rancher.

In 1967, Frison returned to Wyoming, where he was appointed state archaeologist and head of the Anthropology Department at the University of Wyoming. Serving in both positions, Frison investigated and reported on dozens of significant prehistoric sites, not only in Wyoming, but throughout North America. Among his many notable finds within Wyoming was the discovery of the remains of six mammoths near Worland, considered to be one of the most significant Paleo-Indian archaeological discoveries in North America.

Frison has given hundreds of presentations at national and international scientific meetings. He has authored more than 80 journal articles and seven books, including *The Casper Site: A Hell Gap Bison Kill on the High Plains*. Perhaps Frison's best known work within Wyoming is *Prehistoric Hunters of the High Plains*. Considered his most popular work, it has been credited with bringing an appreciation of the past and an understanding of the importance of stewardship of archaeological resources to thousands of Wyoming residents.

Frison's work has been recognized nationally and internationally, not only for his substantive results on Wyoming and Northwest Plains prehistory, but also for his contribution to archaeological method and theory. The recognition of re-sharpening of stone tools, which changes their shape, transforming them into different artifacts, is now widely referred to as "the Frison effect," as he was the first to recognize and widely publicize it. His broad contributions to the field have brought not only him, but the Anthropology Department and the University of Wyoming, an international reputation. The scope of his reputation is evidenced by his recent induction into the National Academy of Sciences. He is the only Wyoming scholar to have been so honored.

During his long career, Frison has taught thousands of students. A recipient of the University of Wyoming's George Duke Humphrey Distinguished Faculty Award, Frison is widely recognized for his excellence in teaching. As the State Archaeologist, he has visited every part of Wyoming, assisting in archaeological excavations, presenting programs about his work and helping local museums to build and maintain their displays. Frison is known and respected in communities throughout the state, for his work in the field of archaeology and his commitment to education.

Frison retired as state archaeologist in 1984, having guided the agency for 17 years. In 1986, he stepped down as head of the Archaeology Department, having presided over its evolution from a newly formed entity to a major teaching and research facility. Oliver Walter, dean of the College of Arts and Sciences at the University of Wyoming, credits Frison with putting "the Anthropology Department on the map as the premier center for high plains archaeological research." Although he retired from the University in 1995, Frison retains emeritus status and continues to pursue research.

MABEL BROWN
1914-

Mabel Brown was born in Golden, Colorado, in January 19, 1914. In 1922, she moved to Wyoming with her family, eventually settling in Weston County. At the age of 17 she left school to marry Charles Wesley Brown. The couple ranched in the Canyon Springs area, near Newcastle, Wyoming, until his death in 1982.

Mabel Brown developed a keen interest in the history of her adopted state and, in keeping with her personality, she acted upon it. She has authored several books on Wyoming, among them a history of the Newcastle area, *And Then There Was One*, co-authored with Elizabeth T. Griffin and first published in 1962, and a biography of Wyoming mining pioneer Harry Thorson, *Inga and Harry* (1995). For 16 years she served as editor and publisher of *Bits and Pieces*, a magazine of western history with special emphasis on northeast Wyoming and the Black Hills. Brown's most popular work, *First Ladies of Wyoming, 1869-1990* (1990), was published by the Wyoming Arts Council as a sanctioned Lasting Legacy Project for the Wyoming Commission for Women.

In 1958, Mabel Brown began hosting a weekly talk show for radio station KASL and she used the forum to promote interest in local history. The following year she was the principal force behind the creation of the Weston County Historical Society. A founding member of the Anna Miller Museum in Newcastle, Brown was director from 1977 to 1984, and worked to expand museum

> *Mabel Brown first learned how to drive at the age of 68. Since then she has traveled Wyoming, educating the populace about the state's historical legacy.*

programs across the state. She has taught numerous courses, workshops and seminars for various institutions such as the Buffalo Bill Historical Center in Cody, Wyoming, and the Trail End Historic Center in Sheridan, Wyoming. Brown has conducted an astonishing 242 classroom presentations in a 180-day school year.

Despite having failed to complete her high school education, Mabel Brown accumulated more than 100 hours of college credits, attending classes at the University of Wyoming, Eastern Wyoming College and the University of Nebraska between 1931 and 1971. And, 40 years after leaving school, at the age of 57, Brown earned her general equivalency degree from Newcastle High School.

Brown has participated in numerous service organizations. She is a lifetime member and past president of the Wyoming State Historical Society, in addition to serving on the Wyoming Historical Foundation Board of Directors. She has been a member of the Wyoming Consulting Committee to the National Register of Historic Places and has served on the board of the Leland Case Library for Western History Studies. Brown has a long affiliation with Blackhills State University in Spearfish, South Dakota, as a frequent guest lecturer, field historian and member of the University Foundation Board.

Brown is the recipient of numerous awards in recognition of her work, and was declared an honorary citizen of Wyoming by Governor Ed Herschler. Brown devoted countless hours to the Wyoming Centennial Celebration, and her service earned her a place among the Centennial 100. She was honored for her work in educating Wyomingites about their heritage by the Wyoming Historical Foundation in 1994.

Mabel Brown first learned how to drive at the age of 68. Since then she has traveled Wyoming, educating the populace about the state's historical legacy. She has visited with school students, lectured to local historical societies, and testified before the state legislature, all in an effort to preserve Wyoming's traditions. Her attributes of independence and determination, coupled with her knowledge of the state and her communication skills, have made her one of Wyoming's most valuable ambassadors.

GEORGE DUKE HUMPHREY
1897-1973

George Duke Humphrey served as president of the University of Wyoming from 1945-1964. *Courtesy of AHC Collection*

class of two. Having passed the teacher's examination that spring, with the highest grade of 132 applicants, he accepted a teaching position at Clements Chapel, Mississippi, for a salary of $42.40 per month. He supplemented his income by farming and continued to teach in area schools.

In 1919, at the age of 22, Humphrey accepted the position of superintendent of the Ripley School District, the largest and only accredited school in Tippah County. His selection caused some concern, in view of his age and lack of a college degree, but Humphrey soon silenced his critics through hard work. In addition to his administrative duties, he played an active role in the local teacher's organization, taught several classes, coached the athletics teams and advised various student groups. During the next four years he also worked toward his degree by taking summer classes at Blue Mountain College, the University of Mississippi and Mississippi Normal.

In 1923, Humphrey successfully ran for superintendent of education of Tippah County. In his six and half years in office, one of his major accomplishments was the consolidation of 90 area schools into 22. It was during this time that he met and married the former Josephine Robertson.

George Duke Humphrey was born near Ivey, Mississippi, on August 30, 1897. His parents were John Washington and Louise Isabel Cheves Humphrey. The family eventually moved to a farm in nearby Dumas, where Humphrey was raised. In 1903, his father succumbed to typhoid fever, leaving his widow to raise their six children, ranging in ages from four to 20.

Humphrey was educated in area schools, graduating from Chalybeate High School in 1915, at the top of a

In 1929, after attending summer classes at various institutions for 14 years, Humphrey earned a bachelor of arts degree from Blue Mountain College, having majored in English, history and education.

In 1930, Humphrey was offered a fellowship from Mississippi's General Education Board that allowed him to study school administration at the University of Chicago. He earned his master's degree in 1931 and returned to his native state, where he assumed the position of superintendent of city schools at Kosciusko. The following year, Humphrey accepted a job in Jackson, the state capital, as state high school supervisor. Soon after he was appointed president of Mississippi State College, a troubled institution that Humphrey was instrumental in turning around. During this period, Humphrey earned his Ph.D from Ohio State University.

Humphrey left Mississippi to assume the office of president of the University of Wyoming in 1945. Under his leadership, the University's physical plant and programs experienced significant growth. During the course of his administration, he supervised 15 major building projects, including new construction and renovation, which doubled the size of the campus. When Humphrey arrived at the university, enrollments numbered less than 1,000; by 1963, the number of students was more than 5,000. Despite this increase, Humphrey managed to maintain a student teacher ratio of 14:1. During his tenure, Humphrey oversaw the creation of several doctoral programs and the addition of four academic programs. As part of his commitment to the recruitment and retention of quality personnel, he used his political skills to persuade the state legislature to support significant salary increases for faculty and staff.

Humphrey advocated the development of the University's football program, insisting that the emphasis was necessary to unify the state and gain support for the University. He oversaw the construction of the War Memorial Stadium and Field House in 1949. But perhaps his greatest contribution to University athletics was the hiring of Glen "Red" Jacoby as athletic director. Working together, these two men built the university's athletic program into a national competitor in collegiate sports.

Humphrey retired as university president in 1964, having presided over the University of Wyoming's greatest period of expansion. The George Duke Humphrey Distinguished Teaching Award, given annually to University professors who demonstrate excellence in teaching, and the G.D. Humphrey Science Center were named in his honor. Humphrey died at his home in Laramie on September 10, 1973.

VELMA LINFORD
1907-

Velma Linford was born in Afton, Wyoming, on May 30, 1907. Her parents, John and Elizabeth Linford, were pioneer Mormons and dairy farmers, who settled in the Star Valley in 1904. She grew up in Afton, along with her five brothers and two sisters. Linford later recalled that she was reared in the frontier tradition of hard work. In 1926, she graduated from Afton's Star Valley High School.

Linford enrolled at the University of Wyoming and came into contact with a number of successful women there, including Dr. June Etta Downey, Dr. Laura A. White and Dr. Grace Raymond Hebard. She was influenced by their example. Linford was an outstanding student, graduating with a bachelor of arts degree in 1930. She returned home to Star Valley, where she taught for the next three years.

In 1934, Linford returned briefly to the University of Wyoming after receiving a teaching fellowship in the English Department. But she left after one quarter, in response to a call for a teacher from the Bosler School in rural Wyoming. Linford later remarked her experiences at the Bosler School were "marvelous" and said she valued the opportunity to learn about rural life in Wyoming. In 1935, Linford accepted a teaching position at Laramie High School, where she remained for the next 20 years. She taught English, history, speech and drama. While working as a classroom teacher, Linford continued to pursue her studies, earning a master's degree from the University of Wyoming in 1935.

Among Linford's better known accomplishments is her textbook, *Wyoming, Frontier State*. She began the treatise while at the Bosler School, but it was a research fellowship from the University of Wyoming in 1945 that allowed her to complete the work. Published in 1947 by the Old West Publishing Company in Denver, *Wyoming, Frontier State* received overwhelmingly positive reviews, with one critic remarking "one of the best friends of the Wyoming high school student is a red-haired schoolmarm — she has written a history of the state as exciting as a western romance and as exhaustive as a mineral survey."

Linford was in demand as a speaker throughout her career, addressing groups and conferences across the state on topics related to education. Known for her effective and dramatic deliveries, Linford invoked in those who heard her speak the feeling that she was personally addressing each member of the audience. It was this skill that served her well when she turned her attention to the political arena.

In 1954, Linford was elected as Wyoming's state superintendent of public instruction, the only Democrat elected to state office that year. She held the position of state superintendent until 1963. As a candidate for public office, Linford was unique for her colorful and largely self-financed campaigns. Referred to by the local press as a "politician educator," Linford was at one time the largest vote-getter in the state of Wyoming. Despite her popularity, her two attempts at national office, as a candidate for the U.S. Senate in 1960 and the U.S. House of Representatives in 1968, were unsuccessful.

Linford left her mark on Wyoming's educational system during her time in the state superintendent's office. During her first term, she established the Wyoming School Foundation Program and implemented requirements for non-degreed elementary school teachers. Linford also presided over the establishment of the Wyoming School for the Deaf in Casper. Re-elected in 1958, she reorganized the State Department of Education, established special education programs and became embroiled in a battle over Wyoming's acceptance of federal aid for education. Linford later recalled this as "the most dramatic period of her career," in which her efforts to ensure the highest quality education for Wyoming's students were overshadowed by partisan political infighting.

In 1963, Linford began a new phase of her career, in Washington, D.C., working first with the overseas dependent school program with the Department of Defense and later with the Department of Agriculture's Extension Services. She eventually began working with Volunteers In Service To America (VISTA), drawing on her own experiences as a rural school teacher and as president of the Department for Rural Education, to coordinate training programs. Despite erroneous reports of her demise (*Laramie Daily Boomerang* 9/16/93), Linford remains vigorous and vital.

Linford has been the recipient of many accolades throughout her long career. She was honored with a citation as an outstanding Wyoming Woman, presented to her by Lady Byrd Johnson. In 1962, Linford was awarded the Wyoming Education Association's Golden Key Award, given annually to an outstanding educator. In 1963, the University of Wyoming presented her with the Distinguished Alumni Award. She was the first recipient of the Hubert H. Humphrey Award for International Service in 1978. That same year, the Albany County School District honored Linford with the opening of the Velma Linford Elementary School in Laramie. Linford remarked that the naming of the school in her honor was paramount of all the recognition she has received in her distinguished career as an educator.

RALPH McWHINNIE
1898-1995

Ralph McWhinnie was born March 14, 1898, at the La Bonte Ranch near Douglas, Wyoming. His parents, settlers and early-day ranchers in Wyoming, were Campbell H. McWhinnie and the former Caroline J. Pollard. McWhinnie was the oldest of six children.

After graduating from Converse County High School in 1916, McWhinnie enrolled in the University of Wyoming. He excelled in his classes and also found time to devote to other activities, including athletics, lettering in basketball. Shortly after arriving in Laramie, McWhinnie and a group of his contemporaries formed a fraternity, Gamma Theta Chi. He was also a charter member, and organizer, of the university's Phi Kappa Phi chapter and served four terms as president of the academic honorary society. He graduated with a bachelor's degree in liberal arts in 1920, having majored in Greek and Latin. McWhinnie later earned a master's degree in political science from Stanford.

McWhinnie served as the registrar and director of admissions for the University of Wyoming for 43 years. He had begun working as a records clerk as an under-graduate and so excelled in this position that he was offered the post of registrar, beginning April 1, 1920, two months prior to his graduation. During his long and distinguished career at the university, he served in numerous capacities, as well as acting as an administrative consultant and unofficial campus historian.

In 1920, McWhinnie began the first bookstore on the university campus, housed in Old Main, and continued as store manager for the next eight years. He edited the university's catalog for 21 years (1942-63), and was secretary for the Committee of Deans for 40 years (1923-1963). He was the first director of the Men' Residence Hall (1928-32) and also served as acting dean of men (1936-37). McWhinnie also took an interest in the university's athletic program and in 1920 he began a 37-year term as scorer for the university's basketball program and the state basketball tournament.

In 1920, McWhinnie succeeded in having Gamma Theta Chi chartered as a chapter of the Sigma Nu national fraternity. As holder of Pin Number 2, McWhinnie worked as the alumni advisor for the

University of Wyoming's Epsilon Delta Chapter of Sigma Nu for 75 years. He also served the Sigma Nu national fraternity as division commander from 1938 to 1954 and held the post of grand historian from 1978 to 1980.

In 1926, McWhinnie joined the Laramie Rotary Club and for the next 69 years achieved an unequaled record of perfect attendance. He served as club president (1931-32) and was appointed district governor for the Rocky Mountain Area (1942-43), after being unanimously nominated. McWhinnie was instrumental in organizing the Charitable Foundation of the Laramie Rotary Club and was a substantial contributor to the Foundation of Rotary International.

McWhinnie retired as registrar in 1963, and spent the next five years editing a compilation of stories by university alumnus from 1920 to 1960, titled *Those Good Years*. In 1971, after the death of his wife, Bernice Appleby, whom he married in 1932, McWhinnie maintained a university scholarship in her name. In 1980, he was presented with the Alumni Association's highest commendation, the Medallion Service Award. In 1992, the university conferred an honorary doctorate on McWhinnie.

McWhinnie died in November of 1995. Services were conducted at St. Matthew's Episcopal Cathedral in Laramie, where McWhinnie was a long-time member, having held the offices of secretary, superintendent of the Sunday school, vestryman and senior warden. At the time of his death, McWhinnie was a senior 33rd Degree Mason and had been a member for 75 years. Often referred to "the man with the crystal memory," McWhinnie was eulogized for his phenomenal ability to recall names, faces and facts.

McWhinnie was remembered fondly after his death for all of the personal attention he had given to countless students throughout the years, as well as his extraordinary career. In 1981, McWhinnie's years of service to the university were honored by the renaming of the former men's residence hall in his honor. At the dedication of McWhinnie Hall, when McWhinnie remarked that the University of Wyoming's "...justification for its existence is educational service, to its public and the state of Wyoming," he could have not more accurately summed up his own career and achievements.

MARY McBEATH ODDE
1918-1990

Mary McBeath Odde was born in Rochester, Texas, on February 18, 1918. Her family eventually moved to Colorado, where she graduated from high school in Littleton in 1935. She attended both Colorado State College and Santa Ana Jr. College and eventually earned a bachelor of arts degree in science education from the University of Wyoming. She earned a master's degree in education from Idaho State University in 1969.

Odde spent 24 years as a classroom teacher in Wyoming, the majority of them in Shoshoni public schools in Fremont County. While science was Odde's major field, she also taught where she was needed, incorporating drama, English, math and physical education into her repertoire. Odde was an advocate of hands-on education. She spent hours setting up special lab experiences for her junior high students and supported the Teton Science School Experience. Odde was known for her willingness to try new ideas when she believed they would enhance the learning process and was instrumental in the Shoshoni school's implementation of flexible scheduling. She did not shy away from controversial issues, such as proposing a sex education class, which she taught, because she felt students needed the information.

Odde's reputation as an outstanding classroom educator earned her respect and recognition from her peers. In 1966, she was selected to attend a National Science Foundation Institute at DePauw University. For three consecutive years (1967-70), she was chosen to attend the Institute of Physical Science, under the joint sponsorship of the National Science Foundation and Idaho State University. She was named Shoshoni Teacher of the Year in 1970 and was also nominated for Wyoming's Teacher of the Year Award. Odde was selected as the Outstanding Earth Science teacher by the National Association of Geology Teachers in 1975 and is the only person to have received both the Wyoming Education Association's (WEA) Golden Key Award, given annually to an outstanding educator, and the Friend of Education Award.

After retiring from the classroom in 1978, Odde joined the staff of the WEA as Wyoming's first female UniServ Director, representing the northwest and northeast districts. She eventually became president of the WEA and in that capacity worked to provide quality in-service education to Wyoming's teachers. Aware of the impact of the political process on thE course of Wyoming's educational progress, Odde decided to seek public office to represent the interests of her particular constituency, teachers, parents and children.

In 1980, Odde was elected to the first of five terms as a Republican member of the Wyoming House of Representatives from Fremont County. Odde, believing her duty was to the people of Wyoming, oftentimes did not vote the party line, choosing to be guided by her conscience and her constituents. Odde served on the Judiciary Committee and chaired the sub-committee on Children and Families. Known for her support of

> *Odde, believing her duty was to the people of Wyoming, oftentimes did not vote the party line, choosing to be guided by her conscience and her constituents.*

legislation to enforce child support agreements, Odde was chosen Legislator of the Year in 1989 by the National Child Support Enforcement Association. Her fellow legislators respected her knowledge of educational issues and recalled Odde as someone who had a true grasp of the meaning of grass roots, always emphasizing the effect that legislation would have on the lives of constituents.

In 1990, Odde announced that she would not seek a sixth term in the legislature, due to ill health. She died September 4th of that year at the age of 71. After her death, her family memorialized Odde's lifelong commitment to education by establishing a scholarship in her name at Central Wyoming College.

DANA VAN BURGH
1932-

Dana Van Burgh was born in Casper, Wyoming, on June 20, 1932, the son of Dana P. and Mary Lucile Geary Van Burgh. He graduated from Natrona County High School. Van Burgh attended Wentworth Military School in Lexington, Missouri, and then Coe College, in Cedar Rapids, Iowa, where he earned a bachelor of arts degree in geology in 1954. The same year he married the former Nora Hoffman; the couple eventually had two daughters and a son.

In 1957, Van Burgh, having completed a three-year stint in the Air Force, was considering the job responsibilities of a company geologist, the direction of his educational path to that date, and decided that "he wanted more involvement with people, particularly young people." Determined to pursue a career in education, he was guided by a desire to arouse students' inherent curiosity in the natural world while encouraging them to reach their full potential. Over the course of 41 years, Van Burgh did just that, teaching, and reaching, more than 6,000 pupils.

Van Burgh taught science, primarily earth science, at Dean Morgan Junior High School in Casper from 1957 to 1995, also serving as department chairman. In 1962, he earned a master's degree in science education from Colorado State College (now the University of Northern Colorado). As a professional educator, Van Burgh has developed numerous programs and curricula, in addition to authoring several publications. In 1964, he and his fellow teacher, Beecher "Ed" Strube, developed a week-long summer school course, "Field Science," for secondary students and teachers, which is still taught in Casper schools.

Van Burgh was a founding force in the creation of the Lee McCune Braille Trail on Casper Mountain, which provides access to information about Wyoming geology and biology to the visually impaired. Van Burgh is also a member of the Bailey Ranch Outdoor Education Center Committee, which works to provide nature education programs, in conjunction with the Audubon Society.

Van Burgh, who officially retired from Dean Morgan Junior High School in 1995, continues to teach as an adjunct instructor in earth sciences at Casper College. Since his particular interest is in helping to train other science teachers, he conducts a seminar for elementary school instructors. He also continues to work with the Summer Field Science Program that he helped to develop.

Van Burgh is the recipient of numerous awards, among them the Presidential Award for Excellence in Science and Teaching (1986). He is also the recipient of the American Legion Wyoming Teacher of the Year Award (1992) and the National Association of Geology Teachers Outstanding Earth Science Teacher Award (1974). But among the most significant accolades Van Burgh has received in his long and distinguished career is the appreciation of his former students.

As one student recalls, Van Burgh's gifts as a teacher, which combine knowledge, enthusiasm and compassion, instill a love of learning in his pupils. By encouraging each of his students to pursue higher education and teaching them the skills they needed to succeed at that level, Van Burgh taught them to value their futures and believe in themselves. Defining his philosophy of teaching as "serendipity," Van Burgh said that as an educator his main goal is to get students to "think, reason and apply information."

Dana Van Burgh taught earth sciences at Dean Morgan Junior High School in Casper for almost 30 years.
Courtesy of Van Burgh Family Collection.

T.A. LARSON
1910-

T.A. Larson was born to Swedish immigrant parents on a farm near Wakefield, Nebraska, on January 18, 1910. Larson attended local schools, where he was quickly persuaded to dispose of the name "Taft" after it became the subject of school yard humor. Thus by a young age he had adopted the more conventional "Al." Larson, editor of his high school newspaper, graduated at the top of his class. He enrolled at the University of Colorado, intending to study journalism. Instead, Larson discovered a love of history, earning both a bachelor's and master's degree in the field. Larson's first exposure to Wyoming came while a college student, he worked in Yellowstone National Park during the summers. He later attended the University of Chicago and received his doctoral degree from the University of Illinois in 1937.

A medieval scholar, Larson came to the University of Wyoming in 1936 as a one-year replacement and taught courses in medieval and English history, as well as western civilization. The following year, Larson sailed to England to study at the British Museum and Public Records Office in London. In 1938, he returned to the University and eventually his success as a classroom professor led to a permanent faculty position, on the condition that he develop a course on Wyoming history. Larson married the former Mary Hawkins in 1949 and the couple had one daughter.

Larson's long years of service to the university are impressive in their scope. He is estimated to have taught more than 16,000 undergraduate students, guided by his personal philosophy of challenging students to the outer limits of their capabilities. Larson directed 80 M.A. theses and six Ph.D. dissertations. Larson served as the chair of the History Department for 20 years, guiding it through its largest expansion and was director of the School of American Studies for nine years. Larson's service to the University was awarded with the George Duke Humphrey Distinguished Faculty Award (1966) and an honorary law degree (1984). The T.A. Larson Graduate Student Fellowship was established in his honor.

In addition to his administrative and teaching duties, Larson found time to excel as a scholar. Larson's first major book, *Wyoming's War Years, 1941-1945* was published by Stanford University Press in 1954. His *History of Wyoming*, first published in 1965, is regarded as the seminal textbook of the state's history. Larson's *History* was recognized with the American Association for State and Local History Award of Merit. In 1970, he received the Louis Knott Koontz Memorial Award for his article "The New Deal in Wyoming" which appeared in the *Pacific Historical Review*. He authored the Wyoming segment of the Bicentennial State History series in 1977. His work received critical acclaim for its unromanticized approach to Wyoming's place in western history.

Larson has also been active in civic and professional organizations. He was a charter member of the Wyoming State Historical Society and served as president. He helped found and later chaired the Wyoming Council for the Humanities. He also served as president of the Western History Association in 1970.

After his retirement from the university in 1975, Larson became the first university professor to serve in the state legislature. As Larson later stated "I made no bones about the fact that education was my number one priority, because I believe firmly education is the most important thing..." His voting record in the house, which included support of raising teacher pay scales and benefit packages, reflected his belief that such a commitment was necessary to maintain the quality of the state's educational system. Larson retired from the legislature after eight years as the Democratic representative for Albany County and now divides his time between Laramie and Southern California.

Larson has often stated his love for his adoptive state, but his affection is tempered by realism. His work as a historian has given him an appreciation of Wyoming's past but he also looks ahead. Believing that wise leadership and planning are necessary to "preserve what is best, to make what is good better," Larson has taught Wyomingites about their history while urging them to develop opportunities for future citizens.

CHAPTER FOUR FINE & PERFORMING ARTS

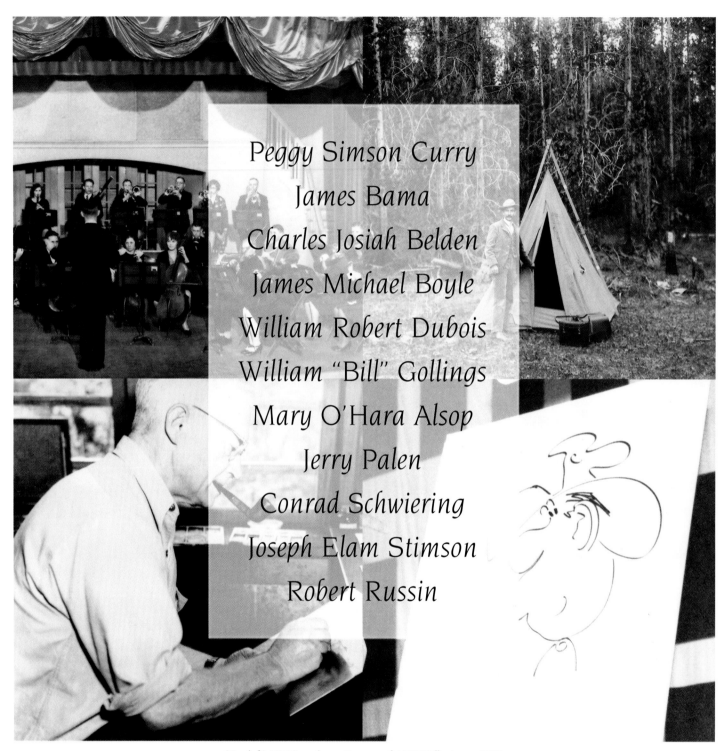

Peggy Simson Curry

James Bama

Charles Josiah Belden

James Michael Boyle

William Robert Dubois

William "Bill" Gollings

Mary O'Hara Alsop

Jerry Palen

Conrad Schwiering

Joseph Elam Stimson

Robert Russin

(Top left) UW Symphony *Courtesy of AHC Collection, c. 1929.*
(Top right) Bill Gollings *Courtesy of AHC Collection, c. 1911.*
(Bottom left) Hans Kleiber *Courtesy of AHC Collection, c. 1950.*
(Bottom right) Jerry Palen *Courtesy of Palen Family Collection.*

INTRODUCTION

Artists in all mediums have been attracted to Wyoming throughout the state's history. Besides its obvious scenic beauty, the opportunity to work in solitude and the state's tradition of fostering and respecting individuality have been factors. Among the first artists to play a prominent role in Wyoming were William Henry Jackson and William Cody. Despite the differences between the careers of the photographer and the performer, both are illustrative of Wyoming's place in western imagery.

Jackson accompanied the Hayden survey to Yellowstone in 1871 and photographed extensively, beginning a lifelong career of recording Wyoming's scenic beauty. As his landscapes and portraits of Native Americans illustrate, Jackson's great gift lay in his realization that it was not necessary to dramatize the west, just record it.

"Buffalo Bill" Cody achieved fame as a frontiersman and entertainer, by virtue of his career as an army scout and promoter of his Wild West Show. At the turn of the century, Cody attempted to develop Wyoming's Big Horn Basin, one of the last areas of the country to be settled. Although the private venture failed, the town of Cody was founded as a result. Cody, an authentic frontier hero, helped transform the real west into the romantic, mythical west still popular today.

Throughout the 20th century, Wyoming's reputation as a true western outpost continued to attract unconventional people, including Caroline Lockhart, a popular author. Lockhart, a successful newspaper reporter in Philadelphia, came to Cody, Wyoming, in 1904 on assignment and made the area her home. She wrote several novels with western themes, some of which were made into movies. Colorful and independent, Lockhart defied contemporary convictions about the role of women and reveled in the Wyoming's acceptance of individualism.

Other artists also drew on the Wyoming experience as the basis of their work, among them Elinore Pruitt Stewart. As a young widow, Elinore accepted a position as a housekeeper with Clyde Stewart, a Wyoming rancher. The two were married soon after. A dedicated letter writer, Stewart's life on the ranch provided her with endless subject matter, ranging from the difficulties of the Wyoming winter to the joys of gardening. Her collected writings were published in 1914 under the title *Letters of a Woman Homesteader.*

Even after the western frontier era ended, public interest in the region remained and some artists built a career upon that fascination. Nick Eggenhofer was a prolific illustrator, known as "King of the Pulps" during a period when that magazine genre continued to popularize the "Old West." By his own estimate, Eggenhofer produced an estimated 30,000 western illustrations in all media, including more than 50 book jackets.

Today Wyoming remains a source of inspiration for a new generation of artists. Whether the medium is painting or drawing, writing or performing, Wyoming is home to a range of artists. As the century closes, Wyoming's community of artists will continue to record and reflect the state's history.

MARGARET "PEGGY" SIMSON CURRY
1911-1987

Margaret "Peggy" Simson Curry was born in Dunure, Ayeshire, Scotland, on December 30, 1911. Her parents were Margaret and William Andrew Simson. When she was still a child, her family immigrated to the United States, settling in Colorado, where her father managed a ranch near Walden. She attended local rural schools, graduating from East High School in Denver.

Curry attended the University of Wyoming at Laramie and occasionally worked as a reporter for the local paper, the *Laramie Daily Boomerang.* She earned a bachelor's degree in English and Journalism in 1936. The following year she married William Seeright Curry. The newlyweds spent the next two years in Illinois, where William taught high school. In 1939, the Currys moved to Midwest, Wyoming, where their only child, Michael Munro Curry, was born. In 1946, the Curry family settled in Casper, Wyoming.

As a writer, Curry produced a large body of work, which includes four novels, two poetry collections, several short stories and a textbook on creative writing. She began her career by writing short stories for romance magazines. By the early 1950s, Curry had expanded her range. Her stories were published in such popular magazines as *Saturday Evening Post* and *Collier's.* She published numerous juvenile stories, a number in *Boys' Life,* and in 1970, a juvenile novel, *Shield of Clover.* She published her first novel, *Fire in the Water,* in 1951.

As her readership increased, Curry's work began to receive critical acclaim, with some comparing her to Willa Cather. Curry's second novel, *So Far From Spring* (1956), was set on a ranch at the turn of the century. A third novel, *The Oil Patch* (1959), was set in a town similar to Midwest. Her work is unique in that it draws on the west almost exclusively for background, setting, character, imagery and theme.

In addition to her personal success as an author, Curry also enjoyed a distinguished career as a teacher of creative writing. In 1950, she began conducting creative writing classes at Casper College. Beginning in the 1960s, she traveled throughout the state with the Mobile Symposium, teaching writing workshops to students at all age levels. She visited schools across Wyoming teaching poetry workshops, laying the foundation for the national Poetry in Schools Program. Curry also taught extension classes in western literature through the University of Wyoming. Her textbook on creative writing, *Creating Fiction from Experience,* was published in 1964.

Curry received many honors in recognition of her work as an author and teacher. Two of her short stories, "The Brushoff" (1957) and "In the Silence" (1970) received Golden Spur Awards as distinguished western stories of the year, presented by the Western Writers of America. She was recognized as a distinguished alumni by her alma matter in 1968. She was the recipient of the Wyoming Writers, Inc. Mygatt Award in 1975 and 1980. Curry was appointed the first state poet laureate in 1981. In 1984, she was honored by the Mountain Plains Library Association for writing that furthered the understanding and appreciation of the mountain plains region. In 1997, Curry was inducted into the Western Writers of America Hall of Fame. Peggy Simson Curry died in Casper, Wyoming, on January 20, 1987.

JAMES BAMA
1926-

James Bama was born in 1926 in Manhattan's Washington Heights. His father, a Russian Jewish immigrant, died when Bama was 14, leaving Bama and his brother Howard to care for their mother, who died four years later. Bama attended the High School of Music and Art in New York City, graduating in 1944. He spent 17 months in the Army Air Corps late in World War II. After his discharge, he enrolled in the Art Students League and after graduating in 1949, he freelanced briefly before joining the Charles E. Cooper Studios, where he worked for 14 years. He then returned to work as a freelancer, illustrating for the *Saturday Evening Post* and Bantam Books.

Bama moved to Wyoming in 1968 after 42 years of living in Manhattan. He established a studio in Wapiti, near Cody, 20 miles from the nearest neighbors. Describing himself as living on an island in a sea of land

and sky, Bama set about painting his surroundings, initially painting mostly still lifes, gradually moving into his now signature brand of western portraiture. Within three years, he gave up commercial art altogether, focusing on his desire to create realistic western art.

As someone who was "weaned on western movies," Bama enjoyed Wyoming's western landscapes and flavor. His philosophy, that the west is heroic and romantic, a blend of myth and tradition, is reflected in the precise imagery of his work. Bama admires the work of illustrator Norman Rockwell and realist painter Andrew Wyeth. His portraits reflect those influences and his work has been described as having a distinctive photo-realistic style.

Bama believes art should tell a story. Thus his Native American portraits, such as "Chester Medicine Crow," "Portrait of a Sioux," or his largest and best known "Contemporary Sioux Indian," reflect both the history of Indians and their current reality. He has captured Wyoming's past with his pictures of Roy Bezona, who described himself as "old man Wyoming," and George Washington Brown, the oldest living stagecoach driver of 24 horse teams. Bama has documented the mountain man phenomenon in such works as "Ready to Rendezvous" and he has illustrated the working west with portraits such as "Dede Fales, Camp Cook," one of his most popular and most often reproduced.

Bama's reputation has continued to grow, he has shared two major shows with Andrew Wyeth and was among the few artists chosen to participate in a 1987 cultural exchange program with China. He, his wife, Lynne, and their son, Ben, continue to live in Wyoming. Bama has described his adopted state as a source of inspiration for him, "a place where I have found what I wanted to say about life and work and what I believe in." Through his art, Bama continues to create a record of Wyoming's contemporary history while capturing the flavor of its past.

James Bama's realistic portraiture captures the essence of the individuality so highly prized by Wyomingites. *Courtesy of James Bama.*

CHARLES JOSIAH BELDEN
1887-1966

Charles Josiah Belden is credited with creating one of the most complete and remarkable pictorial records of early ranch life in Wyoming, documenting the change from the horse and wagon era to modern mechanization. Belden photographed life on the Pitchfork Ranch near Meeteetse, Wyoming, first as a cowboy and then as an owner.

Belden was born into a well-to-do San Francisco family on September 26, 1887. He was one of two children of Charles Albert Belden and Fanny B. Hubbard. He began attending the Massachusetts Institute of Technology in 1906, graduating four years later. While on a tour of Europe in 1909, Belden visited a large photography store in Berlin, Germany, and purchased a Zeiss Palmos camera. Upon his return to the United States, Belden began working at developing his own pictures.

Belden came to the Pitchfork Ranch as a ranch hand in 1914, seeking to experience cowboy lifestyle. The Pitchfork was originally established by Otto Franc, at the headwaters of the Greybull River in Wyoming's Big Horn Basin, east of Yellowstone, in the late 1870s. Franc was killed in an accident involving firearms in 1903 and ownership of the Pitchfork passed to Louis G. Phelps. Phelps expanded the Pitchfork's holdings to 250,000 acres. Belden eventually married Phelps' daughter, Frances, and when his father-in-law died in 1922, the running of the ranch was left to Belden and his brother-in-law, Eugene Phelps. Belden was responsible for the management of the livestock and business aspects of the ranch.

While managing the Pitchfork, Belden continued to perfect his photographic technique and he soon achieved a national reputation as a photojournalist. Action shots were Belden's specialty. He was given assignments throughout the world but his western pictures remain among his best known. Belden's photographs gave the Pitchfork Ranch national exposure, making it one of the most popular dude ranches in Wyoming.

Belden's work remains important today largely because of his expertise as a photographer. Although the majority of Belden's work is in black and white, he also experimented with autochrome color photography as early as 1916. The attention to composition, perspective and light, as well as the sheer artistry of the subject matter Belden chose are evident in each picture. His sympathy with and intimate knowledge of ranch life enabled him to create some of his best work at the Pitchfork Ranch.

Belden left the Pitchfork Ranch after his first marriage ended in divorce. In 1940, he moved to St. Petersburg, Florida, where he settled with his second wife, Verna Steele Belden. In later years he traveled the world, on assignment for national magazines and as a lecturer. In January, 1966, Charles Belden was found dead in his darkroom. The apparent cause of death was a self-inflicted gunshot wound.

The majority of Belden's work is recorded on glass negatives and he eventually built a file of more than 2,700. Through the foresight of his heirs, the majority of these negatives have been preserved. A portion of the collection is housed at the Buffalo Bill Center in Cody, Wyoming, and the remainder was donated to the American Heritage Center in Laramie, Wyoming. Every year, the photos are used and reproduced by many researchers and historians. Belden's legacy to Wyoming lies in his creation of an invaluable documentation of the history of ranch life.

JAMES MICHAEL BOYLE
1910-1996

"a most painterly country." This appreciation for "ever present nature" found an expression in Boyle's artistic philosophy. Art and nature formed the integral core of his vision, he described them as "my sources, my inspiration, my sustenance."

Boyle, who had a reputation as "that modern painter in Laramie," is credited by three generations of students with bringing the world of visual arts to the state of Wyoming. Boyle's vision allowed him to build a department uniquely suited to meet the needs of his constituency. He was well known for the individual attention he gave his students. The large number of graduates with successful careers in the fine arts demonstrates the viability of the department he nurtured.

Boyle taught many classes, including drawing, but he also inspired students with his own work. After arriving in Laramie, he began exploring different mediums, including watercolor. By the late 1950s, his work became more abstract, with stronger colors, emphasizing motion and tension. Throughout the next two decades, Boyle continued to teach and paint. His paintings were uniquely personal, reflecting what his peers referred to as his "impressionistic style." After what was described as a long and productive term as head of the art department, Boyle retired in 1975, after nearly 30 years.

Throughout his career, Boyle worked diligently to further the cause of fine arts throughout the state and region by founding, sponsoring and participating in many of the institutions which promoted art and artists. He supported the Wyoming Artist Association, was a founder of the Western Association of Art Schools and University Museums and served on the Wyoming Council of the Arts from its beginning. Boyle was a longtime advocate for the establishment of an art museum at the University and in 1972 his dream became a reality. His tireless work in promoting and teaching art throughout the region earned him the well-deserved title of "Mr. Art." James Boyle died in Laramie on December 22, 1996.

James Boyle worked to create new opportunities for the people of Wyoming to enjoy art. *Courtesy of Jacques Photography.*

James Michael Boyle was born in Newcastle, Pennsylvania, on January 30, 1910. Boyle, whose father was a steel mill worker, grew up in the mill town of Aliquippa, Pennsylvania, where he attended local schools. Boyle also worked in the mills, while attending the Carnegie Institute of Technology in Pittsburgh, Pennsylvania. He earned a bachelor's degree in 1935 and began to pursue a teaching career, migrating west to Colorado in 1936. Three years later he married June Ott and the couple eventually had two children.

While teaching, Boyle pursued a master of Fine Arts degree from the University of Colorado, completing his studies in 1944. Boyle also created his own work throughout this time. His paintings from this period, which reflected the influence of the Regionalist School as well as a cubistic aspect, often depicted scenes from the steel mills in which he had once labored. The paintings were primarily done in oils.

In 1946, Boyle came to the University of Wyoming in Laramie to head the art department. A believer in the significance of the "real world" in any artistic endeavor, he immediately seized upon the state's natural beauty as an important artistic resource, describing Wyoming as

WILLIAM ROBERT DUBOIS
1879-1953

5—*Sixteenth Street (Lincoln Way) and Business District,*

William Robert Dubois, one of the most prominent and prolific architects in the state of Wyoming for the first 40 years of this century, was born in Chicago in November, 1879. His parents were William John Baptists and Marie Dubois. Dubois attended the Chicago School of Architecture in the late 19th century and then received his architectural training at a firm in Albuquerque, New Mexico. His firm sent Dubois to Cheyenne, Wyoming, in the early 1900s to supervise the construction of the Carnegie Library. He was advised that Cheyenne and the state needed a good architect, and since he had met and fallen in love with his future wife there, Dubois decided to settle in the area. In 1904, he married Dora Slack and the couple eventually had five children.

Dubois was a master of design, utilizing a variety of architectural styles ranging from Beaux Arts Classicism to Romanesque Revival. He quickly developed a large clientele and was responsible for designing both public and private buildings across the state, among them several more Carnegie libraries. Dubois' governmental commissions included the east and west wings of the state capitol and the Supreme Court/State Library Building. Among his other public buildings are the Albany and Laramie County courthouses, as well as the present administrative offices for Cheyenne's schools, formerly the high school. Dubois designed six buildings for the University of Wyoming, including the Half Acre Gymnasium, which was one of several collaborations with Wilbur Hitchcock.

Dubois also designed numerous commercial buildings throughout the state. Two of the most distinctive, the Hynds Building and the Plains Hotel, are part of Cheyenne's historic downtown. The Hynds Building has among its distinctive features a white terra cotta-clad edifice and leaded windows. The Plains Hotel has an exterior typical of contemporary commercial structures but the original interior, now unfortunately largely destroyed, was an eclectic mixture of western designs.

Other Dubois buildings in Cheyenne include the Lincoln Theater and the Elks Club. Not all his work has survived, among the buildings that were demolished were the Henning and Gladstone hotels in Casper, the Consistory Building in Cheyenne and the Eastside Elementary School in Cody. But it appears that people now recognize the value of his work as did his peers, who remarked that "many of the finest buildings on the University campus and in the capital city bear testimony to his worth." Preservationists have worked to preserve his work and the many residences that he designed across the state have increased value by virtue of their provenance.

Dubois was an active member of the Cheyenne community, serving twice as president of the Chamber of Commerce and several terms in the state legislature. He played the organ in many area churches and participated in numerous civic boards and committees. Dubois died in Cheyenne on May 31, 1953. He was described by his contemporaries as the state's leading architect, a man who "has his mark on the state of Wyoming."

WILLIAM "BILL" GOLLINGS
1878-1932

Elling William "Bill" Gollings was born in the mining camp of Pierce City in what was then the Idaho Territory in 1878. His father was Ellick H. Gollings. His mother, Tilla A. Howell, died when he was an infant and Gollings' early years were spent on his grandmother's farm in Michigan. In 1890, his father moved his family to Chicago, where Gollings enrolled in public schools, completing the equivalent of an eighth grade education. His teachers encouraged his interest in drawing and he learned many basic techniques, including the use of perspective and the rudiments of line and form. Following his 1893 graduation, Gollings held a variety of jobs, including draftsman.

Three years later, Gollings traveled to Rapid City, South Dakota, to fulfill his boyhood dream of becoming a "cow-puncher." He later recalled the west "was a country worth living in" that "seemed a paradise to me." He would continue to feel this way about his chosen country for the rest of his life, while accepting that the west he loved was in a period of transition. As Gollings later wrote, "I realized that the cowboy days were about over. The older men... told me as much, and I longed to be a part of at least the last of it." For the next five years, he rode the range in the summer, worked on ranches in the winter, and drew and sketched in his spare time.

Gollings eventually drifted from Montana to northern Wyoming, arriving in Sheridan in 1903. By

this time, he had enjoyed some success with his art and had made an investment in his career, purchasing a box of oil paints and other supplies from Montgomery Ward's mail order catalog. For the next three years he continued to work as a ranch hand, sketching and painting whenever the opportunity presented itself. He spent a great deal of time in the area of the Cheyenne Indian Reservation, making the acquaintance of the residents and using them as subjects in his work.

In 1907, encouraged by his brother DeWitt, Gollings traveled to Chicago to attend classes at the Chicago Academy of Fine Arts. His work was deemed promising by the Chicago art establishment but Gollings himself would remain dissatisfied with certain aspects of his technique throughout his career. Gollings returned to Wyoming and eventually built himself a small studio in Sheridan. After his marriage to Maude Scrivner in 1917, he added a house to the studio. Even Gollings' closest friends described him as a difficult person, often unsatisfied, and this trait eventually led to the demise of his marriage. Gollings continued to work as an artist and although his reputation grew, he was never prosperous. He added to his income by working as a ranch hand during roundups and illustrating for western magazines.

Part of Gollings' inability to support himself solely as an artist arose from his reluctance to promote himself or his work and his low prices. He was a harsh critic of his work, often refusing to sign or sell pieces he didn't like. He would only sign his work, adding his signature pony track, when he was completely satisfied. One of Gollings more successful artistic enterprises began when he started sending Christmas cards, featuring his own work and poetry, to friends in the 1920s. Soon people commissioned these works and Gollings worked steadily to support the demand for these specialized prints.

Gollings died of a heart attack in 1932 at the age of 54. His body of work includes more than 150 paintings, many unfinished works and pen and ink sketches. At his best, particularly in his winter scenes, Gollings successfully captured, in vivid detail, the last of the "old west" in Wyoming.

Bill Gollings, ranch hand turned artist, captured the west of a bygone era in vivid detail. *Courtesy of AHC Collection, c. 1911.*

MARY O'HARA ALSOP
1885-1980

Through her writing, Mary O'Hara created a lasting image of Wyoming's scenic beauty. *Courtesy of AHC Collection, c. 1935.*

Mary O'Hara Alsop was born at Cape May Point, New Jersey, on July 10, 1885. The daughter of an Episcopal clergyman, she grew up in Brooklyn, New York, where she was educated. Alsop's mother died when she was six years old so her maternal grandmother played a large role in her upbringing. Alsop spent time on her grandmother's farm and it was there that she developed her lifelong love of horses.

In 1905, Alsop married Kent Kane Parrot. The couple eventually had one son and a daughter. During her marriage, Alsop lived in California and had a successful career as a screenwriter during the silent film era. After her marriage to Parrot ended in divorce, she married Helge Sture-Vasa in 1922. During the 1920s, she continued her screenwriting career and *Toilers of the Sea* and *Prisoner of Zenda* were among her projects.

During the 1930s, Alsop and her husband came to live in Wyoming on the Remount Ranch, near Cheyenne, and this experience provided the background for her best known books. In 1941, *My Friend Flicka* was published under the pen name Mary O'Hara. The book met with critical and popular success and has been published in 62 languages. It was eventually made into a movie starring the young Roddy McDowell and in the 1950s it became a television series.

Set amongst the windblown hills of Wyoming, *My Friend Flicka* is the story of a 10-year-old boy who lives on a ranch. While his father raises thoroughbreds, the novel's hero prefers a wild filly named Flicka, who is nearly untamable. *My Friend Flicka* has been described as a story about the journey to self knowledge and adulthood. Mary O'Hara caught the imaginations of millions with her vivid descriptions of Wyoming's extraordinary landscapes, breathtaking sunrises and sunsets and extremes of weather.

Although life in Wyoming proved fruitful for O'Hara artistically, her time at the Remount was not successful financially. Attempts to establish a dairy farm, a horse raising operation and a boys camp ultimately failed. In 1943, the Remount was sold and O'Hara and her husband returned to California, where they divorced. She had her maiden name legally restored and eventually returned to the east.

Thunderhead, the sequel to *My Friend Flicka,* was published in 1944 and was hailed as that rarest of commodities, a successful sequel. Critics noted the story had a timeless quality, which would allow it to remain popular for many generations. Of particular note was O'Hara's ability to make the horses, and indeed all the animals, wild and domestic, come alive for the reader without the use of anthropomorphic romanticizing. *Thunderhead* was also made into a movie, with McDowell re-creating his earlier role.

During her lifetime O'Hara published other works, among them *The Son of Adam Wyngate* (1952) and *Wyoming Summer* (1954). *Green Grass of Wyoming* (1946) was also a popular success and was made into a film. She died in 1980 at the age of 95.

Though her time in Wyoming was relatively short, the impact of Mary O'Hara's books will always remain a part of Wyoming's history. People from all over the world continue to make pilgrimages to the Remount Ranch 25 miles west of Cheyenne, drawn by the beauty so aptly depicted in O'Hara's stories. Mary O'Hara Alsop once described Wyoming as "a secret hidden world, unknown to the rest of the country, serene and calm, with a slow heartbeat." Her greatest accomplishment as an author was to reveal that world to her readers.

JERRY PALEN
1943-

Jerry Palen was born in Paris, Tennessee, on July 9, 1943, where his father, an Army colonel, was stationed during World War II. After the war, his family settled in Cheyenne, Wyoming, where Palen grew up and attended local schools. He credits his father, Joe Palen, an acknowledged expert in western art, with developing his artistic sensibilities. Although he was not aware of his father's influence at the time, Palen has recalled that his father "dragged me through every studio and museum in the western United States."

Palen received a Bachelor of Arts degree in political science and economics from the University of Wyoming. When asked why he chose to study sciences rather than art, Palen credits an understanding he had with his mother, who, doubting his ability to make a living in his chosen field, insisted he at least receive an education. Palen studied fine art in Santa Barbara, California, for five years, under the private tutelage of Nicholas Firfires, a prominent artist. Palen returned to Wyoming in 1971, living on the Chalk Bluffs Ranch with his wife, Ann Prosser Palen, and working as a state bank examiner.

Within a year, Palen earned his first money as an artist for eight cartoons that appeared in *Western Horseman*. Soon after, he launched his successful cartoon series, the now famous "Stampede." The series, which features the country couple of Elmo and Flo, was syndicated in 1973. "Stampede" is the largest rural cartoon series in North America, with several million readers.

Noted for its blend of western wit and common sense philosophy, "Stampede" has been praised for its unique representation of the rural point of view. Flo and Elmo have spawned several books and thousands of t-shirts and calendars. Palen is justifiably proud of his success, maintaining that "cartooning is as high an art as there is."

In addition to his cartoon series, Palen is also a successful rancher and businessman, as well as an active member of his community. In 1978, he and his wife purchased part of the historic Wyoming Hereford Ranch. They have built a successful yearling cattle operation with their pioneering use of holistic ranching techniques. The couple also train and show horses. Palen is an original founder and partner in Laffing Cow Press, based in Saratoga, which showcases many Wyoming authors and is one of the leading publishers of country humor.

Palen generously donates art to many community groups, as well as entertaining various civic groups. He is listed in Who's Who in American Art, and is a member of the prestigious National Cartoonist Society. Collectors, who prize his Wyoming viewpoint, seek out his cartoons, limited edition bronzes and watercolors. Constantly in demand as a speaker, Palen travels the United States and Canada as a one of the most visible ambassadors for the Wyoming way of life. He is a broad-based, creative, and talented artist, who uses humor in his cartoons, storytelling and art. There is no question what state he is from and where his roots lie.

Jerry Palen's work as a cartoonist can be recognized by its signature blend of rural wit and common sense. *Courtesy of Palen Family Collection.*

CONRAD SCHWIERING
1916-1985

Conrad Schwiering's unique brand of western art was distinguished by his impressionistic style. *Courtesy of Schwiering Family Collection.*

Conrad "Connie" Oscer Schwiering was the acknowledged dean of the Jackson Hole art colony. Born in Boulder, Colorado, on August 8, 1916, Schwiering grew up in Wyoming. His father worked as the superintendent of schools in Douglas and Rock Springs. It was while living in Douglas that young Schwiering first displayed his artistic tendencies, when, still barely able to walk, he found some crayons and drew "murals" on the walls of his room.

In 1925, Schwiering's father accepted a professorship at the University of Wyoming, where he later became dean of the College of Education. Five years later, while on sabbatical leave, he, his wife and Schwiering's younger brother, traveled to New York City, where they lived while the senior Schwiering earned his doctoral degree. While in New York, Conrad Schwiering enrolled in Stuyvesant High, which had a required course in the fundamentals of drawing. He learned to draw in pencil and because of his skills, was allowed to take a more advanced course, where he learned the use of color.

After the family returned to Laramie, Schwiering completed his high school education, graduating in 1934. He took his first job at a the City Market, a small grocery store. He later credited this experience with teaching him about customer relations. In 1936, his parents persuaded him to enroll in the University of Wyoming, where he earned a degree in commerce and law. It was here that he met his future wife, Mary Ethel Smith, voted the most beautiful girl at the University. The couple married in 1939.

While earning his degree, Schwiering was determined to pursue a career in art and set about learning his craft, studying with Robert Graham, Raphael Lillywhite and Bert Phillips, one of the founders of the Taos art colony. After graduating, he studied art in New York at the Art Students League, with George Bridgemen and Charles Chapman, who became a close friend and mentor. In 1941 he followed the advice of Chapman, who said Schwiering had mastered the fundamentals and should pursue his own artistic path, so the Schwierings returned to Laramie to contemplate their future. World War II put their plans on hold, when Schwiering was called to active duty that same year. He served five years in the army and was discharged at the rank of lieutenant colonel in February, 1946.

Schwiering and his wife arrived in Jackson Hole in June, 1947, and set up house in their travel trailer, where they lived until they eventually built their dream home in Antelope Flats. As an artist, he was stimulated by the clean air and snow-covered mountains of Jackson Hole. In those early years, he later remembered, he would often set up his easel and begin painting in Jackson Hole's town center, in an effort to attract potential buyers. He soon established a gallery in the balcony of the Wort Hotel, one of the town's most attractive tourist destinations by virtue of its open gaming tables. The Wort brothers provided the space for free, in a handshake deal that lasted 12 years.

Among his Jackson Hole works, the Grand Tetons appear most frequently because as Schwiering remarked, "I never tire of using the mountains as a subject over and over, at different times and in different seasons of the year." But his portfolio also included landscapes in Mexico and California, where he and his wife spent their winters in later years. Although Schwiering sometimes painted in watercolor, his favorite medium was oil. His preferred subjects included not only his famous western landscapes, but also what he referred to as "heritage studies," in which he depicted the people and spirit of frontier life. Schwiering was noted for his impressionistic style which set his work apart from the more realistic tradition of western art.

Schwiering died of a heart attack at the age of 69, while painting in Pebble Beach, California. He was buried near his cabin in Jackson Hole. During his career, he completed more than 1,600 oil paintings and thousands of oil sketches and pencil drawings. He recalled his artistic career with satisfaction, "never having sacrificed a moment of my art life to illustration or portrait commission. I have been a really free man who never owed his time to anyone." As an artist and a man Conrad Schwiering managed to capture the essence of the Wyoming way of life.

JOSEPH ELAM STIMSON
1870-1952

Joseph Elam "J.E." Stimson was born on May 18, 1870, in Brandy Station, Virginia. His father, William Stimson, was a doctor who had immigrated from Canada. In 1873, the elder Stimson, his wife, Jenny, and his family of eight children moved to South Carolina and Joseph Stimson spent most of his childhood in southern Appalachia. After his father's death, Stimson was an apprentice for his cousin, James Stimson, who was a photographer in Appleton, Wisconsin. Under his cousin's tutelage he learned the art of portrait photography, as well as the mechanics of wet plate processing and the still relatively new procedure of dry plate photography.

Encouraged by two of his brothers who were employed by the Union Pacific Railroad, Stimson set out for Wyoming determined to establish himself as a photographer, despite having none of the necessary accoutrements of his trade. He arrived in Cheyenne in the spring of 1889, purchased a studio and equipment, and by July was in business as a portrait photographer.

Five years later, two significant events occurred in Stimson's life. On the personal front, he married Anna Peterson, with whom he eventually had two daughters. On the professional front, his career was changed forever when Elwood Mead, the state engineer, brought scenic photos of the Big Horn Mountains to Stimson's studio to be developed. Stimson was intrigued by the beauty of the pictures and the following year he accompanied Mead on a trip to the Big Horns. Although his initial attempts at scenic picture taking were less than successful, (he overexposed the negatives,) Stimson had found his calling, photographing of his adopted state.

Four years later Stimson accompanied Albert Nelson, Wyoming's first game warden, to Jackson Hole and the Tetons. The area became his favorite locale and he returned to photograph almost every year. During the next two years, the quality of Stimson's work improved and he began to sell his efforts and develop a reputation as a scenic photographer.

In 1901, the Union Pacific Railroad hired Stimson as its official photographer. Since he was paid on a per print basis, Stimson was not limited in the number of photographs he took. He traveled the railroad line photographing the 10 western states through which it passed. Stimson's work for the Union Pacific, and other railroads, such as the Burlington and Chicago and Northwestern, went beyond the obvious subjects of locomotives and rail yards; he also photographed city life, rural towns and natural panoramas.

In 1903, Stimson was hired by the Wyoming Commission of the Louisiana Purchase Exposition to produce color photos of scenes across Wyoming. Paid a fee of $875, he spent the summer traversing the state. These black and white photos, beautifully hand-tinted by Stimson, won awards not only in St. Louis, but also at the Louis and Clark Exposition in 1905, and established Stimson's professional reputation.

For the next 10 years, Stimson continued to work for the Union Pacific and the state of Wyoming. He was

Stimson's work, characterized by careful composition, sharp focus and excellent use of light, transcends mere photography to become art.

hired by various state agencies and his work illustrated brochures dealing with topics such as ranching, irrigation and recreation. Most of his state commissions came from the immigration department, which was charged with attracting new residents. Ironically, while Stimson's images may have had little impact on the Wyoming's permanent population, his photos of Yellowstone and other natural wonders were instrumental in establishing the state's tourism industry.

The onset of World War I, with the government taking control of the railroads, meant the end of Stimson's tenure with the Union Pacific. The beginning of the Great Depression meant fewer contracts from the state. Stimson continued to secure work through whatever avenues were available, including more portrait work and projects for local businesses and organizations. During the 1930s, he took photographs for the Civilian Conservation Corps and ranchers throughout the state. And, beginning in 1929, Stimson was commissioned by the Bureau of Reclamation, headed by his old friend Elwood Mead, to create a record of the agency's projects. Unfortunately, few of these, like Stimson's portraits, have been discovered.

Despite his advancing age and the death of his wife in 1938, Stimson continued to work. His actual photographic production slowed but he continued to hand color prints from his extensive files of negatives. In 1948, he was hired by the Wyoming Department of Commerce and Industry to make negatives of his favorite locales, the Tetons and Yellowstone. Four years later, Stimson died of a heart attack. He was buried next to his wife in Cheyenne's Lakeview Cemetery. His photographic collection, gathered during the course of a 62-year career, consisted of more than 7,000 photographs, many of them glass plate negatives. The Stimson collection was purchased by the State of Wyoming for $2,000 in 1952.

Stimson's work, characterized by careful composition, sharp focus and excellent use of light, transcends mere photography to become art, as Stimson himself acknowledged in his own customary signature stamp, "J.E. Stimson, Artist." His legacy remains a pictorial study of life in Wyoming at the beginning of the 20th century.

ROBERT RUSSIN
1914-

Robert Russin's carved white marble trio, "University of Wyoming Family, located in Prexy's Pasture" at the University of Wyoming. *Courtesy of AHC Collection.*

Robert Isaiah Russin was born in New York City on August 26, 1914, the son of Uriel and Olga Russin. He attended the College of the City of New York, receiving a bachelor's degree in 1933 and master's degree in 1935. That same year he received a one-year fellowship for graduate study at the Beaux Arts Institute of Design. It was while studying at Beaux Arts that Russin, who had always considered himself a painter, was introduced to clay. From that point on, all of his work has been three dimensional.

Russin began his career in New York City in the 1930s, working as an artist and a teacher at the height of the Great Depression. He immediately enjoyed some success in both arenas. An early piece, "The Waitress," was exhibited at two World's Fairs; and he taught at Cooper Union and then later at his alma mater. In 1937, Russin married Adele Mutchnick and the couple eventually had three children. A decade later, Russin brought his family to Wyoming to accept a teaching position at the University of Wyoming. From 1976 to 1985 he was the university's Artist in Residence. In 1985, in recognition of his many years at the University, he was named a University of Wyoming Distinguished Professor Emeritus of Art.

Since his arrival in Wyoming, Russin has continued his commitment to public sculpture. After four decades of teaching at the University of Wyoming, his works grace the grounds and buildings. His statue of Ben Franklin offers the key of wisdom to students. Most prominent, the "University of Wyoming Family in Prexy's Pasture," is what Russin himself described as "by far my most significant work on the UW campus." The trio, carved in white marble, provides a focus to the central campus.

Perhaps the best known of Russin's works within the state of Wyoming is the Lincoln Monument, formerly located at the Lincoln Highway, which now sits atop the summit of U.S. Interstate 80, between Cheyenne and Wyoming. The massive bronze bust, perched on a 30-foot base, is designed to appear as a natural outcropping. The Lincoln Monument measures 45 feet from the base to the top of Lincoln's head, standing 12 1/2 feet high atop a 30-foot marble column, and weighs 3 1/2 tons. Completion of the work was a technical as well an artistic triumph. As Russin recalled, "It took nine months to complete the plaster model, do the casting and erect the granite base. A lot of details were involved." Moving the statute from Mexico City to Wyoming via railroad required extensive logistical planning on Russin's part. Russin literally put the finishing touches on the work an hour before the dedication ceremony in October, 1959. Russin has remarked that the statue remains his favorite, "I've always loved Lincoln. The best of America resides in his philosophy."

Russin retired from teaching in 1986. He remains active in his field, maintaining studios in Centennial, Wyoming, and Green Valley, Arizona. In summarizing his career, Russin has maintained that living in Wyoming provided him with many advantages as an artist. Freed from the competitive and somewhat stifling atmosphere of the east coast artistic establishment, Russin had time "to think and expand." Also influential to his stylistic development were "the landscape and the quality of its light." But perhaps most significant, both to Russin as an artist with an abiding interest in expressing the human condition and to the role his art plays in Wyoming's self image, is his belief that Wyomingites "are more intent on real values."

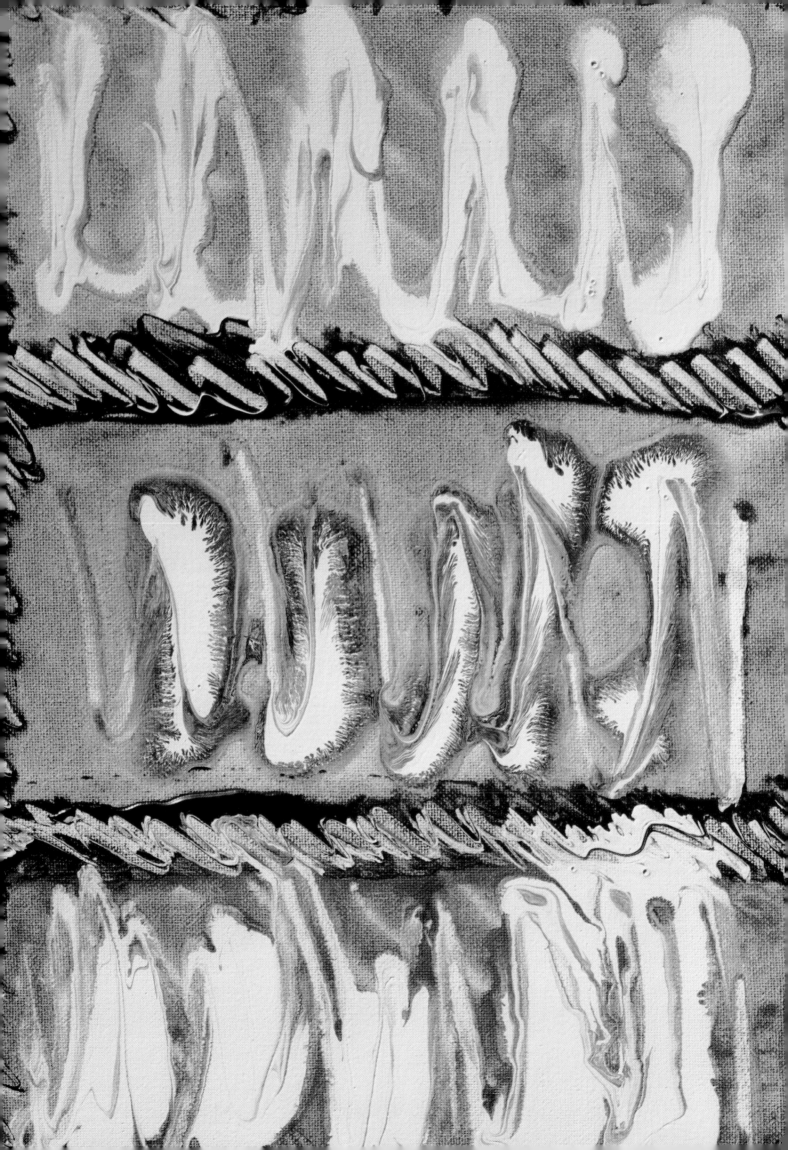

CHAPTER FIVE GOVERNMENT & COMMUNITY SERVICE

Olaus & Margaret Murie

Alan Simpson

Richard B. Cheney

Thurman W. Arnold

Thomas A. Bell

Fred Blume

Clifford P. Hansen

Susan Jane Quealy

John Kendrick

Joseph O'Mahoney

Nellie Tayloe Ross

Thomas Stroock

Michael Sullivan

F.E. Warren

Joseph Watt

Yellow Calf

Edgar Herschler

Teno Roncalio

(Top left) Joe Watt *Courtesy of Watt Family Collection.*
(Top right) Susan Jane Quealy, c. 1915 *Courtesy of AHC Collection.*
(Bottom left) Wyoming State Capitol, c. 1970 *Courtesy of Wyoming Archives.*
(Bottom right) Washington Park, Laramie, c. 1920 *Courtesy of AHC Collection.*

INTRODUCTION

Wyoming's citizens have a long history of service to their state. Government and community services are two categories that encompass a wide range of people, including some of the state's most prominent citizens. Indeed, it is sometimes difficult to distinguish where one person's contributions lie. Some people have claimed that the state's relatively small population makes such an active citizenry inevitable. Others have maintained that the state's designation as the Equality State has created special opportunities for women. Whatever the reasons, Wyoming's 20th century history is rich with stories of people who have given much to their state.

Dr. Oliver Chambers is only one example. Hired out of medical school by the Union Pacific Railroad, he came to Wyoming in 1903. He settled in Rock Springs, serving the community and the surrounding area until his death in 1941. Chambers was extensively involved in community affairs and served in the state legislature. His efforts are still remembered, as evidenced by the many stories about him that are passed among the families in southwestern Wyoming. His work merits recognition because his leadership and values served as an example for those who followed him.

Both Democrats and Republicans have made a name for themselves in national and state politics. Gale W. McGee accepted a position as a professor of American History at the University of Wyoming in 1946. A gifted public speaker and debater, McGee quickly became one of the most popular teachers at the university. Active in democratic politics and with aspirations for elected office, McGee left the University in 1958 in a successful bid for the U.S. Senate, where he served three terms. Progressive on domestic issues, McGee was an internationalist in foreign affairs. His reputation enhanced the stature of Wyoming's congressional delegation.

Following his distinguished service in World War II, Stanley Knapp Hathaway established a law practice in Torrington and became active in the Republican Party. Hathaway ran a successful campaign for governor in 1966 and was re-elected in 1970, becoming the first Wyoming governor to serve two full terms. As governor, Hathaway vigorously promoted economic growth and government reorganization. Perhaps his most significant accomplishment occurred during his last year in office, with the establishment of the Permanent Mineral Trust Fund. In 1975, President Gerald Ford appointed Hathaway as the secretary of the interior.

Women have been in active in Wyoming's communities throughout this century. Thyra Godfrey Thomson served as Wyoming's secretary of state from 1962 to 1986. Harriet Elizabeth Byrd was elected to the Wyoming House of Representatives in 1981, becoming the first African American woman to serve in Wyoming's legislature. She was elected to the state senate in 1989. Johanna Gostas was the state coordinator for the National League of Families of American Prisoners and Missing in Southeast Asia. Helen Bardo of Lusk pioneered efforts to make buildings accessible to the disabled. These individuals represent only a few of the many men and women who have worked to preserve and enhance Wyoming's quality of life for Wyoming's citizenry.

OLAUS & MARGARET MURIE
1889-1963, 1903-

Preserving the elk herd at Jackson Hole was the first of many efforts by Olaus and Margaret Murie to conserve the wilderness in Wyoming and the west.
Courtesy of AHC Collection.

Olaus Murie was born in Moorehead, Minnesota, in 1889. His parents were Norwegian immigrants. As a young man he was fascinated by the natural world. Murie was particularly influenced by the work of the writer and illustrator, Thompson Seton. In 1912, Murie graduated from Pacific University in Oregon. While a student he had worked on two Carnegie Museums ornithological expeditions, one to Hudson Bay, the other to Labrador. During World War I he worked as a balloon observer for the Army Air Force.

In 1920, Murie was hired by the U.S. Biological Survey to conduct a study of the caribou herds that migrated from Alaska to the Yukon Territory. While in Alaska he met Margaret Thomas. Margaret Thomas was born in Seattle, Washington, in 1903. Her family moved to Fairbanks, Alaska, when she was nine. She attended Reed College for two years and then transferred to the University of Alaska, where, in 1922, she became the first female graduate.

The couple married in 1924. During their courtship, Margaret Murie was attracted by her husband's work and knew that when they married, she would be a part of it. For their honeymoon, they explored Brooks Range by dogsled. With their three children in tow, Margaret Murie accompanied her husband on virtually every expedition he made throughout his career. She once described their life together as "one long field trip."

In 1927, Olaus Murie was assigned by the U.S. Fish and Wildlife Department to study the elk herd at Jackson Hole, Wyoming, which appeared to be declining. The couple settled into the area and quickly became part of the community. Margaret was instrumental in establishing the local library. During the course of his research, Olaus became alarmed at the Biological Survey's policy of systematic extermination of predators. By 1931, he was espousing the then revolutionary idea of a more enlightened approach to the management of predator species.

Murie was among the first field biologists to appreciate the delicate nature of each ecosystem. His research eventually led him to conclude that while the decline in the elk herd that had first brought him to Jackson Hole was the result of disease, the extermination of predators was a significant factor in upsetting the natural balance of the area. His work on behalf of preserving the elk herd of Wyoming earned Murie the designation of "Mr. Elk."

In 1943, when President Franklin D. Roosevelt declared Jackson Hole a national monument, the Muries quickly become embroiled in the controversy. There was great opposition to the proposed designation by development advocates, who feared a cessation of growth and conservationists, who objected to Lake Jackson's status as an artificially enlarged body of water. The Muries were instrumental in persuading conservation groups to support the designation. In 1944, Olaus Murie published an article, "The Spirit of Jackson Hole," in *National Parks,* which many have credited with turning the tide in favor of the national monument designation.

In 1954, Murie resigned from Fish and Wildlife to work as the director of the Wilderness Society. Together with his wife, he led the society's push for legislation to protect the last of the wilderness areas. The Muries were a driving force behind the preservation of two major wilderness areas, Grand Teton National Park and the Arctic National Wildlife Refuge. The couple also worked with other conservation leaders to bring about the passage of the 1964 Wilderness Act. Margaret and Olaus collaborated on several publications. She edited his collection of Alaskan bird sketches and they co-authored *Wapiti Wilderness.* Margaret Murie is also an author in her own right and has written her autobiography, *Two In the Far North,* detailing their life together, as well as *Island Between.*

Olaus Murie died in 1963, just months before the passage of the legislation he had fought for created 9.1 million acres of wilderness areas in national forests. As one of the first naturalists to appreciate the concept of ecosystem integrity, he incorporated his work as a field biologist into his personal philosophy. His legacy can be appreciated by the residents of Wyoming who benefit from his efforts at wilderness preservation every time they enjoy the beauty of Jackson Hole.

Since her husband's death, Margaret has continued to campaign for conservationist causes. As a member of the governing council of the Wilderness Society, Margaret Murie was instrumental in the passage of the 1980 Alaska Lands Act, which set aside millions of acres of wilderness. Her years of work in the environmental movement have brought her many honors. In 1980, Margaret was honored with the Audubon Medal and the following year she received the Sierra Club's John Muir Award. In 1998, Murie received the nation's highest civilian honor, the Medal of Freedom. Today, after nearly a century of advocating for wilderness preservation, Margaret Murie continues to live near Moose in the log cabin she and her husband built when they first arrived in Wyoming in 1927.

ALAN SIMPSON
1931-

Alan Simpson was born in Cody, Wyoming, on September 2, 1931. His parents were Milward Lee and Lorna Kooi. After graduating from Cody High School in 1949, he attended the University of Wyoming, where he earned a bachelor of science degree in 1954. That same year he married the former Ann Schroll of Greybull, Wyoming, who was a 1953 graduate of the University of Wyoming. The couple has two sons and a daughter. After a stint in the Army, Simpson returned to the University of Wyoming and earned a law degree in 1958.

Simpson was admitted to the Wyoming State Bar in 1958. The following year he accepted a position as the Assistant Attorney General for the State of Wyoming. From 1959 to 1969, he was city attorney for the City of Cody, while maintaining a private law practice with the firm of Simpson, Kepler, Simpson and Cozzens.

Simpson came from a family with a strong political background. His father served as both a Wyoming governor and United States senator. His brother Peter also served two terms in the Wyoming House. In 1964, Simpson continued in that tradition when he was elected to the Wyoming House of Representatives as a republican representing Park County. From 1973 to 1975, he served as majority whip, moving into the position of majority floor leader in 1975. In 1977, he became speaker of the Wyoming House of Representatives.

In 1978, Simpson entered the national political arena, successfully running for the United States Senate.

He quickly became recognized for his quick wit and sharp criticisms, establishing a reputation as "one of the Senate's most effective speakers, one of its hardest workers and one its most skillful legislators." Simpson himself said serving a state such as Wyoming gave him a particular freedom along with certain responsibilities, noting in his own particular manner that his constituents didn't want "Any white papers or lengthy explanations. They won't allow you to go big dog."

Simpson served on the Veterans Affairs Committee and the nuclear regulation subcommittee. While in the Senate he was known for his work on veteran's affairs and aging issues. Among his successes were a 1981 inheritance tax reform bill and a 1984 wilderness bill that added more than 800,000 acres to Wyoming's wilderness.

Simpson easily defeated Democratic challenges in re-election bids in 1984 and 1990. As a member of the subcommittee on immigration and refugee policy, Simpson sponsored major legislation to reform the immigration process during the late 1980s. True to form, Simpson did not hesitate to support unpopular positions, taking on powerful entitlement and lobbying groups. He also promoted fiscal responsibility, urging his colleagues to slow spending growth.

While in office Simpson never shied away from controversy. His support of abortion rights lost him the backing of republicans both at home and in Washington. A frequent critic of the media, he drew criticism for his characterization of CNN corespondent Peter Arnett as an Iraqi sympathizer in the Persian Gulf War. His attacks on Anita Hill during the Senate confirmation hearings of Supreme Court Justice Clarence Thomas also earned him rebukes from a number of groups.

From 1985 to 1987, Simpson served as assistant majority leader, assuming the position of assistant minority leader in 1987. In 1995, Simpson announced his retirement from the senate, noting that after serving 17 years in Congress, "the old fire in the belly is out... the edge is off." He recalled that when he was first elected to the Senate he promised the voters of Wyoming that he would work hard and make them proud and, in making his decision, felt honestly that he had done both.

RICHARD BRUCE "DICK" CHENEY
1941-

Richard Bruce "Dick" Cheney was born in Lincoln, Nebraska, on January 30, 1941. His parents were Richard Herbert and Marjorie Lauraine Cheney. The family later moved to Casper, Wyoming. Cheney attended Natrona County High School, where he participated in Boys State, played football and was president of his senior class. He married Lynne Anne Vincent in 1964 and the couple eventually had two daughters.

After attending Casper College, Cheney transferred to the University of Wyoming and earned a bachelor's degree in 1965 and a master's degree in political science in 1966. While at the University of Wyoming, Cheney was awarded a fellowship that provided him with the opportunity to work at the state legislature, providing him with practical experience in his chosen field. He attended the University of Wisconsin from 1966 to 1968 for postgraduate studies.

In 1966, Cheney began his career in public service as a member of the staff of Governor William Knowles of Wisconsin. In 1969, he accepted a position as a special assistant to the director of the Office of Economic Opportunity in the Nixon administration. Cheney worked in the White House as deputy counselor from 1970 to 1971, leaving for a position as assistant director at the Cost of Living Council, which he held until 1973. The following year, Cheney returned to the White House, serving on the transition team and then as an assistant to President Gerald Ford. From 1975 to 1976, Cheney served as Ford's chief of staff.

In 1977, Cheney returned to Wyoming to run for the U.S. House of Representatives. Campaigning on a platform that espoused ideas such as "government has a positive creative role to play" but "government can't do everything for everybody," Cheney was elected to serve as the state's sole congressman in 1978. Advocating for making "the American system work the way we here in Wyoming know it should work," he was re-elected five times.

Cheney earned the respect of his republican colleagues, impressing his peers with his work as a freshman on the House Interior Committee. He was subsequently elected to serve as chairman of the Republican Policy Committee and later the Republican Conference and eventually house minority whip. A strong supporter of the agricultural industry, believing it comprised "the backbone of Wyoming's economy," he sponsored the Wyoming Wilderness Bill and the Grazing Bill.

Cheney was named to the post of secretary of defense in the Bush administration in 1989. He was confirmed by a Senate vote of 92 to 0, a measure of the respect he had earned from his peers on both sides of the aisle. Cheney held the post until 1993, presiding over Operation Just Cause in Panama; Operation Desert Storm in the Middle East; and the transition of the U.S. military from the cold war era. In 1991, Cheney was awarded the Presidential Medal of Freedom in recognition for his work during the Gulf War.

After leaving the Bush administration, Cheney was urged to run for the presidency of the United States but ultimately decided against it. His decision to leave politics after 25 years was "final." Cheney eventually accepted a position as a senior fellow at the American Enterprise Institute and has served on the board of directors of several companies, including Proctor and Gamble and Union Pacific. Cheney currently resides in Dallas, with his wife, where he is the president and chief executive officer of the Halliburton Company. The Cheneys also maintain a home in Jackson, Wyoming.

Dick Cheney served Wyoming well in the national political arena. *Courtesy of AHC Collection.*

THURMAN WESLEY ARNOLD
1891-1969

Thurman Arnold had a long history of service to Wyoming and his country, beginning in World War I. *Courtesy of AHC Collection.*

Arnold first saw military service in 1916, when his Illinois National Guard unit was called to serve in General Pershing's Mexican border expedition. The following year Arnold married the former Frances Logan, with whom he eventually had two sons. After his marriage, in response to the outbreak of World War I, he joined the army. In addition to touring Wyoming in a tank to promote the sale of victory bonds, he served as an artillery officer in Europe. Arnold returned to Wyoming after his discharge.

Upon his return to Laramie, Arnold established a law practice and lectured at the University of Wyoming College of Law. Elected to the Wyoming House of Representatives as a democrat in 1920, he was one of the only members of his party to survive the Warren G. Harding landslide. As the lone democrat in the Wyoming House in 1921, he held his own with the majority party. He would frequently announce "the Democratic minority will now caucus" and exit into the cloak room, to return with the news that the minority were divided in their view on the issues and proceed to explain their various concerns at length.

After serving his term in the legislature, Arnold was elected mayor of Laramie. In addition to being an ardent prohibitionist, his term as mayor was also characterized by a drive for the improvement of public works. One

Thurman Wesley Arnold was born in Laramie, Wyoming, on June 2, 1891, to Constantine Peter Arnold and Annie Brockaway. He attended Princeton University, receiving a bachelor of arts degree in 1911. Arnold went on to earn his law degree from Harvard University in 1914. He was admitted to the Illinois bar and practiced law in Chicago until 1917.

of his most controversial acts was the paving of Grand Avenue.

In 1927, Arnold left Laramie to serve as dean of the College of Law at West Virginia University. In 1930, he accepted a permanent faculty position at Yale University Law School. In 1933, he assumed the first of a series of posts within President Franklin Roosevelt's administration. He served first as an assistant to the general counsel of the Agricultural Adjustment Administration, a New Deal agency. In 1935, Arnold assumed a position as trial examiner in Roosevelt's newly created Securities and Exchange Commission.

In 1937, Arnold began his career as a chief trust-buster for the New Deal, as a special consultant to the head of the Justice Department's Anti-Trust Division. As assistant attorney general from 1938 to 1943, he brought more than 200 suits for monopolistic practices. In 1939, he responded to Wyoming Attorney General Kerr's request that he initiate an investigation of a gasoline trust that was believed to be keeping the price of the fuel in the state artificially high.

In 1943, Arnold was appointed to the U.S. Circuit Court of Appeals for the District of Columbia but Arnold resigned from the bench in 1945 to enter private law practice; the firm of Arnold, Fortas and Portas became one of the most influential in Washington D.C. As a lawyer, Arnold's clarity as an interpreter of the law and his stubborn defense of individual freedom made him a force in the decisions of the Supreme Court through the 1950s and 60s.

A popular figure, Arnold was known in Washington for his western humor, in addition to being respected for his extraordinary legal mind. Justice Robert Jackson called Arnold "a cross between Voltaire and a cowboy, with the cowboy predominating." Arnold died at his home in Alexandria, Virginia, in 1969. He is considered by many to be one of most influential Wyomingites of the century in the legal and political arenas. Judge Arnold loved his native state and respected courage and persistence of its people. Thurman Arnold brought the values of Wyoming into the national arena through the New Deal and represented its best qualities in Washington for 30 years.

THOMAS A. BELL
1924-

Thomas A. Bell was born April 12, 1924, in Winton, a mining town north of Rock Springs, Wyoming. His father worked in the town's store and saved enough money to buy a ranch on the North Fork of the Popo Agie River, where Bell spent his childhood. He graduated from Fremont County Vocational School in May of 1941 as president of the student body.

After Pearl Harbor, Bell enlisted in the Army Air Force and was posted to the 455 Bombardier Group. He successfully completed 32 combat sorties and earned the rank of lieutenant. In May, 1944, he was severely wounded while flying a B-24 Bomber mission over Austria, losing his right eye. Despite suffering from shock and a severe loss of blood, he remained at his post. His heroism was recognized with the Silver Star and three Oakleaf Clusters. He returned to the University of Wyoming to major in game management. Before earning his bachelor's degree in 1948, he reactivated the Rodeo Club, founded the Ski Club and served as student president.

After graduating, Bell ran a sawmill and worked in a trout hatchery. Having married, he went to work in the oil and gas industry, and then returned to the University of Wyoming to study range and game management, earning a master's degree. He joined the Wyoming Game and Fish Department and then taught science at Lander High while ranching part time. When the daughters of *Wyoming State Journal* publisher Roger Budrow told their father what a great teacher Bell was, he recruited him to be a columnist. Budrow later remarked of Bell, "Like Socrates was a gadfly to the intellectuals of Athens, Tom Bell was a gadfly to Wyoming."

One of the first issues Bell addressed as a columnist for the *Journal* was the illegal fencing of public lands, which caused tremendous winterkills of game animals. A controversy arose when Bell discovered that sheepman Herman Werner, who had been accused of slaughtering golden and bald eagles, had constructed 69 miles of illegal fences. Bell also found out that the Bureau of Land Management (BLM) had plans to erect a series of fences across the Red Desert. In the ensuing outcry, it was discovered that more than 13,000 miles of illegal fence had been built on BLM land in Wyoming and Montana.

In the course of his work, Bell uncovered several other abuses of the public lands and, in 1968, his discoveries prompted him to found the Wyoming Outdoor Coordinating Council. He eventually took over the *Camping News Weekly* and converted it into a voice of conservation in the west, the *High Country News*. With a circulation of only 1,500, financial difficulties were inevitable. In 1971, the Bells, who by this time had raised their six children, three of whom were adopted, were forced to sell the family ranch to continue to finance the paper. But two years later, the situation had not improved and Bell foresaw the end of his creation. His plight became public and contribu-

"Like Socrates was a gadfly to the intellectuals of Athens, Tom Bell was a gadfly to Wyoming."

tions poured in, enough to pay the accumulated debts and hire two writers, Bruce Hamilton and Joan Nice. 1973 also marked the year that Bell won the American Motors Conservation Award. The following year, exhausted from years of struggling to keep *High Country News* afloat and motivated by religious concerns, Bell decided to move his family to Oregon, leaving the paper to its capable staff.

Bell eventually returned to Lander. He joined the staff of the Fremont County Museum in 1985 to prepare a "one time only" county history book. While that project has yet to be completed, he remained with the museum for 12 years, researching articles for *The Wind River Mountaineer*, a quarterly history magazine focusing on Fremont County with more than 400 subscribers. The Coordinating Council Bell founded, now known as the Wyoming Outdoor Council, has a staff of six and plays a key role in conservation politics. Bell's *High Country News* now has a staff of 15 and a circulation of 20,000.

FRED BLUME
1875-1971

Freidrich Heinrich Blume was born in the Hannover Province of Germany on January 8, 1875. He received his early education in village schools in his native Germany. At the age of 12, he immigrated to the United States, supporting himself by working as a farm hand. At 17, on his way to seek work in the Kansas wheat fields, Blume missed his train and was stranded in Audubon, Iowa. A local lawyer offered Blume a job cleaning his office and was so taken with the young man that he encouraged him to stay in the community.

Blume accepted the offer and continued to work part-time while attending the local high school. He graduated after only two years and went on to attend the State University of Iowa, graduating with a bachelor's degree in philosophy. He studied law as an apprentice and in 1899 was admitted to the Iowa Bar. He achieved his first elective office, justice of the peace for Audubon County, at the age of 23. Blume subsequently served two terms as county and prosecuting attorney for Audubon County.

Blume came to Wyoming in 1905 to practice law in Sheridan and quickly became active in republican party politics. He was elected to the Wyoming House of Representatives in 1906 and to the Wyoming Senate for two consecutive terms, beginning in 1908. He also served as city attorney for Sheridan from 1907 to 1911. As a progressive republican, Blume focused most of his energies on reform, authoring legislation to govern primary elections that remains in effect today. Blume also sponsored the corrupt practices bill, which limited campaign spending and contributions. He advocated fiscal reform, too, helping to enact legislation governing state deposits.

As a member of the Executive Committee of the Wyoming Association of Progressive Republicans, Blume became known as one of the state's most prominent leaders in that movement. Although they created friction within the Republican Party on a number of issues, resulting in some less than spectacular electoral showings for their party, the Progressive Republicans were instrumental in sponsoring democratic reforms designed to mitigate the influence of the cattle and railroad industries in Wyoming.

As a state republican delegate from Wyoming in 1912, Blume refused to support Taft. He resigned as a republican State Senate candidate to campaign for Theodore Roosevelt and the Bull Moose Party. Blume continued to veer from the party line when two years later he ardently supported the democratic candidate for governor, John Kendrick, who was an old friend. Despite these actions and his 1914 bid for Wyoming's lone U.S. House seat as a Progressive on the Democratic ticket, Blume remained an important figure within the Republican Party.

By 1916, most of the reforms advocated by the progressives in Wyoming had become law and Blume became part of the mainstream Wyoming Republican Party, chairing the party's state convention in 1920. In 1921, under the auspices of his old colleague Robert Carey, who had been elected to the governorship on the republican ticket in 1918, Blume was named to the

Wyoming Supreme Court. He was subsequently re-elected for five eight-year terms.

It was as a jurist that Blume made his greatest contribution to Wyoming, authoring 660 opinions in the course of his tenure on the state's highest court. Appointed to the Wyoming Supreme Court at the age of 46, he served as a justice for more than 40 years, almost half of that time as chief justice. His long and active service on the bench resulted in Blume having unprecedented influence on Wyoming law and earned him the sobriquet of "the Grand Old Man" of the Wyoming Supreme Court. His work in the area of interpreting evidence law achieved particular notice, with his studies on this intricate area of legal interpretation being quoted in courts throughout the United States. Blume was hailed by his peers as "the last of that line of judicial giants, famed in American legal history, who moved west in the vanguard of civilization, and helped mold the jurisprudence of a youthful state."

Blume retired from the Wyoming Supreme Court in January, 1963, following the death of his wife of 43 years, Blanche. After his retirement, he remained active, continuing to walk a mile and a half to his office to work every day, accompanied by his German shepherd, Bingo, successor to his well-known companion of many years, Baron the Weimaraner. He died at his home in Cheyenne on September 26, 1971, at the age of 96.

It was as a jurist that Blume made his greatest contribution to Wyoming, authoring 660 opinions in the course of his tenure on the state's highest court.

He was remembered by his successor, Justice Glenn Parker, as "one of the outstanding judicial figures of the century."

CLIFFORD P. HANSEN
1912-

Throughout his tenure as governor, Hansen focused on two central themes, increased economic activity and state's rights.

Clifford Peter Hansen, born on October 16, 1912, was the third of six children of Peter Christofferson Hansen and Sylvia Irene Wood Hansen of Jackson, Wyoming. The elder Hansen came to Wyoming in 1898 and established a homestead which eventually became the family ranch near Jackson Hole.

Hansen's strong family background served him in good stead. Clifford Hansen was sent home after his first day of school and told not return because he suffered from an uncontrollable stutter which led his teacher to declare him unable to learn. Working extensively with a speech therapist, who taught him techniques to overcome his speech impediment, Hansen conquered his handicap. He graduated as valedictorian of Jackson High School's class of 1930.

Hansen attended the University of Wyoming on a scholarship. Following his graduation in 1934, he married Martha Elizabeth Close, with whom he eventually had a son and a daughter. The couple began their married life on 200 acres near Jackson, a gift from Hansen's father, and started ranching with 50 head of cattle to their name.

Both of the Hansens played an active role in their community but it was the controversy surrounding the designation of the Jackson Hole Monument in 1943 that first brought Clifford Hansen wide attention. As chairman of the Teton County Board of Commissioners,

Hansen actively campaigned to negate the designation, fearing a potential loss of tax revenue, grazing rights, and income from big game hunting might be disastrous for the local economy.

In 1962, Hansen ran on the republican ticket and was elected governor of Wyoming. Throughout his tenure, Hansen focused on two central themes, increased economic activity and state's rights. He quickly became embroiled in the controversy surrounding the passage of the "right-to-work" law and called National Guardsmen to the Capitol to prevent potential confrontation during the debate. Believing that the bill would "restore full freedom of choice to the working men and women of Wyoming," Hansen signed the measure into law.

In 1967, Hansen began serving the first of two terms in the United States Senate. Always responsive to the needs of his constituents, he established a unique pilot program of private partnership to save the infrastructure of Rock Springs, which was in danger of collapsing due to the caving in of abandoned coal mines. Hansen also oversaw the battle to designate grass as a crop, protecting livestock interests within the state and legislated the protection of surface rights during strip mining. He sponsored legislation which stimulated domestic oil production and increased federal mineral royalty payments, greatly benefiting Wyoming's economy. Hansen also supported two major tax relief proposals, one decreasing the top capital gains tax rate and another restructuring the method used for tax valuation of family farms and businesses.

After retiring from the Senate, citing health concerns, Hansen returned to ranching and remained active in public affairs. Hansen's long history of service to his state has earned him numerous accolades. He was named Stockman of the Century by the WSGA. Hansen served for many years on the board of trustees at the University of Wyoming and UW has presented him with an honorary law degree, the Distinguished Alumni Award and the Medallion Award. The National Cowboy Hall of Fame inducted him into the Hall of Great Westerners, that organization's highest honor, in 1995. In 1996, the National Western Stock Show and Rodeo named him a Citizen of the West.

SUSAN JANE QUEALY
1870-1956

Susan Jane (Quealey) Quealy was born in Omaha, Nebraska, January 17, 1870, the daughter of Patrick J. Quealey and Bridget Connor Quealey. She attended public schools in Omaha and St. Patrick's Academy. She married Patrick John Quealy (no relation) in 1890. The couple eventually had five sons, two of whom died in infancy. After their marriage, Quealy and her husband moved to Rock Springs, Wyoming. They lived in Rock Springs until her husband, having founded the town of Kemmerer in conjunction with the Kemmerer Coal Company in 1897, moved his family there.

Quealy was an active participant in business, civic and political circles. She was a director and officer of the Lincoln Corporation, the Kemmerer Coal Company and the Frontier Supply Company, all of which were founded by her husband. Until 1947, she operated a cattle and sheep ranch in Shirley Basin. A member of the Wyoming Wool Growers, she was the first woman elected to the Wyoming Stockgrowers Association (WSGA) and the first woman to serve on the Executive Committee. Quealy served as vice president of the First National Bank of Kemmerer and president of the Medicine Bow and LaBarge Oil Companies. She was also a director of the Western Oil Refining Company.

Quealy worked extensively with the Red Cross; she was appointed regional field organizer during World War I. She also chaired the Lincoln County Registration of Women for War Work and National Defense Committees. During World War II, Quealy was state chairman for the Food Supply and Demand Committee. One of the founders of the Lincoln County Library, she served on its board for many years. She donated the 10 acres of land which make up Washington Memorial Park in Kemmerer. Quealy was a major sponsor of Casey's Opera House in Kemmerer and she also chaired the Lincoln County chapter of the American Cancer Society.

Quealy was active in the field of education, a direct result of her interest in promoting domestic science. In addition to serving on both the Rock Springs and Kemmerer School Boards, she was a long time member of the Wyoming State Board of Education (1935-1952). She was a member of the University of Wyoming Board of Trustees from 1940-44 and received an honorary degree from the university in 1955.

Politically active, Quealy attended the first national convention of the Democratic Party in 1908 and the 1919 Womens' Suffrage Convention in Chicago. She was a three time presidential elector, (1932, 1936, 1940) Democratic State Woman's Chairman (1932-1945), and served eight years on the Democratic National Committee for Wyoming (1945-53). She ran unsuccessfully for Wyoming secretary of state in 1942.

Quealy is probably best remembered for her establishment of the Quealy Awards. Conceived by Quealy as way to acknowledge the leadership and industry of women in rural communities throughout Wyoming, she funded the awards program with an annual donation of $500. The first four Quealy award recipients were selected in 1946. Every year four women from four regions are chosen for their leadership and community service and are welcomed at the Quealy Club's annual banquet.

Susan Jane Quealy died in on July 26, 1956. Through her life and work, Susan Quealy illustrated all of the virtues of Wyoming's pioneer spirit. She expanded on the traditional roles allotted to women to become active in her community and personified the energy that is the hallmark of Wyoming's citizenry.

Active in both community and political circles, Susan Jane Quealy (far left) brought the ideal of the "Equality State" to life.
Courtesy of AHC Collection.

JOHN BENJAMIN KENDRICK
1857-1933

Kendrick, a self-made man and successful politician, personified the ideal of rugged individualism. *Courtesy of AHC Collection.*

John Benjamin Kendrick was born on September 6, 1857, in Cherokee County, Texas. His parents were John Harvey Kendrick, who came to Texas as a pioneer and built a plantation, and Anna Maye. His family lost all of their money after backing the Confederates in the Civil War. After the death of his parents, Kendrick was raised by relatives, living for the most part with his half sister, Mary, and her husband, Thomas Harrell Reavis. Kendrick later credited Reavis with instilling in him the "values of thrift, abstinence and hard work" which served him so well throughout his life.

Kendrick set out on his own as a cowboy at the age of 15, breaking horses for room and board. Although he had only seven years of formal schooling, Kendrick used his spare time reading and studying to fill the gaps in his knowledge. In 1879, the Snyder-Wulfjen brothers

of Round Rock, Texas, hired him to help bring a herd of cattle to the grasslands of Wyoming. Kendrick saved his wages and purchased his own small herd from his employers. In 1882, when Wulfjen's holdings were absorbed by the Converse Cattle Company out of Lusk, Wyoming, Kendrick sold his herd for a tidy profit, which he then reinvested in cattle.

Despite the disastrous winter of 1886-87, which forced many cattlemen into bankruptcy, Kendrick, by virtue of sound management, prospered. He signed on as superintendent of Converse Cattle Company and within 10 years had purchased the entire operation. He eventually built a ranching empire that encompassed territories across Wyoming and Montana totaling 210,000 acres of deeded and leased land.

In 1910, Kendrick entered the political arena when he was elected to the Wyoming State Senate from Sheridan County. Three years later, he lost his second race, an attempt to defeat the incumbent republican United States Senator, F. E. Warren. In 1914, he parlayed his reputation into a successful run for the governorship of Wyoming, becoming the second democrat to hold that office. As a democratic governor in a traditionally republican state, Kendrick worked well with his republican legislature, instituting a variety of reform-oriented legislation, including the establishment of worker's compensation and the state public utilities commission.

In 1916, having served only half of his term as governor, Kendrick became the first United States senator from Wyoming elected by popular vote. While in the Senate, he advocated for a variety of legislative programs, but his main area of interest was the reclamation of arid lands. Governed by his overwhelming interest in the western need for water,

Kendrick initiated the legislation which resulted in the appropriations for the Alcova Dam and Reservoir near Casper, Wyoming. He also supported legislation for the Wind River irrigation projects and the Boulder Dam in Arizona.

Kendrick's work on behalf of his constituents made him a popular and virtually unbeatable candidate, despite accusations of corruption and illegal land dealings. Like his one time rival, F.E. Warren, Kendrick was able to build a formidable political machine, benefiting both himself and the democratic party. His controlling interest in the *Cheyenne State Leader* and the *Sheridan Enterprise* allowed him to balance the coverage provided by the Warren political machine's own papers.

Kendrick was at the height of his political power at the end of his third term. A ranking member of the powerful appropriations committee, he was also poised to assume control of the committee on public lands. Thus, people were stunned when he announced his intention not to seek reelection in 1934. Many assumed

In 1916, *having served only half of his term as governor, Kendrick became the first United States senator from Wyoming elected by popular vote.*

he was simply positioning himself to accept his party's selection as their vice presidential candidate in 1936. But it was also noted by those around him that Kendrick, now 76, appeared to be worn out. On November 3, 1933, Kendrick, who had two days earlier slipped into a coma after suffering a cerebral hemorrhage, died at the Sheridan County Memorial Hospital. John Kendrick was remembered by his colleagues as embodying "the leadership and virtues of the old west... courage, straightforwardness, firmness of will and uprightness were as natural to him as the day."

JOSEPH O'MAHONEY
1884-1961

Joseph Christopher O'Mahoney was born in Chelsea, Massachusetts, on November 5, 1884, one of 11 children of Dennis and Elizabeth Shehan O'Mahoney. After his mother's death in 1893, the family moved to Daniels, Massachusetts. He attended Cambridge Latin School until his father's death in 1903, when he moved to New York City to live with his older brother. O'Mahoney found work at a publishing house and paid his way through Columbia University by freelancing.

In 1908, O'Mahoney moved west to Colorado with his younger brother, Frank, who suffered from tuberculosis. He found work in Boulder as a newspaperman and stringer for the Associated Press. By 1913, O'Mahoney had managed to establish himself well enough to bring his longtime sweetheart, Agnes Veronica O'Leary, to Colorado as his bride. The couple eventually had four children.

In 1916, O'Mahoney accepted a position as city editor of the *Cheyenne State Leader,* which was owned by John B. Kendrick. Kendrick was conducting a vigorous campaign for the U.S. Senate and O'Mahoney quickly impressed his new employer with his political skills. After Kendrick's election, O'Mahoney accompanied him to Washington D.C. as his secretary and attended Georgetown Law School, receiving his degree in 1920.

Under the auspices of his mentor, Senator Kendrick, O'Mahoney quickly rose to prominence in the Democratic Party. By 1932, he was a member of the Democratic National Committee and a convention delegate, campaigning on behalf of Franklin Roosevelt. In 1933, he was rewarded for his work with an appointment as first assistant postmaster general. Already on a steady trajectory toward a political career, the death of Senator Kendrick in 1933 brought O'Mahoney into public office. He was chosen by Governor Leslie Miller to fill out the remainder of Kendrick's term and was elected to a full term in 1934, beginning a long and distinguished career representing the state of Wyoming in Washington D.C.

A supporter of the New Deal, O'Mahoney was well known for his independent thinking. This quality was brought to the foreground during the court packing controversy of 1937. O'Mahoney led the opposition to Roosevelt's plan to reform the Supreme Court by adding new justices to ensure no more of the New Deal legislation was struck down by the high court. O'Mahoney was fortunate in that, while he took his position based on principle, his actions were supported by the majority of Wyoming voters, who applauded his independence.

O'Mahoney was often quoted as saying "There can be no permanent political liberty without economic freedom." This philosophy was his guiding principle throughout his 27-year career in the Senate. From 1937 to 1941, O'Mahoney chaired the Temporary National Economic Committee, which had the ambitious mission of inquiring into the economic structure of the country. The committee's final report contained O'Mahoney's signature brand of dynamic democracy, based on his philosophy of preserving free enterprise while promoting equal economic opportunity. O'Mahoney's belief in the power of economic opportunity is further evidenced in his sponsorship of the Maximum Employment Act of 1946. This legislation created the President's Council of Economic Advisors.

O'Mahoney was also a staunch advocate of developing natural resources, an issue of particular concern to his constituency. O'Mahoney was in the forefront of the energy issue in 1943 when he supported the Synthetic Fuels Law, which promoted the production of synthetic fuel from coal and oil shale. He also sponsored legislation aimed at developing the west's oil reserves. The O'Mahoney-Hatch Act (1946) revised the 1920 Mineral Leasing Act to stimulate oil production on public lands. This legislation was credited with significantly increasing Wyoming's oil production.

Senator O'Mahoney was an active crusader for reclamation, another issue of vital interest to his fellow Wyomingites. In 1944, he introduced an amendment to the Flood Control Act to protect the priority of water for irrigation purposes. In 1956, he sponsored the Upper Colorado River Basin Storage Plan, which promoted irrigation and the development of hydroelectric power. Electrification was another issue of concern to O'Mahoney, who was an ardent supporter of the Rural Electrification Authority, which brought power to many rural residents of his state.

O'Mahoney's year career in the Senate was interrupted by his defeat in the Eisenhower landslide of 1952 and he returned to Cheyenne to practice law. The opportunity to return to the Senate presented itself two years later, when his former colleague, Lester C. Hunt, committed suicide. O'Mahoney was drafted to represent his party in the 1954 election. O'Mahoney's victory, which came in spite of scurrilous charges of communist sympathies, gave democrats control of the Senate by a majority of one.

Upon his return to the Senate, O'Mahoney continued his campaign for economic opportunity, introducing legislation to protect small businesses from monopolies and control international cartels. O'Mahoney chose to end his career after he suffered a stroke in 1959, resigning the following year. He died two years later, at the age of 78.

NELLIE TAYLOE ROSS
1876-1977

THE FIRST WOMAN GOVERNOR
Wyoming's Governor
THE WOMAN WHO MADE GOOD

NELLIE TAYLOE ROSS

Businesslike—Able—Courageous. She Has Earned Re-election

Nellie Davis Tayloe Ross was born November 29, 1876, near St. Joseph, Missouri. Her parents were James Wynn Tayloe, a merchant and gentleman farmer, and Elizabeth Blair Green. After her mother's death in 1884, her father and three older brothers raised Tayloe. She was educated in both public and private schools in Missouri and Kansas, graduating from a kindergarten teacher's training school in Omaha in late 1890s. While visiting relatives in Tennessee, Ross met her future husband, a promising young attorney by the name of William Bradford Ross. After their marriage in Omaha, Nebraska, in 1902, the couple moved to Cheyenne. They eventually had four sons, one of whom died in infancy.

In 1922, William Ross was elected governor of Wyoming, a democrat in a traditionally republican state. A strong supporter of Prohibition, he often relied on his wife for counsel because she shared his views. William Ross died suddenly, on October 3, 1924, following complications from a ruptured appendix. His death precipitated the need for someone to stand in the upcoming general election to complete the last two years of his term. Special party conventions convened in Cheyenne in October, with the republicans nominating Eugene J. Sullivan, a Casper attorney, and the democrats nominating the late governor's widow.

Sullivan campaigned vigorously for the next three weeks, but Ross refused to do so. Announcing that she would not campaign, she declared "my candidacy is in the hands of my friends." Her only concession was to allow the appearance of a few small advertisements, in which she declared she would "be governed by the underlying principles by which he and I, side by side, have sought to conduct our lives during our twenty two years together." Ross defeated Sullivan by more that 8,000 votes to become the first, and to date only, woman governor of Wyoming. She was also the first women governor of any state in the union. Although Ross and "Ma" Ferguson of Texas were both elected governor of their respective states on the same day, Ross was sworn into office before Ferguson.

As governor, Ross continued her husband's progressive policies. She advocated tax fairness, improved workplace safety regulations to protect coal miners, and ratification of the Child Labor Amendment to the United States Constitution. In the face of mounting numbers of bank failures, she urged the House and Senate to pass banking regulations and adopt depositor protections. Ross also pushed for legislation to criminalize the purchase of liquor.

In 1926, her party nominated her for another four-year term. Her republican opponent was Frank C. Emerson, state engineer and longtime political adversary of both Ross and her late husband. Ross lost her reelection campaign by a relatively small margin.

Analysts have blamed her defeat on a number of factors; economic conditions, her support of Prohibition, her failure to take a strong stand on the issue of women's rights and the loss of the sympathy votes of republican men and women, many of whom had crossed party lines in 1924. While she later acknowledged she had made an error by not campaigning more aggressively, Ross' best response to her critics was to reply that every four years she voted the democratic ticket but every day she voted for the release of the genius and ambition of the individual woman.

After her defeat, Ross, by now a polished public speaker, was in high demand on the Chatauqua circuit and traveled across the country. She also remained active in Democratic Party politics, eventually serving as National Democratic Committee chairman. Ross made the seconding speech for Al Smith at the Democratic National Convention in 1928 and campaigned on his behalf. In 1932, she directed the campaign for the woman's vote for Franklin D. Roosevelt.

"...every four years she voted the democratic ticket but every day she voted for the release of the genius and ambition of the individual woman."

In 1933, President Roosevelt appointed Ross director of the U.S. Mint. As the first woman to hold that position, she had her likeness imprinted on a mint metal and inscribed on the cornerstone of three government buildings; the gold depository at Fort Knox, the silver depository at West Point and the U.S. Mint in San Francisco. During her 20-year tenure as director, Ross presided over the greatest expansion in mint production.

Nellie Tayloe Ross died in Washington D.C. on November 19, 1977, at the age of 101. After she lay in state in the rotunda of the State Capitol in Cheyenne, she was buried in Lakeview Cemetery. Ross was survived by two of her sons, four grandchildren and six great grandchildren.

THOMAS FRANK STROOCK
1925-

Having served in both elected and non-elected capacities, the former ambassador remains active in political issues as a professor of public affairs at the University of Wyoming. *Courtesy of Stroock Family Collection.*

Thomas Frank Stroock was born in New York City on October 10, 1925. His parents were Samuel and Dorothy Frank Stroock. During World War II, Stroock was a member of the United States Marine Corp. He attended Yale University, earning a BA degree in economics in 1948. In 1949, Stroock married Marta Freyre de Andrade and the couple eventually had four daughters.

Stroock began his career as a businessman in the oil industry at Stanolind Oil and Gas Company in Tulsa in 1948. He left the company in 1952 to become president of his own oil and gas properties firm, Stroock Leasing Corporation in Casper, Wyoming. In 1960, he became a senior partner in Stroock, Rogers & Dymond, also based in Casper. Stroock served as director of the Saks Oil Company of Casper and brokered its merger with the Denver-based Century Oil & Gas Corporation in 1975. Stroock also served as a director of Wyoming Bancorp in Cheyenne and First Wyoming Banks of Casper. He was a member of the National Petroleum Council from 1972- 1977 and is a member of the Rocky Mountain Oil and Gas Association. In 1980, he

assumed the presidency of Alpha Leasing Corporation, and with the exception of the time he spent in government service during the Bush administration, continues today as chief executive officer and chairman.

Stroock has also been active in politics. Stroock served as a republican precinct committeeman from 1950 to 1968. He was president of the Natrona County School Board from 1960 to 1969 and president of the Wyoming State School Board Association from 1965-66. Stroock also chaired the Wyoming Higher Education Council. He served five separate terms in the Wyoming State Senate, representing Natrona County, beginning in 1967. While in the Senate, Stroock chaired the Wyoming Health Reform Commission and co-chaired the Joint Appropriations Committee. In addition to his duties as vice president of the Senate, Stroock was a member of the Select Water Oversight Committee and the Steering Committee of the Education Commission of the States. A member of the executive committee from 1954-1960, Stroock was chairman of the Wyoming State Republican Committee from 1975 to 1978, following an unsuccessful candidacy for Wyoming's lone seat in the United States House of Representatives. He was a regional coordinator in both of George Bush's presidential campaigns. Beginning in 1989, Stroock served as United States ambassador to Guatemala. Stroock is a co-founder, past-president and member of the Wyoming Committee on Foreign Relations.

In 1984, Stroock and his wife endowed the Stroock Professorship of Natural Resource Conservation and Management for the College of Commerce and Industry at the University of Wyoming. Stroock also sponsors the annual Thomas Stroock Lecture Series through the College of Arts and Sciences. He was awarded the Distinguished Visiting Professor Award in 1996 in recognition of the classes he taught at the University as a Distinguished Visiting Professor of Public Policy. In recognition of his service to the University, Stroock was awarded an honorary doctor of law degree in 1995.

MICHAEL "MIKE" JOHN SULLIVAN
1939-

Michael "Mike" John Sullivan was born in Omaha, Nebraska, on September 22, 1939. He was the second of three children of Joseph B. and Margaret E. Sullivan. Soon after his birth, the family moved to Douglas, Wyoming, where he attended Southside Grade School and graduated from Converse County High School in 1957. He earned a bachelor's degree in Petroleum Engineering from the University of Wyoming in 1961 and graduated from the University of Wyoming Law School, with honors, three years later. While attending the university, Sullivan met and married the former Jane Metzler and the couple eventually had three children.

Sullivan practiced law in Casper, Wyoming, for 22 years before being elected as Wyoming's 29th governor in 1986. During that period, he was actively involved in community and professional organizations, serving as president of Casper Rotary, chairman of the Natrona County Hospital Board and chairing the Wyoming Board of Bar Examiners. He is a member of the Wyoming State Bar and the American Bar Association.

Sullivan's successful bid for the governorship was his first attempt at political office, motivated by what he jokingly referred to as mid-life crisis. In reality, Sullivan's motivation was his belief that he "could contribute to the campaign in a positive and constructive way, and, if I got elected, that I might be able to learn enough to be good governor." He was re-elected in 1990 by the largest margin in Wyoming's history. While in office he earned a national reputation, chairing the Western Governor's Association and working actively with the National Governor's Association, as a member of the executive board, and on committees dealing with natural resource and educational issues and Indian gaming. In 1992, he was one of only two governors to earn the Cato Institute's highest rating for fiscal policy.

Sullivan assumed the governor's chair at one of the most difficult times in the state's history, a period when Wyoming's economy was in rapid decline following several years of rapid growth brought on by the energy boom of the previous decade. In his first inaugural speech, Sullivan encouraged Wyoming's citizens to "ask each other for a full measure of dedication and energy." His personal philosophy of governing, one which encouraged participation from all sectors, private and public, as well as consensus building, proved to be particularly effective at guiding the state during hard times. And his belief that "economic growth and Wyoming's lifestyle are not incompatible" was a message that all could support. While in office, Sullivan focused his attention on stabilizing the state's sagging economy and reducing its dependence on the energy industry by courting new businesses.

After serving two terms as governor, and an unsuccessful run for the United States Senate, Sullivan returned to private law practice in 1995. He continues to be active in civic and political affairs, serving on the board for the Institute of Environmental and Natural Resources at the University of Wyoming, and the advisory board for the University Law School and the College of Engineering. He is also a member of the Board of Trustees for the Buffalo Bill Memorial Association and is trustee of the Catholic Diocese of Wyoming. During 1996, he held an Institute of Politics Fellowship at the Kennedy School of Government at Harvard. Sullivan assumed the post of United States ambassador to Ireland in 1999.

As governor during difficult economic times, Mike Sullivan was greatly admired for his leadership abilities.
Courtesy of AHC Collection.

F.E. WARREN
1844-1929

Francis Emroy "F.E." Warren was born in Hinsdale, Massachusetts, on June 20, 1844. At the age of 18 he enlisted in the Union Army as a member of the 49th Massachusetts regiment. Warren distinguished himself in battle at Port Hudson, Louisiana, and was awarded the Medal of Honor. After his discharge, he held a variety of jobs, finally settling in Wyoming in 1868. Three years later, Warren married Helen Marie Smith and the couple eventually had two children, a son and a daughter.

After his arrival in Cheyenne, Warren was employed by Amasa Converse, first to tend his sheep herd and later to clerk in his store. By 1871, Warren acquired a half interest in that business, becoming a full partner in the firm of Converse and Warren. Six years later, Warren bought out Converse and created the Warren Mercantile Company.

Warren also ventured into sheep and cattle ranching on a large scale, establishing one of the first corporations in Wyoming, the Warren Land and Livestock Company, in 1883. In addition to his mercantile and ranching enterprises, Warren eventually owned or had an interest in utilities, as head of Cheyenne Light, Fuel & Power Company; banks, including the First National Bank of Cheyenne; and railroads, having established the Cheyenne and Northern. By 1909, Warren was the richest man in Wyoming, worth a reported $5 million.

Warren was active in the civic affairs of Cheyenne, serving first in 1871 as a trustee, then as president of the city council and later mayor, overseeing the construction of the city's water and sewer systems. He was also active in the territorial government, as a legislator, treasurer and finally governor. By 1885, Warren was emerging as the dominant figure in Wyoming's Republican Party, eventually creating one of the strongest political organization the state has ever seen. When Wyoming was granted statehood in 1890, Warren was elected governor, but served only briefly before being selected as a U.S. senator. He served until 1892 and was reelected to the Senate in 1895.

The underlying theme throughout Warren's long career in the Senate was the development of Wyoming and the protection of the state's interests. Warren served on the committees on irrigation and reclamation, military affairs and appropriations. As a member of the Senate Committee on Public Buildings and Grounds (1902-1912), Warren secured in excess of $1 million in federal funds for the construction of public buildings throughout the state. He fought for protective tariffs on foreign wool, hides and beef, to the benefit of ranchers. Citing Wyoming's belief in women's suffrage, he supported the national suffrage amendment. Arguing that the Prohibition question was a state's rights issue, he voted against the Eighteenth Amendment. Warren sponsored reclamation of arid lands, diverting millions of federal dollars to the west in the form of reservoir projects. He was a leading proponent of the construction of a flood control dam on the Laramie River that led to the development of the Wheatland area.

Warren worked to assure that Cheyenne's Fort D.A. Russell (now F.E. Warren Air Force Base) remained open, at a time when many of the army's other posts in the west were being phased out. He oversaw the modernization of the post, including electrification. Warren used his influence to guarantee that military units were continuously assigned to Fort D.A. Russell, thus preserving a military presence in the state that continues today.

From the start of his political career, Warren was vilified by his opponents as a land baron who fenced public land to discourage settlers. He was blamed for precipitating the Johnson County Cattle War, in which ranchers and businessman attempted to intimidate homesteaders. Warren was criticized for siding against white miners in favor of Chinese laborers following the Rock Springs Massacre in 1885. He was hung in effigy by silver miners who objected to his failure to support the Silver Purchase Bill. Warren was accused of fraud, wielding undue influence in judicial appointments, nepotism and tax dodging. He withstood every attack.

In 1902 the senator's wife, a well-known member of Washington society, passed away. His daughter, Frances, acted as his hostess until her marriage in 1905 to General John J. Pershing. In 1911, at the age of 67, Warren married again. His bride, Miss Clara LaBaron Morgan was 35.

Francis Warren died on November 24, 1929, while planning to run for yet another term in the Senate. During his 37 years in office, he served through eight administrations. Before being laid to rest with full military honors in Cheyenne, Warren received a state funeral in the United States Senate Chamber and lay in state in the Wyoming capitol rotunda. A week after his burial, a presidential declaration changed the name of Fort D.A. Russell to Fort Frances E. Warren. Warren was honored for all he brought to Wyoming as an enterprising and progressive individual, who used his force, energy and enthusiasm to promote his home state.

JOSEPH WATT
1905-

Joseph "Joe" H. Watt was born on a homestead on Buffalo Creek near Moorcroft, Wyoming, in 1905. His parents were Franklin Vance Watt and the former Katherine Oelkers. One of two children, Watt grew up working on his family's ranch. He started school at the age of four because the local school needed at least three students to warrant a teacher. When he was 13, he moved to Moorcroft to begin high school. He completed his final two years of secondary education in Buffalo, graduating at the age of 16 in 1922. He briefly attended the University of Wyoming but his father's financial difficulties forced Watt to curtail his education.

Watt returned to the family ranch, established himself as a homesteader, and in 1928 married Arlene Bundy, a schoolteacher from Gillette. For the first winter of their marriage, Watt worked in the mines of North Lily Mining Company in Eureka, Utah. Then, in partnership with his wife, Watt assumed active management of the Watt ranch in 1929, starting with the five head of calves they had received as a wedding present and the purchase of their first 330 acres of land. Whenever the opportunity presented itself, Watt would acquire more land, "sometimes for as little as fifty cents an acre... this was a slow process... it took me thirty years to build and own my ranch."

In addition to ranching, Watt also tried dry farming, planting "Gehu corn and raising hogs." The 1930s were some of the most difficult times the Wyoming agricultural industry had ever seen, as Watt

> *In 1962, Watt, along with his brother Robert, established the Watt Brothers Scholarship Fund, donating yearling Herefords to aid students in the colleges of law and agriculture.*

later described them "the years of the great drought and grasshoppers and crickets." Despite this rocky start, the Watts managed to build the Triangle T Ranch, based near the original homestead established by his father in 1898, into a 64,000-acre cattle operation which was hailed as a model of efficient management practices.

Watt's reputation as rancher spread within the livestock industry. In 1967, he was elected second vice president of the American National Cattlemen's Association and was named regional vice president the following year. He was also named to the board of directors and served in that capacity for many years. He served as president of the Wyoming Stockgrowers Association and was named Wyoming Stockgrower of the year in 1972, the first member in the history of the organization to be so honored. Watt did not limit his business activities to ranching. He was named president of the National Bank in Newcastle, Wyoming, in 1970. That same year, Watt became a director of the Teton National Insurance Company and eventually assumed the chairmanship of the board of directors.

Watt has also been an enthusiastic supporter of the University of Wyoming. In 1962, Watt, along with his brother Robert, established the Watt Brothers Scholarship Fund, donating yearling Herefords to aid students in the colleges of law and agriculture. Watt and his wife also established three other funds; the Joe H. Watt Scholarship in Engineering Honoring H.T. Person, the Elliot G. Hays Wyoming Internship and Small Business Development Fund and the Western History Research Center Fund. Watt was a leader in the capital campaign to develop the American Heritage Center at the University. A life member of the University Foundation's Board of Directors, Watt is a recipient of the institution's highest honors; an Honorary Doctor of Law Degree and the Alumni Association's Medallion Award.

Watt began to divest himself of his ranching interest in 1966, and by 1973 he had sold his cattle, horses and equipment and leased the ranch, moving permanently into Sheridan, where he still resides. In 1983, he sold the Triangle T, ending 68 years on the Moorcroft ranch. In recalling his life, Watt maintains "I can say that I have enjoyed every bit of it, and hope to be around many more years."

YELLOW CALF
1860-1938

Yellow Calf (George Caldwell) was a Northern Arapaho religious figure, chief and member of the Arapaho-Shoshone Joint Business Council. Yellow Calf lived, and thrived, in two distinctly different eras. Born in 1860, his life spanned the transition from the heyday of Plains Indian life to the poverty which characterized the early reservation period, and finally to the onset of a new era of political and economic activism.

Though too young to serve as a scout for the United States Army during the Plains Indian wars, Yellow Calf reportedly volunteered for service anyway, claiming to have participated in the 1878 conflict with the Bannocks. Upon the relocation of his people to the Shoshone Reservation (now Wind River), he gradually made a name for himself, both as politician and

religious leader. He was a member of the Arapaho Indian police force during the 1880s, a common avenue of political and social advancement for young Indian men during the early reservation years.

At the same time, he also established his credentials as a religious figure. In 1890 or 1891, he reportedly had a powerful spiritual experience which led him to promote a religious ceremony, the Crow Dance, among his people. Under Yellow Calf's leadership, the Crow Dance thrived for a time, passed away, and then was revived in the early 20th century.

Yellow Calf's political career really began in 1904 when he took the place of his half-brother, Wallowing Bull, on the Shoshone-Arapaho Business Council. The youngest member of the group, Yellow Calf also was the only member who had not been a warrior in pre-reservation times. Even though he went to great lengths to highlight his service in the Bannock campaign, his selection marked a passage of time and generations.

As council member from 1904 to 1928, Yellow Calf was an important figure in numerous negotiations with the Shoshones and American authorities, and was a prominent figure in delegations to Washington, D.C. He led the unsuccessful opposition to a 1905 land cession agreement that resulted in the cession of 1.48 million acres of the Wind River Reservation, including the site of Riverton, Wyoming. He also complained vigorously that the terms of that agreement, namely per capita payments and the surrender of certain lands, were not being honored. He was part of a 1908 delegation to Washington which, among other things, protested the exploitation of Indian laborers on reservation projects. This delegation succeeded in gaining an increase in the minimum wage paid to Indian workers, a promise to renew per capita payments to children and a relaxation of restrictions on the Sun Dance ceremony. In 1913, he headed another delegation which expressed opposition to high water charges and protested Wyoming's attempt to control water rights on the reservation. In this respect, his activities anticipated the Arapahos' more successful water rights litigation in the 1970s.

Yellow Calf was one of the two most important Arapaho councilmen, representing the Ethete district while Lone Bear represented the Lower Arapaho. After Lone Bear's death in 1920, Yellow Calf became the head councilman. Through all of this, Yellow Calf carefully presented himself to authorities as a "progressive" Indian, willing and able to promote change, while still acting like a traditional Arapaho leader: in other words, securing aid for his constituents and doing what was right for them. In this connection, his American name, given to him by Agent Herman Nickerson around the turn of the century, and his facility with English, symbolized Yellow Calf's ability to operate in two cultures. The fact that he rarely used the name George Caldwell, and generally chose to speak Arapaho over English, indicates that he was first and foremost Arapaho.

While the most outward manifestation of Yellow Calf's influence lay in his political activities, the basis of his authority derived from his position as a religious leader. In addition to his famous vision, Yellow Calf was "beeteet," meaning that he had a special relationship with supernatural powers, and was a member of the Dog Lodge, an age-graded organization that combined political, social and religious activities. These organizations rank among the most important groups in facilitating the Arapahos adjustment to reservation life, in that they allowed the Arapahos to preserve their traditional ways. Later in life he also was responsible for the revival of the Crow Dance, and served as its spiritual advisor. Yellow Calf's religious influence even extended to Christianity. In 1910, he and Seth Willow sold a parcel of land to Bishop Nathaniel Thomas, land upon which Thomas constructed St. Michael's Episcopal Mission. This property, "iiOeti" or "good" in Arapaho, came to be known as Ethete.

Yellow Calf remained active right up to the end of his long life. In 1933, he graduated from St. Michael's Mission where he learned reading and arithmetic, and in 1934 he led the opposition to the Indian Reorganization Act, remembering as he said, broken promises from the past. Yellow Calf died in December, 1938. He was buried at Ethete, Wyoming.

EDGAR "ED" JACOB HERSCHLER
1918-1990

Edgar "Ed" Jacob Herschler was born on October 27, 1918, in Kemmerer, Wyoming. His parents were Edgar F. Herschler and Charlotte Jenkins. He was raised on his family's ranch in the Fontenelle Creek region of Lincoln County, which had been homesteaded by his grandfather, Jacob Herschler, in 1888.

Herschler's elementary education took place in a typical rural tradition; he rode his horse to a small schoolhouse located on Fontenelle Creek. When he reached high school age, because there were no buses available to transport him to Kemmerer, he boarded with a local family. After graduating, he enrolled at the University of Colorado in Boulder to study chemical engineering.

Herschler's studies were interrupted after only one year by the onset of World War II, when he answered the call to arms by enlisting in the Marines in 1942. He saw extensive action in the Pacific and was eventually promoted to sergeant. In 1944, during an amphibious landing at Bougainville in the Solomon Islands, he was severely wounded while attempting to evacuate his fellow soldiers, who were trapped by enemy fire. Herschler returned stateside to recuperate and was presented with the Purple Heart and the Silver Star Medal for "conspicuous gallantry and intrepidity in action."

After his discharge, Herschler married his college sweetheart, Katherine Sue "Casey" Colter, of Springerville, Arizona. The couple returned to the Herschler family ranch and eventually had two children. But Herschler soon realized that life as a rancher was not enough to satisfy his ambitions so he returned to college and, in 1949, earned a law degree from the University of Wyoming. Herschler settled his family in Kemmerer and established a successful law practice. After serving as Lincoln County's prosecuting attorney for eight years, he realized that he had a real knack for politics.

In 1959, Herschler successfully ran for the state legislature on the democratic ticket. He represented Lincoln County for five terms and was known for his skill as a legislator, as well as his ability to work with members from both sides of the aisle. In 1970, Herschler made an unsuccessful bid for Congress. However, his political career was not over.

Four years later, Herschler entered Wyoming's gubernatorial race. Herschler traveled the state to meet and greet and shake the hands of countless voters. His hard fought campaign, which he remembered as the hardest work he had ever done, was successful. A self described "good ole boy country lawyer," Herschler enjoyed unparalleled levels of popularity among Wyoming's voters.

Believing that he was "supposed to be governor 365 days a year and not just during office hours," Herschler made himself available to the public in a way never before seen in the state, often answering phone calls from voters at his home. Herschler won re-election in 1978, becoming only the fourth governor in the state's history to win a second term. And then he made history in 1982 when he was elected to an unprecedented third term as governor.

While in office, Herschler presided over a period of great growth in Wyoming, resulting from the development of the state's energy-related resources. During his 12 years in office, he focused on managing the social and economic impacts of that growth. Despite the increasingly partisan nature of state politics, Herschler continued to strive for a partnership approach to governing.

Herschler once summed up his personal philosophy of life by saying, "The worst thing you can do is worry. Just do the best you can, and don't get excited." It was an idea that served him well, particularly toward the end of his public life, when he had more than his share of things to worry about, both political and personal. As he embarked on his third term, Wyoming's economy began to falter in the face of a national recession and there were charges of corruption in his administration. Financial difficulties also forced Herschler to file for personal bankruptcy.

In 1986, despite his continuing popularity with the voters, Herschler chose not to run for a fourth term. He died on February 6, 1990, following a bout with cancer. Herschler once said of his three terms as governor, "I enjoy the job, I like the work." It was that attitude which accounted for his popularity, prompting his successor, Governor Mike Sullivan, to remember him as "one of the true giants of Wyoming history."

TENO RONCALIO
1916-

> *In addition to assignments on the Interior and Veterans committees, Roncalio fought for the people of Wyoming — taking stands against gun control and for improved social security and education programs.*

Teno Roncalio was born in Rock Springs, Wyoming, on March 23, 1916. His father was a coal miner. By the time Roncalio was 10 years old, he had gone to work as a bootblack to help support his family. He became a barber's apprentice at the age of 16 and subsequently passed the barber board exam. Roncalio attended local schools, graduating from Rock Springs High School in 1932. Within two years, he began working as a reporter and ad salesman for the *Rock Springs Rocket.*

Roncalio eventually left Rock Springs to enroll in the University of Wyoming, where he worked as the business manager for the student newspaper, *The Branding Iron,* and served as student body president. He left the university in 1941 to accept a position with Senator Joseph O'Mahoney and worked as a research clerk in the United States Senate Library. The following year he was drafted into the army, serving in campaigns in North Africa and Europe as a combat army infantry officer. Roncalio was discharged after serving 33 months, having earned the rank of captain and a Silver Star for gallantry in action. He returned to his studies at the University of Wyoming, enrolling in the law school and earning his degree in 1947.

Roncalio was admitted to the bar shortly after graduation and quickly established himself in Cheyenne. In 1950, he began working as editor of the *Wyoming Labor Journal* and was appointed deputy county attorney for Laramie County, a position he held for the next six years. He married Cecilia Waters Domenico in 1962 and became stepfather to her four children, and eventually the father of two sons.

It was during this period Roncalio became active in the state's Democratic Party, assuming the post of Democratic State Central Committee chairman in 1957. Despite his vigorous espousal of party philosophy, Roncalio maintained cordial relations with his counterparts from the Republican Party. Roncalio ran successfully for the United States House of Representatives in 1964. He later gave up his house seat in a failed bid for the Senate but successfully ran for Congress, again in 1970. While in Congress, Roncalio was identified with liberal issues. In addition to assignments on the Interior and Veterans committees, Roncalio fought for the people of Wyoming — taking stands against gun control and for improved social security and education programs.

While labeled a "dove" during the Vietnam War, Roncalio is quick to point out that he fully supported the troops, visiting the Vietnam battlefields with other combat veterans of World War II at the request of President Lyndon Johnson. Roncalio was an outspoken opponent of the El Paso Natural Gas Company and Atomic Energy Commission's Wagon Wheel Project, which was a plan to detonate several nuclear bombs over a 20-year period in an effort to stimulate gas production. Roncalio described the proposal as a misdirected effort to find a peaceful use for the atom bomb and noted that it was the only time he "actually fought to kill a project that would have brought employees and federal dollars" to his constituency. Roncalio served four terms (1970-1978) before retiring from politics. He continues to reside in Cheyenne and remains active in the community.

CHAPTER SIX HEALTHCARE, SCIENCE & TECHNOLOGY

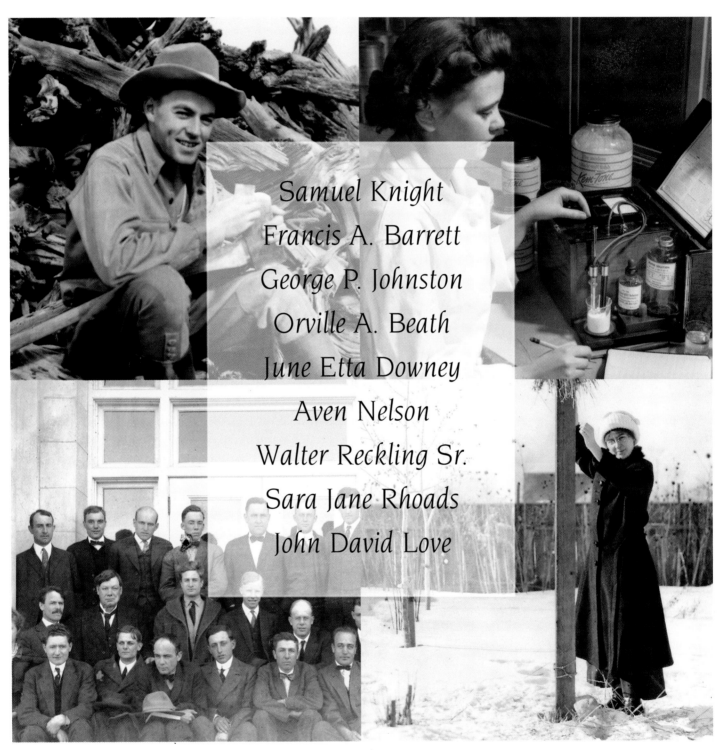

Samuel Knight

Francis A. Barrett

George P. Johnston

Orville A. Beath

June Etta Downey

Aven Nelson

Walter Reckling Sr.

Sara Jane Rhoads

John David Love

(Top left) John David Love *Courtesy of Love Family Collection.*
(Top right) Sara Jane Rhoads *Courtesy of AHC Collection.*
(Bottom left) O.A. Beath, seated first row, far left, c. 1915 *Courtesy of AHC Collection.*
(Bottom right) June Etta Downey, 1917 *Courtesy of AHC Collection.*

INTRODUCTION

Throughout the 20th century, the fields of healthcare, science and technology have played an important role in Wyoming's development. It is a legacy dating back to the state's early days. New residents required medical care and although quality of care was sometimes lacking, the state soon attracted qualified professionals and standards were quickly established. In a tradition that continues into the present day, larger communities soon had access to state-of-the-art facilities while the state's rural residents depended on so-called country doctors, often among the best practitioners, for their healthcare needs.

With the establishment of the University of Wyoming, the importance of scientific and technological developments, particularly to the state's agricultural industries, became more formalized. The presence of the Experimental Agricultural Station serves as proof of this, but the relationship had been in existence since the inception of ranching and farming in the state.

Then, as now, ranchers relied on the latest developments in veterinary and animal science to preserve and increase their herds and flocks. Without the evolution of so-called dry farming, agriculture would never have achieved its place in the state's economy. Farmers in Wyoming have always depended on technology, in the form of irrigation and reclamation, to provide them with water. The work of the Experimental Agricultural Station, made available across the state in the form of published bulletins, made farmers and ranchers privy to the latest advances in agriculture and animal husbandry.

Today, Wyoming boasts many large medical facilities, such as the United Medical Center in Cheyenne and the Casper Medical Center. Working in conjunction with businesses and other interests across the state, the University of Wyoming continues to play an important role in both scientific and technological developments. As Wyomingites prepare to cross over into the next century, they can expect that advances in the fields of healthcare, science and technology will play an important role in bringing their state into the new era.

SAMUEL HOWELL KNIGHT
1892-1975

Sam Knight's (shown here in 1916) many years as a teacher and scientist earned the title of "Mr. Wyoming University." Courtesy of AHC Collection.

Samuel Howell Knight was born in Laramie, Wyoming, on July 31, 1892. His parents were Emma Howell Knight and Wilbur Clinton Knight. Knight attended elementary and secondary school in Laramie. He received a bachelor of science degree from the University of Wyoming in 1913 and then attended Columbia University in New York City, receiving a doctor of philosophy degree in geology in 1929.

In 1916, having completed his graduate course work at Columbia, Knight returned to Laramie and was appointed assistant professor of geology. In 1917, he was promoted to full professor. During World War I, Knight served as a lieutenant in Army Intelligence. Upon his discharge from the army, Knight returned to the Geology Department of the University of Wyoming, where he remained until his retirement.

Knight was famous for his abilities as a teacher. In the course of his 50-year classroom career, Knight taught "Introductory Geology," a required class for geology majors, to about 15,000 students. A commanding figure, Knight was noted for his ability to simultaneously lecture and draw three dimensional diagrams with colored chalk. Students were also awed by his capacity for drawing perfect circles, using his arm as compass. Knight was also a firm believer in a hands-on approach to learning. In 1925, in conjunction with Professor J.F. Kemp of Columbia University, he established a science camp in the Medicine Bow forest to provide geology students with field experience.

Knight was instrumental in establishing the University of Wyoming Department of Geology and Geophysics as among the best in the nation. Under his chairmanship, the department faculty increased from one to eight and he oversaw the development of the department master's and doctorate degree programs. As a result of his efforts, in 1953 the University of Wyoming awarded its first doctor of philosophy degree through the geology program.

Within the field of geology and geophysics, Knight's contributions were numerous. His monograph on the depositional environments of late Paleozoic formation in southeastern Wyoming appeared two decades before such interpretive studies became standard. In collaboration with Professor O.A. Beath, Knight produced a groundbreaking study on the distribution of selenfiuorus rocks and soils in Wyoming. In what many consider his most important work, Knight's study of the cretaceous and tertiary rocks of southeastern Wyoming supported the theory that development of mountains within the state was not a single event but a series of geologic episodes occurring from the late Mesozoic to the early Cenozoic periods.

A prominent member of the university community, Knight was president of the Alumni Association from 1920-23. He also served on the faculty athletic community and organized the football program's first homecoming game activities in 1922. Knight chaired the planning committee for the university's 50th and 75th anniversary celebrations. Knight was dean of the graduate school from 1951-52. And, in keeping with his pursuit of academic excellence, he was president of the local chapters of Phi Beta Kappa, Phi Kappa Phi and Sigma Xi.

Knight also served as an ambassador for the university throughout the state and beyond. He was Wyoming state geologist from 1933-40. In 1962, he was the first member of the university faculty to participate in a statewide lecture series. In 1941, 1942 and 1944, as part of the American Association of Petroleum Geologist Distinguished Lecturer Series, Knight presented lectures across the nation.

Although he officially retired in 1963, Knight remained active within the university's geology program. The legacy of his work remains visible to all who visit not only the geology museum but also the campus. Knight painted the large murals in the university's Geology Museum and mounted the apatosaurus that remains among the museum's most important displays. He also constructed the large, copper-plated tyrannosaurus rex, a campus landmark which greets all visitors.

Knight's contributions did not go unnoticed. He was made an honorary member of the Wyoming Geology Association in 1952. In 1953, the university awarded him an honorary law degree and in 1954, the Alumni Association named Knight a distinguished alumnus. In 1955, Knight received Omicron Delta Kappa's Outstanding Faculty Award. The American Association of Petroleum Geologists made him an honorary member in 1959. In 1974, the University's geology complex was named the S.H. Knight Geology Building. In April, 1997, the College of Arts and Sciences posthumously granted Knight a Distinguished Former Faculty Award.

Samuel Howell Knight died on February 1, 1975, in Laramie.

FRANCIS A. BARRETT
1920-1998

A self-described country doctor, Francis Barrett incorporated current medical practices into his work. *Courtesy of Barrett Family Collection.*

Francis A. Barrett was born in Omaha, Nebraska, on June 29, 1920. He was one of three children of Alice and Frank Barrett, who was a United States congressman, governor of Wyoming and a United States senator. Raised in Lusk, Wyoming, Barrett attended local schools, graduating from Lusk High School in 1938. He entered Creighton University in Oklahoma and later completed medical school at the University of Michigan. After an internship at Providence Hospital in Washington D.C., Barrett served as a captain in the Army Medical Corps during World War II. In 1951, having finished his surgical residency at Providence, Barrett and his family settled in Cheyenne, Wyoming.

Barrett established a medical practice and quickly became a fixture in his community, serving as arena doctor at Cheyenne Frontier Days for 25 years. He and his wife, the former Harriet Permelia Holland, had eight children, the first six of whom were boys. The birth of the Barretts' seventh child, a daughter, generated the headline "Barretts Break Boy Bonanza," in the local paper. A traditional country doctor, despite the relatively urban nature of his practice, Barrett often made house-calls and accepted payment in foodstuffs.

Barrett was a well-respected member of the medical community. He authored numerous scientific articles and served as an editor of the *Rocky Mountain Medical Journal*. A clinical associate professor of surgery at the University of Colorado School of Medicine, he was recognized as an outstanding faculty member in 1975. Barrett was a member of the staff of DePaul Hospital in Cheyenne since 1951 and served as chief of surgery and chief of staff for that institution. As district surgeon for the Union Pacific Hospital Association, Barrett assumed responsibility for administering the medical care for that organization's 1,000 employees.

Beginning in 1963, Barrett worked diligently as a member of the Western Interstate Commission on Higher Education, serving on the executive committee and as commissioner. He was involved in the recruitment of doctors and the establishment of Family Practices throughout the state of Wyoming. Barrett also participated in the development of post-graduate programs in medicine at the state's institutions of higher learning, among them nursing and mental health.

In addition to his work in the medical profession, Barrett also became a rancher, purchasing Mountain View Ranch, where he ran cattle. In 1966, Barrett entered the political arena and was elected to the Wyoming State Senate, where he served for five years. Barrett was a member of the Board of Directors of the Cheyenne Chamber of Commerce, the Laramie County United Fund and the American National Bank of Cheyenne.

Barrett's life was described by one of his sons as encompassing all of the change that has occurred in Wyoming during the 20th century. Barrett, through his involvement in the fields of medicine, education, ranching and politics, participated in Wyoming's change from a rural state to a modern one. Though Francis Barrett himself was most proud of his accomplishments as a father and grandfather, his work on behalf of the state of Wyoming throughout his life truly makes him a Citizen of the Century. Barrett died on September 29, 1998.

GEORGE P. JOHNSTON
1863-1956

George P. Johnston was born in Greene County, Ohio, on March 6, 1863. He graduated from the Medical College of Ohio in Cincinnati in 1891, arriving in Cheyenne, Wyoming, the following year to establish his practice. Johnston recalled dealing with outbreaks of scarlet fever, diphtheria and the grippe in the early days of his practice in Wyoming, which reached epidemic proportions on an annual basis. Typhoid fever and Rocky Mountain Spotted Fever, both characterized by skin rashes and often confused in diagnosis, were also common. Johnston later recalled consulting with Dr. H.T. Ricketts, the Montana State Board of Health physician responsible for clarifying the relationship between ticks and Rocky Mountain Spotted Fever, during Ricketts' tour of Wyoming army posts. Having established a reputation as a surgeon, Johnston performed the first appendectomy in the state and the first abdominal section surgery.

Johnston quickly established himself, not only as a physician, but also as a community leader in Cheyenne. He worked with fellow physicians Dr. Samuel Miller and Dr. M.C. Barkwell for passage of the medical licensing act that was passed by the state legislature in 1899. Prior to this act, licensing consisted of simply registering one's diploma with the county clerk of the area in which one wished to practice. The revelation that diploma mills in Iowa, Illinois, Wisconsin and Missouri had manipulated this system, coupled with the public outcry generated by the arrival in Wyoming of what were described by observers as "a troop of migrating quacks," convinced the legislature to initiate more stringent regulations. Johnston was the first physician licensed under the statute, thus earning the distinction of holding Wyoming Physician License Number One.

A member of the Cheyenne City Council during the typhoid fever epidemic of 1900, Johnston noted that most cases were centered around homes which had private wells. He then pioneered the use of water testing to trace the source to the contaminated wells. To care for victims of the epidemic, Johnston brought the first registered nurse to the state and established a ward at St. John's Hospital, under somewhat primitive conditions. The building had no plumbing, stoves were the only source of heat and kerosene lamps provided lighting.

Johnston married Fanny Phelps in 1912. The couple eventually had two sons. Both husband and wife were among Cheyenne's prominent civil and social leaders. In more than 60 years of practice in Cheyenne, Johnston delivered over 11,000 babies. At the time of his death Dr. Johnston was the oldest member of the American Medical Association's House of Delegates, having represented Wyoming in that body for more than 50 years. Johnston died on September 18, 1956.

> *Having established a reputation as a surgeon, Johnston performed the first appendectomy in the state and the first abdominal section surgery.*

ORVILLE A. BEATH
1884-1965

O.A. Beath was born on a farm near Verona, Wisconsin, on November 11, 1884. He attended the University of Wisconsin, earning a degree in chemistry in 1908. Beath's first teaching position was at Wauwatosa High School in Milwaukee, where he taught science until 1910, before returning to the University of Wisconsin for graduate work. After supporting himself as an assistant chemist for the U.S. Forest Products Laboratory, he completed the requirements for a master's degree in chemistry in 1912. Shortly thereafter he married Katherine Helen Shepard, with whom he had one daughter, Mary Elizabeth.

Upon graduation Beath accepted a position as an instructor in chemistry at the University of Kansas, where he remained until 1914, when he accepted a post as an assistant research chemist at the University of Wyoming. In 1922, he was named head of the Department of Research Chemistry, and remained in that capacity until 1955, when he resigned and was appointed professor emeritus of Agricultural Research in Chemistry. Beath's friends and colleagues recalled him as someone who was known for his "dedication to the mysteries of science and his love of nature" but was also "an adamant sports fan."

As a member of the College of Agriculture Experiment Station faculty at the University of Wyoming, Beath eventually headed up a research team, which included Harold Eppson, Carl Gilbert and Irene Rosenfeld. This group of scientists and researchers studied plant chemistry, the poisonous constituents of western range plants, seleniferous vegetation and the chemical valuation of native forage plants. Beath directed their investigations into the problems of the Wyoming livestock industry from a chemical viewpoint for 40 years.

Beath's work had practical applications for the farmers and ranchers of Wyoming, His team's research, both in the laboratory and on the range, explored the nature of forage plants, as well as stock water and feeds. Beath was particularly dedicated to warning about the dangers of livestock poisoning and approaches to prevention. Among the subjects he dealt with were potent alkaloid poisoning from larkspur or death camas, the control of halogeton and ragwort as a potential source of poisoning. A representative sample of this work can be found in the Experiment Station's Bulletin 324, "Poisonous Plants and Livestock Poisoning."

Ultimately, nearly 50 years of Beath's life were devoted to significant selenium research, beginning with lab and field investigations into the geologic source of the element selenium in 1916. Selenium is an element that is naturally occurring in soils, plants and animals and which also has many industrial uses. When plants and water absorb selenium from the soil it can become toxic to birds, humans and animals. Beath and his team of researchers made the University of Wyoming Agricultural Experiment Station the world center for selenium research.

After laboring in relative obscurity for more than 30 years, Professor Beath's work on selenium became internationally known. Hailed as the authority on the toxicity of selenium, Beath authored and co-authored almost 30 publications related to this subject. Among his better known works were, *Selenium* (1949), his breakthrough treatise written in conjunction with Dr. Samuel F. Trelease of Columbia University, *Selenium: Geobotany, Biochemistry, Toxicity and Nutrition* (1964), written with his longtime colleague Irene Rosenfeld, and the 1963 classic, *The Story of Selenium in Wyoming.*

Beath won acclaim for his work in uncovering the problem of selenium poisoning in humans and livestock. He was the first to recognize the significance of geologic occurrence and plant relationship of selenium, demonstrating a pattern of distribution. Through his research, Beath was able to prove that certain plants accumulate selenium, while some plants have an obligate requirement for the element. His hypothesis of the role of converter plants in making selenium available to other plants is among his most significant discoveries.

A respected member of his profession, Beath was a member of the American Chemical Society, the Botanical Society of America, and the Colorado-Wyoming Academy of Science. Beath died in August, 1965, after a long career that brought prominence to his adopted state and the university. After his passing, he was memorialized by the Faculty Senate as "...an outstandingly productive man." His colleagues recalled that "Professor Beath was exceptionally mentally alert throughout his mature years. Many young staff members have learned and profited from his accounts of past experiences of research in Wyoming and his unfailing intellectual curiosity and interest in new lines of research."

JUNE ETTA DOWNEY
1875-1932

June Etta Downey was born in Laramie, Wyoming, on July 13, 1875. She was one of eight siblings born into a prominent family. Her mother was Evangeline Victoria Owen. Her father, Colonel Stephen Wheeler Downey, was a prominent attorney and delegate to the Wyoming Territorial Legislature. A founder of the University of Wyoming, he served for many years as president of the Board of Trustees.

June Etta Downey received her early education in Laramie's public schools, before attending University Preparatory. She graduated from the University of Wyoming in 1895, having written the school's alma mater. After graduation, Downey taught for a year in Laramie public schools. She then attended graduate school at the University of Chicago, earning a master's degree in 1898. Downey returned to Laramie, where she joined the faculty of the university, teaching English and Philosophy. She maintained a lifelong interest in study of aesthetics and was a published poet. A collection of some of her work was published under the title *Heavenly Dykes.* Her work has been described as introspective and mystical, with a continuing theme of appreciation for the beauty to be found in nature and art.

In 1901, Downey attended a summer session at Cornell University where she was introduced to the experimental procedures of Edward Bradford Titchener, which would greatly influence her course of study. Downey, who had long been intrigued by the field of psychological research, developed a particular interest in motor procedures and differences in temperament. Having been made a professor of philosophy at the university in 1905, she returned to the University of Chicago the following year on a fellowship. In 1907, Downey was awarded her doctoral degree, having completed her thesis "Control Processes in Modified

Handwriting: An Experimental Study." Downey argued that each individual manifests a tendency toward a definite type of covert behavior in which his/her handwriting characterizes his/her will temperament. She was the first graduate of the University of Wyoming to earn her doctorate.

Downey returned to Laramie, where she was made head of the Department of Philosophy. She continued to serve the university community, presiding over the Graduate Committee and as principal of the Department of University Extension Studies from 1908 to 1916, while continuing her research. In 1915, she was made a professor of Psychology and Philosophy and was assigned to preside over both departments.

Throughout the course of her professional career, Downey combined her interest in psychological research and aesthetics. Among her professional publications were "A Musical Experiment" (1897), "The Imaginal Reaction to Poetry" (1911), "Literary Self Projection" (1912), "Program for the Psychology of Literature," and "Creative Imagination" (1929). Her areas of research included mental imagery, color blindness, graphic function, muscle reading, the study of expression and the significance of measuring non-intellectual traits to support intelligence tests. Downey's work in developing will temperament tests, which arose from her doctoral research, was among the first attempts to measure personality objectively. Her 1919 publication article "The Will Profile: A Tentative Scale for Measurement of the Volitional Pattern" earned her an international reputation. Downey's book, *Will Temperament and Its Testing* was published in 1925, followed two years later by *The Kingdom of the Mind*.

Well respected by her peers in the psychological community, Downey served on the Council of the American Psychological Association and was an editor for the *Journal of Applied Psychology*. In one of Downey's last projects she cooperated with Professor C.H. Warren in preparing terms on graphic function for the *Dictionary of Psychology*. Downey became ill while attending a professional convention and she died in Trenton, New Jersey, on October 11, 1932, following an unsuccessful operation. She was buried in Laramie.

AVEN NELSON
1859-1952

Aven Nelson (standing far right) originally came to the university to teach English but ended up building a successful career as a botanist. Photo c. 1891 *Courtesy of AHC Collection.*

Aven Nelson was born on a farm in Lee County, Iowa, near the town of Summerville, on March 24, 1859. His parents were Norwegian immigrants. He received his primary education in local rural schools and eventually attended State Normal School in Kirksville, Missouri, earning a bachelor's degree in English in 1883. After graduating from the State Normal School, Nelson pursued a career in education. He tutored at Drury College in Springfield for two years before becoming principal of the public schools at Ferguson, Missouri.

In 1887, Nelson journeyed west with his family. He was the first faculty member to arrive on the campus of the newly formed territorial university in Laramie, Wyoming. Hired to teach English, Nelson was asked if he would become the university's first biology teacher. He agreed and began teaching botany and zoology, and, since there was no mathematics teacher, geometry.

Along with a colleague, Nelson was placed in charge of the physical education program and became the calisthenics instructor, which he later recalled "came near to being my undoing, for the girls mischievously failed to follow directions..." Nelson also assumed the post of university librarian for two years, another difficult undertaking, "No books could be purchased, for we had no money." With typical determination, by the end of his tenure as librarian, Nelson had built a collection of 256 books, mostly textbooks he had persuaded publishers to donate.

In 1891, the univeristy established the Agricultural College and Experimental Station and Nelson became, in addition to a professor of biology, the botanist of the experiment station. Believing that he needed formal training to perform well in his new position, Nelson and his family traveled to Boston, where he earned a master's degree in botany from Harvard over the course of a year. He returned to Laramie to assume his new duties, and his work on behalf of the Agricultural Experiment Station brought him into contact with farmers throughout the state. He actively promoted opportunities for economic development in Wyoming, especially in farming. For example, Nelson's bulletins for the Experiment Station were influential in the development of orchard farming in the Big Horn Basin.

Realizing that the Rocky Mountain Region had flowers and plants about which little was known, Nelson set about the arduous task of classifying them. It was this work that resulted in the establishment of the Rocky Mountain Herbarium. He later reminisced that "collecting plants was my avocation and filled every summer full." In 1904, Nelson received a doctoral degree from the University of Denver, "based upon the many papers I had published upon the new plants of the Rocky Mountains."

In 1912, Nelson was appointed acting president of the University of Wyoming and remained in that capacity until 1917, when he became the university's ninth president. He remained as president until 1922, when he retired to return to his botanical studies, stating his desire to return to the Botany Department and "round out my botanical career by some teaching in these riper years, and by publications... I hope to leave the Herbarium in such shape that it may be justly considered a real contribution... "

Nelson was able to fulfill each of these goals. He remained a popular instructor, as evidenced by his continuing high enrollments. He published many scholarly works on the plants of Wyoming and the region, including the *New Manual of Botany of the Central Rocky Mountains,* co-authored with J.M. Coulter, the standard reference on Rocky Mountain plants for many years. His other works include *Report of Flora of Wyoming, Trees of Wyoming* and *How to Know Them, Key to Rocky Mountain Flora* and *Spring Flora of the Intermountain States.*

Under Nelson's direction, the University of Wyoming's world-famous Rocky Mountain Herbarium, formally established in 1899, grew into the largest and most representative collection of indigenous plants from the central Rocky Mountain region. By 1936, the collection contained more than 145,000 sheets of specimens and was growing at an average rate of 5,000 items annually. The Rocky Mountain Herbarium was recognized during Nelson's lifetime as "an indispensable fount of data for investigators, an invaluable treasure store of references for students."

Nelson established an international reputation and enjoyed the admiration of his peers. His election as the president of the American Society of Plant Taxonomy was one indication of his success. Recognized as the foremost authority on western flora, Nelson was chosen as president of the Botanical Society of America at the age of 75. And he was often referred to as the father of the Colorado-Wyoming Academy of Science, of which he was the first president.

Aven Nelson remained active in his field throughout the remainder of his life. After the death of his first wife, Alice Calhoun, in 1929, with whom he had two daughters, he married Ruth Ashton. At the age of 89, Nelson, who continued active research, began an unofficial association with the botany department at the University of Oklahoma, where he and his wife spent their winters. Nelson died in on March 31, 1952, in Colorado Springs.

By the time Aven Nelson retired in 1942, he had served the university and the state for 55 years. In his resignation as president of the University of Wyoming, Nelson appropriately used a botanical metaphor to describe the institution he served so long and so well. "We speak of the university as an educational plant... Those educational plants that have grown into magnificent proportions have had very few gardeners, but these gardeners have fertilized the soil with unflinching devotion and have watered, if need be, with their own tears." The legacy of Aven Nelson's contributions to the university and the state are proof of the truth that lies behind his words.

WALTER ERVIN RECKLING SR.
1899-1963

Walter Ervin Reckling Sr. was born in West Salem, Illinois, on January 20, 1899. His parents were William Frederick Reckling, a German immigrant, and Clara Kuntz Reckling. He was a junior attending West Salem High School when he interrupted his studies to enlist in the army during World War I, feeling his German descent obligated him to demonstrate his patriotism. At the age of 15, Reckling was sent overseas with the Medical Corps.

Reckling returned from the war in 1919 to find that both of his parents had died in the influenza epidemic. He completed his high school education the following year and journeyed west. Reckling enrolled at the University of Colorado, and working his way through college, earned his medical degree in 1926. While interning at Mercy Hospital in Denver, Colorado, Reckling met the surgical nurse who would become his wife, Daisy Jean Brower. The couple eventually had two sons and one daughter. The Recklings also adopted two sons and two daughters.

In 1927, Reckling established a medical practice in Kansas. Four years later, Reckling moved his family to

Lusk, Wyoming, where he took over the practice of Dr. Ernest Sheldon Watson. He quickly built a reputation as a physician who cared more about patients than payments, and as someone who would treat both humans and animals with equal care. He once estimated that one third of his practice consisted of charity work. Many grateful ranchers recalled how he had prolonged the lives of prized livestock because he did not distinguish his patients by species.

A member of the International College of Surgeons, Reckling soon became recognized as specialist in surgery, drawing patients from across the state. He was particularly known for his pioneering work in the use of prosthetic devices and the reattachment of severed limbs. In April, 1941, Reckling established the Spencer Hospital, the last privately owned medical facility in the state.

Named after the woman who put her faith in Reckling and provided the start up money for his venture, the hospital was a success. Starting out with eight and soon 16 beds, within four years the hospital had admitted 3,000 patients. Eventually the facility provided care to an average 1,000 patients annually from Lusk and Niobrara County. Built in the former Henry Hotel, Spencer Hospital was as modern a medical facility as could be found in the state at that time.

Reckling was an active member of his adopted community, serving as county health officer and during World War II as county director for the American Red Cross. All three of his children attended Lusk High School and Reckling, who was known for his interest in young people, was an active supporter of the band, raising funds for uniforms and instruments, and the football team, providing free physicals to all student athletes. Reckling served for many years on the Niobrara County Fair Board. He was also the creative force behind the staging of the *Legend of the Rawhide,* which provided funding for buildings at the county fairgrounds.

Reckling assisted a graduate student working on a master's thesis at Denver University, in recording the local legend of the reputed incident on the Emigrant Trail near Lusk. Reckling spearheaded the dramatization, gathering advertising and writing the copy for the pageant booklets. An annual production, *Legend of the Rawhide* was usually staged on the Saturday night preceding Frontier Days, beginning in 1946.

The story concerns a caravan of would be forty-niners on their way to the California gold fields. One man in the group, Clyde Pickett, ambushed and murdered an Indian woman and the members of the caravan were in danger of being massacred if they failed to surrender the guilty party. Eventually, Pickett gave himself up to the Sioux to save his fellow travelers and was flayed alive at or near the Big and Little Rawhide Buttes.

Reckling was a colorful figure, known throughout Wyoming and the Rocky Mountain West. Red Fenwick of the *Denver Post* referred to him as "Wyoming's Sagebrush Philosopher." Reckling achieved a certain degree of his fame as a result of his association with "Mickey, The Talking Dog." Mickey, a German Shepherd, was known to accompany Reckling on his calls to patients in the country. The animal was the subject of numerous press mentions, by virtue of her prodigious talents. Mickey knew elementary mathematics, musical scales and possessed a small but impressive vocabulary, all taught to her by Reckling. After her death, at the age of 11, in April, 1952, Reckling buried her in his backyard and erected an appropriate monument to his canine friend.

In 32 years of medical practice, Reckling delivered 2,224 babies. His lifetime of service and achievement was recognized by his peers when he was named as the second recipient of the A.H. Robins Award for Community Service from the Wyoming Medical Society. The citizens of Lusk also honored all of his work on their behalf, declaring August 17, 1963, "Doc Reckling Day."

Reckling became seriously ill in the spring of 1963 and died that year. He was survived by his second wife, Kitty Brower, a longtime nurse at Spencer Hospital, whom he married after his first marriage, to her sister, ended in divorce. He was buried in Moravian Cemetery in West Salem, Illinois, beside his first wife, who preceded him in death by five years. A self described "country croaker," Doc Reckling was remembered by his friends as a man whose only vice was helping others.

SARA JANE RHOADS
1920-1993

Sara Jane Rhoads earned international recognition for her work in the field of organic chemistry. *Courtesy of AHC Collection.*

Sara Jane Rhoads was born in Kansas City, Missouri, on June 1, 1920, one of six siblings. Her parents were Charlotte Kraft Rhoads and Errett Stanley Rhoads. She attended Kansas City public schools through junior college. In 1941, she graduated from the University of Chicago with a degree in chemistry. She worked in industrial research and development until 1943 when she accepted a position as an instructor of science at the Radford School in El Paso, Texas. In 1944, she relocated to Hollins College in Virginia, where she was a chemistry instructor. In 1945, she began her graduate studies at Columbia University in New York City.

Rhoads joined the faculty of the University of Wyoming in September, 1948, and one of her first tasks was to gain accreditation for her department. Successful in that, she was instrumental in initiating the undergraduate research program in the Department of Chemistry. As one of the first faculty members to receive a National Science Foundation grant, Rhoads was able to continue her research interest. One year after arriving in Laramie, she completed her doctorate in organic chemistry from Columbia. She advanced to full professor in 1958 and served as acting head of the Chemistry Department from 1967 to 1968.

Her peers regarded Dr. Rhoads as an outstanding researcher. She made significant contributions to the study of pericyclic reactions in the field of physical organic chemistry and produced almost 30 publications over the course of her career. To translate into laymen's terms, Rhoads' research into the mechanisms by which organic chemicals rearrange their internal structures led to increased understanding of chemical reactions, which has both scientific and practical applications. The significance of her work was recognized not only by the National Science Foundation, which awarded her four research grants, as well as a post-doctoral fellowship, but was also funded by the American Academy of Arts and Sciences.

Rhoads colleagues and students often referred to her as an excellent instructor, who inspired people with her infectious intellectual curiosity. She herself believed that the university's prime purpose was "to transmit knowledge." She established high academic standards but also demonstrated real concern for students. Students took particular pleasure in her ability to make the material relevant by incorporating the latest technical research available into every subject.

During her tenure at the university, Rhoads directed several master's students as well as guiding the careers of at least a dozen doctoral students, both at the University of Wyoming and other institutions. Among the Ph.D. students Rhoads advised was her longtime friend and colleague, Rebecca Raulins. Typical of the interest Rhoads took in her students' careers were the detailed and personal recommendations she wrote for them. She extended every effort to ensure that her students pursued the course of study best suited to their individual needs and goals.

Rhoads held many visiting scholar positions throughout her career, at diverse institutions such as the California Institute of Technology, the Brookhaven National Laboratories and Redding University in England. She participated in several professional organizations, serving as chair of the Wyoming section of the American Chemists Society (1960-61) and as President of the Colorado-Wyoming Academy of Science (1959-60). Rhoads also found time to be an active participant in the university community, serving as a faculty advisor, a member of the Faculty Senate's Executive Committee and on the Academic Planning Committee.

Among the many awards Rhoads received was the Manufacturers' Chemists Association Teaching Award (1964), American Women in Science Woman of the Year (1968) and the George Duke Humphrey Award (1974). Rhoads was also awarded the American Chemical Society's prestigious Garvan Medal in recognition of her position among both the foremost American women organic chemists and the country's physical organic chemists in 1982.

To honor Dr. Rhoads excellence in research, the Wyoming Chapter of the American Chemical Society established the Sara Jane Rhoads Graduate Students Research Award. In 1992, in recognition of her contribution to the Department of Chemistry, an annual lecture series in organic chemistry was established at the University of Wyoming in honor of Dr. Rhoads and her colleague, Dr. Rebecca Raulins. The first lecturer in this annual series was Dr. Richard E. Smalley, Rhoads' nephew and a pioneer in the field of supersonic beam laser spectroscopy. Rhoads retired from the university in 1984, but continued to reside in Laramie and Centennial. Dr. Sara Jane Rhoads died May 1, 1993.

Characterized as "an ideal blend of teacher and researcher," Dr. Sara Jane Rhoads was unique not only by virtue of her professional successes but also as a woman in a field traditionally dominated by men. Early in her career, Rhoads stated that "in order to advance in science women must be better qualified than men and just as ambitious." She later recalled that she herself had experienced little in the way of discrimination, attributing her ability to progress in her field to the opening up of new endeavors to women after the end of World War II. Perhaps it was the qualities of intellect and a personal drive that allowed her to escape the barriers faced by so many women in the sciences. Rhoads defined what she termed the five elements of success necessary for women to excel in the sciences; education and training, incorporating precision of thought and expression; seriousness of purpose; self esteem, based on realistic self-assessment; determination and opportunity. With the exception of the fifth quality, which she may have created for herself, Rhoads personified her own definition.

JOHN DAVID LOVE
1913-

John David Love has spent more than 40 years studying the geology of his native state. *Courtesy of Love Family Collection.*

John David Love was born in Riverton, Wyoming, on April 17, 1913. His parents were John G. and Ethel P. Love. Love spent his early childhood on a remote ranch in northeast Fremont County in central Wyoming. He enrolled in geological studies at the University of Wyoming in 1929, studying under Dr. Samuel Knight. He earned a bachelor's and master's degree in 1933 and 1934, and worked intermittently at the Geological Survey of Wyoming until 1937 while completing advanced studies at Yale, University, where he was awarded a doctorate in Geology in 1938. Upon leaving Yale, Love worked as field assistant for the United States Geological Survey before joining Shell Oil Company as a research geologist, a position he held until 1942.

In 1942, Love accepted a post with the United States Geological Survey, and remained with that agency for the next 46 years. Love established and served as director of the Wyoming Fuels Branch (1942-43) and was director of the Wyoming Office of the Geologic Division from 1943 until 1987. He was chief for the Compilation of State Geologic Maps for both the 1955 and 1985 Wyoming Projects. During the course of his career, Love completed more than 220 published works and conducted uncounted site specific investigations, making him the foremost authority on Wyoming geology.

Throughout his career, Love made many significant contributions to the understanding of Wyoming's geological history. Beginning in 1945, Love spent nearly every summer field season in Jackson Hole, Wyoming, and is recognized as the authority on the state's geology. Love has studied the Teton Range and Granite Mountains extensively. His 1951 discovery of the Pumpkin Buttes uranium district was the forerunner of the state's uranium industry. Love also discovered the location of the western end of the Owl Creeks, under the Absarokas. At the time of his retirement in 1987, Love assumed the rank scientist emeritus.

Among his honors are an honorary degree from the University of Wyoming (1961) and the UW Distinguished Alumni Award. His work was also recognized by the Wyoming Geologic Association, which granted him an honorary membership and a distinguished service award, in addition to establishing the J. David Love Wyoming Field Geology Fellowship Program at the University of Wyoming. Love also received the Meritorious and Distinguished Service awards from the Department of the Interior.

Love married Jane S. Matteson in June, 1940. The couple eventually had four children. Love and his wife, who holds a master's degree in geology, collaborated on the Wyoming Geologic Survey publication *Roadlog: Jackson to Dinwoody and Return.* Love was also the central character in John McPhee's *Rising From the Plains.*

CHAPTER SEVEN MILITARY

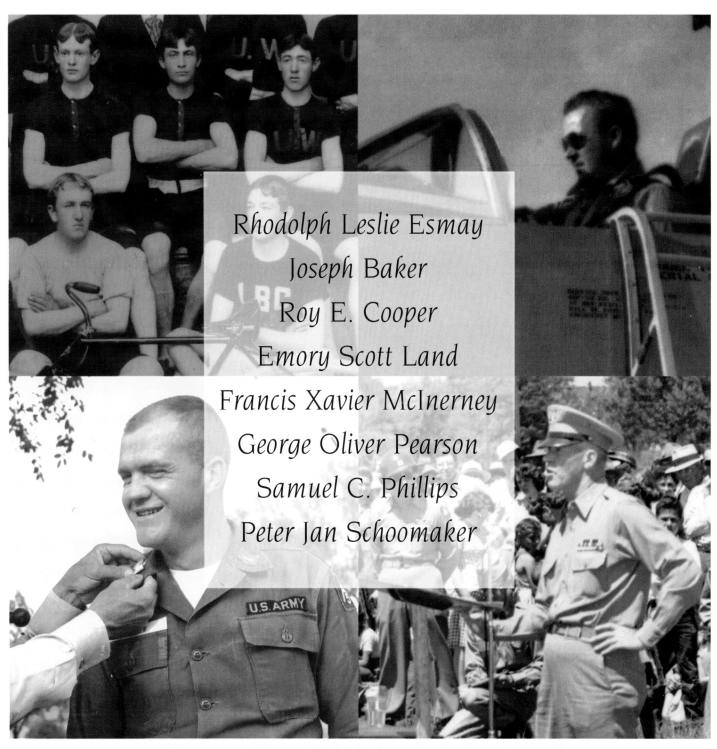

Rhodolph Leslie Esmay

Joseph Baker

Roy E. Cooper

Emory Scott Land

Francis Xavier McInerney

George Oliver Pearson

Samuel C. Phillips

Peter Jan Schoomaker

(Top left) Emory Scott Land, back row, far left. UW Athletics Club, 1897 *Courtesy of AHC Collection.*
(Top right) Roy Cooper *Courtesy of Cooper Family Collection.*
(Bottom left) George Pearson, left *Courtesy of Pearson Family Collection.*
(Bottom right) General Esmay *Courtesy of Esmay Family Collection.*

INTRODUCTION

Many of Wyoming's early prominent citizens, such as Medal of Honor winner F.E. Warren, were veterans of the Civil War. This tradition of military service continues to the present day. The first test of Wyoming's citizen soldiers came during the Spanish American War. When the new century was less than two decades old, many members of Wyoming's National Guard were dispatched during the United States' border dispute with Mexico.

When World War I began in 1914, Wyoming, like the rest if the country, felt removed from the conflict in Europe. By 1917, when U.S. involvement seemed inevitable, the majority of Wyomingites threw themselves wholeheartedly into the war effort. More than 12,000 of the state's citizens served in the conflict, and almost 500 of them died during the war.

During World War II, more than 20,000 of Wyoming's men and almost 600 of the state's women served in the war effort. The efforts of these men and women in the service of their country were heroic. Among the many that served was Sergeant Charles F. Carey, Jr. In 1945, Carey, in command of an antitank platoon in Rimling, France, rescued and evacuated several wounded soldiers in the face of enemy fire. He was later struck down by sniper fire. Carey's leadership was recognized with the Medal of Honor.

Wyoming also sacrificed many of its citizens in the Korean conflict and during Vietnam. Major William Edwards Adams, Medal of Honor recipient and native Wyomingite, was one of many who served. Major Adams distinguished himself in May, 1971, while serving as a helicopter pilot in Vietnam. His helicopter was damaged by enemy fire during an attempted rescue of wounded comrades. Despite Adams exceptional skills as a pilot, no one survived the crash that followed.

In subsequent conflicts in Panama, the Middle East and Europe, Wyoming continues to provide soldiers for all branches of the armed forces. This sacrifice is in keeping with the state's tradition of military service.

RHODOLPH LESLIE ESMAY
1898-1965

General Esmay served his state and country in war and peace time. *Courtesy of Esmay Family Collection.*

Rhodolph Leslie Esmay was born in Sabula, Iowa, on May 15, 1898. His family moved to Douglas, Wyoming, around 1900, and his father established J.H. Esmay Contracting and Building. Esmay attended local schools, graduating from Converse County High School in 1916.

Esmay's military career began in 1915, when at the age of 16 he enlisted as a private in the Wyoming National Guard. After his graduation from high school, he assumed active duty status with the National Guard and was dispatched with his unit to serve during the border dispute with Mexico. In 1916, Esmay joined the United States Army, completing the course of instruction at the Officer and Non-Commissioned Officer School in Cheyenne, Wyoming. The following year he graduated as an infantry second lieutenant from the U.S. Army Officer Candidate School in Presidio, California.

During World War I, Esmay served in Europe with the 32nd Infantry Regiment of the 91st Division. He was twice wounded in the Meuse-Argonne campaign and participated in the St. Mihiel advance, two bitterly fought operations in the French theater. He also fought in the Lyse Scheldt campaign in Belgium. Esmay was discharged from active duty in 1919.

From 1921 through 1923 Esmay served as the Adjutant General for the state of Wyoming. After resigning his post he worked in the family business and also attended the University of Wyoming. He assumed the position of Adjutant General again in 1929 and remained in that post until his retirement in 1962, serving for a total of 35 years. Under his leadership the framework for the contemporary Wyoming National Guard took shape. He presided over a succession of changes, both tactical and technological, which brought the state's National Guard into the 20th century.

Esmay was a charter member of the American Legion, the Veterans of Foreign Wars, the Disabled American Veterans and the Reserve Officers Association of the United States. He served on the National Guard Association's executive committee and was a member of the Adjutant Generals' Association. Upon his retirement, his portrait was placed in National Guard Memorial Building in Washington, D.C. Esmay himself believed the National Guard afforded a "training ground for citizenship, discipline and high incentive."

During World War II, Esmay headed the state's Selective Service organization, delivering almost 60 percent of Wyoming's servicemen for induction. His administration earned the state a reputation for efficiency with the Selective Service National Headquarters. In 1941, under congressional authorization, the state legislature provided for a State Defense Council, with Esmay serving as executive vice chairman. The first task of this body was to establish a state guard to assume civil protection duties in the absence of the National Guard, which had been called to active duty. Esmay also supervised test blackouts and when necessary, assisted the Wyoming Emergency Relief Board.

Esmay died of a heart attack in Cheyenne on November 13, 1965, at the age of 67. He remained as the state's selective service director at the time of his death. His wife and their two sons survived Esmay. Flags on the Capitol and state buildings flew at half-staff in tribute to Esmay's years of service. He held the Legion of Merit, the Purple Heart and the Distinguished Service Medal of the National Guard, as well as the service commendations for World I, World War II and the Mexican Border Campaign.

Esmay was buried with full military honors after funeral services at St. Mark's Episcopal Church, where he had been an active member of the congregation for many years. Governor Clifford Hansen praised Esmay not only as a "great soldier and a military administrator but a tireless worker for the common good in civilian affairs as well." As someone whose military career spanned the age of horse cavalry to the missile era, Esmay is truly representative of Wyoming's military history in the 20th century.

JOSEPH BAKER
1919-

> *"I was a soldier with a job to do and I did it."*

Joseph Baker was born in Cheyenne, Wyoming, in 1919. Orphaned at the age of four, when his parents were killed in an automobile accident, Baker and his two older sisters were raised in Cheyenne by his grandparents. His grandparents provided a stable home life. His grandfather worked as a railway brake inspector, providing a certain degree of financial security, and insisted that Baker attend school. Despite their efforts, as a young man Baker was often in trouble and at the age of 11 he was sent to Father Flanagan's Boys Town in Nebraska. Baker later recalled that his grandfather "thought it would straighten me up — and it did." In 1933, Baker left Boys Town, enrolling in high school in Clarinda, Nebraska, and earning his diploma.

Baker returned to Wyoming in 1939, accepting a position as a porter on the Union Pacific Railroad. Dismayed by the pervasive racism and seeking a more challenging career, Baker joined the army two years later. Despite the army's segregation of black soldiers, Baker thrived in the structured atmosphere and was selected for officer training. He eventually rose to the position of staff sergeant and in 1944 was sent to Italy. He quickly saw action and was wounded during an encounter with a German sniper. Promoted to second lieutenant, he returned to active duty after two months of recuperation in a segregated hospital, as a platoon commander in the all-black 92nd Infantry, known as the Buffalo Division.

On a spring morning in 1945, Vernon led 25 men in an assault on the heavily fortified Castle Aghinolfi in northern Italy, as part of a larger effort to make a final push to force the Germans to retreat, in preparation for the advance of the Fifth Army. Despite a tactically difficult position below the castle, where "every time they moved, they would shell us," Baker's platoon took out a German observation post, two bunkers and three machine gun nests. Baker's platoon inflicted heavy losses on the Germans and Baker himself is estimated to have killed nine enemy soldiers. After suffering 18 casualties among his own men, Baker ordered his seven remaining men to retreat, while he drew enemy fire. The following day Baker led the remains of the battalion back up to the castle and realized that his mission to dislodge the Germans had been successful because "There wasn't a shot fired. They were gone."

Baker was honored for heroism with the Distinguished Service Cross and subsequently promoted to first lieutenant. He was denied higher honors as a result of what was eventually found to be a systematic refusal on the part of the military to acknowledge fully the heroism of black soldiers. Not until the army initiated a re-examination of World War II records for black Medal of Honor candidates did Baker receive the full recognition he was due.

In 1997, Vernon Baker was awarded the Congressional Medal of Honor, the nation's highest military award for valor, along with six other black veterans, who received their medals posthumously. Baker himself maintained that he felt no bitterness at the long overdue honor, "I was a soldier with a job to do. And I did it."

Returning from Italy in 1947, Baker remained in the army and made the military his career. In 1953, he married Fern Brown, with whom he had four daughters. He retired from the service in 1968 and worked with the Red Cross in Fort Ord, California, counseling military families. When his first wife died in 1986, Baker left the Red Cross and settled in northern Idaho, where he still resides. He married the former Heidi Pawlik in 1993. Baker is also co-author of *Lasting Valor,* which details his military exploits during World War II while providing a first-hand account of his personal struggle with racism.

ROY E. COOPER
1923-

Roy E. Cooper was born on November 23, 1923, in Nampa, Idaho. He spent his childhood in Grand Island, Nebraska, where he attended grade school and high school. He enrolled in Kansas State University, but the outbreak of World War II interrupted his studies in 1942, when he entered United States Air Corps Cadet Training. After completing his training, Cooper was commissioned as a second lieutenant. He was stationed in Europe with the Eighth Air Force. Cooper flew P-51 Mustangs and completed more than 200 combat hours. He was awarded the Distinguished Flying Cross and released from active duty in February, 1946.

Upon his return to the United States, Cooper became a leading proponent for the organization of the Air National Guard. Wyoming was one of the first states to respond to the call, forming the Wyoming Air National Guard in August, 1946. As one of the first pilots in the newly formed unit, Cooper decided to settle in Cheyenne. He married the former Mickey Harms and the couple eventually had two children.

Cooper's belief in the necessity of the Air National Guard became a reality when the Wyoming Air National Guard was called to active duty in response to the Korean Conflict in 1951. Again a member of a P-51 unit, Cooper lost nine of his fellow pilots in Korea. After the unit was released from active duty, Cooper returned to Cheyenne.

Cooper turned his attention to reorganizing the Wyoming Air National Guard to meet the demands of the jet age. He soon realized that Wyoming lacked the necessary airport facilities, particularly longer runways, to adequately service jet based units. Cooper lobbied the Army Corps of Engineers to approve the necessary construction projects to bring the Wyoming Air National Guard into the new era. Wyoming became the only air guard unit in the United States operating jet aircraft from a base at an altitude of more than 6,000 feet. As an added benefit, these improved facilities also brought civilian airlines, with jet service, to the state.

Throughout the 1950s, Cooper continued to serve as a leader of the Wyoming Air National Guard, in its new role of providing round-the-clock air defense for the northern tier of states during the height of the Cold War era. In 1961, Cooper again foresaw the necessity of the Air National Guard changing its role to meet new demands. He was instrumental in the Guard's conversion from fighter aircraft to a world transport fleet. These transports, bearing Wyoming's bucking horse logo, have traveled the globe, including numerous missions in Asia and the Far East.

With the ending of the Vietnam War, during which Cooper flew numerous combat support missions, he again realized that the Wyoming Air National Guard needed to update its aircraft. He led the conversion process, attending the required training to bring the updated C-130s to Wyoming, securing a vital role for the guard well into the next century.

Cooper has served his adopted state for many years, working to maintain Wyoming's place as a viable member of the nation's military team. The significance of his contributions in providing for federal spending within the state for Wyoming's economy cannot be measured. But most importantly, Cooper's continued ability to negotiate successfully the intricacies of the federal and military bureaucracies have ensured the future of Wyoming's Air National Guard.

Roy Cooper has been instrumental in keeping Wyoming's Air National Guard in a state of readiness. Courtesy of Cooper Family Collection.

EMORY SCOTT LAND
1879-1971

Emory Scott Land was born in Canon City, Colorado, on January 9, 1879. His parents were Scott E. and Jennie Taylor (Emory) Land. He grew up in Colorado and attended local schools. After his family moved to Laramie, Wyoming, where his father had taken a job at a local fish hatchery, Land enrolled in the University of Wyoming. During his four years at the university, Land was an outstanding football player and all-around athlete. He graduated with a bachelor's degree in 1898.

While at the University of Wyoming, Land became enchanted with the idea of joining Theodore Roosevelt's Rough Riders in the Spanish American War. Since his parents opposed the notion, Land and a friend went to Cheyenne, where he enlisted in the army. His family intervened and according to Land's own recollection, he was summoned to the office of Senator F.E. Warren, who advised him he could better serve his country by taking the competitive examinations for the United States' Naval Academy. Land took the exams and won an appointment to Annapolis.

Land excelled at Annapolis, both as an athlete and a student. He won fame for his touchdown in the Army Navy game of 1900 and was presented with the Sword for General Excellence in Athletics. He was Cadet Commander of his battalion his final year and, at sixth in his class, graduated cum laude. Too ill to participate in the 1902 graduation ceremonies presided over by President Theodore Roosevelt, and confined to the

infirmary, Land received a memorable visit from his idol, and the two "reminisced about cow-punching, Cloud's Peak, Paint Rock lakes and the splendor of Wyoming scenery."

A mere 135 pounds while a plebe, Land went on to earn the title of "the busiest little guy in the Navy." Land's first assignment was a two-year stint at the Asiatic Station on the *U.S.S. Oregon*. He was then appointed assistant naval constructor. He did post-graduate work at MIT and received a master's degree in 1907. In 1909, he married the former Elizabeth Stiles.

In 1912, Land was commissioned Naval Constructor with the rank of lieutenant. From 1914 to 1916, he served in that capacity on the staff of the Commander of the Atlantic Fleet. During World War I, Land the navy assigned Land to the Bureau of Construction and Repair. Land won recognition for his work in the design and construction of submarines and was awarded the Navy Cross for his service. In 1918, he served on the Allied Naval Armistice Commission and the following year was appointed assistant naval attaché at the American Embassy in London.

Land was subsequently transferred to the Navy's Bureau of Aeronautics, qualified as a naval aviation observer, and was appointed to the Army and Navy Helium Board and the Post Graduate Council of the Naval Academy. From 1926 to 1928, he served as assistant chief of the Bureau of Aeronautics and on the National Advisory Committee for Aeronautics. He then took leave to work with the Daniel Guggenheim Fund for the Promotion of Aeronautics and during that time qualified for his pilot's license. After returning to active service, Land was assigned to the Office of Naval Operations as chief constructor and chief of the Bureau of Construction and Repair. He retired at the rank of rear admiral in 1937.

The outbreak of war brought an abrupt end to Land's retirement. Described as "a peppery man with an active dislike of red tape," he became something of a legend in the nation's capital during World War II. As chairman of the Maritime Commission, beginning in 1938, and head of its companion agency, the War Shipping Administration, he supervised the greatest crash program of ship building in the history of the industry.

Land's new role landed him in *Life* magazine and on the cover of *Time,* which described him as a "casual dispenser of lurid and effective seagoing profanity."

Using his "phenomenal energy and whiplash tongue," Land battled Congress and the unions to produce an astounding 55 million tons of ships for the fleet. He oversaw the operation of the Merchant Marines, as well as chairing the Strategic Shipping Board and administering the War Shipping Administration. At President Franklin Roosevelt's request, Land attended the Quebec Conference in 1944 and the Yalta Conference in 1944. In 1945, he attended the Potsdam Conference as an advisor to President Truman.

Land resigned from government service for good in 1946, after a 48-year career. A special act of Congress raised his rank to vice admiral. He subsequently accepted the presidency of the Air Transport Association, a position he held until 1963. During this period he was also president of Air Cargo, Inc., and board chairman of Aeronautical Radio Inc. Beginning in 1957 he had a long association with General Dynamics Corporation, as a consultant and director. In 1958, he published *Winning the War With Ships*. Charles A. Lindbergh, who was Land's cousin, wrote the introduction to his book, which recounted Land's work during World War II.

Land received numerous awards throughout his career, including the Distinguished Service Medal. Knight Commander of the Order of the British Empire, Commander of French Legion of Honor, and Commanders Cross of Saint Olav from Norway were among the honors Land received from foreign governments in recognition of his services during World War II. He also had a glacier in Antarctica and a mountain peak near his birthplace named in his honor. In 1953, Land was the first recipient of the University of Wyoming's distinguished alumnus award.

Emory Land died on November 27, 1971, at the age of 92. He was remembered as "a major architect of the victory of the allied forces" during World War II. His legacy at the University of Wyoming lives on in the form of the Admiral Emory S. Land Award, presented annually to the outstanding university athlete and non-athlete student who have contributed to the advancement of inter-collegiate athletics.

FRANCIS XAVIER McINERNEY
1899-1956

Francis Xavier McInerney was born on March 28, 1899, in Cheyenne, Wyoming. His parents were Thomas and Phyllis O'Neal McInerney. He attended local schools and after completing high school, enrolled in the University of Colorado at Boulder. In 1917, he received an appointment to the U.S. Naval Academy for Wyoming.

McInerney graduated from Annapolis with the class of 1921 and was commissioned ensign and assigned to the USS New Mexico, flagship of the Commander in Chief of the Pacific Fleet. During the next six years he served on destroyers in the Pacific and Atlantic fleets. He was subsequently assigned to the Naval Torpedo Station in Newport Rhode Island for two years, at which time he returned to sea for a three-year stint on the USS Dobbin.

In 1932, he reported for post-graduate instruction in law, under the supervision the Office of the Judge Advocate General of the Navy. He attended George Washington University Law School and, after receiving a bachelor of law degree, was admitted to practice in the District Court for the District of Columbia in 1935. He was later admitted to the U.S. Court of Appeals for the District of Columbia. From 1935 to 1938 McInerney served on the USS Concord with the Pacific Fleet, before returning to shore duty as an instructor at Annapolis.

McInerney assumed command of the USS Smith in 1940. When the United States entered World War II the following year, McInerney was at the forefront of the action as commander of a destroyer division. In February, 1942, he became the senior officer of destroyers attached to the ANZAC squadron in the South Pacific and participated in the early strikes in the Solomons. After the Battle of the Coral Sea he received a letter of commendation from the commander in chief of the Pacific Fleet for "exemplary action."

In March, 1943, McInerney assumed command of Destroyer Squadron 21, first of the new 2,100-ton destroyers. His squadron operated in the Solomons and participated in the laying of mines and bombardment of Japanese positions, for which he was awarded the Bronze Star. He commanded three of these destroyers in the first and second Battle of Kula Gulf and was honored for his "extraordinary heroism" and "conspicuous gallantry" with the Navy Cross and the Silver Star. McInerney also oversaw rescue operations for the survivors of the torpedoed USS Helena, for which he received a Presidential Citation and the Legion of Merit.

In August, 1943, McInerney was selected representative of Commander Destroyers in the South Pacific. The following year he was named chief of staff for Commander Operational Training for the Pacific Fleet. He assumed command of the battleship Washington in 1945, returning to the United States to join the Atlantic Fleet as part of the so-called "magic carpet" bringing veterans home from Europe.

In October, 1946, McInerney reported to San Francisco as commanding officer of the Naval Receiving Station at Treasure Island. He was promoted to rear admiral in 1947. In 1948, he assumed command of Cruiser Division 15 and the following year he took over Cruiser Division 5.

His conduct and accomplishments were recognized by the U.S. Navy, which named a nuclear-guided missile frigate in his honor.

In 1950, McInerney became commander of the Pacific Fleet's Amphibious Training Command, later assuming command of both Group Three and Service Squadron Three. He saw extensive action in the Korean conflict and was awarded a Gold Star for his command of amphibious training exercises. He also received notice for his development of a technique of underway replenishment, which allowed continuing logistical support for combat units in Korean territory.

In 1953, McInerney was detached from Service Squadron 3 and ordered to report as a senior member of the West Coast Section of the Board of Naval Inspection and Survey in San Francisco. The following year, he assumed the presidency of the Permanent General Court Marshall for the 11th Naval District. He retired from active duty in June, 1955, and was advanced to the rank of vice admiral on the basis of his combat service awards.

McInerney died in San Francisco in 1956. McInerney, both in leadership and action, through his distinguished service in World War II and Korea, brought honor to his native state. His conduct and accomplishments were recognized by the U.S. Navy, which named a nuclear guided missile frigate in his honor.

GEORGE OLIVER PEARSON
1903-1998

George Oliver Pearson was born on August 15, 1903, in Sheridan, Wyoming. His parents were Nels A. Pearson, founder of the N.A. Pearson Construction Company, and Anna Oliver Pearson. Pearson attended local schools and eventually graduated from Sheridan High School. His military career began in 1920 when he joined Troop B, 1st Cavalry Regiment of the Wyoming National Guard.

Pearson enrolled at the University of Wyoming and later transferred to University of Minnesota, where he earned a degree in architectural engineering in 1928. While at Minnesota, Pearson was commissioned a second lieutenant through ROTC and was assigned to the 6th Coast Artillery. After graduation he returned to Sheridan, where he worked in the family business. In 1932, Pearson married Sarah "Sally" Leightner and for

the next nine years the couple and their two daughters resided in Sheridan. Pearson was eventually assigned to the Sheridan Unit of the Wyoming National Guard, assuming command of Troop B of the 115th Cavalry Unit, the last of the combat horse squadrons, in 1937.

In 1941, the Pearsons left Sheridan with the 115th for Ft. Lewis, Washington, as a result of the World War II mobilization of the National Guard. While there, Pearson served as a troop commander, squadron commander and regimental executive officer. In December, 1942, Lieutenant Colonel Pearson was assigned as G2 Intelligence Officer for the 11th Airborne Division at Camp McCall, North Carolina. He was called to combat in the Pacific Theater. The 187th was considered by General Douglas MacArthur to be one of the best combat units in the army and their reduction of Mt. McLeod in the Philippines is regarded as one of the most successful combat operations in the area. In recognition of Pearson's leadership of the 187th he was promoted to regimental commander.

On August 30, 1945, the 187th, under Pearson's command, was the first regiment into Japan, charged with establishing security for General MacArthur's landing. The following year Pearson was assigned to the Manila Engineering District and acted as Area Engineer for Reconstruction of Manila, Batangas and Clark Field. In June, 1947, he was reassigned to the 11th Airborne Division as commander of the 187th RCT and as Island Commander of Hokkadio.

Pearson was subsequently assigned to the Office of the Secretary of Defense, the Industrial College of the Armed Forces, the Office of the Acting Chief of Staff G3 Operations at the Pentagon and the 508th Airborne Regimental Combat Team at Fort Benning, Georgia. Between 1953 and 1957, Pearson served as assistant commander of the Berlin Command, with the Southern Commander at Munich and as chief of staff, COMLANDENMARK-NATO. While at the Presidio in San Francisco in November, 1958, Pearson retired from the army at the rank of colonel.

Pearson returned to Wyoming and was appointed assistant army general. In 1961, he accepted the position of state adjutant general. Serving in that capacity during the critical period of the Cold War, Pearson was credited with updating the Wyoming National Guard and raising troop morale. Upon his retirement in 1967, he held the rank of major general.

Pearson, who once noted "there is no such thing as being too ready when called upon to do your mission," earned numerous honors throughout his military career. Among his military awards were the Silver Star, two Bronze Stars, two Legions of Merit and two Commendation Ribbons. He was also the recipient of the 1967 Freedom Foundations Award and the Wyoming Distinguished Service Medal. In 1990, the National Guard Armory and U.S. Army Reserve Center in Sheridan was dedicated in Pearson's honor. Pearson was known by his peers as a commander, who in leading by example, "showed a great deal of empathy for his men." Pearson died on March 20, 1998.

SAMUEL C. PHILLIPS
1921-1990

Phillips brought the Apollo Program to its pinnacle, with Neil Armstrong's 1969 walk on the surface of the moon.

Samuel C. Phillips was born in Springerville, Arizona, on February 19, 1921. His family later moved to Cheyenne, Wyoming, where he was raised. He graduated from Cheyenne High School in 1938 and enrolled in the University of Wyoming. While at the University of Wyoming, Phillips completed the Officer Reserve Training Corps program and received a degree in Electrical Engineering in 1942. He later attended the University of Michigan, earning a master's degree in Electrical Engineering in 1950.

Phillips was a pilot during World War II. He served with distinction, earning the Flying Tiger Pilot Trophy, the Distinguished Flying Cross, WW II Victory Medal and the Legion of Merit. Following the end of the war, Phillips pursued a career in the Air Force, rising to the rank of colonel. By the late 1950s, Phillips was assigned to the Strategic Air Force Command in England.

In 1959, Phillips became director of the Minuteman Intercontinental Ballistic Missile Program (ICBM) for the United States Air Force. Phillips assumed responsibility for management analysis, engineering technology and testing, bringing the program from the design to the operational stage. He oversaw the successful development of this new generation of long-range solid propellant intercontinental ballistic missiles, which eventually comprised the United States' primary nuclear deterrence. And he was able to meet the revised launching schedule, which moved the project forward one year.

Under Phillips' leadership, the Minuteman Missile became an operational ballistic system. Planning for this nuclear deterrent provided for the creation of underground launch silos in several interior states, including Wyoming. Implementation of the system required the construction of 200 underground missile launch silos, 20 feet in diameter, at a depth of 80 feet. 200 Minuteman missiles, each equipped with a nuclear reentry vehicle warhead, were placed in the silos. To support these silos, 20 Launch Control Centers, self-sufficient two-person stations, were constructed. The silos made of concrete and steel, and the launch centers, were constructed to withstand near-miss nuclear detonations, while providing facilities to support the crews throughout a nuclear attack.

All of the missile silos and launch control centers are interconnected by underground electric cables and free air radio communications. The ground level of above the 220 components of the Minuteman System is protected by chain link fences, control doors and electronic surveillance systems. Since its construction, the Minuteman System has remained on almost continuous alert.

The infrastructure for the Minuteman System in Wyoming represents an investment of billions of dollars. Within the state the missiles and their supporting facilities are assigned to the 90th Space Wing, formerly known as the 90th Strategic Missile Wing, at F.E. Warren Air Force Base in Cheyenne. The cost of the initial construction, missile installation, reentry vehicle attachment, launch crew and maintenance personnel required to operate the system, as well as the cost of continuing technological updates, has had a tremendous positive impact on Wyoming's economy.

In 1964, having made the Minuteman System a reality, Phillips went on to become the deputy program director for the Apollo Program at NASA. He was quickly promoted to director of the Apollo Manned Lunar Landing Program. During the next five years, Phillips brought the Apollo Program to its pinnacle, with Neil Armstrong's 1969 walk on the surface of the moon.

Having achieved success with the Apollo Program, Phillips subsequently commanded the Space and Missile Organization in Los Angeles and served as director of the National Security Agency. His final posting, as commander of the Air Force Systems Command in Maryland, ended with his retirement in 1975. After retiring from the Air Force, Phillips went on to work in the private sector, as vice president and general manager of the Energy Systems Management Division of TRW, a major defense contractor. He was later named vice president of TRW Defense Systems Group.

In 1986, Phillips returned to NASA to oversee the troubled Space Shuttle Program in the wake of the *Challenger* disaster. He was in charge of the eight month review of NASA management procedures. The result of that review, with its emphasis on safety procedures, revitalized the Space Shuttle Program. Ironically, the finding that Morton-Thiokol, a NASA contractor, was largely to blame for the *Challenger* disaster echoed Phillips' earlier condemnation of another NASA contractor following the death of three *Apollo* astronauts in a 1967 training accident.

Phillips earned many honors during his long and distinguished career, including an honorary degree from the University of Wyoming, the Simon Ramo Medal from the Institute of Electrical and Electronic Engineers and the General Thomas D. White Space Trophy from the National Geographic Society. He was one of only 14 recipients of the Langley Medal, awarded to him by the Smithsonian Institution in 1971. Other recipients of the Langley are the Wright Brothers and Charles Lindbergh.

Phillips died on January 30, 1990, at his Palo Verdes estate in California. He was remembered as laconic and unflappable by his colleagues, qualities that no doubt contributed to his success as a manager of such massive projects. His military career resulted not only in tangible benefits to his native state, but, through his work as a pioneer in the space program, brought honor to Wyoming.

PETER JAN SCHOOMAKER
1946-

"The people of Wyoming have a great sense of pride and admiration for this special man."

— Senator Al Simpson

Peter Jan Schoomaker was born in Detroit, Michigan, on February 12, 1946. He attended the University of Wyoming. Schoomaker, known as an outstanding defensive tackle, played football for the Cowboys, lettering in 1966, 1967 and 1968. He played in the Sun Bowl in 1966 and was part of the legendary football team that went to the Sugar Bowl in 1968. Schoomaker also excelled academically. In 1969, he was elected to Omicron Delta Kappa's Men's leadership Honorary.

While at the University of Wyoming, Schoomaker began his military career as part of the Army ROTC program. He was an outstanding member of the cadet corps, selected as brigade commander and Distinguished Military Graduate. He was also selected by the U.S. Armor Association as the outstanding graduate in armor. After graduating in 1969 with a degree in education, Schoomaker was commissioned in armor. Over the next decade he served in a succession of assignments, in Germany, Korea and throughout the United States as an infantry reconnaissance platoon leader, rifle company commander armored cavalry troop commander, and squadron commander.

In 1977, Schoomaker was assigned to special operations, serving with the army's top-secret Delta Force and Special Forces, popularly known as the Green Berets. His special operations assignments included detachment, company, battalion and group level commands. Between 1979 and 1990, Schoomaker participated in Desert One, during the Iran hostage crisis, Operation Urgent Fury in Grenada, Operation Just Cause in Panama and served in Lebanon. He served in both Desert Shield and Desert Storm in the Persian Gulf and Uphold Democracy in Haiti.

Schoomaker has received numerous military decorations and commendations. In 1992, Schoomaker was promoted to brigadier general. Senator Al Simpson spoke on his behalf, noting that "the people of Wyoming have a great sense of pride and admiration for this special man." Over the next five years Schoomaker was selected for some of the Army's most important general officer positions, including assistant division commander of the 1st Cavalry Team, deputy director for Operations, Readiness, and Mobilization for the Headquarters of the Department of the Army, and commanding general of the Joint Special Operations Command.

In 1997, General Schoomaker assumed command of the U.S. Special Operations Command (SOCOM) at MacDill Air Force base in Tampa, Florida. He assumed responsibility for overseeing the training and equipping of all of the special operations forces, including the Navy Seals, the Air Force's Special Tactics Squadrons and the Army's Special Forces and Rangers. As special operations commander, he has 47,00 active and reserve soldiers in 140 countries under his command. Schoomaker, who reports directly to the secretary of defense and the chairman of the joint chiefs of staff, also serves as an advisor to the president.

Schoomaker has maintained his ties to his alma mater as a member of the Alumni Association. He takes an active interest in mentoring army and air force ROTC cadets at the University of Wyoming. He was recently inducted into the Wyoming Football Hall of Fame.

CHAPTER EIGHT MINERALS, OIL & GAS

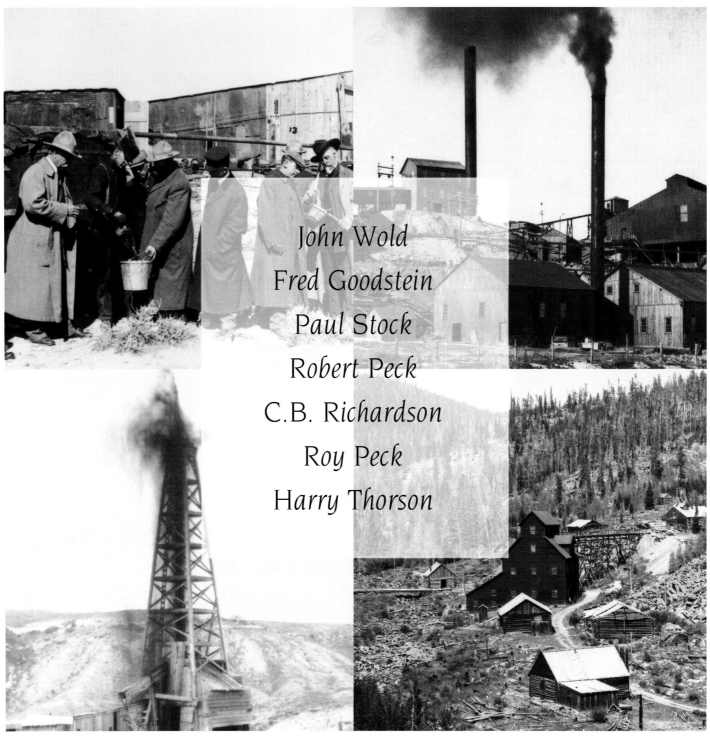

John Wold

Fred Goodstein

Paul Stock

Robert Peck

C.B. Richardson

Roy Peck

Harry Thorson

(Top left) Oregon Basin Field, c. 1912 *Courtesy AHC Collection.*
(Top right) Cyrus Iba and family *Courtesy of AHC Collection.*
(Bottom left) Gusher coming in on the South Rim of the Elk Basin Field, c. 1917 *Courtesy of AHC Collection.*
(Bottom right) Keystone Mining Camp, c. 1905 *Courtesy of AHC Collection.*

Wyoming: A 20th Century History of its Citizens, Businesses & Institutions

INTRODUCTION

The mineral, oil, and gas industries have played a significant role in Wyoming's history. It was actually the Indians who first commercialized oil, gathering crude oil and selling it to settlers as grease for their wagon wheels. Soon whites saw the potential offered by this natural resource and during the 1850s began what was probably the first commercial marketing of Wyoming's petroleum; collecting oil and mixing it with flour and selling the product to emigrants for axle grease.

By 1867 Wyoming had its first oil well, located near Fort Bridger. Less than 20 years later Cy Iba placed the first location stake in the area now known as the Salt Creek Oil Field. But it was not until the early 1900s that sufficient financial backing was acquired to develop fully the Salt Creek Field. From that point on oil became a dominant force in the state's economy.

Mining, particularly coal, has also played an important role in Wyoming's economy. Coal fueled the railroads that brought people to Wyoming. By the 1870s mining was a growth industry. A century later large expansion in mining, particularly trona, bentonite, iron ore and uranium, emphasized the importance of extractive industries. The construction of new pipelines, spurred by new discoveries, also meant that the 1970s saw continued growth in Wyoming's oil and gas production.

While these industries are by nature cyclical and rely heavily on the laws of supply and demand, they have offered immense opportunities for those individuals willing to take chances. Men like Dave True and Glenn Nielsen were able to build their fortunes through hard work. Today the legacy of the oil, mineral, and gas industries remains an important part of Wyoming's identity.

JOHN WOLD
1916-

John Wold is the first professional geologist ever to have served in the U.S. Congress. As the member from Wyoming, Congressman Wold served on the House Interior Committee and was the original sponsor of the National Mining and Minerals Policy Act of 1970 in the House of Representatives. The act extols the need for a strong, domestic, free-enterprise mineral industry to strengthen national security.

He holds a bachelor's degree from Union College, a master's in geology from Cornell University, and an honorary LLD from the University of Wyoming. His oil field career started in 1939 with Socony Vacuum's Magnolia Petroleum Company in Oklahoma and Texas. He was an early 1941 World War II volunteer officer with the Navy Bureau of Ordnance, later serving as Gunnery and Executive Officer of a destroyer escort in the Atlantic and Pacific Theaters. In 1946, he returned to the oil fields with Barnsdall Oil Company's gulf coast operations, moving to Wyoming as Rocky Mountain Division Geologist and then becoming an independent oil and gas producer in 1950.

In the late 1960s and early 1970s, he moved into joint venture coal exploration and acquisition programs on a nationwide basis with Peabody and Consolidation Coal Companies. He is reputed to have assembled more coal properties than any entity in the country, introducing Exxon, Mobil, Sun, Mapco and other major players to the coal resources of the Rocky Mountains.

In 1973 he founded Wold Nuclear Company, and with Page T. Jenkins. Wold and Jenkins discovered and developed Wyoming's Christensen Ranch, a major uranium ore body. He was a principal in the development of the Highland Uranium Mine, in Converse County, Wyoming, which became the largest uranium solution mine in the world.

At the present time, John heads Wold Trona Company in Casper, Wyoming, which is developing the sixth mine and soda ash plant in the Green River Basin. The program involves new technologies developed by Wold Trona at Hazen Research of Golden, Colorado. The processes have the potential of revolutionizing Green River operations which currently produce one-third of the world's soda ash. Wold family ventures, with sons Peter and Jack, include operation of a 30,000-acre, Hole-in-the-Wall Cattle Ranch of southern Johnson County, Wyoming, a locale renowned in the annals of Butch Cassidy and the Sundance Kid.

This spectrum of interests has given John's business activities an exposure which may be unique: significant activity in five of Wyoming's major minerals — oil, gas, uranium, coal and soda ash — in addition to serious commercial ranching.

In a parallel political career, John has served in the Wyoming Legislature where he was Chairman of the House Labor Committee. He is a two-term Wyoming Republican State chairman, Republican State Finance Chairman, member of the Republican National Committee and the executive committee of that group. He was Chairman of the Western Republican State Chairmen's Association and Wyoming Republican candidate for the U. S. Senate in 1964 and 1970.

He has served as Wyoming Engineering Representative on the Interstate Oil Compact Commission, a director of the Federation of Rocky Mountain States, vice president for Wyoming and South

Dakota of the Rocky Mountain Oil and Gas Association and President of the Wyoming Geological Association.

In 1968, he was chosen by the Associated Press and United Press as Wyoming Man of the Year, and in 1978 he was picked as Wyoming Mineral Man of the Year.

He is a past director of K-N Energy; Empire State Oil Company; Midland Energy Company; National Association of Manufacturers; past chairman and CEO of Nuclear Exploration & Development Company; and director of Sierra Madre Foundation for Geological Research sponsored by the geology departments of Cornell, Harvard and Yale. He is a recent director of the Plains Petroleum Company and of Coca Mines, Inc. and has been the Chairman of the Wyoming Natural Gas Pipeline Authority.

As a longtime trustee of Union College, Schenectady, New York, and former President of Casper College Board of Trustees, he has with his wife, Jane, endowed a Geology Chair at Union as well as the first fully endowed chair at the University of Wyoming, the Wold Centennial Chair of Energy. Their concern for science in college academics made possible the Wold Science Hall at Casper College.

John is a founder and first president of the Wyoming Heritage Foundation, a 1,200-member, nonprofit organization dedicated to the education of Wyoming citizens on the benefits of the free-enterprise system.

Wold has been especially interested in recreation and conservation. He played an important personal role in the development of Casper's Hogadon Basin ski area as founding president. He has been a Little League Baseball Manager and Chairman of Advance Gifts of Casper United Fund. An Eagle Scout, he was a Boy Scout troop committee member and also served as a Sunday-school teacher, vestryman, and warden at St. Mark's Episcopal Church in Casper.

He is a member of the American Association for the Advancement of Science, the Council of the American Geographical Society, Sigma Xi, American Association of Petroleum Geologists, Independent Petroleum Association of America, American Petroleum Institute, Sigma Gamma Epsilon, Geological Society of America, Wyoming Mining Association and Alpha Delta Phi.

FRED GOODSTEIN
1897-1983

Goodstein was responsible for the development of much of downtown Casper, including the old Sears store, the Goodstein Building and the Petroleum Building.

Fred Goodstein was born in Denver, Colorado, in 1897. His parents were Myer and Leah Goodstein. In 1912 Myer Goodstein established the American Pipe & Supply Company, a scrap metal business. Fred Goodstein grew up working in the family firm. He later recalled that as a small boy his father had sent him through sluice boxes of abandoned mines in Colorado, sweeping tailings with a feather duster.

Goodstein attended Denver public schools and established a reputation as an amateur boxer, developing a habit of physical fitness that would remain with him throughout his life. After graduation from high school he served in the Navy Air Corps during World War I. In 1922 he married Ida Goldburg, with whom he eventually had one daughter.

In 1923, Goodstein and his family settled in Casper, Wyoming, where he established his own branch of the family's scrap iron business. Under Goodstein's leadership, American Pipe and Supply Company received contracts to remove scrap from area oil fields. Eventually, Goodstein had literally built a mountain of scrap and in 1939, when the threat of war in Europe caused prices to soar, he sold the pile for a sum reputed to be as high as $1 million.

Goodstein expanded his interest to include the oil business, eventually becoming the owner and operator of Trigood Oil Company. A firm believer in the possibilities of scientific research and methods in oil exploration, Goodstein's decision to enter the oil business arose from his belief that new technologies would greatly increase production in the Salt Creek and other large fields. Between 1931 and 1932 he acquired the Carter Oil Company's most productive properties in the Salt Creek Oil Field. His oil operations gradually extended to the Lance Creek Oil Field near Lusk and other major fields across Wyoming.

Always interested in new projects, Goodstein was a director and one of the organizers of the Rocky Mountain Pipeline, which was the first pipeline to carry oil from the Lance Creek oil field to Denver. Goodstein next focused his interest on the possibilities of natural gas, serving as director of the Montana-Dakota Utilities Company and becoming a major stockholder and president of Northern Gas.

Goodstein eventually amassed a fortune estimated to be between $300 million and $500 million. In the 1980s he sold his 20-percent share of stock in Northern Utilities for an estimated $48 million. He was responsible for the development of much of downtown Casper, including the old Sears store, the Goodstein Building and the Petroleum Building.

Goodstein was active in his community, giving to the Natrona County Hospital, the Salvation Army and Meals on Wheels, among other organizations. He established the Goodstein Foundation, which financed the Goodstein Library at Casper College, as well as a visual arts center.

Fred Goodstein died in Palm Springs, California, on November 9, 1983, at the age of 86, having remained active in business and as sharp as ever until the end. He was widely known and respected as a man of keen business judgment. While some of his business associates speculated as to the key to his success, given that he had only a high school education, Goodstein himself observed: "There's nothing like the scrap iron business to sharpen your wits." He was remembered as man whose business dealings were marked by honesty and reliability.

PAUL STOCK
1894-1972

Paul Stock, standing far right, left school at the age of 15 to make his fortune in the oil fields.
Courtesy of Mountain Fuel Supply Collection, AHC.

Paul Stock was born in 1894 in Florence, Colorado, the sixth of Hugh and Kate Stock's seven children. Hugh Stock was a prominent oilman in Colorado, credited with drilling the first producing well in Florence. In 1902 Stock's father and older brother, James, formed the Stock Oil Company and began drilling in the Salt Creek field north of Casper, Wyoming. In 1905, at the age of 15, Paul Stock left school and began working as a roughneck for the Stock Oil Company. He later roughnecked in Cuba and Mexico, working as a tool dresser and driller.

Stock returned to Casper in 1914 and began work as a contract driller in the Salt Creek field. He married Genevieve Ellen Dragoo in Basin, Wyoming, in 1917. After her death in 1930 Stock married Bertha Larson. After the death of his second wife in 1948, he married Eliose J. McGinnis.

During World War I he served as a sergeant in Company C of the 13th Ammunition Train. After his discharge from the army, Stock worked in the oil fields of Texas and Oklahoma. By 1923 he and Genevieve had moved to Cody, Wyoming. Stock began working in the oil fields around Cody, successfully using the first rotary rig in the Oregon Basin and Byron-Garland fields. He soon became the president and largest stockholder of

Stock Oil Company and Yale Oil Company. In 1937 the companies were reorganized under the name of Yale Petroleum Corporation, with Stock remaining as president. Yale Petroleum merged with Texas Oil Company in 1944 and Stock became the largest shareholder in the newly created Texaco. During this period, Stock was elected president of the Rocky Mountain Oil and Gas Association.

In addition to his success as a businessman, Stock was also active in his community. He served as mayor of Cody from 1940 to 1948. In 1958 he and his wife organized the Paul Stock Foundation, which has as its mission assisting students in obtaining a higher education. He was a generous patron to the city of Cody, donating among other things, the city swimming pool and auditorium. In 1969 the Stock Scholarship, for graduates of Cody High School, was established. Stock was also a generous contributor to the Buffalo Bill Historical Center in Cody and the Goettsche Rehabilitation Center in Thermopolis, Wyoming. He was named the Grand Old Man of Petroleum Production at the International Petroleum Exposition in 1966 and the following year he was named Wyoming Oil Man of the Year. Paul Stock died in 1972.

ROBERT PECK
1924-

Robert Peck's
Riverton Ranger
publishes an annual
Mining Edition,
regarded by many as
the industry bible.

Robert Peck was born on October 7, 1924, in Riverton, Wyoming. His parents were LeRoy Ellsworth Peck and the former Elvira Sostrom. Peck grew up on his family's dairy farm, the Morningstar Dairy, which was established by his father. He attended local schools and was a three-time winner of the Fremont County Spelling Bee. In his junior year at Riverton High School he won the National Journalism Institute scholarship competition. He graduated in 1942 as salutatorian with a perfect 4.0 grade average, having lost the valedictorian position in a coin toss.

Peck attended Northwestern University on a full scholarship and was elected president of his freshman class. The outbreak of World War II brought a halt to Peck's college career when he volunteered for military service in 1942. Serving with the 5th Infantry, he was wounded three times in combat and received the Purple Heart.

After returning home from Europe in 1947, Peck began attending the University of Wyoming. He was editor of the student newspaper, *The Branding Iron* and also edited the Wyoming Education Association Newsletter. Peck graduated Phi Beta Kappa after having been named outstanding senior in the journalism department in 1949. In October of that year Peck married the former Cordelia Ruth Smith and the couple eventually had three sons.

Peck and his bride settled in his hometown of Riverton, where he and his brother, Roy, along with their wives, purchased and began operating a weekly newspaper, the *Riverton Ranger*. The Pecks went on to build a respected publishing enterprise, turning the *Ranger* into a daily and winning numerous awards for excellence. They also purchased papers in communities throughout Wyoming and Montana. Believing in the importance of community newspapers, Peck has adopted a unique approach, hiring on-site publishers who have the opportunity to purchase the business. Under this program he eventually sold all but three of the 11 papers he purchased. Peck remains as publisher of the *Riverton Ranger,* which today employs 52 people and 100 newspaper carriers.

Beginning in 1956 the *Ranger* began publishing an annual Mining Edition, a statewide profile, regarded by those in the industry in Wyoming as their "bible." It was during this period that Peck and his brother founded the Wyoming Mining Association. Peck has long recognized the vital role that all facets of the mining industry play in Wyoming's economy. He serves as director of the National Mining Hall of Fame in Leadville, Colorado, and has chaired numerous statewide panels on the state's mineral industry, including the Wyoming Uranium Roundtable in 1977. Peck has been honored as a Wyoming Mining Man of the Century and his support for mining has been called by those within the industry steadfast and without equal.

Peck has always taken an active role in community affairs. During the 1950s he helped to found the Riverton Kiwanis and chaired the committee that arranged for the paving of the city's streets. He founded the Riverton Museum Board and laid the cornerstone for the museum in 1969. A longtime member of Arts in Action, he aided in the establishment of the Wind River Arts Foundation and the Peck Summer Theater. Peck chaired the Riverton Golden Jubilee Committee, the Riverton Bicentennial Committee, and the Riverton Diamond Jubilee Committee, which endures today as the Riverton Rendezvous, an annual summer celebration. Peck donated the land for the Fremont County Library.

Peck has a long-standing interest in education, beginning in the 1950s when he began planning for the founding of Central Wyoming College. Prior to the establishment of the college, Peck organized the gift of the land on which the campus now stands. That explains why the address of the college is 2660 Peck Avenue. He has served on the board of trustees for 15 years, including 14 terms as president, and engineered three successful bond issues to improve and expand the campus. He was also the moving force between a creative public-private partnership that financed the construction of the arts and theater complex that bears his name, the Robert A. Peck Arts Center. Peck continues to serve the college as a member of the foundation and received the CWC Medal of Honor.

A member of the University of Wyoming Business Advisory Committee, Peck serves on the board of directors of the Wyoming Taxpayers Association. He was a founder of two local economic development groups, Riverton Economic Betterment and IDEA, Inc. In 1991 Peck was appointed to serve the remainder of retiring State Senator Frank Dusl's term in the Wyoming Legislature. He has won re-election twice and is a past chair of the Senate Transportation Committee and current head of the Joint Revenue Committee.

He continues to look to the future of the town and the state to which he has dedicated his life. He has formed Target 200, a Fremont County group dedicated to identifying the challenges of the new century. Peck serves on the Tax Reform 2000 Committee, appointed by Governor Jim Geringer. Those who nominated Peck for Citizen of the Century noted that "his record of service and achievement spans all of the nomination categories," thus making him truly qualified for consideration as Wyoming's Citizen of the Century.

CLARENCE B. RICHARDSON
1867-1961

Clarence B. Richardson was born in Pittsburgh, Pennsylvania, on September 7, 1867. Three years later, his family moved to Cheyenne, Wyoming, where his father worked as an editor for the *Cheyenne Daily Leader*. Clarence Richardson began his business career selling his father's paper on the streets of Cheyenne as a boy. Richardson then learned the printing trade, joining the Wyoming Typographical Union No. 184. Although he eventually rose to the position of reporter, Richardson became convinced that there was no money to be made in the newspaper business and decided to seek his fortune elsewhere.

In 1888 Richardson joined his brother-in-law, Iver Johnson, in an unsuccessful mining venture at the Silver Crown Mines. By 1892, Richardson had moved on to Granite, Colorado, where he established a stamp mill. Searching for capital for his venture, Richardson traveled east and then to Paris, where he was able to persuade a French count to invest in his project. By his own account, he "operated the mill for four or five years, sometimes at a profit, most of the time at a loss."

It was during this time that Richardson first became interested in the oil fields of central Wyoming. Seeking funding for development, Richardson traveled to New York City and unsuccessfully attempted to persuade John D. Rockerfeller to invest. In 1895 and again in 1897 Richardson went to England to recruit investors and met with greater success in this attempt. Three different expeditions were sent from London to the Salt Creek field. As Richardson later recounted, "We had

Clarence Richardson "contributed greatly to the development of Wyoming's natural resources."

operations on nearly all the oil land in central Wyoming, representing over 300,000 acres, and it covered most all of the Salt Creek field and practically all of the now famous Teapot Dome."

Richardson then became caught up in the "great Klondike excitement" of 1898 and made his way to Alaska. Realizing that there was more money to be made supplying the miners than in mining, Richardson first sold doughnuts and later lemons and cigarettes, and reaped a substantial profit. Richardson, who was accompanied by a Henry Rothberger, a photographer, had many adventures during his travels in Alaska. Richardson sent narratives and photos to his brother, Arthur, editor of the *Cheyenne Sun-Leader*, who published his accounts.

After receiving an appointment as Commissioner-in-Chief for the State of Wyoming to the St. Louis Exposition in 1904 and later the World's Fair in Portland, Oregon, in 1906, Richardson accepted a position as head of one the largest lumber companies in Mexico. Headquartered in Chihuahua, Richardson's position with this American-owned enterprise placed him in the midst of the Mexican Revolution, where he encountered both Pancho Villa and General John Pershing.

Richardson returned to Wyoming and the Salt Creek field in 1916, and after the discovery of the Muddy oil field the following year, decided to focus his attention on his oil interests. He founded and presided over the Consolidated Royalty Oil Company of Casper and served as president of the Western Exploration Company. He was also a founding director of the Wyoming National Bank in Casper.

Having become a millionaire by virtue of his leading role in the development of Wyoming's oil industry, Richardson became a philanthropist in his later years. In 1901 he had married the former Anna May Stanley. Richardson donated much of his fortune to worthy causes, including the construction of laboratory facilities at Cheyenne Memorial Hospital and the establishment of student scholarships at the University of Wyoming. Clarence Richardson died in 1961 at the age of 94. He was eulogized as an "interesting and colorful" man, one who "contributed greatly to the development of Wyoming's natural resources."

ROY PECK
1922-1983

Because Fremont County was home to both uranium and iron mine mills, Peck developed an interest in extractive industries.

Roy Peck was born in Rugby, North Dakota, on May 16, 1922. His parents were LeRoy Ellsworth Peck and the former Elvira Sostrom. Shortly after his birth, the family moved to Riverton, Wyoming, where he grew up. In 1931 LeRoy Ellsworth Peck founded the family business, the Morningstar Dairy, in which his family retained an interest after his death in 1954.

Roy Peck graduated from Riverton High School in 1940 as class valedictorian. He attended the University of Wyoming, where he worked as editor of the student newspaper, *The Branding Iron.* Peck graduated with a degree in journalism.

During World War II Peck enlisted in the Army, where he served with the 84th Infantry Division in Europe. He was awarded the Bronze Star, the Silver Star and the French Croix De Guerre for combat action. While serving in France, Peck met his future wife, Margaret Elizabeth MacFayden, who was with the American Red Cross. The couple married the following

year and eventually had four children. In 1946 Peck was discharged with the rank of captain.

After his discharge, Peck returned to Wyoming, where he joined the staff of the athletic department at the University of Wyoming as publicity director, track and cross country coach and ticket manager. In 1949, he left the university to found the *Riverton Ranger,* a weekly newspaper, with his brother Bob. By 1960 the Pecks' newspaper business had expanded to include the *Kemmerer Gazette* and the *Powell Tribune.* During the 1970s they acquired the *Red Lodge News* and the *Lovell Chronicle.*

During the Korean War, Roy Peck was recalled to active duty in the armed forces. Between 1951 and 1952 he served in Germany as company commander in a psychological warfare group. After his return to Wyoming, Peck served the first of two terms on the University of Wyoming Board of Trustees and later he became a member of the University of Wyoming Foundation. He was a supporter of vocational education programs and served on the founding committee of Central Wyoming College.

In addition to his military service and his interest in education, Peck was an active member of the business community, and not just as a newspaper publisher. Because Fremont County was home to both uranium and iron mine mills, Peck developed an interest in extractive industries. He was a charter member of the Wyoming Mining Association and was instrumental in its founding in 1956. The following year, he began serving as vice president of the Allied Nuclear Corporation, remaining as a director until 1968. Peck also helped found Western Standard Corporation in 1955, becoming president 15 years later. From 1967 until 1970, Peck headed the Wyoming Department of Economic Planning and Development.

A lifelong member of the Republican Party, Peck was unsuccessful in his first attempt at public office, a run for Congress in 1966. He ran a successful campaign for the Wyoming House of Representatives in 1970 but gave up his seat four years later in a failed bid for governor. He returned to public office in 1977, when he was elected to the Wyoming State Senate. He served in the Senate until his death in the spring of 1983.

HARRY THORSON
1902-1976

Noted for his political acumen and support of the Republican Party, Thorson was also credited by many with guiding the successful economic development of Wyoming's natural resources.

Harry Thorson was born in Milan, Minnesota, on August 12, 1902. He was the oldest of five children and his parents, of Norwegian descent, were Anne Graves and Gulman Thorson. Shortly after his birth, Thorson's family settled near Carrington, North Dakota, attracted by the homesteading possibilities. Although circumstances were primitive at first, and the family lived in a tarpaper shack; they prospered as farmers and gradually acquired more land.

Because he was a farmer's son, Thorson's education was frequently interrupted, but he attended local schools and managed to earn his high school diploma by the time he was 16. Thorson wanted to continue his studies, so he went to Fargo, North Dakota. He procured a job as bookkeeper at the YMCA where he lived. Thorson worked his way through college, eventually securing a position as an assistant instructor at the North Dakota Agricultural College. But long hours of indoor work and a severe bout with illness during the influenza epidemic of 1918 left Thorson with a lingering lung ailment. Advised by his physician to seek a different climate, he accepted a teaching position in Colorado.

While on his way to his new job, Thorson stopped overnight in Casper, Wyoming. After exploring the local oil fields, Thorson decided to stay in Wyoming. He began working as a collector for the local paper, the Casper Herald. He soon left that job to work in an accounting office. It was at this time, while attending services for the Lutheran Church, that Thorson met his future wife, Inga Gysland.

Preferring to work outdoors, Thorson went to work for Illinois Pipeline (ILCO). He was quickly promoted to foreman and in 1927 was transferred to Osage, Wyoming, as district manager. Two years later he married Inga Gysland and brought his bride to live with him in the oil fields of Osage. In 1932, after seven years with ILCO, Thorson began working as superintendent for the Osage Trust. For the next several years, Thorson, whose family eventually grew to include two sons and a daughter, continued to work in the oil fields, managing operations. He was briefly sidelined after a natural gas explosion, which leveled the family's company house and left him with third-degree burns.

In 1939 Thorson was presented with an opportunity to invest some of his own money in the Osage field. When the Lambi lease became available through a sheriff's sale, Inga Thorson sold some stock she had purchased before her marriage to provide part of the $10,000 purchase price. Thorson was able to increase production and make a profit and the following year he purchased another lease from the Osage Trust.

In 1941, Thorson entered into bentonite mining, using his capital to buy mining equipment. The Black Hills Bentonite Company, formed by Thorson in 1947 in partnership with Al Harding, was a success. The company continued to purchase new deposits and in 1964, after making a large purchase near Kaycee, Wyoming, decided to build a new plant in Casper to process their supply. Thorson's Black Hills Bentonite Corporation and Kaycee Bentonite Corporation entered into a partnership with Bethlehem Steel, which financed the building of the plant in return for stock. This arrangement assured the Kaycee Corporation of a market for its product while guaranteeing Bethlehem with a steady supply.

While building his business, Thorson also was involved in politics. A lifelong republican, he served as Weston County's State Committeeman from 1949 to 1955. From 1955 to 1960 Thorson was Chairman of the Wyoming State Republican Party and for the next four years he served as Republican National Committeeman. But these titles do little to reveal the extent of Thorson's influence in Republican Party politics within the state. Given titles such as "Mr. Republican," the "Sage of Osage" and "Kingmaker," Thorson promoted many successful candidates for state and national office, including Milward Simpson, Clifford P. Hansen and Stanley K. Hathaway. Thorson also served as chairman of the Wyoming Recreation Commission, the Land and Water Conservation Commission (1965-67) and the Governor's Commission on the Reorganization of State Government (1967-69).

Thorson maintained an active interest in business affairs and his community. He was a member of the U.S. Chamber of Commerce and the Wyoming Mining Association. He was named Mineral Man of the Year by the Wyoming Chamber of Commerce in 1973. Thorson served on the board of directors of the Wyoming National Bank of Gillette and the Wyoming National Holding Corporation. He was chairman of the Board of directors of the Weston County Hospital and actively involved in the Wyoming Division of the American Cancer Society.

In September of 1976 Harry Thorson died in a Casper hospital, after suffering a fatal cardiac arrest, the result of injuries sustained in an automobile accident. He was 74. Friends and colleagues were uniform in their praise for Thorson, who was remembered by all as an honest and modest man. Noted for his political acumen and support of the Republican Party, Thorson was also credited by many with guiding the successful economic development of Wyoming's natural resources.

CHAPTER NINE RELIGION

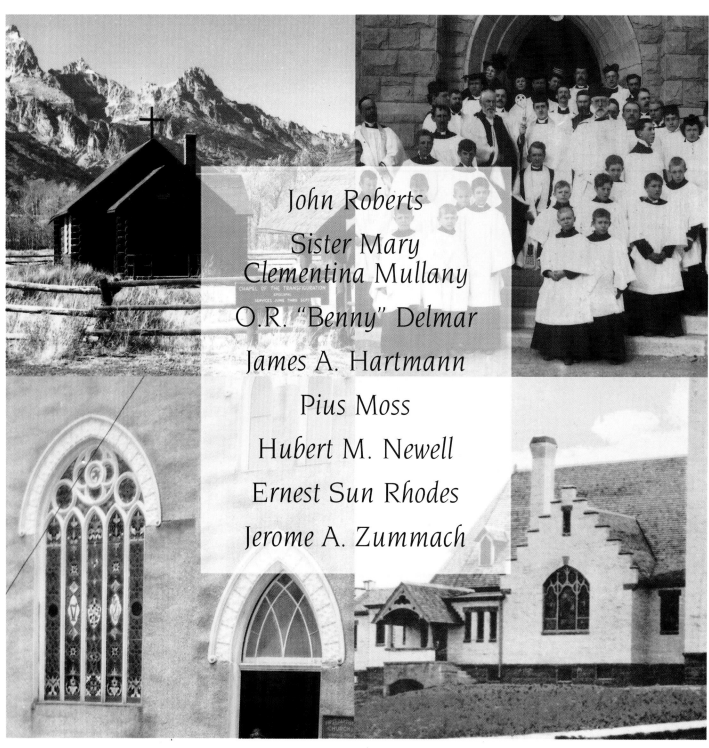

John Roberts

Sister Mary
Clementina Mullany

O.R. "Benny" Delmar

James A. Hartmann

Pius Moss

Hubert M. Newell

Ernest Sun Rhodes

Jerome A. Zummach

(Top left) Photo c. 1950 *Courtesy of AHC Collection.*
(Top right) Dedication of St. Matthews Cathedral, Laramie, Wyoming, 1942 *Courtesy of AHC Collection.*
(Bottom left) Cheyenne, Wyoming church, c. 1925 *Courtesy of AHC Collection.*
(Bottom right) Presbyterian Church, Sheridan, Wyoming, c. 1910 *Courtesy of AHC Collection.*

INTRODUCTION

Religion has always played an important role in the lives of Wyoming's people, for natives and non-natives alike. For American Indians the challenge has often been in reconciling their traditional beliefs with new ideas brought in by white missionaries. For non-natives the issue has been not only a missionary one, of bringing their religion to new peoples, but also a practical one, of establishing their own churches in an area where none had previously existed.

Missionaries like Ethelbert Talbot and W.B.D. Gray sought to meet those challenges, while Indians, like Sherman Coolidge and Yellow Calf struggled to reconcile two different belief systems. Both Talbot and Gray journeyed into unknown territories to do what they believed was necessary, spread the gospel as they believed it to be true. Both Coolidge and Yellow Calf confronted the differing doctrines of Christianity and native religion. Coolidge choose to embrace Anglo society, converting to Christianity, marrying a white woman and eventually becoming a missionary. By contrast, Yellow Calf advocated an adherence to traditional religious beliefs but was able to function successfully in both worlds.

As churches became more established in Wyoming they began to broaden their mission to meet more than the religious needs of their congregations. During the latter half of the 19th century a new kind of missionary came to Wyoming. John Pattison was recruited from Ireland to meet the expanding needs of the western states. In addition to providing spiritual guidance to the members of the First Presbyterian Church in Cheyenne, he also became a prominent civic leader and helped to found the Wyoming Children's Home Society.

Lay people have also played an important role in the development of the state's religious institutions. Margaret Prine is only one example of the many individuals who have worked to enhance their communities. An active member of the First Baptist Church of Laramie, Prine serves on numerous community, state and national boards. She has dedicated much of her time to solving problems and addressing issues that directly impact the people of her state.

The efforts of these individuals are reflected in the religious lives of Wyoming's people, both past and present. St. Mark's Episcopal Church in Cheyenne lays claim to being the first church built in the state. Today, in towns across Wyoming, virtually every denomination, including white and Indian creeds, are represented and the people of the state have the opportunity to worship as they choose.

JOHN ROBERTS
1853-1949

John Roberts' ministry spanned two centuries and several generations. *Courtesy of AHC Collection.*

John Roberts was born in the county of Flint, North Wales, in 1853. As a child he attended Welsh grammar schools and later St. David's College. He was made an Episcopal Deacon in 1878 and served for two years in the Diocese of Litchfield before embarking on his missionary career. Roberts volunteered for service in Africa but was sent instead to the West Indies, where he ministered to a leper colony. In 1881 he was ordained to the priesthood. He came to the United States in 1883 and the following year married Laura E. Brown. The couple eventually had five children and adopted numerous others.

After his arrival in the United States Roberts traveled west. He was eventually assigned to minister to the Shoshones and Arapahoes under the auspices of the Board of Domestic and Foreign Missionary Society. As

Roberts soon discovered, the difficulty of his task was compounded by the "vast differences... in languages, religions and methods of living." Having taken eight days to complete a 150-mile journey, Reverend Roberts arrived at his new posting in the midst of one of the most brutal winters on record.

Roberts set about his work by learning all he could about Native American customs and beliefs, feeling that by the knowing the people he hoped to minister to he would be more effective. He eventually learned the native languages and with the assistance of tribal members was able to translate the Lord's Prayer, the Apostles' Creed and portions of the Bible. Fluent in both Shoshone and Arapahoe, Roberts maintained that Shoshone was "the most difficult of the Indian tongues." After having been on the reservation less than a year,

Roberts officiated at the burial of an Indian woman reputed to be Sacajewa, who accompanied Lewis and Clark on their famous expedition.

Roberts soon impressed his superiors with his labors. After an 1885 visit to Roberts' mission, Bishop Spaulding remarked upon Roberts' "zeal, earnestness, and self-denial." Spaulding noted that Roberts gave half of his $840 annual salary to his helpers, despite having a growing family to support. Roberts often said the object of his work among the Indians was to make them self supporting. With this in mind he established two schools, the Indian Boarding School at Ft. Washakie and the Shoshone Indian Mission Boarding School. He also oversaw the construction of a gristmill and a water system.

Roberts cultivated friendships with tribal leaders, including Chief Black Coal and Chief Washakie, whom he later baptized. Roberts remembered Washakie as "an intelligent, honest man." It was Washakie who gave Roberts the 160 acres where he built his school for Shoshone girls. Roberts earned the trust of the tribal leadership and was often involved in their negotiations with agents of the federal government. The Indians acknowledged Roberts' fairness in dealing with them by giving him the name Dambaivie, or Elder Brother.

Roberts also ministered to the non-natives of the state. He established Episcopal churches in towns across Wyoming, including those in Dubois, Lander, Riverton, and Thermopolis. Roberts retired from active missionary work in 1921 but continued to live on the reservation. Upon his retirement Roberts commented on the great changes in the lives of the Indians during the time he spent with them. His early years at the mission saw the Indians supporting themselves by hunting. In his first winter they sold in excess of 3,000 buffalo and elk hides. Over time, farming and ranching replaced the hunting culture. Having overseen the education of three generations of Indians, Roberts felt he had succeeded in the object of his mission.

Roberts was recognized for his many years of work by the University of Wyoming, which awarded him an honorary degree in 1923, and by the state legislature, which commended his career the following year. Roberts died in June, 1949, at the age of 97.

SISTER MARY CLEMENTINA MULLANY
1882-1963

Sister Mary Clementina Mullany was born on July 22, 1882, in Chicago, Illinois, in the family of Patrick and Ann (Rachward) Mullanies. She attended Catholic and public schools through the seventh grade. From the Sisters of St. Francis who taught her, young Mary Mullany learned about the Indian Mission at St. Stephens. Before she had ever seen Wyoming, she was determined that her life's work would be devoted to helping Native Americans at Wind River.

Sister Clementina first arrived at St. Stephens Mission in 1909 and from that moment dedicated the next 52 years of her life to education and work among the Arapaho and Shoshone Indians on the Wind River Reservation. Her only absence from St. Stephens was between 1932 to 1935 when she was assigned at St. Andrews Mission on the Umatilla Reservation near Pendleton, Oregon.

Through half a century Sister was a highly successful teacher for some three generations of Indian youth. Those who experienced real hunger, families who needed clothing for children, the homeless and the sick who needed attention found that Sister Clementina not only taught but also practiced the corporal works of mercy. In conversation with those who remember, it is obvious that she was always available, always willing to listen and always inspirational.

In the earliest years of her work at St. Stephens, Sister Clementina was assigned the task of teaching the children of the primary grades, who neither knew nor understood English. She accomplished this task through cooperation with another young educator, Arapaho Tribal Member Susanna Behan, who helped her as an interpreter.

After many years of teaching, Sister Mary Clementina began the first of four terms as Religious Superior of the Franciscan Sisters at St. Stephens Mission. In her first term, the Mission was struck by two of its gravest crises. A meningitis epidemic, which first appeared in December of 1927 and lasted well into the spring of 1928, devastated the Mission. There was little time to recover before a disastrous fire on January 20, 1928, destroyed the Mission's main buildings. Those who lived through this difficult period recalled that despite sickness, fires and other hardsips, Sister Mary

Clemetina was "right there with her special gifts and her sense of humor."

In later years, Sister Mary Clementina's administrative duties limited her teaching opportunities, but her love and devotion for the Indian people never diminished. She initiated the earliest efforts in arts and crafts and home economics programs at the school with instructions in sewing, weaving and ceramics. During her time at St. Stephens she saw many changes in mission life. Sister Mary Clementina is fondly remembered as a

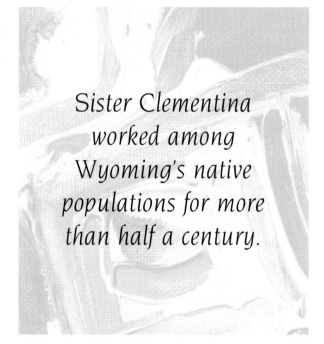

Sister Clementina worked among Wyoming's native populations for more than half a century.

"pioneer of Catholic education" who accomplished a great deal in her ministry with the Arapaho and Shoshone people.

In 1959 the students of St. Stephens Indian School dedicated their yearbook to Sister Mary Clementina Mullany. Two years later, at the age of 80, Sister Clementina retired and left the reservation. Throughout her long life Sister Clementina enjoyed remarkable good health. It was often said that she was "a nurse, not a patient." After a brief illness Sister Clementina died in St. Joseph Hospital in Pendleton, Oregon, on October 12, 1963. Many who knew her point with pride at the small but practical little gifts which were her signature. For those who remember Sister Clemintina, her legacy is one of love and compassion.

O.R. "BENNY" DELMAR
1918-

Brother Benny Delmar traveled Wyoming as a missionary for the Southern Baptist Convention. *Courtesy of AHC Collection.*

O.R. "Benny" Delmar was born in Seminole, Oklahoma, on August 23, 1918. At the age of 13 he was first called to his religious pursuits, becoming a member of the First Baptist Church of Seminole. While still a teenager, Delmar was called to preach. He was formally trained for the ministry at Oklahoma Baptist University, which he attended on a boxing scholarship. In 1948 Delmar earned a master's degree from Southern Baptist Theological Seminary.

After completing his theological studies, Delmar moved to Arizona and began mission work. Three years later he was asked by a group of citizens in Casper to preach a revival, in an effort to build a Southern Baptist Congregation. The revival was a success, resulting in the establishment of the First Southern Baptist Church of Casper, and Delmar remained as pastor. He never returned to Arizona, although his early missionary work in Wyoming continued to be sponsored by the Arizona Baptist Convention.

Delmar soon assumed the directorship of all mission work for the entire state. During the most intensive years of his mission work, Delmar traveled between 50,000 and 70,000 miles annually. He had a simple philosophy that guided his mission work — anywhere he found two Southern Baptist families he placed an ad in the local paper and held a meeting the following Sunday. This method, coupled with his extraordinary

success in persuading other ministers to pursue mission work in Wyoming, resulted in a rapid expansion of the number of Southern Baptist congregations across the state. Under Delmar's leadership, what became the Wyoming Southern Baptist Convention now encompasses 77 churches and 16,000 members, comprising the largest evangelical group in the state.

Delmar also expanded his mission work into Montana and South Dakota. His strategy of beginning with major population areas and using those centers as the basis for new missions, has proven successful. Believing that the purpose of his church is to reach people, Delmar has always advocated home visits and Bible studies. A self-described "local church man," Delmar earned a reputation as a "powerful and impassioned" preacher. He was a staunch advocate of the Baptist Faith and Message long before that doctrine became a formal component of the Southern Baptist teachings. Among the basic tenets held by Delmar and the ministers he recruited is a belief in baptism.

Delmar has been supported in his mission work by Jo Delmar, his wife of many years. His work has been recognized by the Southern Baptist Convention, which named him Missionary of the Year West of the Mississippi. Known as "the last of the suitcase missionaries," Delmar continues to advocate the propagation of his church.

JAMES A. HARTMANN
1884-1973

James A. Hartmann was born in St. Michael, Minnesota, on November 10, 1884. He decided at an early age to follow his religious calling and pursued his seminary studies at Pontifical College Josephinum. While in the seminary he was recruited for the Diocese of Cheyenne by Bishop James Keane. Erroneously informed that a large German community within the state was in need of his proficiency in that language, he arrived in Wyoming in the summer of 1915.

Hartmann was immediately sent to a parish in the northern part of the state but within a few months was recalled to Cheyenne to assume the post of pastor of St. Mary's Cathedral, which he held for the next 46 years. Soon after becoming pastor, he was appointed as Chancellor of the Diocese. In that capacity he oversaw the apprenticeship of most of the area's newly ordained priests and through them, Hartmann's influence was felt across the state.

Hartmann established a reputation as an industrious worker who was extremely responsive to the needs of his community. His financial expertise was also widely acknowledged, and his frugality and austerity were legendary. Seeing the need for recreation and meeting space for his constituency, Hartmann purchased a large parcel of land to the west of St. Mary's. In 1920 construction commenced for the building that would be Cathedral Hall. During the next 50 years the building served as a meeting place for various churches and civic organizations, for City League basketball games and for the USO during World War II. The property was eventually sold to the federal government and today is known as the O'Mahoney Building.

In 1922, in accordance with his widespread building program, he set out to improve Olivet Cemetery, a desolate and unkempt area. With the help of volunteers, Hartmann used horses and wagons to straighten markers, grade roads and fence the land. He also planted his garden at the site and produced vegetables that were unrivaled in the city.

In 1926, Hartmann, having found that there were few German speakers in need of his abilities but many who spoke Spanish, took a year's leave to attend Catholic University and learn the language. Upon his return in 1927 he established a relationship with Cheyenne's Spanish-American community that lasted throughout his life.

In 1929, in addition to his duties at St. Mary's, Hartmann became the administrator of the newly established St. Joseph's Parish in South Cheyenne, serving in a dual capacity until 1938. It was during this period that he also assumed the role of Catholic Chaplain of the Veterans Hospital. In 1933 the parish purchased a private Catholic school, the Holy Child Academy, and Hartmann served as administrator, as well as teaching German and religion classes. He became known as a strict disciplinarian but was also renowned for his skill in the classroom. Over the course of the next decade Hartmann presided over a series of building projects that made St. Mary's School one of the best facilities in the state. It had a new high school building, a convent to replace the old academy building, a new grade school building, and later an addition connecting the high school and grade school.

Hartmann's years of service were recognized by Pope Pius XII, who elevated him to Domestic Prelate with the title of Right Reverend Monsignor. Despite his new status as prelate, Hartmann still considered himself a parish priest and advised his parishioners to address him still as "Father." Failing health forced Hartmann to retire in 1959. With typical forethought, he had previously purchased for the parish a small property on 24th Street in Cheyenne where he lived during his final years.

Despite his supposed retirement, Hartmann still ministered to his community. He continued his custom of visiting each and every patient in the local hospital, which he had done ever since arriving in Cheyenne. He also continued to play an active role at St. Mary's School, serving as chaplain to the Dominican Sisters and passing out cookies in the school cafeteria. Hartmann died in Cheyenne in April 1973.

PIUS MOSS
1914-1998

Pius Moss was born on May 3, 1914, on the Wind River Reservation. His parents were Alonzo and Victoria (Warren) Moss. They received permission to bestow the Indian name "Young Chief" on their infant son. Moss later recalled that he learned the traditional ways of his people from his mother and father, who also taught him about nature and what to expect from the changing seasons. Above all they "gave him a good foundation in regards to respecting and responding to the world around him."

Among the most important gifts he received from his mother was his ability to orate. Moss recounted that as a small boy his mother roasted a meadowlark, gave him a small bite, "and told me to ask for the skill of speaking well." He credited his father with teaching him about the necessity of doing every task he undertook to the best of his ability.

A member of the Northern Arapaho tribe and a descendant of Chief Black Coal, Moss was associated with St. Stephens Indian Mission from the age of five. This association was a continuation of a tradition began by his grandfather, Chief Black Coal. When the Mission was founded in 1884, Chief Black Coal was a tribal leader and frequently visited the school. He stressed to the students that their best hope lay in education, "the new way" because the old buffalo culture was gone forever.

After the death of his mother Moss began attending first grade at St. Stephens in 1919 as a boarding student. He entered the school speaking only two words of English and later recounted that he was very lonely. Moss gradually adjusted to mission life. He remembered that while the sisters could be kind they were also very strict. "They acted with complete parental authority. If our behavior was unacceptable the punishment would be very harsh." Moss attended the school at a time when the students were punished for speaking their native language, but he harbored no ill will toward the teachers, priests and sisters who enforced this rule.

After he graduated from the eighth grade at the mission school, Moss worked with the land and livestock at St. Stephens for the next 30 years. In 1936 he married the former Mary Behan and eventually became the father of five children. Pius purchased his own land and went into cattle ranching. He did not hesitate to describe himself as a success, crediting his experience at St. Stephens Mission with allowing him to acquire the skills he needed.

Like his grandfather, Moss believed that education was vital to the preservation of his people. Moss encouraged his people to embrace both the old and the new ways of learning. He helped establish an Indian Office and a scholarship fund at the University of Wyoming for eligible Arapaho students. As a cultural teacher Moss

> *Like his grandfather, Moss believed that education was vital to the preservation of his people. Moss encouraged his people to embrace both the old and the new ways of learning.*

was instrumental in teaching the Arapaho language and the ancient Arapaho ways. Moss worked closely with University of Massachusetts Anthropology Professor Zdenek Salzmann in developing a 16 character phonetic alphabet for the Arapaho language. In 1991 Central Wyoming College awarded Moss the prestigious Medallion of Honor in recognition of his achievements in preserving and teaching Arapaho customs.

Pius Moss died on November 1, 1998, on the Wind River Reservation and is buried in the Arapahoe Catholic Cemetery at St. Stephens, Wyoming.

HUBERT M. NEWELL
1904-1987

In 1947 Bishop Newell was consecrated a bishop and appointed Coadjutor to Bishop Patrick A. McGovern. McGovern had administered the Diocese of Cheyenne since 1912 and felt the need of assistance in governing the growing Wyoming diocese. After McGovern's death in 1951 Bishop Newell succeeded him as head of the Catholic Church in Wyoming.

As Bishop of the Diocese of Cheyenne, Newell presided over the Catholic Church in Wyoming during a period when the state's population nearly doubled. In response to the increased needs of his congregates, Newell embarked on a building program that greatly increased the number of churches, rectories, schools and convents throughout the state. Newell also oversaw the creation of the *Wyoming Catholic Register,* a publication which continues to enhance communication throughout the diocese. As Bishop he presided over the establishment of the church's board of education, Wyoming Catholic Social Services and the Priest's Senate. He reorganized the Chancery Office and the Marriage Tribunal and created the Office of Education, the Vocation Office and the Building Commission.

During his tenure, Newell also focused on less concrete aspects of the church to meet the growing needs of the community. He emphasized a modern management style and created a collegial, consultative, and cooperative atmosphere to bring about his vision of helping people in need throughout the state. Newell also worked to create programs to maximize the effectiveness of church personnel, including the Diocesan of Catholic Women, which has affiliates in every parish, and the Diocesan Pastoral Council, a group of representative priests, sisters and laity who advise on matters of diocesan policy.

Newell retired in 1978, after 48 years of service as a priest and bishop, at the age of 78. He died in Denver, Colorado, on September 8, 1987.

Bishop Hubert Newell directed the Catholic Church in Wyoming for almost 30 years. Courtesy of AHC Collection.

Hubert M. Newell was born in Denver, Colorado, on February 16, 1904. He and his twin bother, Raymond, were the youngest of six children and the second set of twins born to Thomas and Nellie Taney Newell, who emigrated from Ireland in the 1890s.

Newell attended Annunciation Grade School and Sacred Heart High School in Denver. He went on to Regis College, receiving his degree in 1926. Like his twin, also a priest, and his older brother, a Jesuit missionary, he decided to dedicate his life to the Catholic Church and was ordained on June 15, 1930. Newell's first assignment was an assistancy at St. Mary's Parish in Walsenburg, Colorado, where he served until 1933, when he was assigned to the staff of the cathedral in Denver.

Three years later Newell began graduate studies at the Catholic University of America in Washington, D.C., receiving a master's degree in educational administration in 1937. That same year he was appointed superintendent of Catholic education for what was then the Diocese of Denver, including the entire state of Colorado. In 1943 the Archdiocese of Denver was created and a separate Diocese of Pueblo, encompassing the remainder of Colorado was created, with Bishop Newell continuing as state superintendent of Catholic schools.

ERNEST SUN RHODES
1914-1987

Ernest Sun Rhodes was remembered as someone whose "genial manner and infectious humor" brought a prevailing spirit of harmony to the contentious discussions.

Ernest Sun Rhodes, a descendant of Chief Sharp Nose, was a respected tribal teacher, elder and Eucharistic Minister at St. Stephens for many years. He was born on August 27, 1914, to Dominic and Ruth (Norse) Sun Rhodes on the Wind River Reservation in Wyoming.

Sun Rhodes was educated at St. Stephens Indian School. He had a strong commitment to education, working at St. Stephens School as a coach and boys' prefect of the mission dormitory. Sun Rhodes also taught religion to the mission students. He served on the board of education of the Arapaho school and was a member of the St. Stevens Indian Education Association and a 4-H leader.

Ernest Sun Rhodes managed to accommodate both Christian beliefs and tribal customs in his life and activities. He was an Indian dancer and a drum keeper of the Northern Arapaho Tribe. He was also a very active member of St. Stephens Church. He served as Eucharistic Minister and offered traditional cedar blessings at special ceremonies in the church. Ernest worked with a tribal committee and others to translate the Mass and the "Lord's Prayer" into the Arapaho language. He was chosen as a special delegate to the Washington D.C. reception for Pope John Paul II and was accompanied by his daughter, Mrs. Colleen Addison. Ernest Sun Rhodes was also designated a representative of the Arapaho people for the Beatification of Kateri Tekakwitha, the first Native American Indian to be considered for sainthood, in Rome, Italy, in 1981.

Ernest Sun Rhodes was a prominent force in tribal life. A rancher and a game warden, he served as a Wind River Reservation police chief and tribal council member. He was particularly devoted to issues affecting older tribal members. He was a member of the Wyoming Governor's Commission on Aging and a member of the Silver-Haired Legislature. He was instrumental in getting a Senior Citizens Center built in Arapaho, Wyoming.

Sun Rhodes also worked with the reservation youth. He was tireless in his efforts to engage young people in meaningful activities. He organized youth groups to participate in the annual Tekakwitha Conferences, which fostered ongoing educational programs throughout the year.

Ernest Sun Rhodes was married to Ruth (Bitner) Sun Rhodes and, after her death, Victoria (Warren) Sun Rhodes. He died on September 12, 1987, on the Wind River Reservation and is buried in the Arapaho Catholic Cemetery, St. Stephens, Wyoming. He was remembered as someone whose "genial manner and infectious humor" brought a prevailing spirit of harmony to the contentious discussions.

JEROME A. ZUMMACH
1913-1998

Father Zummach was a devoted priest who earned the respect as well as the friendship of the Arapaho and Shoshone people of the Wind River Reservation who gave him the name "Big Eagle."

Jerome A. Zummach was born on December 16, 1913, in Milwaukee, Wisconsin. His parents were Harry and Josephine Zummach. He attended Marquette High School, later continued his education at St. Louis University and studied theology at St. Mary's College in Kansas and St. Charles College in Lousiana. In 1947, after being ordained into the priesthood and having completed his Jesuit studies, Father Zummach was assigned to St. Stephens Indian Mission to serve as a religion teacher, advisor and coach at the school.

Father Zummach was successful in combining church policies and teachings with traditions and customs of Native Americans. He strived to learn the culture of both the Arapaho and the Shoshone People. He made use of their cultural items and designs — beads, eagle feathers and incense — in religious ceremonies. Zummach adopted traditional greetings and gestures to identify with the ways of the people he was ministering to. He believed native children needed and deserved an education in order to better equip them for the future. Zummach also saw the school as an instrument to help them preserve their traditions.

While working in the mission school, Zummach employed sports, especially basketball, to motivate the students to attend school and teach them the value of teamwork. With his athletic prowess and skills, Father Zummach was able to serve as a special influence to lead the young students of St. Stephens high school and grade school to a notable degree of success. In the late 1950s to mid-1960s, he promoted championship teams that became well known all over the state of Wyoming.

Due to financial reasons, the high school at St. Stephens Mission closed in 1966. Father Zummach was appointed pastor at the mission's station church, Blessed Sacrament at Fort Washakie, which for the most part served Shoshone tribal members. Father Zummach was instrumental in gaining the help of the Catholic Church Extension Society for the erection of another station church, St. Joseph's, in order to serve the Arapaho people who resided about Ethete, Wyoming.

Father Zummach was a devoted priest who earned the respect as well as the friendship of the Arapaho and Shoshone people of the Wind River Reservation who gave him the name "Big Eagle." He spent nearly 27 years of his priesthood at St. Stevens Mission and is remembered by former students as a devoted teacher, coach, leader and advisor.

Due to failing health, Father Zummach had to leave the mission in 1976 and returned only for short visits, including the celebration of his 50th anniversary as a Jesuit in 1982. He always considered St. Stephens his home and expressed his wish to be laid to rest among the people he loved. Father Zummach died in 1998 and was buried near St. Stephens at Arapahoe Catholic Cemetery. In his eulogy it was said "You called him 'Big Eagle' because he soared for you. He wanted to walk in your moccasins, and you let him. He was always there for the people."

CHAPTER TEN SPORTS

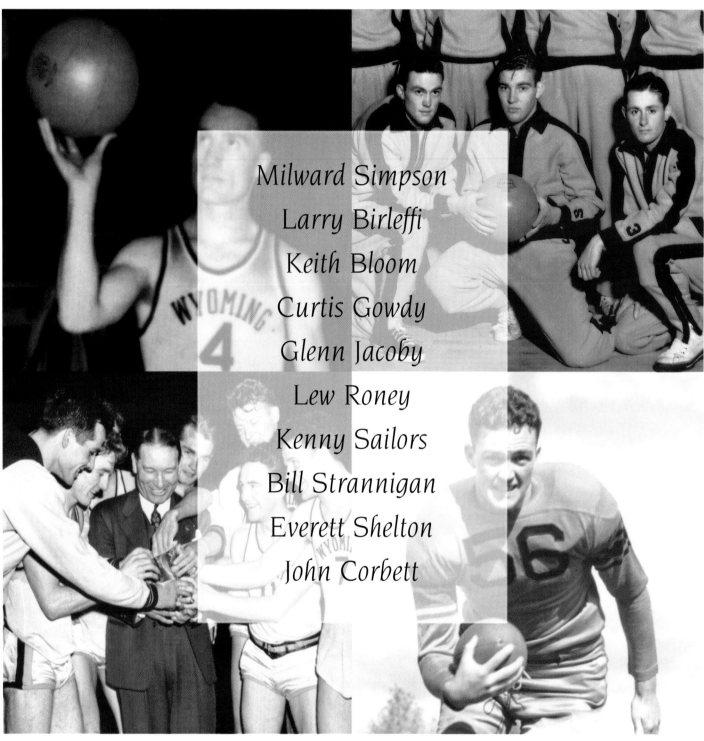

Milward Simpson
Larry Birleffi
Keith Bloom
Curtis Gowdy
Glenn Jacoby
Lew Roney
Kenny Sailors
Bill Strannigan
Everett Shelton
John Corbett

(Top left) Kenny Sailors, c. 1942-43 *Courtesy of AHC Collection.*
(Top right) UW basketball team *Courtesy of AHC Collection.*
(Bottom left) University of Wyoming, 1943 NCAA Championship Team *Courtesy of AHC Collection.*
(Bottom right) Bill Strannigan, c. 1941 *Courtesy of AHC Collection.*

INTRODUCTION

Wyoming is known as the "Cowboy State" not only because of its western heritage, but also because of the ideals personified in the image of the cowboy, among them individualism and perseverance. The history of sports in Wyoming shows that the state's residents bring those values with them to the playing field. Whether as individuals or a team, Wyomingites always compete to the best of their abilities and take great pride in bringing honor to their state.

Since soldiers first began playing baseball during the Civil War, the sport captured the interest of the country, and the people who came to Wyoming brought baseball with them when they came to the new territory. With the founding of the University of Wyoming, wrestling, track and field and eventually basketball also became popular, with men as well as women students participating. Younger athletes also had opportunities to play. During the first half of the 20th century, as the state's secondary schools expanded, so did opportunities for team sports. And Little League Baseball has been a Wyoming tradition throughout the 20th century.

By the onset of World War II, community leaders across the state realized the importance of providing young people with access to organized sports. During this period the University of Wyoming greatly expanded both the football and basketball programs. As new facilities were built, the university's sports program earned a national reputation and secured the loyalty of fans across the state.

Since the creation of Yellowstone National Park in 1893, Wyoming's abundance of natural beauty has also meant that outdoor recreation has come to hold a special place, with skiing, hiking, rock climbing, and mountain biking enjoying a wide constituency. Many of Wyoming's outstanding athletes have gone on to compete at the national level, and the state has even produced Olympic contenders. Today Wyomingites remain loyal fans to local and university teams, as well as participating in a full range of sporting activities.

MILWARD SIMPSON
1897-1993

Milward Simpson was a three-sport standout during his career at the University of Wyoming. *Courtesy of AHC Collection.*

Milward Simpson was born in Jackson, Wyoming, on November 12, 1897. He was the youngest of three children of Margaret Burnett and William Lee Simpson. William Simpson, a native of Colorado, trailed cattle into the Jackson Hole area in 1884 and settled in Wyoming, later establishing himself as a prominent attorney.

Milward Simpson spent his early years in Lander, where his father, as Fremont County prosecutor, obtained a conviction against Butch Cassidy, the infamous outlaw. The family later moved to Meetetsee and eventually settled in Cody. Simpson attended public schools in Cody, Wyoming, and the Tome School in Maryland, graduating from Cody High School in 1916. In 1918 Simpson enlisted in the U.S. Army. He was commissioned as second lieutenant in the Infantry the following year.

Simpson attended the University of Wyoming from 1917 to 1921, where he lettered in three sports. Considered by many to be one of the greatest natural sportsmen in the history of the state, Simpson is the only athlete in the university's history to be selected team captain for the football, basketball and baseball teams. In 1918 he was the university's leading scorer in basketball, averaging 11.6 points per game. Simpson, who played the halfback position, was a member of the Kodak All-American Football Team in 1920. Perhaps his best sport was baseball. His performance on the diamond was so outstanding he fielded offers from major league baseball teams. In 1921 he earned his bachelor's degree. That same year he married Lorna Kooi. The couple eventually had two sons, Peter and Alan.

Simpson was dissuaded by his father from pursuing a career in baseball, opting instead to pursue a law degree at Harvard. However, he continued to play baseball while in the East, traveling in the semi-pro leagues. Simpson left Harvard law in 1925 to return to Wyoming in response to a family crisis. His father had been charged with murder and the younger Simpson needed to take over his practice for the duration of his trial. He received a special dispensation from the state district court to practice until he passed the bar. His father was later acquitted on the basis of self-defense because the deceased, enraged at having lost a lawsuit against Simpson, had attacked him on a public street.

Simpson's first foray into the political arena was in 1926, when he was elected to the Wyoming House of

As governor, Simpson was noted for his enthusiasm in promoting the state of Wyoming.

Representatives. His second attempt at electoral office was an unsuccessful attempt to unseat Senator Joseph O'Mahoney in 1940. In 1939, he was appointed to the Board of Trustees for the University of Wyoming. He spent 16 years as a member of that body, 12 of them as president. During his tenure, he was instrumental in securing an endowment that allowed the construction of Coe Library and the creation of the School of American Studies.

Milward Simpson was elected governor of Wyoming. In 1954, he ran for governor on a platform of efficiency and equality, defeating his formidable Democratic opponent, Scotty Jack. As governor, Simpson was noted for his enthusiasm in promoting the state of Wyoming. He is credited with modernizing the state's tax code, closing down illegal gambling and creating a foundation program to fund state schools. He was a defender of state's rights and opposed to capital punishment. Since Simpson was considered by many to be one of the best governors in the state's history, it was a surprise when he was defeated by Joe Hickey in his 1958 bid for reelection. Political analysts have blamed his defeat on a highway squabble that put in him in disfavor with residents of Sheridan County, losing him their votes and the election.

Simpson returned to politics in 1962 and was successful in his second attempt at the U.S. Senate, ironically defeating his former gubernatorial opponent, Joe Hickey, in 1962. He served in the Senate until 1967 when health problems forced him to retire. Simpson died from complications of Parkinson's Disease on June 11, 1993. He was 95 years old.

LARRY BIRLEFFI
1918-

Larry Birleffi was born in Hartville, Wyoming, on April 17, 1918. His parents were Louise and Victor Birleffi, former mayor of Hartville, and he was one of three boys. Birleffi grew up in Hartville and attended school in Sunrise, a neighboring community. While attending the University of Wyoming, Larry Birleffi began his career in journalism in 1937 as a columnist for the student newspaper *The Branding Iron* and a sports writer and later editor for the *Laramie Daily Boomerang*.

Birleffi graduated with a bachelor's degree in journalism in 1942 and married his college sweetheart, Lois Ann Sturtevant, with whom he eventually had three daughters. During World War II Birleffi served in the Army as public information officer for the 92nd Infantry Division. He served for four years and was discharged with the rank of major in the G-2 Intelligence Division, having served in Italy and earning a Bronze Star.

Birleffi returned to Wyoming and began a long career as a daily sports columnist and newspaper reporter in Cheyenne. He became sports editor for the *Wyoming Eagle* and by 1947 had expanded into the broadcast medium at station KFBC in Cheyenne, later developing one of the first nightly call-in sports shows.

By the early 1950s Birleffi had assumed the position of director of sports for KFBC-TV and continued to serve in that capacity for more than 30 years. In 1960 he became the director of sports for radio station KFBC and later took over the post of station manager.

Birleffi had assignments with ABC's "Wide World of Sports" and was one of the first to broadcast a rodeo on television. Throughout his radio and television career he continued writing for *The Wyoming Eagle* and the *Wyoming Tribune-Eagle*. His popular column, published three times weekly, became a fixture on the sports page, earning him a reputation for "wit, insight and a long memory."

Birleffi began covering the University of Wyoming's football and basketball games in 1947 and soon became known as the "Voice of the Cowboys." He eventually bought KFBC and acquired the broadcast rights for the Cowboys' games. For 38 years Birleffi covered every University of Wyoming football and basketball game. Birleffi announced his retirement in 1986 but continued to travel with the university's football team and write columns for the *Tribune-Eagle*. Most recently, he has had his weekly spot on KGWN-TV. Birleffi has received many honors throughout his broadcast career, the Wyoming Broadcasters Association named him Broadcaster of the Year in 1954, and the press area at the University of Wyoming's War Memorial Stadium was named in his honor in 1992.

Birleffi has a long history of service to the state and the University of Wyoming. A member of the Rotary and the Wyoming Jaycees, he chaired the State Heart Fund Drive and the Cancer Fund Drive and is a past president of the Quarterback Club and a member of the Cowboy Joe Club. In recognition of his work on behalf of the athletic program, Birleffi was inducted into the University of Wyoming's Intercollegiate Athletics Hall of Fame in 1996.

KEITH BLOOM
1927-

Keith Bloom was born in Powell, Wyoming, in 1927. He graduated from Powell High School, having earned 12 letters and all-state honors in football, basketball and track. After a stint in the U.S. Navy, he began attending the University of Wyoming on a basketball scholarship in 1947 and became the last three-sport letterman undergraduate at the school.

Bloom played basketball, football and baseball for the University of Wyoming. He lettered in basketball all four years of his college career, starting every game his junior and senior years and playing in every game of both seasons. In 1950 Bloom was basketball team captain and most valuable player. Bloom also lettered in football in 1947 but an injury ended his participation in that sport. In 1948 Bloom switched to baseball, although he had never before played, and lettered his sophomore, junior and senior years, playing first baseman for the Cowboys.

After graduation, Bloom pursued a career in professional sports, playing professional basketball in Denver for the Frontier Refiners in the National Basketball League, as well as playing baseball in the Brooklyn Dodgers' Organization. In 1952 he changed his focus, opting to work as a teacher, coach and athletic administrator in his native state, beginning at Evanston High School. The following year he married Joyce Swenson and the couple eventually had two children, a son and a daughter.

In 1954 Bloom accepted a position at Powell High School and he remained there for 38 years. Bloom, who earned a master's degree in physical education and athletic administration from Indiana University in 1958, enjoyed an outstanding coaching career, winning state, regional and conference championships in football, basketball, track and tennis. In addition, he was honored as Coach of the Year several times. In 1974 he initiated the Powell High School tennis program, serving as coach until his retirement as athletic/activities director in 1992. In recognition of his influence on the school's athletic program, the Keith Bloom Leadership Award is given annually "to recognize one who has been a tremendous example to countless students from the Powell High system for many years."

Bloom has been active in numerous professional organizations throughout his career, serving as president of the Wyoming Association of Health, Physical Education and Recreation, the Wyoming Coaches' Association, and the Wyoming Interscholastic Athletic Administrators' Association. As president of the Western Wyoming Athletic Conference for three different terms, he was instrumental in developing rules and regulations for the newly formed conference. He served on the executive board of the Wyoming Coaches' Association Hall of Fame for nine years, three of them as president, and helped to develop the philosophy and criteria for that body.

Bloom has received many awards in recognition of his years of service, among them the Wyoming Coaches' Association's Bill Farthing Award, the National High School Athletic Director of the Year for District Seven (1991), and the Wyoming High School Activities Association's Meritorious Service Award. In 1984 he was inducted into the first class of the Wyoming Coaches' Association Hall of Fame, and 10 years later he was a member of the first class and the first Wyoming high school coach inducted into the National High School Coaches' Association's Hall of Fame. He was inducted into the University of Wyoming Athletic Hall of Fame in 1996. Since his retirement, Bloom has remained active in his chosen field, serving on the Wyoming Coaches' Association Hall of Fame Committee, the Milward Simpson Outstanding High School Athlete Awards Committee, and as president of the Wyoming Chapter of the National Football Foundation and College Hall of Fame.

After a successful stint as a college and professional athlete, Keith Bloom had a long coaching career. Courtesy of Bloom Family Collection.

CURTIS "CURT" EDWARD GOWDY
1919-

Curtis "Curt" Edward Gowdy, who believes the job of the sportscaster is to report the game, is recognized as one of the premier sports announcers in the nation. He was born in Green River, Wyoming, on July 31, 1919. His parents were Edward and Ruth Gowdy. They had one other child, a daughter, Margaret.

Gowdy's father worked as chief dispatcher for the Union Pacific Railroad and in 1925 the family moved to Cheyenne, Wyoming. Gowdy excelled at sports from an early age, playing both basketball and baseball. During his senior year at Cheyenne High School, Gowdy was the leading scorer in basketball for the state, as well as a member of the National Honor Society. After graduating from high school in 1937, Gowdy worked as an electrician's apprentice for the Union Pacific and played Class A softball.

Gowdy began attending the University of Wyoming in 1938, where he lettered in basketball and tennis his sophomore, junior and senior years. Gowdy received a bachelor's degree in statistics from the university in 1942. After graduation, Gowdy enlisted in the service as a second lieutenant. During air force pilot school he suffered a back injury that resulted in his discharge and ended his active participation in sports. In 1944 Gowdy returned to Cheyenne and embarked on a career as a sports reporter for the Wyoming Eagle. Gowdy's first job as a sports announcer was for KFBC in Cheyenne, which he received after he impressed the station manager with his attempt at describing a local six-man football game. From there he went to Oklahoma City, where he was an announcer in the Texas baseball league. Gowdy married the former

Jerre Dawkins, a student at the University of Oklahoma, in 1949. The couple eventually had two sons and a daughter.

In 1949, Gowdy went to New York City to assist Mel Allen in play-by-play coverage of the New York Yankee games. By 1951 Gowdy had begun a 15-year run as the play-by-play announcer for the Boston Red Sox. He hosted his own local sports show at station WHDH in Boston and also worked for NBC broadcasting college football and professional basketball. In 1957 he was forced to reduce his work schedule after an altercation with a drunk driver who had run into Gowdy, aggravating his pre-existing back condition, but by 1958 he was fully recovered.

In 1961, Gowdy began broadcasting American Football League games and college football games for ABC. In 1965, when the AFL switched its games to NBC, Gowdy resigned his position in Boston and stayed with the network, where he began "The Game of the Week," a play-by-play report of the week's outstanding major league baseball game. In 1967, Gowdy broadcast the first Super Bowl game between the Green Bay Packers and the Kansas City Chiefs.

The first installment of Gowdy's Emmy Award-winning "The American Sportsman" series, which began a 20-year run in 1964, was shot on the Platte River in Wyoming. During the course of his career, Gowdy broadcast 16 World Series, 12 Rose Bowls, eight Super Bowls, and eight Olympic games. He eventually expanded his interests to include ownership of radio and television stations, including KFBC, the Cheyenne station where he had begun his career.

Curt Gowdy has received numerous awards in recognition of his career. In 1967 the National Association of Sport Writers and Sports Broadcasters named him Sportscaster of the Year. Curt Gowdy State Park, near Cheyenne, was named in his honor. A recipient of the prestigious Peabody Award for "distinguished achievement in television sports coverage," Gowdy was given the American Academy of Television Arts and Sciences Lifetime Achievement Award in 1992. Gowdy has been elected to six different Halls of Fame, including the Baseball Hall of Fame and the American Sportscaster Hall of Fame.

GLENN JACOBY
1907-1973

> Jacoby is credited with the recruitment of the university's most successful coaches, including Bowden Wyatt, Phil Dickens, Bob Devaney, Lloyd Eaton and Fritz Shurmer.

Glenn Jacoby was born in Lake Nebagamon, Wisconsin, on September 2, 1907. He attended the University of Idaho in Moscow, earning a bachelor's degree in 1928 and a master's degree in 1932. While a student at Idaho, Jacoby was considered to be an outstanding athlete, earning nine varsity letters. In 1935 he married Dorothy Fredrickson. The couple eventually had two sons.

In 1941, Jacoby was enrolled in the Ph.D. program at Columbia's School of Education when he was called to active duty in the Army. During World War II Jacoby served in North Africa, Europe and the Pacific Theater. He was also stationed at Fort F.E. Warren in Cheyenne, Wyoming. By 1944 Jacoby had achieved the rank of colonel.

Upon his discharge, Jacoby accepted a position as head of the department of physical education at the University of Idaho. During his posting in Wyoming, Jacoby made the acquaintance of Tracy McCraken, a Cheyenne newspaper publisher and University of Wyoming trustee. McCracken recommended Jacoby to the university's president, George Duke Humphrey, for the position of athletic director. Persuaded by Humphrey's promise that the university was committed to a complete reorganization of the athletic department, Jacoby accepted the position. Jacoby served as the University of Wyoming athletic director for 27 years until his retirement in 1973.

During his tenure as athletic director Jacoby transformed the university's program. Known for his unexcelled organizational ability and sound judgment, he quickly built a national reputation as one of the finest athletic directors in collegiate sports. When he arrived in 1946, the bleachers in Corbett Field served as a football stadium and the inadequate Half-Acre Gym was the basketball arena. Under his leadership the university constructed War Memorial Stadium, War Memorial Fieldhouse, a 55-acre athletic complex, and the university golf course, later named in his honor.

Jacoby is credited with the recruitment of the university's most successful coaches, including Bowden Wyatt, Phil Dickens, Bob Devaney, Lloyd Eaton and Fritz Shurmer. He was an integral player in the Founding of the Western Athletic Conference. Under his leadership Wyoming basketball repeated the successes of the 1930s and 1940s and the now defunct Wyoming baseball program participated in four NCAA tournaments. During his tenure the ski team earned top NCAA honors and the wrestling team consistently finished in the top 12 at the national tournament. Jacoby's crowning achievement as athletic director came in 1968, when the Cowboys earned their fifth bowl appearance, to the Sugar Bowl in New Orleans.

Jacoby also presided over one of the most controversial incidents in the history of university athletics, the "Black 14" episode. When 14 black football players protested discrimination by opponent Brigham Young University, Coach Lloyd Eaton dismissed them from the team. Jacoby supported Eaton's decision and the case ultimately had a negative effect on the university's recruiting efforts.

Jacoby received many honors for his work. In 1960 he was selected to serve on the United States Olympic Committee. A testimonial dinner attended by prominent figures from across the state marked Jacoby's 25th anniversary with the University of Wyoming. In February, 1973, he was elected to the National Association of Collegiate Directors of Athletics Hall of Fame. In December 1972 Jacoby had announced plans to retire the following summer, but in the early part of the 1973 he was diagnosed with cancer and died in March. Jacoby was posthumously elected to the Wyoming Athletic Hall of Fame in 1993.

LEW RONEY

University of Wyoming, 1943 NCAA Championship Team *Courtesy of AHC Collection.*

Lew Roney was raised in Laramie, Wyoming, and attended local schools. While attending Laramie High School he excelled in football, basketball and track and field. He also served as student body president and graduated second in his class. He set state records in the hurdles and led his team to the state championships in football (1964) and basketball (1964 and 1965). He played shortstop for the American Legion League in Wyoming, batting over .500 in one season.

Roney turned down offers from Philadelphia and the Chicago Cubs to pursue his education at Yale University, where he excelled in track, basketball and football. After winning the Bobby Hertz Trophy as outstanding freshman football player, he played on three Ivy League championship teams (1967, 1968 and 1969). Roney also earned three varsity letters in basketball during his college career. He was near the top of the collegiate rankings as a hurdler before an injury curtailed his track and field career. Roney graduated in 1970 with a degree in engineering.

Roney returned to Wyoming in 1971. He accepted a position as a math teacher at Central High School and served as assistant basketball, football and track coach.

Two years later he was named head coach of the basketball team. During the course of 21 seasons, his basketball team won more than 300 games and five state championships. During his tenure with the football program, Roney worked with five state championship winners. In 1991 Roney began a four-year stint as head football coach at Central High. Roney also presided over eight state championships in track and served as meet director for the Jim McLeod Meet of Champions for eight years.

A two-time Wyoming Coach of the Year, Roney was inducted into the Wyoming Coaches Association Hall of Fame in 1993. His work as a teacher has also garnered him recognition. The Cheyenne Teachers Education Association named him Teacher of the Year in 1992 and he is a recipient of a Presidential Certificate of Honor for Excellence in Science and Mathematics Teaching. A member of the Board of Directors of the Wyoming Chapter of the National Football Foundation since its inception in 1993, Roney is also currently chairman of the Athlete Selection Committee, charged with nominating Wyoming athletes for recognition and scholarships.

KENNY SAILORS
1921-

Kenny Sailors is widely credited with inventing the jump shot. *Courtesy of AHC Collection.*

Kenny Sailors was born in Bushnell, Nebraska, on January 14, 1921. He grew up in Wyoming, living first in Hillsdale, and later in Laramie. After graduating from high school, Sailors attended the University of Wyoming and played basketball for the Cowboys. He lettered in the sport and in 1943 he led the Cowboys to the NCAA Basketball Championships, winning the Most Valuable Player Award. That same year he married a fellow student, the former Marilyn Corbin. The couple eventually had a son and a daughter.

Sailors' collegiate career was interrupted by the onset of World War II. He enlisted in the U.S. Marine Corps and was commissioned as a second lieutenant. After serving in the South Pacific campaign he was discharged as a captain. He returned to the University of Wyoming and continued to dominate on the basketball court. Sailors' forte was his innovative jump shot, which allowed him to dribble the basketball, pull up short in front of his opponent, leap into the air, and shoot the ball over the outstretched arms of the player guarding him. Sailors credited his inventiveness to circumstances, recalling that playing pickup basketball games with his older, and taller, brother drove him to develop his signature move; "Bud was big and he was fast enough to stop my drive. I just did it out of necessity."

Sailors' performance on the court earned him numerous accolades. It was his jump shot and his ability to dribble the ball around his opponents that dazzled national sports writers, one of whom remarked, "This Sailors can do everything with a basketball but tie a seaman's knot. And, given time and a chance to dribble two steps, he'd probably do that." Sailors was the only University of Wyoming player to earn All-American honors three times. He was awarded the Sullivan award, given annually to the nation's top amateur athletes. He was also the recipient of the Chuck Taylor award as outstanding basketball player of the year. He was twice voted College Player of the Year, in 1943, by unanimous selection, and again in 1946. That same year he was named the Helms Foundation college player of the year.

After graduation, Sailors pursued a professional sports career in the new National Basketball Association for five years, earning about $7,000 a season. He played for the Cleveland Rebels, the Providence Steamrollers, the original Denver Nuggets, the Boston Celtics and the Baltimore Bullets. During the off-season, Sailors returned to Wyoming, working in Cheyenne as a recreation director.

Sailors eventually became involved in state politics, successfully serving as a representative for Laramie County for two terms. In the 1950s he moved his family to Jackson Hole, where he established his own business, the Heart 6 Ranch, a dude and hunting guide service. Sailors also remained active in politics; he was state campaign chairman for Barry Goldwater's presidential campaign and a candidate for the U.S. House of Representatives. In 1965, Sailors and his family relocated to Alaska and founded a guide and outfitting service. After retiring, he and his wife returned to Casper, where they still reside. Sailors was inducted into the University of Wyoming Athletics Hall of Fame in 1993.

BILL STRANNIGAN
1918-1997

Strannigan lettered in football, baseball and basketball while at Wyoming. He ran the single wing offense as a football tailback in 1940. He was a pitcher for the baseball team and was selected for the All-Skyline Conference Team in 1941 and 1942. But basketball was his best sport and having led the team in scoring, he is credited with bringing the Cowboys back from two consecutive losing seasons to a 1941 conference title. His efforts were recognized when he was selected for the Chuck Taylor All American team his junior year.

During World War II Strannigan served in the U.S. Navy. After his discharge, he embarked on a career in sports, beginning with a two-year stint in the AAU Basketball League. In 1948 Strannigan took his first coaching job at a high school in Loveland, Colorado. He accepted the post of basketball coach at Colorado State University in 1950 and during his four years there established a winning record. In his last year at CSU he led his team to the Skyline Conference Championship. From 1954 to 1959 Strannigan was head coach for the Iowa State University Cyclones. He continued to succeed as a coach, with his teams placing in the top three in the Big Eight Conference three out of five years.

Strannigan returned to University of Wyoming in 1959 as head basketball coach, one of only three graduates of the university to hold that position. During his career as head coach, Strannigan won 179 games in 14 years, the second highest total in the Cowboys' history. Known for his "up-tempo" coaching style, Strannigan was selected as Western Athletic Conference Coach of the Year in 1967. Strannigan led the Cowboys to one NCAA tournament and in 1967 and 1969 his team tied for the Western Athletic Conference Championship.

Strannigan retired from coaching after 14 seasons with the Cowboys. In recognition of his accomplishments, he was inducted to the University of Wyoming's Athletics Hall of fame in 1994 and the Iowa State University Athletics Hall of Fame in 1997. Strannigan died in September of 1997.

An alumnus of the University of Wyoming, Bill Strannigan had the second best record for a basketball coach in the school's history. Courtesy of AHC Collection.

Bill Strannigan was born in December, 1918, in Dalry, Scotland. Two years later his family moved to Rock Springs, Wyoming. He attended local schools and earned a reputation as an outstanding athlete. In high school, Strannigan earned All-State recognition in football, basketball and track, earning eleven varsity letters. Embarking on his college career, he played freshman and sophomore basketball at the University of Colorado, earning all-conference recognition. He transferred to the University of Wyoming and completed the remainder of his amateur play as a member of the Cowboys.

EVERETT SHELTON
1899-1974

Ev Shelton, who served as the Cowboys basketball coach for two decades, won more games, 328, than any other coach in the university's history. He was born and raised on his family's farm near Cunningham, Kansas. Shelton was an all-sport standout at Little River High School in Kansas. He particularly excelled in baseball, playing catcher, and was good enough to be offered summer jobs with semi-pro teams in Oklahoma his junior and senior years.

In the fall of 1917 he entered Bethany College in Lindsburg, Kansas, but he quit after only a few months, called to duty by the outbreak of World War I. He

> *Ev Shelton won more games than any other coach in the University's history.*

enlisted in the Marines and served as sergeant with the 11th machine gun platoon in France. After his discharge in 1919 he enrolled in Phillips University, in Enid, Oklahoma, where he earned 12 letters in football, basketball and baseball and was twice named all conference quarterback.

Shelton started his coaching career at the high school in Claremore, Oklahoma, where he coached all sports, after graduating from Phillips in 1923 with a degree in chemistry. He returned to his alma mater in 1924, serving three years as head football and basketball coach, as well as athletic director. From 1928 to 1929 he coached the Sterling Milk Amateur Athletic Union (AAU) basketball team in Oklahoma City, developing his innovative moving screen with a five-man weaving offense. During the next 10 years he

worked with three AAU teams: Cripes Baker at St. Joseph, Missouri, Denver Safeway and the Antler Hotel team from Colorado Springs. His Denver team won the national AAU championship in 1937 and took second the following year. Known affectionately as The Fox, and then toward the end of his 30-year career as The Old Man, he achieved "almost phenomenal coaching success."

Shelton came to the University of Wyoming in 1939. His basketball teams won eight Skyline Conference titles and appeared in four NCAA championship tournaments. In 1943, with a record of 31-2, he lead the Cowboys to their first NCAA Championship. After winning the NCAA title the Cowboys went on to defeat St. John's, Madison Square Invitational. Overall, his teams complied a record of 328 wins and 200 losses, a .612 percentage.

Before the 1943-44 season, the onset of World War II made it impossible for the Cowboys to field an adequate team, so Shelton took a temporary job coaching the Dow Chemical AAU basketball and softball teams out of Midland, Michigan. While with Dow, Shelton remarried Kay Shelton, who was the mother of his son, Steven. Shelton returned to Laramie and resumed his duties in time for the 1944-45 season.

Shelton also coached the university's baseball team during the 1940s. He was instrumental in raising funds for the construction of the War Memorial Stadium and War Memorial Fieldhouse. Shelton was elected to the National Basketball Hall of Fame in 1982 and the University of Wyoming Hall of Fame in 1993.

Following the 1958-59 season, his worst season, Shelton announced his retirement. Although some of his critics felt it was time for him to move on, many viewed his leaving as signifying the end of an era. Shelton moved to Sacramento State College in California, where he coached until 1969, when he became the first commissioner of the Far Western Intercollegiate Athletic Conference.

Shelton died of a heart attack while vacationing at San Juan Capistrano Beach. He was 75. Shelton, who was often quoted as saying he loved the game of basketball, was remembered by his fellow coaches and associates as an "authentic gentleman," who achieved success by virtue of hard work, sacrifice and patience.

JOHN CORBETT
1896-1947

John Corbett was born in Cambridge, Massachusetts, on November 14, 1896. Corbett attended Harvard University, where he played football and baseball in addition to ice hockey, tennis and polo. In 1891 he was named as a halfback on Walter Camp's All-American Football Team. Corbett graduated from Harvard in 1894 and seven years later he married Mary Kingsley. The couple eventually had five children.

Corbett began his career as director of athletics at Ohio University (1908-1910), before moving on to a similar position at Oklahoma A & M in 1912. Three years later, he accepted a position as the first director of the University of Wyoming Physical Education Department in Laramie. His teaching responsibilities, in addition to a variety of physical education classes for both men and women, included courses such as anatomy and the physiology of exercise.

As the university's first professional coach, Corbett coached all sports, including track and field, football and baseball, as well as basketball, posting a 7-2 season in 1918 and a 10-1 season the following year. He introduced programs in boxing, wrestling, fencing and gymnastics. Corbett also instituted the practice of giving physical examinations to incoming freshmen.

Corbett, who became known as the "grand old man" of Wyoming athletics, worked diligently to expand intercollegiate athletics at the university. He was the originator of the present intramural program and inaugurated inter-collegiate wrestling, boxing, swimming, gymnastics, fencing and track and field. In 1922, working with alumni and assisted by Dr. Samuel Knight, Corbett oversaw the construction of what later became known as Corbett Field. He was also instrumental in beginning the State High School Basketball Tournament.

Corbett was an active member of the community outside of the university. A veteran of the Spanish American War, he participated in veteran's organizations as well as the Lions Club, of which he served as president. He also worked extensively with the Boy Scouts of America. Corbett served on the Laramie City Council for six years. In collaboration with his wife, he originated an outdoor pageant that became an annual event, first on campus, and later at Vedauwoo. Corbett died on February 21, 1947, and was buried in Laramie.

Corbett's work on behalf of the athletics program at the University of Wyoming was honored with the dedication of the John Corbett Physical Education Building in 1976. In 1995, Corbett was inducted into the University of Wyoming's Athletics Hall of Fame, where he was remembered as the Founding Father of Wyoming Athletics. Corbett's career exemplified his belief in Plato's dictum that a sound mind and healthy body go hand in hand.

As the first professional coach at the University of Wyoming, John Corbett developed virtually every intramural program.

Partners in

Wyoming

Wyoming

AGRICULTURE & RANCHING
Holly Sugar..170
Warren Live Stock Company......................................172
Willow Creek Ranch At The Hole-In-The-Wall, The..........174
Wyoming Stock Growers Association.........................176

BUILDING A GREATER WYOMING
Fowler & Peth..177
Reiman Corp..178

BUSINESS & FINANCE
American National Bank...179
United Bancorporation of Wyoming, Inc...................180
First Interstate Bank...183
Big Horn Federal...186
Ed Murray & Sons...188
Hilltop National Bank...190
Norwest Bank..192
SafeCard..193
Natrona County School Employees Federal Credit Union.......194

MANUFACTURING & DISTRIBUTION
Crum Electric Supply Company..................................195
Unicover Corporation...196
Wyoming Machinery Company...................................198
Vision Graphics, Inc..199
Waterworks Industries Inc..200
Westech/Wotco...201

MARKETPLACE
Coliseum Motors & Big Wyoming...............................202
Eastridge Autoplex, Inc..205
Sierra Trading Post..206
Taco John's International, Inc......................................208
Halladay Motors, Inc...210
Spradley Motors, Inc...211
Webster Chevrolet...212

MINERALS & MINING
RAG Coal West, Inc...213
Solvay Minerals, Inc..214
Black Hills Bentonite..216
Wyodak Coal...217
Hillcrest Spring Water...218

NETWORKS
Questar Corporation..219
Cheyenne Light, Fuel and Power Company................220
Bighorn Airways..224
Wyoming Newspaper Group..226

OIL & GAS
Petroleum Association of Wyoming............................228
BP Amoco..229

Exxon Company, U.S.A. 230
McMurry Oil. 232
True Companies. 234
Wold Companies, The. 236
Fleischli Oil Company, Inc. 238
Marathon Oil Company. 239

PROFESSIONS
AIA Wyoming, A Chapter of the American Institute of Architects. 240
Gorder|South Group Architects. 242
Lathrop & Rutledge. 244

QUALITY OF LIFE
American Heritage Center. 245
Wyoming Business Alliance/Wyoming Heritage Foundation. 246
Blue Cross Blue Shield of Wyoming. 248
Church of Jesus Christ of Latter-day Saints, The. 250
Sheridan VA Medical Center. 252
Cheyenne VA Medical Center/Cheyenne VA Regional Office. 253
Kemmerer Legacy, The. 254
Kennedy-Western University. 256
Teton County and Town of Jackson. 258
University of Wyoming. 262
Wyoming Medical Center. 264
Buffalo Bill Historical Center. 266
Martin-Harris Gallery. 267
National Museum of Wildlife Art. 268
National Outdoor Leadership School. 269
Wyoming Business Council. 270
Ucross Foundation. 271
Wyoming Game and Fish Department. 272
United Medical Center. 273
Wyoming State Historical Society. 274

RESORTS & RECREATION
Sinclair Oil Corporation/Holding's Little America. 276
Cheyenne Frontier Days. 278
Elk Country Motels, Inc. 279
Hitching Post Inn. 280
Hotel Wolf. 281
Lost Creek Ranch & Spa. 282
Old Baldy Club. 283
Parkway Plaza Hotel. 284
Powder Horn Ranch and Golf Club, L.L.C., The. 285
Saratoga Inn Resort and Hot Springs Spa. 286
Spring Creek Ranch. 287
Wort Hotel, The. 288

TECHNOLOGY
Advanced Computers. 289
UniLink Software. 290
Union Telephone Company. 292

Holly Sugar

The Holly Sugar company was founded in 1905 in Holly, Colorado, near the Kansas border. Its founder, Kenneth Schley, liked the name Holly because holly berries were traditional symbols of friendship and good cheer. By 1915, the expanding company built a factory in Sheridan, under the auspices of the Sheridan Sugar Company, of which Holly Sugar was the main shareholder. Over the next 15 years, under the leadership of A.E. Carlton, the company expanded aggressively, adding 10 new factories, including those in Worland and Torrington.

Research in Sheridan in the 30s

The Worland factory had been built in 1917 by the Wyoming Sugar Company. Holly acquired it in 1925, along with some area farms that grew beets for the factory. By 1939, the beet receiving station could handle more than 70,000 tons of beets — it was the largest receiving station in the world at the time. In the 1940s, Holly started leasing its Worland-area farms to tenant farmers. Part of the lease included sheep, fed with wet pulp and molasses from the sugar plant, producing natural fertilizer to be used on the farm.

The Worland area's sugar beet production has increased significantly over the years. The per-acre yield today is about three times what it was in 1917. By 1997, the Worland plant's annual payments to growers exceeded $19 million.

Holly built its Torrington factory in 1926, using equipment from a factory in Huntington Beach, California, where oil production displaced sugar beet production. Its capacity was 2,000 tons. When running at full capacity, the factory could produce 7,500 to 8,000 100-pound bags of sugar every 24 hours. Full capacity employed 850 people, as well as 150 at beet receiving stations and up to 2,000 laborers on individual growers' harvests.

The open house for Holly's Torrington factory, in the spring of 1928, featured a Denver dance band playing in the company warehouse. Amidst Prohibition, no alcohol was served, but 3,000 people ate sandwiches and ice cream and danced well past midnight. Now, the Torrington factory has about 120 employees and another 250 during the 150 days of "campaign."

Torrington, in southeast Wyoming near the Nebraska border, lies in the fertile valley of the North Platte River. The area attracted Holly's attention because of its phenomenal yields, averaging 17.5 tons of beets per acre in 1919 when the rest of the valley averaged just 11.8 tons per acre. Today, sugar beets remain a vital part of Goshen County's economy.

In the early days, campaign workers were known as "sugar tramps." At both Worland and Torrington, many were young Mormons. Others were families from Japan, Russia, Germany and Mexico. When local men went away for World War I, women and children (schools closed during the harvest) topped and harvested the beets, then loaded them into horse-drawn carts.

In Worland, the "Sugar Tramps Club" has held an annual picnic each August for the last 72 years, the last big get-together before harvest begins. The club also sponsors an annual spring dinner/dance to celebrate the end of campaign.

From the 1920s to the 60s, Holly factory locations nationwide also served as cattle feedlots, taking advantage of the beet pulp and molasses byproducts of the sugar beet manufacturing process. These operations were phased out as the company pursued additional efficiency and profitability. Holly's other complementary ventures have included the Holly Oil

Company, which drilled for oil on the site of the Huntington Beach factory.

Roger Hill, president of Holly Sugar, grew up in Lingle, Wyoming, near Torrington, in the 1950s. As a child he helped weed, irrigate, cultivate and harvest his family's sugar beets. Like many in grower families, he referred to himself as a beet picker. He would hand-top the beets with beet knives, and scoop them onto trucks or wagons for transport to the receiving station. After graduating from the University of Wyoming, he went to work for Holly in Worland in 1963. Working his way from the ground up, Roger Hill has been president of the company since 1988.

Holly established an agricultural research station in Sheridan in 1936. It sought to develop new beet seed varieties to increase sucrose content and yields. The Sheridan sugar factory, in operation since 1915, was dismantled in 1947, though the old buildings are still used for seed storage and processing.

[Holly Sugar] produces enough sugar each year to satisfy 68 million people.

Today Sheridan serves as headquarters for all of Holly's nationwide beet seed research and development. Its objective is to make beets more productive — and disease-resistant — in all localized growing areas.

Holly has an alliance with Advanta, a world player in the seed market. Advanta leverages worldwide research expertise with modern biotechnology to produce sustainable agriculture as well as high-quality, safe food products at competitive prices for a growing world population. For example, "sustainable plants" can thrive on less water and less nitrogen than their ancestors. This means they are less likely to deplete soil, and can better survive drought. By breeding resistance to diseases, insects and herbicides, Holly and Advanta can reduce plants' dependence on chemicals.

In 1988, Holly merged with Imperial Sugar Company,

becoming Imperial Holly, a publicly traded company. With equal capacities for beet and cane sugar, the company could smooth production peaks. Additional acquisitions in the late 1990s helped the company branch into foodservice supply and organic sweeteners. In 1999 the company — now America's largest processor of refined sugar — reverted to the name Imperial Sugar Company.

In 1915, Holly Sugar produced 60,000 hand-sewn 100-pound bags of sugar, processing 600 tons of beets a day. Today, the company can process 40,000 tons of beets a day. Totally, it produces enough sugar each year to satisfy 68 million people. The company works with 2,500 growers on 310,000 acres in eleven states. During the peak season, more than 2,700 employees work for the sugar beet company, and 1,250 work year-round.

Holly's factories and facilities are one of Wyoming's largest employers. Yearly contributions to the economy — through beet grower payments, payroll, equipment purchases, taxes and other expenses — were estimated in 1994 at over $65-70 million.

Through all the changes of the past years, including improving technologies and tighter links with global markets, two key principles continue for Holly. The first is its relationship with the state of Wyoming: applying advances in global research to help improve the yields of the state's farmlands and the lives of its residents. The second is the holly leaves and berries that adorn Holly Sugar containers, stationery, buildings and vehicles, symbolizing that continued friendship and good cheer.

Modern seed operations in Sheridan

Agriculture & Ranching

Warren Live Stock Company

At the Warren Live Stock Company, cattle and sheep graze together as peacefully as twin lambs. Never mind that clashes between Western cattlemen and sheepmen reached warlike proportions in frontier-day Wyoming. The Warren Live Stock Company proved that cattle and sheep could inhabit the same range without robbing each other of vital forage or water.

Pole Creek Ranch, headquarters of Warren Live Stock Company

Warren Live Stock Company was founded in Wyoming in 1874 and incorporated in 1883, making it one of the oldest corporations in the state. Its founder was Senator Francis E. Warren, a Massachusetts native who found success in real estate and ranching in the wild Wyoming pioneer town of Cheyenne. He entered Wyoming politics and in 1885 was appointed territorial governor. When Wyoming gained statehood in 1890, Warren was elected to the governorship; however, in that same year he was also elected to the U.S. Senate and, subsequently, left the state capital for Washington, D.C., where he remained for seven terms.

In spite of a busy political career, Warren ran the livestock company through some tough times, including the national economic panic of 1893. It was then that the bottom fell out of the market and the company lost $233,500. After 17 months in receivership, the company settled its debts and was on its way to another 70 years of Warren family ownership.

After Sen. Warren died in 1929, his son, Frederick E. Warren, took over the operation. He used technology to bring the company from an Old West-style open range operation to a modern and efficient ranch. Strategically

placed lambing camps, updated sheering facilities, new water wells with large storage capacity to serve cattle and sheep and new ranch roads were among the improvements. These updates were vital in keeping the company competitive in times of economic uncertainty.

Efficiency was not only important to the ranching process, it became the trademark of the company's main product as well. Frederick E. Warren and Dr. John Hill, the dean of the University of Wyoming's School of Agriculture, developed the Warhill breed of sheep, known for its inclination to produce twins. Although each twin lamb is born weighing less than the average single lamb, they weigh more combined than a single lamb, thus increasing the company's production at sale time. The Warhill sheep are well suited to the open grass range of the Warren Live Stock Company's southern Wyoming ranch holdings. Warren Live Stock Company is one of the country's most fruitful producers of sheep for replacement breeding animals, meat and wool. By the time of Frederick E. Warren's death in 1949, he had become one of the West's best-known and respected livestockmen. Around that time, U.S. sheep production began a startling decline from a peak population of 53 million sheep. Sheep growers say several factors are to

(From left to right) Paul Etchepare Jr., John Etchepare and their father Paul Etchepare in front of one of the ranch's original shearing sheds

blame, including consumer's taste for beef over sheep; the use of synthetic fibers in clothing; the limitations in the control of animals that prey on sheep; taxes and grazing fees; international competition; and a decline in the number of herders willing to spend long periods in isolation tending to the flocks.

Rounding up cattle in Trail Creek country

The reins of the Warren Live Stock Company were taken up after Frederick E. Warren's death in 1949 by his son, Francis E. Warren II. He further modernized the business, using technology to improve communication between sections of the vast ranch. But realizing that no one in his family would take over the business after his own death, he offered to sell the 334,000-acre ranch.

Paul Etchepare, a well-respected livestock and rural real estate businessman, along with a group of Colorado investors, purchased the Warren Live Stock Company in 1963. As a condition of the sale, Etchepare moved from Denver to Wyoming and became manager of the ranch.

Etchepare learned about sheep in part from his father, John, a Basque sheepherder from the French Pyrenees Mountains. John arrived in the United States in 1890, coincidentally, the same year Francis E. Warren was elected to the U.S. Senate. After several years of herding, John Etchepare started his own successful sheep ranch. He died in 1937 and the ranch was sold. But his son, Paul, having been exposed to ranching as a child, returned to the sheep-raising life of his father.

In 1973, Paul Etchepare's Colorado partners sold their interest in the business to the Etchepare family. The Etchepare family is now the sole owner of the Warren Live Stock Company. Etchepare and his sons, John and Paul Jr., worked to greatly increase the multiple birth rate of the sheep but also to diversify the operation in order to reduce its heavy reliance on the unpredictable sheep market. They have developed the mineral assets of the ranch, cultivated 12,000 acres of farmland and continued to raise cattle in addition to sheep. Because of this diversity and their modern ranch management practices, they have been able to get the most out of the sheep market, selling lambs in the spring when fewer are available than during the typical fall lamb sale period.

One highlight of Paul Etchepare's long successful career was being named *Record Stockman* magazine's 1994 Man of the Year in Livestock. He was honored for his achievements at the national Western Stock Show in Denver, at age 83. He died in 1997, leaving the operation of the company to his sons.

John Etchepare is president of the Warren Live Stock Company, and his brother Paul is the secretary and treasurer. Together they value the same principles that were important to the company's founders, such as hard work and constant stock improvement. Although they may not be able to control the market, the availability of workers, the popularity of synthetic fibers, people's preferences for burgers over lamb chops, or predation on their vulnerable lambs, they take pride in knowing that the Warren Live Stock Company is able to compete with sheep producers from all over the world.

Band of Warhill ewes and lambs

The Willow Creek Ranch
At The Hole-In-The-Wall

The Willow Creek Ranch At The Hole-In-The-Wall is a beautiful 57,000-acre traditional working cattle, horse and sheep ranch, operating much as it did more than a hundred years ago, and recently operating also as a guest ranch. It is located on the South Big Horn — Red Wall Back Country Scenic Byway — 60 miles north of Casper and 35 miles southwest of Kaycee, Wyoming. It lies at the southern end of the Big Horn Mountains, and the elevation ranges from 5,200-8,200 feet. Its geography varies from flat open range to rolling hills to canyon country and on into the high country of the Big Horn Mountains proper. The famous Red Wall, approximately 350 feet high and composed of red sandstone, forms about 18 miles of the ranch's boundary on the east and south sides and is home to many species of birds. As the sunlight changes throughout the day, the wall becomes the focal point for photographers and artists attempting to capture its awesome beauty.

The famous Red Wall Country of Wyoming

The Willow Creek's history is unique and somewhat mysterious. Kenneth McDonald, the founder, was kidnapped as a year-old baby with his nanny and taken on board a ship to Australia. He never knew his real name or anything about his family or native country. His nanny died at sea and he was raised by an Australian family who taught him the sheep business. When he was 12 years old, he sailed with a sheepshearing crew to California to shear for the summer. At summer's end, the crew sailed home with his wages, but without him. He went to work for sheep ranchers, and in a few years he owned several bands of his own sheep. In time, he walked his sheep from California to Rawlins, Wyoming, and began to ride circle looking for a place of his own. He found what he sought under the Red Wall and put together the Willow Creek Ranch in 1882. Through inheritance, it remained in the same family until its sale to the present owners, Gene and Sammye Vieh.

Historical evidence of a colorful past is abundant on the Willow Creek. It is the actual location of the Hole-In-The-Wall Gang's hideout along the Outlaw Trail, which extended from Canada to Old Mexico, and was made famous by Butch Cassidy and The Sundance Kid. The hideout, tucked into the mouth of Buffalo

(Right) Around the campfire on the trail

(Far right) Holding up the mine payroll re-enactment

Creek Canyon, was remote and easily defended. The outlaw cabin foundations are slowly being covered over by earth as the years pass. Not far away is the Hole-In-The-Wall trail up and over the Red Wall. It is challenging and fun to climb on foot. Nearby, on Smith Hill, is located a stone monument and plaque marking the site of a gunfight between an alleged rustler and the foreman and cowboys of the CY Ranch who were trying to round up their stolen cattle. Bob Smith, a rustler, was shot and killed by Joe LeFors, then a stock detective, and later a marshal, who was riding with the CY outfit.

Sunset brings out the colors along the Red Wall.

This area of the ranch has not changed much in the last hundred years. It is still remote, undeveloped and beautiful with magnificent, red rock formations and flat-topped mesas reminiscent of classic Western movies.

Also on the Willow Creek Ranch are the foundations of old Fort Houck, a "road ranch" originally built to protect an Army marching road and stagecoach route. It served as a way station for the stage between the towns of Buffalo and Arminto, Wyoming. The high walls and caves of nearby Buffalo Creek Canyon still contain the names and dates of soldiers stationed at the fort, in addition to numerous Indian petroglyphs. A Sioux Indian trail crosses the ranch, and was once part of the Army wagon road and stagecoach route. There is evidence of Indian campsites with tepee rings still intact.

The dilapidated remains of several old pioneer homesteads are scattered over the ranch and there is an ongoing project to restore and preserve some of them. A bunkhouse, originally built in 1890, has been recently refurbished and now serves as a guesthouse. Family-style meals are served in the same kitchen used since 1890, around a large table with lodgepole pine benches and a view from the window of a small herd of genuine Texas Longhorn's grazing in the meadow. In the evenings after dinner, it is a special treat to feed and socialize with the beautiful cattle that so efficiently helped feed a nation intent on westward expansion and survival.

The Willow Creek Ranch is host to the "Hole-In-The-Wall Endurance Ride," an annual event held on Labor Day weekend. The American Endurance Ride Conference-sanctioned event features a 25 and 50 mile endurance ride daily.

The Willow Creek Ranch also abounds in wild game, and the fall hunting season is enjoyed by hunters from all over the world who stay in the ranch bunkhouse and have meals there provided by the staff. There are several small streams and reservoirs with trout, both natural and stocked, for the fishing enthusiast.

The Willow Creek Ranch At The Hole-In-The-Wall is not a "dude" ranch. There are no swimming pools, spas, tennis courts, golf or TV. It is an old, rawhide and very unique operating cattle and sheep ranch with lots of U.S. and Wyoming history, and deep ties to its rich, Western heritage.

(Far left) The ladies take a holiday.

(Left) Inspecting the Will Taylor Homestead Cabin

Wyoming Stock Growers Association

In a Cheyenne livery stable in 1872, five men gathered. Their mission: the organization of a vigilance committee to address the growing problem of cattle rustling. A system of brand inspection was the eventual result. This was, and is, the backbone of the Wyoming

Wyoming Stock Growers meet in Basin, Wyoming, for their 1919 annual convention.

Stock Growers Association, the organization that grew out of that meeting.

The history of the Stock Growers is entwined with the history of Wyoming. It was the first association formed in the territory, and cattle the first industry. As both grew, the Stock Growers would see plenty of hard times, not the least of them the brutal winter of 1886 that destroyed entire herds. When Wyoming became a state four years following, there were only 183 members and a $29 treasury, but the Stock Growers pressed on. Today, 1,400 members support an industry made up of 1.5 million head of cattle across the state.

Cattle being gathered and moved to fresh pasture on a modern-day ranch

The Stock Growers claim many distinguished members and leaders. Four past presidents went on to be elected governor. David H. True, also a former president, is one of 10 finalists for the Wyoming Citizen of the Century Award from the American Heritage Center. Among others nominated for the award were former presidents Clifford Hansen, Manville Kendrick, Ken Kirkbride and Joe Watt, as well as former executive vice president Dean T. Prosser.

WGSA is the only organization in the state focused on serving the needs of the cattle industry, the largest segment of Wyoming's agricultural production. Its

mission is to serve that industry by protecting its economic, legislative, regulatory, judicial, environmental, custom and cultural interests. That means lobbying, tracking issues at the state and national level, and working closely with state and federal agencies that write regulations affecting the industry. The association also participates in litigation on critical issues and works on public relations and beef promotion.

Its quarterly magazine, *Cow Country*, helps keep producers informed, as does the newsletter that is published monthly. *Periodic Advisories* inform members about key issues, and meetings with producers, members and non-members alike, provide an opportunity to hear their concerns. The Stock Growers offers both a scholarship program and leadership training, geared not only to those becoming leaders in the agriculture industry, but also in the state.

As a keeper of both Wyoming and cattle industry history, its collection is one of the most valuable sources of Western Americana in the country, housed in the University of Wyoming's American Heritage Center in Laramie.

The Stock Growers' most recent leadership includes the immediate past president, Nels J. Smith, from Sundance; president Robert J. Hendry, from Lost Cabin; first vice president Jack Turnell, from Meeteetse; and executive vice president James H. Magagna, from Rock Springs. All are confident that the Wyoming cattle industry will play a major role in the economy and culture of the state in the 21st century, just as it did in the 19th and 20th. The cattle business is the very symbol of Wyoming, drawing both residents and tourists. Many of its small communities are nearly totally dependent on agriculture for their survival, so the future of the state is linked to the cattle industry, and therefore to the Stock Growers. As the industry continues to face many age-old issues, the goal is to bring a fresh approach to addressing them. After 127 years, there is still work to be done.

Fowler & Peth

Take two investors with $2,000 each and one man with a car and an idea, put them together and what do you get? In 1948, this combination produced Fowler & Peth (F&P), a long-lasting company that has successfully evolved to reflect changes in the market-place since its inception.

More than 50 years ago, William Peth traveled the roads of Wyoming and Colorado selling treated fence posts. During his travels, he struck up a friendship with a customer of his, Herb Fowler. When Peth suggested starting up a wholesale lumber company, Fowler and another friend, C. Forrest Perdue, backed the idea. They contributed the necessary start-up money, while Peth, lacking funds, contributed his car.

Thus, F&P came into existence in Cheyenne in 1948. The men had discovered a novel niche in the market, leading to early prosperity. However, in the late 50s and early 60s, the lumber industry underwent an enormous change. Large forest products companies started to enter the distribution business, threatening independent distributors like F&P. In response, Bill Peth redefined his business, narrowing the company's focus to roofing distribution in the Denver area and moving F&P's headquarters to Denver.

This move allowed F&P to successfully recapture a niche by focusing solely on the distribution of roofing and related products, despite the closure of the Cheyenne branch. F&P also set itself apart by introducing rooftop loading (placing roofing materials on the customer's roof) to the region.

Co-founder Bill Peth

The relative lack of competition in the 60s gave way to a revolution in the roofing business in the 70s. Until that time, asphalt had been the major component of roofing. With prices skyrocketing, other industries developed new roofing products. Nonetheless, F&P continued to prosper by offering excellent products and customer service. This decade saw the addition of Bill Peth's sons to the company. Eric ("Ric") Peth joined in 1975 as the branch manager in Casper, and younger son Kurt joined in 1979 as the branch manager for the newly reopened Cheyenne branch.

During the 80s and 90s, F&P's success continued as it addressed the changing needs of the market. Three new branches opened: Colorado Springs in 1984; Scott's Bluff, Nebraska, in 1996; and Rifle, Colorado, in 1997. F&P's fully interactive Web site includes not only product and service information, but also information on the constantly changing residential and commercial roofing products. In the late 90s, F&P again led the market in rooftop loading with its innovative use of Hiab knuckleboom cranes, permitting the company to provide more efficient service.

Through a series of evolutions over the 50-plus years of its existence, F&P has proven that remaining flexible and changing with the times are keys to prosperity. As current president Ric Peth proudly states: "Fowler and Peth has survived as the largest family-owned independent distributor of residential roofing products in the Rocky Mountain Region."

Fowler & Peth's Hiab knuckleboom crane in front of company headquarters

Reiman Corp.

Reiman Corp., a general contracting and construction management firm, is recognized for high-quality work throughout Wyoming and the Rocky Mountain region. In a half century of operation, the company has completed more than a thousand projects, including commercial and public buildings, highway and railroad bridges, and concrete-paving and pile-driving work as well as structural remodeling. Reiman managers work carefully to develop positive relationships with architects, suppliers and subcontractors to meet client needs in a timely fashion — using local resources wherever possible and providing safe work environments. Success in meeting these goals has given the business a solid reputation for integrity and skill. Company contracts totaled $20 to $25 million yearly in the late 1990s. In that period Reiman employed 140 people year round, with up to 60 additional seasonal workers on projects in Wyoming, Colorado, New Mexico and western Nebraska.

This bridge over the Shoshone River near Yellowstone National Park is a "signature" for Reiman Corp.

Major Reiman projects in Cheyenne include the Laramie County Government Complex and Laramie County Library, the Science Center at Laramie County Community College, the Civic Center and Fire Station, the George Cox Parking Structure, the B and E stands at Frontier Park, the United Blood Services Center, Johnson Junior High School, Central High School, and the Hathaway and Barrett state office buildings. Additionally, the company built most of the Central Avenue viaduct crossing the Union Pacific rail yard, an award-winning project from the American Institute of Steel Construction in 1984.

Reiman Corp. also constructed the top tiers of the University of Wyoming football stadium in Laramie, a job that required special forms to pour concrete for arc-shaped end supports. The firm was the general contrator on high schools in Rock Springs, Douglas, Glenrock, Wheatland and Torrington as well as Eastridge Mall, and the Cottonwood, Aspen Creek and Union Oil office buildings in Casper. During a 12-month period in 1982 and 1983, Reiman crews built 29 bridges for the Chicago Northwestern Railroad. The company's "signature" bridge, completed in 1959, is a span of the Shoshone River between Cody and Yellowstone National Park. The largest out-of-state Reiman project to date is a $9 million highway interchange near Roswell, New Mexico.

The firm's founder, W.R. (Bob) Reiman, enlisted in the Navy after graduating from the University of Cincinnati with a civil engineering degree during World War II. He was assigned to a "Seabeas" unit in the Philippines, where he met Bill Lowe, a serviceman from Billings, Montana. Reiman joined Lowe and Russ Riedesel, another builder from Billings, in a business partnership after the war. Reiman became managing member of Riedesel-Lowe, the company they formed in Cody, Wyoming, in April 1948. The firm moved to Cheyenne in 1950 to build the Barrett Building. It has maintained its headquarters in the capital city since then. Through ownership changes, Riedesel-Lowe Co. became Riedesel-Reiman Co., Reiman-Wuerth Co., Reiman Construction Co., Engineered Structures of Wyoming, Inc. and finally Reiman Corp., which is owned and operated by Bob Reiman's sons — Tom, Wally and R.C.

The company is committed to professional excellence in construction supervision, subcontractor relations, scheduling, procurement, coordination, claims resolution, bonding, insurance and risk management. Says R.C. Reiman, "We plan to continue building Wyoming and bridging the Rockies well into the future."

American National Bank

Since opening its doors in 1919, American National Bank in Cheyenne has been, according to its logo, "Big enough to deliver, small enough to care."

An early test proved those words true. After World War I, declining livestock values, high feed prices and severe winter weather caused livestock loan defaults and statewide bank failures. Two of the four national banks in Cheyenne were among them. But American National Bank, only a few years old at the time and also closely associated with the livestock industry, remained open.

Changes since those early days include a relocation and many stages of expansion. Having started at 16th and Capitol, the bank moved down the street to a five-story building at 20th and Capitol in 1960. North of the building is a motor bank facility with eight drive-through lanes and two commercial windows. Other additions include four full-service ATM machines and two cash-dispensing machines throughout the community, a branch in the Pointe Frontier Retirement Community, a sales and service center inside Albertson's, and a full-service branch on the F.E. Warren Air Force Base. The newest addition is a branch in Casper, which opened in July of 1999.

The banking industry has also changed considerably in the past 80 years, and American National Bank has stayed on the cutting edge of the developing technology. It was one of the first banks in Wyoming to introduce check imaging, a paper-saving process that all banks are expected to adopt in the future.

What has not changed is the bank's commitment to the community. The bank has been a major contributor to the Cheyenne LEADS, promoting economic development in Cheyenne and Laramie County. It supports area youth groups as well as the Laramie County Community College. The bank has also been a pacesetter for the United Way campaign, and it earned the Gold Award for the sixth consecutive year in 1999.

This community involvement starts at the top. Mark A. Zaback, the CEO, president and chairman of the board, was named Person of the Year for 1999 by the Greater Cheyenne Chamber of Commerce. His work ethic and values infuse the bank and its staff. A strong belief in Cheyenne means that the bank makes every effort to help and promote the city. The 90 bank employees are encouraged to get involved in the community through volunteer efforts, and they are given time to do so during work hours.

Another leader encouraging strong community presence is Donald Sturm, the majority shareholder whose name appears on *Fortune*'s Top 100 list. He believes in community banks that make their decisions independently and locally.

American National Bank is one of Wyoming's largest, with assets of $140 million. Yet it is still very much a hometown bank. The staff knows its customers and goes out and visits them on a monthly basis. The employees' philosophy dictates that they create the kind of place they would want their own kids to work. Staff morale reflects the emphasis on positive motivation and atmosphere at work.

Joining Mark A. Zaback on the board of directors are Gary Mammel, Gus Fleischli, Jay Dee Fox, April Brimmer Kunz, Donald J. Lawler, J. Michael Powers and Robert C. Willits. They, and all the bank's employees, look forward to serving Cheyenne for many more years.

The bank building at 20th and Capitol in Cheyenne

United Bancorporation of Wyoming, Inc.

In an era characterized by mergers creating fewer, larger and often impersonal banks, it is significant that each of the three banks comprising the United Bancorporation of Wyoming has maintained its own identity, integrity and unique style of hometown friendliness. Whether at the Jackson State Bank in Jackson Hole, the Shoshone First Bank in Cody, or the Sheridan State Bank in Sheridan, customers expect and receive exceptional, personalized service, and have access to sophisticated banking services usually found only in larger metropolitan areas.

Dating back to the early 1900s, the Jackson State Bank and Shoshone First Bank are the oldest and largest banks in their respective communities and played significant roles in the growth and development of the Wyoming economy. Founded in 1984, the Sheridan State Bank is now the third-largest bank in that community, and an important resource for its residents. With 220 employees and assets of more than $570 million, UBW is currently the largest bank holding company domiciled in Wyoming.

The driving force behind UBW, and the architect of its successful banking philosophy, is founder, Chairman and CEO W. Richard Scarlett, III. A native of Philadelphia who was raised on a Wyoming ranch, Scarlett graduated from the University of Wyoming with a degree in business administration. His wife Maggie is a Wyoming native and also a graduate of UW. Scarlett has held leadership positions and served on a number of boards including the Teton Music Festival, the University of Wyoming Business College and the Federal Reserve Bank of Kansas City, Denver Branch. He was recognized as a Distinguished Alumnus by UW in 1996.

Each of the UBW banks is managed by a local board of directors whose members have deep roots in the community. "We operate our banks as community banks," explains Senior Vice President David R. Landis. "Each bank has decision-making authority and is supportive of hometown activities and events, giving both time and monetary support to local projects." Each institution strives to make the banking experience a pleasant and comfortable one for the customer, a philosophy that extends to the warm, inviting decors featuring works by local artists.

UBW banks are among the leaders in the use of cutting-edge banking technology, offering access to

Jackson State Bank

services usually found only in larger towns. In addition to seven banking locations and 24 ATMs, the three affiliate banks were the first in Wyoming to offer Online Banking through the Internet, with bill-paying capacity. They are also recognized as high-performance banks by their peers.

In addition, UBW banks were among the first in the state to offer 24-hour automated telephone banking. Additional services include a wide variety of checking, savings and deposit accounts, the VISA® check card, in-house investment centers offering full brokerage services, and personal and business loans. Realizing that mortgage and construction loans fuel community growth, UBW banks are strong real estate lenders that even offer lot financing, a rarity in banking.

Jackson State Bank

Jackson State Bank is the largest member of the UBW family, and the largest and oldest bank in Jackson. Founded in 1914, it was the first bank in Jackson and has always been an integral part of the town. Its formation is arguably one of the key reasons for Jackson's prosperity and growth. In the early 20th century, few people lived year-round in Jackson because of the isolation and harsh winters. The ranchers in the valley decided the best way to encourage full-time residents was to establish reliable, permanent commercial institutions. So with Robert Miller as its first president, $10,000 capital and no reserves, the Jackson State Bank opened its doors on July 22, 1914 in a small rented building on the town square.

When President Hoover ordered the closure of U.S. banks after the stock market crash in 1929, the Jackson State Bank defied the order. The bank officers felt it was crucial to keep commerce flowing in the isolated valley. In the ensuing years, during the worst of the Great Depression, the bank remained open despite small deposits and scarcity of paper currency. Because Jackson was a gambling town, there was however, an ample supply of silver dollars! While many banks across the country failed in the 1930s, the Jackson State Bank survived the greatest financial crisis in American history, due in large part to the grit and determination of its leadership.

Acquired by UBW from the Buchenroth family in 1981, the Jackson State Bank is one of the largest year-round employers in Teton County, with assets of more than $370 million, compared to assets of $50 million in 1978.

Jackson State Bank has a long tradition of making Jackson its first priority, as illustrated by its commitment to St. John's Hospital. In the early 1950s, the town's only

hospital was facing severe financial difficulties and was in danger of closing. The Jackson State Bank not only organized fund-raisers for the hospital, but also covered its checks until the hospital's finances improved.

Jackson State Bank is also committed to providing customers with the newest and most convenient services and products. In a county with only 15,000 full-time residents, the Jackson State Bank has three locations, 13 drive-up banking lanes and 14 ATMs. The West branch has seven drive-up lanes and an ATM, making it one of the largest facilities of its type in the state.

W. Richard Scarlett, III

The first bank in the state to have a Web site, the Jackson State Bank offers an array of big-city services with a small-town flair, including the exchange and transfer of 26 different foreign currencies. And through The Silver Buffalo Club, the bank offers a comprehensive concierge banking service for customers maintaining $100,000 in deposits. Because of Jackson Hole's popularity as a world-renowned resort area, the bank's customers include tourists from all over the world, including Fortune 500 CEOs, dignitaries, movie stars and other celebrities.

Shoshone First Bank

Located in Cody, Wyoming — the town named for Buffalo Bill Cody — and founded in 1901, Shoshone First Bank is the largest and oldest financial institution in Cody. The bank was the idea of Col. Frank J. Williams, a cashier at the First National Bank of Lander who convinced two of the owners, E. Amoretti and S.

Shoshone First Bank

Conant Parks, to open a bank in Cody. In 1901, the bank began operations in the lean-to of the Cody Trading Company, with $10,000 capital. Three months later it moved to new quarters in a building, which, though remodeled and renovated several times, remained its home for 90 years.

As it grew with the town of Cody, the bank also went through several name changes. The original name, Amoretti, Parks and Company became Shoshone National Bank in 1905. Later it merged with First National Bank and became Shoshone First National Bank, and now bears the name Shoshone First Bank. In 1984, it became the second subsidiary of UBW. In 1993, UBW built a new, 28,000-square-foot facility on Sheridan Avenue, just a few blocks from the original location.

With 70 employees and current assets of more than $150 million, Shoshone First Bank offers the latest in full-service banking amenities, and places top priority on providing quality service to each customer. The first bank in Wyoming to open a branch in a grocery store, the bank now boasts three convenient locations, including a second grocery store branch in Powell. In addition to other innovative services, Shoshone First Bank offers an investment center managed by a certified financial planner and provides concierge services through its Silver Buffalo Club.

Sheridan State Bank

The youngest of UBW's banks, Sheridan State Bank was founded in 1984 by Joseph R. and Jerralee A. Lyman in the town of Sheridan at the base of the beautiful Big Horn Mountains. It was originally the Sheridan National Bank and was located on North Main Street. In November 1987, the bank moved to its present location in Sheridan's downtown business district, and eight months later it was purchased by the holding company Drake-Lyman Bancshares, Inc. In 1994, UBW purchased the bank and renamed it Sheridan State Bank.

At the time of the acquisition by UBW, Sheridan State Bank was the fourth-largest bank in Sheridan. After reorganizing the staff and assembling a board of directors from the Sheridan business community, bank services were refocused with an emphasis on commercial, agricultural and real estate financing. As a result, the full-service bank has become a major competitor in Sheridan County and assets have increased 67 percent, from $37 million to $62 million, making it now the third-largest bank in Sheridan.

Sheridan State Bank

First Interstate Bank

In 1893, in the newly created state of Wyoming, the tiny town of Sheridan took a step upward in status and a step forward in the convenience and security of its residents with the establishment of its first bank. Located in the Dutch Lunch Restaurant building, the former restaurant's signs still prominently displayed, the fledgling Bank of Commerce was capitalized at $30,000 and had no president. It had three employees — a cashier, an assistant cashier and a bookkeeper.

Sheridan evidently thought banks were a good thing, as it kept adding them. Thirteen years later, Sheridan boasted six banks. The first was still the biggest, however, with more than twice the assets of any of its rivals. Within another decade the rapidly growing bank had acquired two of its competitors, the Sheridan Banking Company and the Sheridan County Savings Bank, and had moved for the fourth time, into the mammoth Whitney Building, widely regarded as the finest structure in the Northwest. The bank was relegated to the back half of the bottom floor. The rest of the building was occupied by doctors, dentists, lawyers and the Sheridan Chamber of Commerce. No one at the time, of course, had any inkling that one day the Bank of Commerce would own, occupy, and more than once extensively remodel the entire edifice.

The first home of Bank of Commerce, the former Dutch Lunch restaurant building, 1893

When the Depression closed its grim fist around the country, banks across the nation closed their doors. Panicked patrons stood outside those doors, unbelieving that their savings of a lifetime were lost. The Bank of Commerce was a relative eye of calm in this economic tornado, its leaders guiding it sure-footedly through the wreckage. In 1934, in the midst of the chaos, the bank executed the largest single transaction in the city's history, acquiring the Sheridan Trust & Savings Bank. *The Sheridan Post* reported that "a king's ransom" was moved the day of the physical relocation, which was excitingly attended by guards with machine guns and various hand artillery. Service charges at the time included 1 cent for the cashing of cream checks.

As the Depression finally released its hold on the United States, with 85 percent of the population unable to establish bank credit, the Bank of Commerce, now the largest bank in the state, proved itself a bank with a heart and established a Personal Loan Department. Savings bonds, savings stamps and earnings credits made an appearance. A hard-working, young construction engineer named Homer Scott moved to Sheridan to open a branch office for the contracting firm of the Peter Kiewit Company.

Although some years would pass before Homer Scott's life became inextricably intertwined with the Bank of Commerce, the bank it became — the multifaceted banking entity it is today — is largely the result of the vision, foresight and practical sense of this remarkable man. At age 7 Homer Scott was already evidencing the thrift and industry that took him so far, milking six cows morning and night with his small hands and helping daily with milk deliveries around his family's Nebraska

Homer Scott Sr.

farm. As an adolescent and young adult, he sometimes worked as many as three jobs, at whatever work he could find — grocery store clerk, engine wiper on the Burlington Railroad, mechanic's helper, construction laborer on various crews. He worked his way through engineering school, somehow finding time to compete as a top-notch prizefighter, then hooked up with Peter Kiewit to help develop Kiewit's small masonry firm into the huge contracting and mining company it became. He spent his early years in Sheridan immersed in this task.

In the meantime, the Bank of Commerce continued its steady, inexorable growth. In 1945 it changed its relationship with the Whitney Building from lessee to owner. In 1950, its board of directors included the only woman bank director in Wyoming. Assets totaled more than $9.5 million. That year also the bank gave its building a whole new interior, beginning and completing extensive remodeling within the year.

The centerpiece of the bank's new look was an immense, stunning mural depicting the history of the Sheridan area. The artist, Bernard Thomas, finished this 47-by-7.5 foot masterpiece of a scene in 60 days, putting in nearly half a normal work year's worth of hours in that time. His finished creation is rendered in almost inconceivable detail and includes representations of Sheridan's industries, transportation systems, crops, livestock, scenery, notable institutions, and figures of local lore.

By now Homer Scott had long since diversified, both as a key man in the Peter Kiewit Company, which had branched into coal mining as well as construction, and individually, as owner-operator of the Padlock

Ranch near Sheridan. Under his management the Padlock Ranch was soon succeeding on a relative scale to match the Bank of Commerce, and in 1961, having established his business endeavors as concerns so thriving that he could turn his attention to other matters, he accepted an appointment to the board of the Federal Reserve Bank of Kansas City. While so serving, first as member, then as chairman, he discovered he had an interest in and aptitude for banking. In 1967 he joined the Bank of Commerce board of directors and the next year bought the controlling interest in the bank.

Within a year the opening of Sheridan's first drive-through bank marked the beginning of a physical expansion of the Bank of Commerce that would eventually reach near-empire proportions. In-house, the trust department took a leap in growth and MasterCard became available, introducing the novel concept of credit cards. Assets were $23 million. That year Homer Scott received a telegram of congratulations from President Richard Nixon, acknowledging his outstanding contributions to his county and community.

These contributions, and contributions to come, which have made Homer Scott's banks almost synonymous with community action, stemmed from his personal and business values, which took sincere account of the needs of those around him, from his employees to his colleagues to his family to his fellow Sheridan and Wyoming citizens. Homer Scott was a people person. He condensed his credo into a phrase: "We don't have any illusions about being the biggest, but we do want to be the best." People and organizations, he believed, are known not by what they say, but what

First Interstate BancSystem, Inc. board of directors (standing left to right): John Heyneman; Dan Scott; Jim Haugh; Jim Scott, vice chairman; Joel Long; and Homer Scott Jr., chairman (seated left to right): Randy Scott; Lyle Knight, president and COO; and Tom Scott, CEO

of the third Scott generation to participate in bank management.

As part of an unusually thorough sales and service culture training program, First Interstate Bank has memorialized Homer Scott's strategic vision in booklet form for distribution to its employees, some of whom have been with the bank for nearly half a century. The vision in short form is: "To provide a range of financial services which meet or exceed market expectations, to be recognized as clearly superior to our competitors, to meet the needs of our shareholders, to exercise business leadership, to assist in making our communities a better place to live and work, and to nourish a strong and positive corporate culture." This vision, these concepts — based on common sense, fair dealing, and walking the extra mile — have proven a formula for extraordinary success. First Interstate Bank is eagerly and vigorously embarked on its second century of service.

Former Whitney Building, present Sheridan First Interstate Bank building, 1931

they do. Scott, his wife and his banks are famous for their philanthropy, having gifted millions of dollars over the years to better the lives of the people in the communities the banks serve.

In 1984, Bank of Commerce became a franchisee of First Interstate Bank, a California company, and over the next decade and a half witnessed the California parent company's involvement in a boggling series of maneuvers, mergers, takeovers, and other complicated transactions, primarily concerning its corporate banks, rather than its franchise banks. When the flurry finally subsided, the former Bank of Commerce was the sole holder of the First Interstate Bank name.

A glorious centennial celebration marked the bank's 100th birthday in 1993. The festivities culminated in a drawing for the grand prize of a trip for two to anywhere in the Continental United States, Canada or Mexico.

In 1999 First Interstate Bank, with $2.5 billion in assets, is perhaps the largest privately held bank in the country. The Scott family owns 80 percent of its stock, with the remaining 20 percent primarily owned by its directors, officers and employees. Thirty-eight branches describe a far-flung circumference of thousands of square miles in Wyoming and Montana — very different from banks its size in metropolitan areas, where one can almost throw a rock and hit all the branches. Homer Scott's family has become a dynasty in the banking industry. Sons Tom and Homer Jr. (Scotty) are First Interstate Bank's chief executive officer and chairman respectively. Son James is vice chairman and directs the bank and family foundations, disbursing large sums each year to support the banks' communities, with a special emphasis on the Native American communities. Son Dan is on the board of directors and also oversees the family's Padlock Ranch. Grandsons Randy Scott and John Heyneman are board members, marking the advent

Headquarters of First Interstate BancSystem, Inc., a multistate holding company — tallest building in Montana

Big Horn Federal

In the frightening economic climate of 1933, a small group of businessmen from the half dozen sparsely populated towns of northwest Wyoming's Big Horn Basin met to discuss the needs of their growing communities and their families. The construction of new homes was an obvious priority. They set about creating an entity to encourage and facilitate the building of homes in the basin. Their model for the new entity was the earliest form of savings and loans, the cooperatives of the 1800s, and the cornerstone for the model they envisioned was member ownership.

group in the Big Horn Basin spent two years obtaining the required approval and authority and establishing its directorate. Because of the small population and the size and scope of the geographic area to be served, the fledgling institution's charter was approved on the basis that one person from each of the major communities in the Big Horn Basin serve as a director. In 1935 the Big Horn Basin Federal Savings & Loan Association was officially born as a mutual institution — an institution owned by its depositors and borrowers. Then, as now, it provided two essential services: a safe place for savings

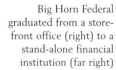

Big Horn Federal graduated from a store-front office (right) to a stand-alone financial institution (far right)

The cooperatives, which came into being long before banking was regulated, were member-owned and member-operated. Participants committed to monthly deposits, and when sufficient monies had accumulated — a paltry few hundred dollars in those days — they could bid to obtain homebuilding funds. The bidder who agreed to the highest interest rate received a loan for the specific purpose of building a house. His repayments, plus the continued contributions of the other members, built up the fund for the next bid.

The Great Depression of the 30s caused the federal government to take stabilizing regulatory measures supportive of financial institutions. Its efforts to mitigate the panicked runs on banks resulted in congressional legislation that put into place the original banking laws that, among other things, backed accounts with insurance. As a result of these new laws, chartering a new financial facility suddenly became more complicated, and the little

(accounts were then insured to $5,000) and affordable mortgage funds for home purchases. By the end of the year its books reflected $100,000 in assets, $35,000 of which came from the U.S. Government and the Federal Home Loan Bank System.

The original home office was situated in Greybull, the central location for the six basin communities — Powell, Thermopolis, Cody, Worland, Lovell and Greybull. For many years it operated part time, sharing office space and employees with a Greybull accounting firm. In 1973 Big Horn Federal graduated to a full-time financial institution. By the mid-70s, the need to expand inspired the first branch office in Powell, followed during the next decade by branches in Thermopolis, Cody, Worland and Lovell. All of these offices, including the home office, came into being as simple store-fronts, small unimposing offices in the middle of the block, serving a limited number of walk-in customers.

Today, five of the six branch locations are site-aesthetic, stand-alone, full-service facilities erected on bank property. The sixth branch, currently a storefront, is slated for conversion to a full service facility soon after the turn of the century.

The bank's name has also metamorphosed over time. The institution has long outgrown its bare beginnings as a simple, straightforward provider of the fundamental services of holding savings and lending monies for residential mortgages. Its present name, Big Horn Federal Savings Bank, more accurately depicts the comprehensive banking services it offers today.

The institution's leaders have never lost sight of the fact that their original charter was for the benefit of the Big Horn Basin communities. Where many similar small-town institutions purchase loans from outside their geographic areas, Big Horn Federal originates loans for the benefit of its customers in the four counties of the Big Horn Basin — Big Horn, Hot Springs, Park and Washakie — estimated population 47,000. Throughout its history, up to and including the present, the bank has been active in its communities. Bank directors, officers and employees are members, directors and officers of local commissions and boards and have helped charter and held office in many new civic and service organizations. Bank personnel coach little leagues, support fine arts and recreation departments and have otherwise contributed to and enhanced the quality of life for the residents of the Big Horn Basin.

One reward for Big Horn Federal's community orientation is its highest-possible Community Reinvestment Act rating of Outstanding by the U.S. Treasury's Office of Thrift Supervision, which has praised the bank's volume of lending as "remarkable." Throughout the regulatory tenure of the Community Reinvestment Act, the bank has maintained this Outstanding rating, a direct result of the bank's lead-

ing status as a provider of loans within its market area. In fact, the bank has consistently ranked highest of all financial institutions in its market area in loans as a percentage of deposits. The bank's percentage of loans to low- and moderate-income borrowers is proportionate to the percentage of families at those income levels.

Independent analysts Bauer Financial and VeriBank also reward the bank with their top ratings, Five Stars Superior and Three Stars Green respectively.

Today, while still faithful to its cooperative spirit of more than 60 years ago, Big Horn Federal has come a long way from its beginnings. From the original $100,000, green eyeshades, pen-and-paper recordkeeping and part-time status in 1935, Big Horn Federal has grown into a sophisticated state-of-the-art electronic bank of $100 million in 1999. No longer limited to savings

and loans, it has expanded its original services from deposit holding and home financing to include checking accounts, credit cards, wire services, safe deposit accounts, ATMs, TeleBanking, Internet banking and loans for agriculture, business and personal needs. Subsidiaries provide insurance and investment services.

The Big Horn Ram logo is proudly displayed and instantly recognized throughout the region of the Big Horn Basin.

Current board, original values — (seated left to right) Dixie M. Cummings, Secretary, Greybull; John J. Coyne Jr., Chairman, President & CEO, Greybull; James A. Linton, Director, Powell; (standing left to right) John B. King, Executive Vice President, Greybull; Hack Jolley, Director, Lovell; Charles N. Stump Jr., Director, Thermopolis; Donald M. Robirds, Director, Cody; and W.R. Shelledy Jr., Director, Worland

Big Horn Federal, serving you with interest

Ed Murray & Sons

A few generations ago, Edward Murray was a college graduate and a professional baseball player with the St. Louis Browns. But when World War I called, he left the team to become a pilot in the Army Air Corps. After the war ended, many young men were bitten by the adventure bug, and Ed and his older brother James, also a military pilot, were no exception.

Bill Murray, co-owner of his family's longtime business

(Far right) Garth Boreczky, co-owner of the business

In 1922, Ed and his wife Mae left their Connecticut home to head west, where Ed joined his brother as a flyer with the post office's brand new airmail service. They were among the first to fly the mail in and out of Cheyenne, Wyoming, and points west.

It wasn't long before Ed and Mae fell in love with Cheyenne and decided to make it their permanent home. Mae felt that Ed could better appreciate their new community from the ground, however, and convinced him to find safer employment.

Meanwhile, it was 1923, and a man named C.W. Riner was celebrating 46 years as owner of Wyoming's first insurance agency. C.W. Riner and Company specialized in fire, plate glass, and accident insurance, as well as noninsurance commodities like coal, wood and feed. Riner was looking to add a new man to the payroll and hired the young Ed Murray.

After a few years of hard work learning his new profession, Ed used his earnings to purchase the business from Riner in 1926 and Ed Murray & Sons was born.

Ed and Mae had three sons, all of whom graduated from the University of Wyoming in Laramie, and joined their father in the family business. By 1956, Bill, Ed Jr. (known as Ned) and Don were co-owners of the insurance business. The elder Murray died in 1971, leaving his three sons to carry on the family tradition.

Only for a brief period in the 1980s was the business owned by someone other than a Murray family member. Robinson-Conner, a now-defunct insurance brokerage, purchased the business in 1983 and made it part of one of the largest insurance agencies in the United States. Around that time Bill retired, but Ned and Don continued to operate the business. A few years later, the two men had an opportunity to purchase the brokerage back from Robinson-Conner. Because of proposed changes to the business that they felt could result in a loss of service to customers, they grabbed the chance. In 1989 the Murray family bought back their business.

Bill died in 1990, and a few years later, both Ned and Don wanted to retire. On January 1, 1996, Bill's son, also named Bill, and his partner Garth Boreczky, became the new owners.

Today, the company's business is focused on property and casualty insurance, with an estimated ratio of 85 percent commercial customers and 15 percent personal customers. It represents eight out of the 10 largest insurers. It is a large provider of medical malpractice insurance, and is a key insurer in the moving and storage industry. The agency also provides unique products to associations such as the Wyoming Liquor Dealers Association, Wyoming Medical Society and others.

The new owners credit the company's longevity and good reputation, combined with their progressive business practices, for making Ed Murray & Sons one of the best performers in the insurance industry today. The company has grown at least five percent annually since the early 1990s. The partners attribute this growth to the agency's quality products and service staff, and to its policy of staying competitive with agencies in large cities. Efficiency is one of the best ways to be competitive, so the company has invested heavily in state-of-the-art computer hardware and software, making daily procedures less paperwork-intensive than it is for many of its competitors.

Murray and Boreczky have worked hard to provide service to people in small communities and rural areas that don't have the same buying clout as those in larger cities. They recognize that the higher the annual premium volume the company generates, the more clout it will have with the big insurance companies for good rates and fair settlements. That is why in 1997 Ed Murray & Sons, the oldest insurance brokerage in the state, purchased Wyoming's second oldest brokerage, Barnard Insurance. Barnard has offices in Casper and Douglas, Wyoming. Combined, these offices have an annual premium volume of $20 million.

Soon the partners hope to make Ed Murray & Sons a regional brokerage. The acquisition of Barnard Insurance has moved the company in that direction. They plan to add offices in Northern Colorado, Western Nebraska, Idaho, Montana, South Dakota and Utah.

Ed Murray & Sons has been deeply involved with the community of Cheyenne outside of its role as an insurance brokerage. The elder Bill Murray spent many years in service in both local and state government. He and the rest of the family have contributed financially and through volunteer labor to many Cheyenne institutions, such as the annual Frontier Days festival. Today, Boreczky and the younger Murray serve on a variety of community agency boards and with insurance agency organizations. The company's employees also are heavily involved in community activities.

The business has been headquartered within a six-block area of downtown Cheyenne since the beginning, moving only a handful of times as it outgrew its office

space. The younger Murray attributes the company's longevity and stability to the "New England values" instilled in the family by his grandparents Ed and Mae. Order, propriety, honesty, integrity and commitment to customers are values that the third generation of this family-owned business feel still have importance today.

A framed sign on the office's boardroom wall reads: "Blessed are those who sweeten the bitter pill of providence, for they shall be called insurance people." It is unknown if any of the new generation of Murrays or Boreczkys will grow up to provide insurance to soften the blows of fate under the banner of Ed Murray & Sons. The partners feel that the business will flourish because the approximately two dozen employees care about the company's history as much as its future. They'll carry on the tradition long after the current generation has retired.

Ed Murray & Sons' headquarters in downtown Cheyenne

Ed Murray Sr., (seated) is surrounded by his sons in this picture from the company's photo archives. Standing left to right are Bill Murray Sr., Ed Murray Jr. and Don Murray

Hilltop National Bank

When Hilltop National Bank opened its doors July 27, 1964, Casper was the financial hub of Wyoming, boasting five banks.

Original organizers Don and Jim Chapin, Hardy Ratcliff, Bill Barnard, John Hoover, L.V. Stafford, Tom Sandison and Tom Hockaday opened the bank with just $350,000 in capital. Five employees offered more than a dozen services to mostly east-side customers from the original location in the corner of Hilltop Shopping Center. Indeed, an early advertising slogan dubbed it "The Young Bank for Young Adults."

By 1971, the bank had grown to 26 employees and nearly $8 million in assets. It needed more space, and during the next year Hilltop added 3,500 square feet. The addition doubled the number of teller windows, allowing for yet another customer convenience — drive-up banking. Hilltop National Bank was the first bank to add a modern pneumatic drive-up system and was considered to be the most progressive bank in town. The local media covered the first customer to use the drive-up banking system as a gala event.

N.P. Van Maren Jr., chairman of the board, speaks of those early days as a time of slow and tenuous growth, long hours and difficult decisions. "You spent all your time putting out fires," he says. Some banks had jumped in to the oil industry with a vengeance, dominating the lucrative commercial lending market.

Hilltop had always found itself in the position of competing with Goliath, developing and keeping a philosophy of customer service that would sustain it where the others failed. Though regarded by some as overly conservative in the boom days of the 70s, Hilltop was better positioned to assist the many small businesses verging on bankruptcy during the 80s. Robert Sutter joined Hilltop in 1976, remaining there today as president. He says that Hilltop has a wise lending philosophy, exchanging unsustainable growth rates for a steady 15 percent. "Maybe this is nothing more than a function of having people around for a long time. Bigger banks may have access to more funds, but we have been able to weather the ups and downs."

In 1977, Casper oilman H.A. "Dave" True Jr. visualized the benefits of bringing together his businesses and a community bank, and as a result, purchased Hilltop. Van Maren and Sutter agree that the decision was a good one. The two entities shared the same fundamental principles and the transition was seamless. Under True's guidance, the assets expanded, and the search began for a new main office headquarters. Shortly thereafter, a modern precast concrete structure was erected to house the expanded services. The headquarters are light, airy and feature regular art shows.

The early 1980s saw the economic pendulum swing from boom to bust almost overnight as the uranium

Original main office of Hilltop National Bank

Country Club Road
main office

industry crashed, and the oil and gas rig count dropped dramatically. "The Trues gave moral as well as factual support," says Van Maren. "They had a lot of insight as to what was going on in the oil industry. Because of Dave True, we avoided many of the problems the other banks experienced with their oil industry lending."

By 1985, just as the businesses in Casper were beginning to take some shaky steps towards recovery, a drop in oil prices added the second recession of the decade. Most banks reacted fearfully, refusing to lend money to their customers. Hilltop again maintained a middle-of-the-road philosophy. A local CPA noted that the bank's reputation went from "the most conservative in town to the most aggressive in town," when really the philosophy hadn't changed at all. "The goal has always been to not just be here today but to be here tomorrow," says Sutter. Hilltop has developed a reputation as a reliable source for small business with sound ideas, known statewide as the "Source for Financial Straight Talk."

Under its holding company, in 1981 the bank added its second location, Mountain Plaza National Bank, which is now a branch of Hilltop National Bank. Three more branch offices were added in the 1990s including a Glenrock office, a downtown office and a drive-up motor bank. The staff has increased to 140, and a recent seven-figure investment has been made to maintain progressive technological advances.

Looking at the nuances of the community and anticipating the needs of its customers, Hilltop was the first bank in the region to introduce a check imaging product called *SnapShot Checking*, a technological advancement in checking account transactions. As with drive-up banking nearly 30 years before, once again, Hilltop was ahead of the curve. Gary Trapkus, vice president of marketing, says the 30 percent market share Hilltop enjoys means the bank is able to offer choices. "We're a nice size. We're large enough to be able to provide the new services the customers require, but not so big that the customer is lost in the technology."

Through the gradual evolution of Casper's economy, the company has been able to diversify its asset base and offers many banking options to its customers. "As technology changes, we will continue to take advantage of the innovations and offer our customers up-to-date banking convenience," says Trapkus.

The board of directors is made up of a broad cross-section of local business owners, including Bill Barnard, one of the original members. Decisions are based on local conditions, and a large staff allows the bank to be involved in nearly every facet of the community.

It's unusual for banking institutions to enjoy the kind of continuity Hilltop is noted for, down to the name. "Just the fact that we have had the same name for 35 years is amazing in and of itself," says Sutter. N.P. Van Maren notes, "When you're working hard, but you're enjoying it, you're successful. That's the best of times I think. Creating sensitivity to what goes on in central Wyoming is Hilltop National Bank's specialty. No doubt it will continue to be the premier bank in central Wyoming."

Norwest Bank

The roots of Wyoming's Norwest Banks date back to the early 1900s, with the origin of Wyoming National Bank of Casper in 1914. Wyoming National observed as its clientele grew from basically a livestock town with a population of 3,000 to an oil boomtown boasting a populace of more than 20,000.

Former Governor of Wyoming Bryant B. Brooks and other community leaders, seeing the need for a secure banking institution in Casper, procured a private bank with the initial capital of $50,000. By year's end, deposits at Wyoming National totaled more than $270,000.

Soon after its inception, Wyoming National outgrew its existing site and was relocated. The new bank was

In 1921, Wyoming National Bank relocated to the Midwest Building at Second and Wolcott in Casper.

situated in Casper's Midwest Building, the largest office building in Wyoming at the time. Soon after, Wyoming's thriving economy, complemented by the oil boom, necessitated the annexation of five national and two state banks.

By 1950, Wyoming National was extensively remodeled to accommodate its ever-growing clientele. Seven years later, it was renovated again. Within the 19-year period from 1946-1963, the bank's assets increased from about $15,900,000 to $59,115,000. Wyoming National prevailed until 1970, when it was purchased by a small group of Wyoming citizens who created the Wyoming National Corporation.

In the early 1980s, Wyoming National Corporation acquired the First National Bank and Trust Company of Cheyenne, one of the oldest chartered banks in the state.

A decade later, the Norwest Corporation requisitioned Wyoming National Corporation, then the second-largest finance system in the state in terms of banking assets.

Concurrently, Norwest initiated its slogan, *To the Nth Degree*, proffering the highest degree of financial services obtainable to its customers. Wyoming's Norwest Banks have since lived up to that maxim.

In October of 1998, the Norwest Corporation merged with Wells Fargo & Company, which is now a wholly owned subsidiary of Norwest. In 1978, Norwest's assets were valued at $11 billion. Twenty years later, following the merger, the company boasts 61,000 stores nationally and 15 million customers. Norwest is now the seventh-largest banking corporation in the United States, with $202 billion in assets.

Although Norwest will officially be named Wells Fargo by the year 2000, the quality of its financial services will not change. To date, Norwest is rated No. 1 in the nation in mortgage lending. Norwest Mortgage, Inc. offers low down payments, personalized mortgage counseling and quick loan decisions. The corporation also has a consumer lending facility, Norwest Financial, in every state.

Included with Norwest's professional services are: online banking and the upcoming online bill pay feature with an e-mail option for customers' queries; four convenient savings plans; 24-hour phone banking; four distinct checking account options; home equity loans — and a great deal more.

Wyoming's banking system has grown to exceed the dreams of its financial forefathers. It is proud to have Norwest as part of its heritage and pleased that Norwest can so comprehensively fulfill all the financial demands of Wyoming's citizens.

Since 1969 SafeCard has been the leader in providing credit card registration, credit report monitoring, travel reservations and other services through credit card issuers. More than 125 clients and 10 million of its customers are served by SafeCard, the first company of its kind, providing a solid foundation for the company's future growth.

SafeCard's service programs are varied but have several advantages in common, including reasonable price, universal appeal, convenience, money and time savings, and value.

The year 1992 will go on record as the most eventful for SafeCard in its 30-year history with the move of its headquarters and operations from Fort Lauderdale, Florida, to Cheyenne, Wyoming. Realizing that people are key to the success of any company, the move was predicated on the strong work ethic of the people of the West and the excellent quality of life. Given the highly sensitive and confidential nature of SafeCard's business, employee loyalty is essential. These are among the many reasons SafeCard chose to move its operations to Cheyenne.

In 1996, CUC International, one of the leading online consumer services with a strong presence in Internet commerce, acquired SafeCard. CUC, a consumer-services membership company, linked consumers to a huge array of products and services through home shopping, travel, dining, automotive, financial and other programs via telephone and through the rapidly emerging World Wide Web.

A merger in 1997 between HFS Inc., a leading service provider in the travel and real estate industries, and CUC International created SafeCard's current parent company, the Cendant Corporation. Headquartered in New York City, Cendant has more than 30,000 employees and operates in 100 countries. Its financial strength, industry leadership and growth potential provide excellent opportunities for employees.

SafeCard's 550 employees occupy a 145,000-square-foot facility located on 14 acres in the center of Cheyenne. Customer service representatives for the aforementioned products respond to incoming calls 24 hours a day, 365 days a year. Departments that support customer service activities include finance, member services, fulfillment, information technology and office services. SafeCard is proud of its employees, secure in the knowledge that each member receives personal service from polite and helpful staff.

SafeCard is happy to be firmly entrenched in the community of Cheyenne. Proud to be a good corporate neighbor, SafeCard and its employees are actively involved in numerous charitable events, such as the Relay for Life, the March of Dimes WalkAmerica and the Cheyenne Frontier Days Challenge Rodeo. Fund-raising

SafeCard's state-of-the-art 145,000-square-foot facility sits on 14 acres in the center of Cheyenne.

events, such as the Stride Learning Center's Men's Culinary Cup, and employee participation in Habitat for Humanity enable the company to give something back to the community. SafeCard is honored to be a part of Progress and Prosperity: The Next Dimension, a campaign to raise economic development funds for Laramie County to improve infrastructure, work force development and quality of life for residents.

Optimistic about a bright future, SafeCard looks forward to providing top-quality service to its customers, challenge and opportunity to its employees, and financial performance to its shareholders in the years to come.

Natrona County School Employees Federal Credit Union

For more than 60 years, the city of Casper has been home to the Natrona County School Employees Federal Credit Union. Formed by Natrona County schoolteachers in 1936, its first repository was a cigar box; its first location the back of someone's truck. By the end of the first year, there were 100 members and the operation had found a home in the basement of McKinley School. In the ensuing years, it grew slowly but steadily, necessitating a move to its first independent site at 12th and Jackson streets in the 1970s. Continued growth took the credit union to 1301 S. Wisconsin Street in 1984, and then to its present location on Werner Court in 1995. The staff — originally one

employee — also grew to 18 people. And the membership has expanded from a group that was made up exclusively of teachers to include virtually all education-related groups in the area: Casper College faculty and students, day-care workers, YMCA employees and Natrona County School District employees.

Today, the Natrona County School Employees Federal Credit Union is a full-service financial institution with nearly 8,000 members and more than $30 million in assets. It offers checking, savings and money market accounts, as well as Individual Retirement Accounts, overdraft protection, ATMs, debit and Visa cards. It also provides a wide variety of financial assistance in the form of mortgage, automobile, consumer, debt consolidation

and home equity loans. The National Credit Union Administration has consistently given a superior rating to the Casper institution, and the independent evaluator *Bauer Financial Reports* gave it a five-star rating — the highest possible — as one of the safest credit unions in the United States.

In the era of mega-mergers among financial institutions, the credit union has remained true to its roots, providing financial services in a reliable and genuinely personable manner. It is a quintessential hometown institution, Casper-born and -bred, as it were, and staffed by people who are its members' neighbors. As a nonprofit, member-owned entity, it is dedicated not to quarterly earnings but to serving the community. "Our total focus is on helping our members," explains Jackie Hotle, the credit union's CEO, "not on making a profit."

The credit union contributes to numerous local and national charities. And it contributes to the community in a significant way by helping members realize their financial goals — to build or buy a home, or save for their children's education or their own retirement. This is accomplished not only through an excellent program of traditional financial services but also through education, which is an integral part of the credit union's mission. It is reaching out to the next generation as well, working with the school district to teach students financial responsibility and financial skills such as how to maintain a checking account, how to apply for a loan, and the value of saving.

Because its definition of "helping" is a broad one, and because most of the staff members are long-term employees who have come to know the members and their families, the Natrona County School Employees Federal Credit Union's relationship with the community is a special one. "We like our members and we show it," Jackie Hotle affirms. "Once a member, always a member."

Crum Electric Supply Company

Crum Electric Supply, Wyoming's leader in multi-branch electrical distribution, began in 1976 in what President and CEO Dave Crum affectionately calls his "little tin shed" in Mills, Wyoming. "Mary and I started from scratch. It was just me and an answering service, with Mary teaching 4th grade to support our young family of four," Crum says.

Crum Electric has since evolved into one of the largest corporations in the Northern Rockies, with the diminutive shed in Mills expanding into nine branches — one in South Dakota, two in south-central Idaho and six in Wyoming: Casper, Cody, Gillette, Evanston, Rock Springs and Cheyenne. The company's major markets are industrial, commercial, residential and institutional.

The reason for Crum's tremendous success? Diversity, for one. Wyoming's economy has begun to diversify, and Crum Electric Supply is meeting the demands of the state's ever-changing commerce. Crum also attributes his success to a roster of nearly 3,000 steadfast customers, an invaluable asset to his company's prosperity.

Wyoming's oil boom in the late 1970s spurred an industrious progression for Crum Electric. However, Crum ascended to the top of the corporate ladder, only to topple over the summit with Wyoming's depression of the mid-1980s. The economic collapse taught Crum the "rights of survivorship," and gave the business the upsurge it needed to persevere.

The shifting economy in the state has created a broad range of markets and Crum Electric has seized the new opportunities.

In 1982, Dave Crum received the Small Businessman of the Year award in Wyoming. Two years later, Crum Electric was recognized by *Inc. Magazine* as one of the Top 100 fastest-growing private companies in the United States. Ten years later, manufacturers voted Crum Electric Supply the 1994 Western Distributor of the Year.

Crum Electric Supply was also featured in *Electrical Wholesaling* in 1998 for the addition of a new data communications division. The new division has all the electronic products necessary for the installation of LANs, or local area networks, and other data and voice communications systems. The new products accommodate not only home and office computers, but are used in the automation of industrial processes.

Crum says the technology of electronics and electrical equipment are merging, and the difference is becoming less and less apparent. Jeff Hockin, Crum Electric's vice president and general manager says, "It is very exciting to be involved in such a vibrant business at a time when technology is rapidly changing the products we sell and the way we conduct business."

Another aspect of Crum Electric's success is the availability of and easy access to its products. The company's state-of-the-art computer and Extranet communication system allows customers and employees immediate access to its entire inventory. Crum's customers can communicate via e-mail or by visiting the corporation's Web site, placing orders, soliciting quotations, or requesting specific product information online.

Crum Electric's products, too, lend credence to the company's reputation as the No. 1 electrical supply distributor in the Northern Rocky Mountain area. The company's product basket includes: transformers and motor starters, conduits, fittings, lamps, ballasts, micro switches, meters and test instruments, wiring devices, and most every kind of fixture, gadget or component necessary in the cybernetic industry.

Crum Electric Supply Company adheres to its maxim, and truly allows its customers to "Plug Into Quality."

(From left to right) David M. Crum, technical sales specialist; Jim Roden, operations manager; Mary Crum, secretary/treasurer; Jeff Hockin, vice president and general manager; David H. Crum, president

Unicover Corporation

When thinking of Wyoming exports, oil, gas and cattle come to mind, but probably not postage stamps, coins or other collectibles. However, since 1968, these are just what the Unicover Corporation has marketed and exported from its headquarters in Cheyenne, Wyoming.

Unicover's philatelic and numismatic customers are concentrated in the United States and Canada. Its market includes 38,000 cities, towns and villages, housing 7 million stamp collectors and 14 million coin collectors. Hundreds of thousands of individual hobbyists purchase items from Unicover each year. These customers receive information about the latest collectible coins and stamps through Unicover's widely distributed catalogs. They can also research potential purchases and order directly from the company's Web site.

Unicover is one of five U.S. companies that is a security printer of postage stamps. Other than facilities operated by the federal government, the Cheyenne plant prints more stamp designs than almost any other plant in the nation. Although stamps and coins are low-tech items, Unicover uses modern, high-tech equipment employing efficient digital proofing, plating, printing, perforating, packaging and distribution to create and market high-quality products.

Marketing and shipping collectibles is a huge endeavor, but Unicover does not stop here. It commissions national and international artists to create original artwork that complements the collectible postage stamps and coins. The artwork is printed on the First Day Cover, which also features the stamp, the first day of issue postmark and authoritative historical information about the stamp. Fleetwood, a company that started creating much-admired First Day Covers in 1929, formed the core of Unicover in 1968. Unicover continues to manufacture First Day Covers with the Fleetwood imprint, giving today's hobbyists the opportunity to possess this highly valued collectible.

Unicover now produces First Day Covers for every new stamp issued by the United States and the United Nations, and for selected stamps of virtually every other nation. The First Day Cover created in 1993 to accompany the U.S. Elvis Presley commemorative stamp sold more copies than any other Cover in history.

Unicover's facility is a modern, 100,000-square-foot facility on the outskirts of Cheyenne.

Unicover also serves customers other than individual collectors. The postal administrations of France, Russia, China, New Zealand, Australia, the Marshall Islands, Belgium, Sweden, Germany and Slovenia are all Unicover customers. When the People's Republic of China was opened to international trade in the late 1970s, Unicover was one of the first companies to enter into a contractual agreement with that nation. The U.S. government is also a steady customer, as is the State of Wyoming, for which Unicover prints and distributes tourist information and other materials.

Also popular with collectors are Unicover's coin packages. Although the company does not mint coins, it markets them on behalf of its many worldwide governmental customers. Coins are marketed individually or in thematic packages. As with stamps, Unicover's emphasis is on new issues, minted in limited quantities, which are offered at original issue or face-value prices, in proof or uncirculated condition. Some of Unicover's collectible products combine coins, stamps and postmarks.

Co-founder and President James A. Helzer wants Unicover to be a "single solution company" for all types of customers. For the philatelist and numismatist, that means stamps and coins, First Day Covers, albums, publications and accessories are all available from one source. For governmental customers, products can be marketed, sold and shipped from a single location.

Unicover strives to create a quality product that collectors will treasure...

To deliver such a diversified range of services, Unicover has a 100,000-square-foot facility, completed in 1979, which houses approximately 170 employees. Its printing plant operates two to three shifts a day, seven days a week.

Running a company with a $4 million payroll in a city of 50,000 can be challenging. Many companies of Unicover's size might be tempted to locate in more populated cities where there is a large pool of skilled labor. Unicover originally located in Cheyenne because it was Helzer's home. He and Executive Vice President James A. Willms admit they've needed to be "creative" to overcome the disadvantages of time and location. But they feel that Cheyenne offers more advantages than disadvantages, like being central to the time zones where their customers are concentrated, as well as making telephone contact, shipping and other aspects of customer service efficient.

Although Cheyenne's labor pool is small, its people have a strong work ethic and possess other core Wyoming values: loyalty, honesty, sincerity, commitment, enterprise and self-reliance. Helzer and Willms believe Unicover has succeeded in the marketplace because the organization itself is a model of these core values.

Unicover's success has had a strong impact on the local economy.

Besides providing well-paying jobs, the company generates money from outside the state. Approximately 90 percent of what it produces and sells is exported to customers outside Wyoming. That means that most of the money that flows into the Cheyenne area is new money, not simply "recycled" from one business to the next.

Unicover sees its business evolving. It plans to continue serving the individual collector, but acknowledges that since the late 1980s product development and fulfillment for other enterprises have grown dramatically, and now account for approximately one-third of the company's business. It expects that proportion to increase in the next few years.

Stamp and coin collecting have long been popular hobbies, and Unicover sees developing new hobbyists as part of its role in the collectibles industry. People collect because they want to own something of beauty and value. Unicover strives to create a quality product that collectors will treasure while providing an important service in a diversified but rapidly shrinking world. "We sell art, history, testaments to culture," Willms explains. "We help nations show people what they are all about."

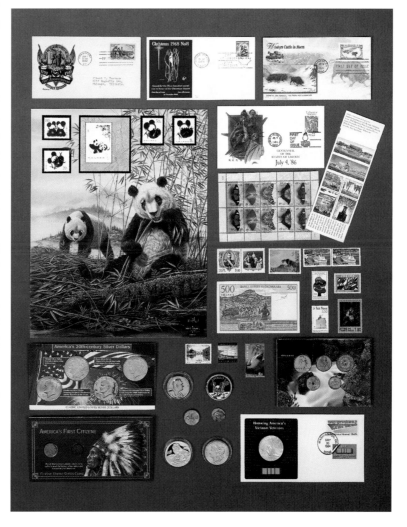

A collage of Unicover's products marketed to coin and stamp collectors

Wyoming Machinery Company

Wyoming Machinery is the authorized Caterpillar dealer for 16 counties in Wyoming. It is a family-owned-and-managed business, marketing products built by Caterpillar through a sales and service agreement. The main store is located in Casper, with branch stores in Gillette and Cheyenne.

Wyoming Machinery is a product of two predecessor companies: Wortham Machinery, the Caterpillar Dealer for Wyoming prior to 1969, and Wheeler Machinery Company, the Caterpillar Dealer for Utah. Richard E. Wheeler, current CEO of the company, represents the third generation of Wheelers to hold the Caterpillar franchise. Wheeler's son, Rich, hopes to become the family's fourth generation of Caterpillar dealers.

The company as it is known today had its beginning in the fall of 1969. New facilities were constructed in Cheyenne in 1972, Casper in 1976, and Gillette in 1978. The Gillette facilities have been expanded twice and the Cheyenne shop has doubled. The company grew in employees from less that 50 in 1969 to over 400 in 1980.

The demise of the uranium industry and the slump in oil exploration during the early 1980s precipitated a dramatic drop in sales and resultant downsizing of the company. Employment fell below 200 employees in 1987, which was also the low point in sales volume. Wyoming coal mining in the 1990s provided growth opportunity bringing sales back to 1980 levels and employment to 340 people.

Company headquarters in Casper

The Caterpillar product line comprises 25 families of earthmoving, paving, compaction and agricultural machinery, material handling lift trucks, and a broad range of engines.

The primary market for the company's products are mining, construction and governmental. The mining market demands track-type tractors, wheel tractors, off-highway trucks, excavators, motor graders, front shovels, scrapers and wheel loaders. The contractor's call is for track-type tractors, motor graders, excavators, scrapers, off-highway trucks, soil compactors, integrated tool carriers, backhoe loaders, wheel loaders, compactors and pavers. Cities, counties and state governments have a need for track-type tractors, motor graders, landfill compactors, loaders, integrated tool carriers and backhoe loaders. Mining utilizes the largest machines and represents the largest dollar-volume opportunity. Caterpillar machinery has long been a favorite with contractors and local government bodies. Other machines that have limited markets in Wyoming are belted track-type tractors and combines for agriculture, log loaders and skidders for forestry, pipelayers, track loaders and articulated trucks.

Wyoming Machinery Company is also the distributor of Load King Trailers, light plants, Multiquip air compressors, electric generators and compactors. Additionally, they sell many attachments manufactured by others for use on Caterpillar machines.

The company sells and leases new and used machinery and new Caterpillar parts, and provides trained technicians to accomplish repairs and perform warranty services. Product support capability ranges from the most basic service and adjustments to complete tear-down and rebuilding.

President and CEO Richard Wheeler says, "This is a great business to be in. We represent the best products. We have a uniquely amicable relationship with Caterpillar. Our customers are honest, hard-working, up-front kind of people and our employees are family. We have loyal, conscientious, dedicated associates. There is a bit of a little boy left in all of us that we never completely grow out of. We like the machinery and we still like to see it move dirt."

Vision Graphics, Inc.

On a spotless floor in a spacious building in northern Colorado, a high-tech printing press hums busily. Barely out of packing crates, the German-made, six-color Man Roland is flicking out huge sheets of brightly inked paper at a rate of 15,000 an hour. A beautiful brochure for a mountain golf course is taking shape, and Mark Steputis is pleased. As president of the company started by his uncle in Cheyenne in 1952, Steputis sees Vision Graphics, Inc. as a regional printing power, serving Wyoming capably, but competing elsewhere as well. With yearly sales increases of 40 percent in the late 1990s, the firm is on its way to that reality.

The business began in a downtown Cheyenne office building. Francis Brooks ran a profitable one-room employment agency there, but the focus changed when he bought a mimeograph machine to replicate his office forms. Soon he had more calls for copy work than job or worker inquiries, so he sold the agency and opened a printing business called Frontier Letter Shop.

Although mimeograph machines are now a forgotten technology, they were a staple in short-run printing in the 1950s. Laboriously typing the required stencils himself, Brooks made $36 in his first month as a printer. Eventually he involved a friend, LeClercq Jones, and in 1959 they moved the shop (by then known as Frontier Printing and Mailing Co.) to the firm's main location of today on West Lincolnway. Brooks invested in an A.B. Dick press, which soon paid for itself in increasing sales, and which remained in production for two decades. Earnings were invested in new equipment and facilities, including a blueprint service to serve the needs of engineers installing Atlas missile sites around Warren Air

Force Base, a development that greatly expanded Cheyenne's economy. Tireless workers, Brooks and Jones served well the printing needs of local businesses, government offices, the University of Wyoming in Laramie and, especially in the 1980s, the area's financial institutions. The name was again changed in 1972 to Frontier Printing, Inc.

Steputis began working for his uncle in 1986. Born and raised in Southern California, he had been a marketer for Aetna Life Insurance Company, but he left that position to test his business instincts in the less complicated world of southeast Wyoming. He began as a salesman for Brooks. By 1991, Steputis was made vice president of the firm. In that same year, Brooks bought an adjacent store building, had it razed and installed a four-color Heidelberg 72VP press in a modern building he and Steputis erected on the site. This mechanical upgrade helped generate a seven-fold revenue increase in six years. In 1994, the firm became known as Vision Graphics, Inc.

With prospects improving, Vision Graphics has bought more Lincolnway property. According to Steputis, however, available downtown real estate is limited. For survival in the now quick-paced Rocky Mountain business world, he says, mid-sized printers have two choices: downsize or upsize. His choice is to grow. By continually reinvesting in technology, selling aggressively and delivering well-printed materials "a day sooner" than competitors, he expects to triple sales volume. "My uncle built this business with sheer determination and fortitude," Steputis says. "I plan to do the same in expanding it."

Francis Brooks, left, and Mark Steputis are pleased with the work of their new Heidelberg 72VP speedmaster press in 1991.

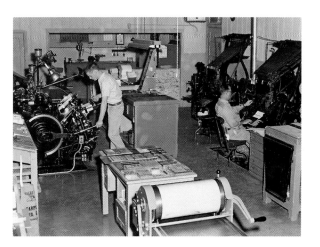

Frontier Printing & Mailing Co. workers operate a letter press and linotype equipment in 1964.

Waterworks Industries Inc.

In virtually every community — urban, suburban or rural — utility companies deliver water for household and commercial use, and then take away the sewage for processing and disposal. This is accomplished through a largely unseen network of equipment, products and technical systems. In much of Wyoming, these water/wastewater transmission systems are supplied by Waterworks Industries Inc. Founded in 1971 by G.W. "Jerry" Russell, who began with only an idea, $5,000 in borrowed capital and a single vacant room in a moving company warehouse, Waterworks has persevered and grown into one of the state's largest suppliers in the field.

G.W. "Jerry" Russell, founder and president of Waterworks Industries Inc.

Waterworks Industries distributes virtually every piece of equipment or system needed to transport water from its source — mainly water treatment plants or wells — to the end user. The company also supplies the gravity sewer pipe and equipment that transports the wastewater discharge to the lagoon or sewage treatment plant. It provides such items as brass fittings, clamps and couplings, ductile iron pipe and fittings, PVC pipe, valves, water meter equipment and fire hydrants. It also sells a wide variety of engineered pump systems and sewage lift stations, including centrifugal/submersible pumps, slurry pumps, sewage grinder systems, and solar pumps for watering agricultural stock. As a manufacturer's rep and distributor, Waterworks sells the products of approximately 30 top-of-the-line manufacturers. "We represent only the very best in the field," Jerry Russell explains. That includes such companies as Mueller, Tyler, Griffin, Sensus, Smith-Blair, ETI, Gorman-Rupp, Patterson, Cornell and Warren Rupp.

Waterworks Industries Inc. has developed relationships with a wide-ranging and multifaceted market during its first 28 years, dealing with municipalities, contractors, commercial institutions, power plants, mining companies, and rural water and sewer systems. From its Casper office, it serves all of Wyoming, as well as the Nebraska panhandle and western South Dakota; a branch office in Billings, Montana handles engineered pump systems for that state. The company, like other companies that are intent on staying ahead of their competitors, is computerized in most facets of the operation, in the office as well as in the field.

Over the years, Waterworks has grown to 20 employees, including eight outside sales and service personnel, and two inside marketing employees. Led by Jerry Russell and vice presidents Ed Sommers, Joe Norfolk and Buck Patterson, it is a unique and expert group of people who are skilled in a variety of areas, including pump hydraulics, electronics, sales and technical services. The group also works with consulting engineers in the design and application of specialized equipment. Waterworks also makes a substantial investment on an ongoing basis for its employees' continuing education. "You can't be complacent," Russell remarks. "Our field is always changing because of engineering and product advancement — and because of government regulation. We make it a point to keep abreast of all of the changes. It's one of the things that gives us a competitive edge."

Not surprisingly, Waterworks Industries has earned a reputation as a solid, progressive and ethical company, one with demonstrable expertise in an increasingly complex field. Its business may not be glamorous, but it is certainly vital, especially in a region with great stretches of undeveloped land between towns and cities. In the coming years, it will grow as Wyoming grows — slowly but steadily, on a well-planned course.

Westech/Wotco

Western Technology Services International, Inc., ("Westech") one of the world's leading steel fabrication companies, originated in 1938 in Laramie, Wyoming, as a subsidiary of Manning Drilling. It was named Western Oil Tool Company, or Wotco, and was launched to support the state's increased oil and gas industry.

In 1940 the company relocated to Mills, Wyoming, at the present site of Wotco. Within 10 years, Wotco had expanded its facilities to include Williston, North Dakota, Rangely, Colorado, and Snyder, Texas, while also incorporating a mobile machining facility for servicing drilling projects on site.

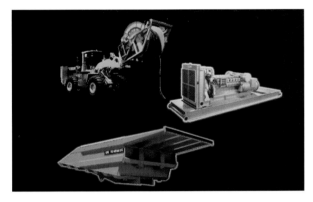

The decline of the oil industry, offset by tremendous growth in the mining and construction industries in Wyoming, induced Wotco's management to expand their machine shops into metal fabrication and engineering design for custom industrial products. Wotco began developing and producing new products and services for those new Wyoming industries.

Through the introduction of new Wotco products, a relationship was established with Caterpillar, and by the late 1960s, Wotco began manufacturing components for the crawler tractors for Caterpillar, Inc. The early 1970s yielded the design and manufacture of 100- and 150-ton coal wagons, and the introduction of the new 85-ton trucks, which led to Caterpillar's selection of Wotco as the "Approved Source" for the bodies of these new trucks. To date Wotco has produced more than 7,500 truck bodies ranging from 50-ton to over 300-ton that have been shipped worldwide.

Westech/Wotco is involved with the design and initial production of many new and unique products such as: Auger Scraper for Caterpillar; Large Sugar Cane Wagons and Pineapple Trailers for Hawaii; a special Elevating Scraper in New Zealand; Cable Reels; and Truck Bodies and Tailgates for any application and any brand truck. Wotco has custom engineered products for the mining, construction, agricultural, petroleum and sanitary landfill industries worldwide. In 1988 Wotco became the first Wyoming company to receive the President's "E-Award" for Excellence in Exports.

In 1985 Wotco was purchased by Wotco employees through the means of an ESOP, or Employee Stock Ownership Plan, and Wotco became 100 percent employee-owned.

The parent company, Westech, was formed in 1992, and plans were formulated to establish an additional manufacturing plant. Three years later, Global Mfg. Inc. was founded near Charleston, South Carolina.

Today Westech's strategically placed manufacturing facilities, with more than 300,000 square feet of manufacturing space, can accommodate the production and delivery of its medium/heavy metal fabrications to any major city in the world. The company primarily champions Caterpillar products such as truck bodies and attachments, and the assemblages of large-engine generator sets. Wotco also produces drag-line buckets, shovel dippers and front-end loader buckets for ESCO Corp.; sub-assemblies for CMI Corp.; and is a certified supplier to many other major OEMs in the mining and construction industries.

Westech supports Wyoming's economy through Wotco, employing more than 250 machinists, grinders, welders, painters, and an extensive shipping and receiving department. Westech has a catalogue of permanent clientele and a steady production ratio.

Since its inception, Westech has been a boon to Wyoming's economy and the production industry of rugged, heavy equipment, confirming the aphorism that its "manufacturing excellence is built-in."

Cable Reel Attachment, Generator Set and Ultra Lite Mining Body are a few of the many products manufactured by Westech.

Wotco manufacturing facility on the banks of the North Platte River in Mills, Wyoming

Coliseum Motors & Big Wyoming

Few businesses can claim almost 100 years of serving the public — especially in a state that is barely 100 years old. Such longevity is attained only by companies that stand above the rest in product, ownership, employees and attitude. The Coliseum Motor Company can legitimately make that claim, and also has the distinction of having conducted business in the same location for its entire existence. The record of its ingenuity, perseverance and neighborliness mirrors the pioneering spirit and history of Casper and Wyoming.

A Freewheeling Spirit

At the turn of the 20th century, Casper was a typical Western town — freewheeling and fast-moving, with a small but optimistic population. Few roads led into or out of town, and those were little better than rutted pathways. As a result, no one owned a car. The first rail line had reached Casper in 1888, but it was not until the second one arrived in 1913 that the foundation was laid for the arrival of the automobile. Prior to that time, delivering new cars from Omaha or other towns by driving them over the long, treacherous roads was simply not practical.

One of Casper's leading citizens at the time was Patrick J. O'Connor, an Irish engineer who had emigrated to Wyoming. O'Connor was a prominent Democratic politician and public orator, a behind-the-scenes mover who had been active in acquiring oil leases and penny oil stocks. He had also made a fortune by building irrigation canals and roadbeds for the railroads. Early in the century's second decade, O'Connor used the leftover lumber from a railroad construction project to build a large wooden structure on the corner of 5th and Wolcott. He named it the Coliseum Amusement Hall (after its Roman namesake), and, with the help of investors, made it into a multipurpose facility that was alternately a dance hall, skating rink, wrestling auditorium, bowling alley (Casper's first) and theater that showed silent movies. Because most of those activities were scheduled in the evening, O'Connor decided to use the building during the day as a garage to sell automobiles. Casper's population was still less than 3,000 people in 1913, and so the evening enterprises failed. The car business, however, survived under the management of J.W. Bingenheimer and was soon thriving.

P.J. O'Connor, the founder of Coliseum Motor Company

Monte Robertson, first generation automobile dealer

O'Connor and his associates had chosen a fortuitous time to launch an automobile agency. Until 1908, no one in the town had owned a car. Five years later, the market was still mostly untapped. It was also a market that was economically primed to purchase cars, thanks to a sudden prosperity — an oil boom had begun in 1912, and mining was just getting started after finds were made in silver, gold, lead, copper, galena and asbestos. At first, Coliseum sold Chandler cars, and the supply could not keep up with the demand. O'Connor applied to Dodge Brothers for a franchise and received it, and before long, his agency was selling several brands, including Paige, Hudson, Franklin, Pierce Arrow, Peerless, Cadillac and seven makes of trucks. By the time the company was incorporated as the Coliseum Garage Company in 1917, it had become the largest automobile agency in Wyoming.

The Robertson Era

During the early years, many people made significant contributions to Coliseum's successful launch. P.J. O'Connor's son, Ed, managed the parts and service department with an expertise that was renowned. The founder's daughter, Mary, was an important stockholder, and remained so until her death in 1997. And many of the early stockholders went on to have distinguished careers, most notably A.W. Peake, who later became president of Standard Oil. Under such capable leadership, the agency became the number one Dodge truck dealer in the entire United States during the development of the Salt Creek oil fields in the 1920s.

Of all the contributors to the company's growth, P.J. O'Connor's choice for manager had the greatest and longest impact. M.E. "Monte" Robertson, who was hired in 1921, was a former school teacher and school superintendent with some business experience. Robertson would manage the Coliseum Motor Company, as it was now known, for 34 years and see it through its early years to becoming a stable, established business. He also acquired a 25 percent interest in the company.

Around the same time that Robertson took the helm, Coliseum officers established a new company that fueled the agency's growth: the Finance Corporation of Wyoming. In the 1920s, banks and manufacturers did not finance new car purchases, and Coliseum often sold cars on no more than the buyer's promise to pay when he could. The finance company not only alleviated that risk but expanded Coliseum's market by opening up car ownership to a broader segment of the population. As a result, new car sales increased dramatically. The company's success was also helped by the addition of a large, full-service shop which soon outgrew its space, necessitating an addition to accommodate the ever-increasing business.

The Great Depression hit at the end of Coliseum's prosperous decade, but Monte Robertson managed to keep the business open. His farsighted stewardship also kept the agency's doors open through World War II, when the federal government froze the sales of new automobiles. It was a daunting challenge, but Robertson managed by shifting the company's focus from sales to service — selling gasoline, washing cars, fixing flat tires and performing general repairs. After the war, when many dealers were selling their inventory at twice the retail price in an attempt to make up for lost profits, Robertson refused to gouge his customers. A firm believer in the "golden rule," he bucked the trend by selling Coliseum's new cars at the regular retail price. The foundation for much of the company's later repeat business was undoubtedly laid in those crucial post-war days. When Coliseum's founder, P.J. O'Connor, died in 1946, Monte Robertson was elected president in his place.

Robertson continued as manager and president of Coliseum Motors for the next 10 years, steering the

R.M. Robertson, second generation automobile dealer

The current owners (left to right): Mike Holland, Clay Hawthorne, David Mertz, Bill Nolen

Big Wyoming Oldsmobile, Buick, Cadillac, Pontiac-GMC

of 74 years ended, but only in the sense that a Robertson no longer headed Coliseum Motors; the new ownership was very much a part of the Coliseum family. The president and principal owner, Bill Nolen, had been with the company for almost 20 years. In 1977, he had joined the dealership as the first ever fleet manager. Nolen was promoted to used car manager two years later, and then to the position of sales manager, where he helped make the company prosperous again after the Chrysler near-fiasco. In 1991, he became general manager of Big Wyoming, setting the stage for the 1994 buyout of the Robertsons.

Coliseum Motors is one of a handful of original Dodge dealerships still operating in the United States, and it is the only remaining original Dodge dealership west of the Mississippi River. From its inception, it was successful and grew, but it grew even faster under the leadership of the Nolen group, now employing 85 people at its various locations. Like the previous ownership, the new group had a keen eye for opportunities. In 1997, it purchased the franchises of Nagel Motors, a respected multifranchise dealership that had operated in Casper for almost a half-century. Nagel's Jeep franchise moved to Coliseum Motors, and its remaining three franchises — Cadillac, Pontiac and Buick — were incorporated into Big Wyoming, creating an impressive and diverse dealership in one convenient location. To reflect the expansion, the company's name was changed to Big Wyoming Oldsmobile, Buick, Cadillac, Pontiac-GMC. The Nolen group also continued another Coliseum tradition: an award-winning service department that is dedicated to excellence and customer satisfaction.

company through the new prosperity of the 50s. The decade also saw the transition to the second generation of Robertsons who would run the company. After serving in World War II and then graduating from the University of Wyoming in 1948, Monte's son, Rob, began working at Coliseum. He was also being groomed to replace his father, and when Monte retired in 1956, Rob Robertson was named manager of the company. For the next 38 years, Rob and his wife, Marie, ran the company and were its principal stockholders. Rob became the president, and in 1977, Dale Perry — who would work for Coliseum for nearly 50 years — succeeded him as general manager. Like Monte Robertson before them, they judiciously shepherded Coliseum through boom-and-bust cycles, prospering during the oil and uranium boom of the 1970s, and surviving both the statewide recession that occurred when those same industries went bust and the near-collapse of the Chrysler Corporation in the early 1980s.

The Coliseum Motor Company not only survived, but it flourished once again. In 1989, it expanded its number of automobile franchises by acquiring another business with a long history. Big Wyoming, an Oldsmobile and GMC Truck dealership dating back to the 1930s, became a wholly owned subsidiary of Coliseum Motors, and would play an important role in the decade to come.

A Tradition Continued

Rob Robertson retired in December of 1994, selling his interest in the company to William Nolen, Michael Holland, David Mertz and Clay Hawthorne. A tradition

After almost 100 years, Coliseum Motors still has a reputation for integrity, fairness, honesty, friendliness and a belief in Wyoming. It is a reputation that keeps customers — some of whom bought their first cars from Coliseum in the 1920s — coming back, year after year. An impressive 45 percent of the company's sales are repeat business and customer referrals. The key to such unusual success is no secret. "For 74 years, Monte and Rob Robertson preached and practiced the golden rule," Bill Nolen explains. "If they said they were going to do something, they did it. And we've carried that through." As a result, the company is stronger than ever. Coliseum Motors already has a plaque commemorating 75 years of serving the people of Casper and central Wyoming. The 100-year plaque is a virtual certainty.

Eastridge Autoplex, Inc.

Eastridge Autoplex, Inc. is one of the most visible car dealerships in Casper, Wyoming. Occupying nearly five acres on bustling Wyoming Boulevard, just off Interstate-25, it sits adjacent to the state's largest shopping mall.

A prime location is important, but it isn't the only factor in the dealership's visibility. The numerous volunteer activities of its employees set the stage for an even higher level of recognition among Casperites. From Habitat for Humanity to 4-H, the Casper Symphony to United Way, its 33 employees contribute their time and money to many worthwhile causes.

As with any business, the ownership sets the tone. Robert Womack and Larry Miles, who purchased the business in 1994, are active volunteers. Womack's favorite volunteer activity is Rotary Club, while Miles is a member of the board of the National Minority Automobile Dealers Association for Lincoln-Mercury. They authorized thousands of dollars of contributions by Eastridge to numerous Casper charities in 1998.

The dealership dates back to the 1970s as Tripeny Motors. It opened its doors under the new name on December 4, 1994. The prestigious Lincoln-Mercury line, as well as Nissan and Hyundai, are represented in inventory.

As with most dealerships, the service department is the heart of the business. A tour of the service area reveals abundant computerized diagnostic equipment. This allows the technicians to repair virtually any model on the road.

Upstairs is a classroom with computers and videoconferencing capabilities. It offers the service technicians and other associates the convenience of on-site education. Courses range from technical repair subjects to salesmanship and customer service. There are even courses offered by Lincoln-Mercury to assist the general manager in doing his job.

The well-lighted service area is always busy. Service is the cornerstone of any auto dealership.

General Manager Ron Roth says that the pieces are in place for continued success. Key staff changes over the last two years have made for a team that shares the importance of being customer-friendly. From sales associates to service technicians, everyone is pulling in the same direction.

Amid the paintings and photographs of native Wyoming outdoor scenes in the general manager's office are assorted axioms pertinent to the business and to life in general. On the marker board: "A sure way to miss success is to miss the opportunity." In a frame on the wall behind the desk is a quote attributed to Abraham Lincoln: "Better to remain silent and be thought a fool than to speak and remove all doubt." Beside it is an unattributed framed quote: "Truthfulness is the cornerstone of character, and if not firmly laid in youth, it will ever be a weak spot in the foundation..."

Eastridge Autoplex occupies five acres in a prime location in Casper, Wyoming.

Such philosophies are central to the character of the business and the enthusiasm of its people. There is a sense of purpose evident throughout the operation. The staff is focused and determined. The combination of positive factors — location, high visibility, customer service and enthusiasm — ensures the continued viability of Eastridge Autoplex.

Sierra Trading Post

Leaving Reno in 1992 posed some risk for Keith and Bobbi Richardson, but it was no gamble. Economic developers in Cheyenne had showed them that business costs in the Wyoming capital were far less than what they were used to in Nevada. To the upbeat owners of Sierra Trading Post, a discount mail-order firm specializing in outdoor clothing and equipment, numbers were a powerful incentive. The Richardsons were also pleased at the prospect of moving to a smaller community. And when they considered Wyoming's allotment of the Rocky Mountains, especially the Tetons and the Snowy Range, they were ready to sign papers and call movers.

The transition has been rewarding. Cheyenne residents often visit Sierra's retail outlet, which resembles a tastefully decorated mountain home, and many travelers come through the door, including truckers who notice the words "Espresso Bar" on the company's billboards along Interstate 80.

Sierra Trading Post is truly a family business. One Richardson son is the company's Web site director. Another, a skilled artist, draws finely detailed sketches of merchandise for Sierra's distinctive catalogues. Throughout the facility, from store to warehouse to customer-service phone banks, the atmosphere is one of dedicated purpose and genial informality. One or two German short-haired pointers might be seen wandering the place, gaining occasional pats on the head from workers. (Keith and Bobbi show and hunt with dogs of this breed as a hobby.)

According to a well-defined business philosophy, Sierra customers receive utmost attention and care. The Richardsons will point to a pair of shoes they once replaced even though the buyer, who had problems with them from the beginning, wore them for years before returning them. The dilapidated shoes are mounted on a board bearing the customer's letter of concern and the slogan "We Guarantee Satisfaction." Additionally, department managers work hard to minimize costs so Sierra goods can be offered at 35 to 70 percent price reductions. Since its inception in Cheyenne, the company has gone from 60 employees to 350, and from 30,000 square feet of operational space to 150,000. In the firm's first year in Cheyenne, catalog print runs totaled 8 million. As the century neared its close, Sierra was generating 30 million-plus catalogs annually.

From their home on the high prairie west of the city, the Richardsons see much to be thankful for, including sunny skies and the lovely purple of larkspur blooming in prairie grass in the spring. Moreover, they have a sense of community. Mindful of their city's needs, the two contribute faithfully to service groups. Jack Crews, the leader of the economic development team that brought the Richardsons to Cheyenne, notes that their generosity extends to "virtually every organization" in the area.

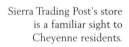

Sierra Trading Post's store is a familiar sight to Cheyenne residents.

In coming to Wyoming, the Richardsons felt assurances deeper than business calculations. Their confidence stemmed from earlier decisions they had made. In 1979, for example, Keith left an accounting position to work for Sportif USA, an outdoor clothing company in Reno. Sportif's owner hired Keith as company president. One day in 1986, however, the owner told Keith he wanted the position himself. Keith could take another place in management, but the president's office was no longer his.

That surprise clarified a truth the Richardsons recognized to some degree already — that God is faithful to those who reverently acknowledge Him. At times Keith had thought of striking out on his own, but he was unsure, so he decided to pray and read the Bible daily for a month. "After about 30 days I had a mental picture of myself standing on a cliff," he says. "It was as if God was saying to me, 'You think your job with Sportif, or any job you might have, is solid ground. It is not. It is only a mist. I am the only solid ground you have, and I am encouraging you to make a change, a leap in faith. I will take care of you. My accountability in this will be so remarkable in retrospect that you will realize you could never have done it on your own. Let me show you. Jump!'"

Although he had no business concept and little in the way of initial capital, Keith resigned from Sportif. The next day he had a thought: buy name-brand clothing and equipment overstocks and sell them at discount through the mail. Manufacturers need to dispose of overages without compromising their markets, and consumers will buy well-made items outdated by only a few months in terms of color or fashion detail — especially at low prices. Liking the idea, Keith and Bobbi anchored their thinking with resolve indicated by an Old Testament proverb: *Commit to the Lord whatever you do, and your plans will succeed.* Keith then did some figuring and saw how short they were of start-up money. In time, they remembered a friend — a man of

The Richardsons' prized short-hairs — Ava, Giff and Greta — agree to pose for a family portrait in the courtyard in front of Sierra Trading Post.

means and shared faith who eventually agreed to silent partnership and remained as a silent partner until 1992. Keith devised fulfillment and marketing strategies. Bobbi, who had worked in Macy's stores, developed a retail outlet. The business took hold. Then, in 1990 when Nevada's commercial costs increased, the Richardsons began to explore other options and discovered Wyoming.

Observing that God does not promise material prosperity, the two take nothing as a given. They say they will trust in the Lord whether their business continues to prosper — or if by some unforeseen circumstance it falters.

While candor about their relationship with God extends to company literature, including catalogues, the Richardsons ask no more of their employees than to work diligently and abide by the Golden Rule. If queried, they will say Jesus is the source of anyone's ability to live by that high standard. Early in their marriage the two studied the New Testament book of John, in which Jesus described the unique spiritual awakening available through him. "Finally, after years of skepticism, the light came on," Keith says. "We realized he was telling the truth, and we are grateful that God made our hearts receptive to that."

Taco John's International, Inc.

The story of Taco John's International, Inc. began in 1968 in Cheyenne, when John Turner opened a restaurant he called the Taco House. The following year he sold its franchise rights to Harold Holmes and James Woodson, also from Cheyenne. They changed the name to Taco John's and began to expand the company.

Super Nachos — always a popular item at Taco John's

Harold Holmes, who also owned a mobile home manufacturing company called Holmes Camper, got the contract to build the restaurant's second unit. It was the first of many modular 10 foot-by-30 foot Taco John's he built, and he finished it in eight days so it could be open in time for Cheyenne Frontier Days. Jim Woodson, who also owned Woodson Realty, negotiated the land lease for that second unit, installed on Carey Avenue. The next 100 franchises were similar modular units, and it was not uncommon to see a tractor-trailer hauling a Taco John's down the highway to its new home.

By the end of 1969, eight franchised Taco John's were open. In 1975, there were more than 75, all within 600 miles of Cheyenne. Five years after that, more than 250 restaurants spread from Washington to Michigan. Today, more than 450 franchises serve 24 states.

Changes along the way include the addition of customer seating to the original units, drive-through service, a mansard roof and vinyl awnings. The Taco "Juan" pictured on the logo has also changed with the times, his face and hat undergoing various transformations. Beginning in 1995, Taco Juan metamorphosed into the brighter and more modern Taco John looking down from the signs today. All Taco John's restaurants will make that change by the end of 2000. Designs for a whole new building and new interior, displaying

Paul Fisherkeller, president and CEO, in a newly re-imaged Taco John's

Mexican art and artifacts, will be installed in stores over the next three years, contributing to the restaurant's unique environment and reflecting its Western heritage.

The desire to appeal to contemporary tastes brought additions to the menu, which originally stuck to tacos and burritos. In 1979, the company introduced Potato Olés®, one of its most successful offerings. Focus on the kinds of items people want today, such as all-white chicken breasts and lean cuts of beef, drive the new product development. Every menu item features authentic Mexican flavors.

That taste is written into the company's "Promise," which is posted in every Taco John's restaurant. It pledges generous portions and that menu items will be prepared fresh from the best ingredients, service will be efficient and friendly, and restaurants clean and comfortable.

Taco John's invests considerable energy in partnering with its franchisees, in order to bring the Promise to life. Each owner is involved in every stage of the business, from strategic planning to restaurant operations. The company credits its success to its franchisees, a diverse group that includes schoolteachers, athletic directors, bankers and corporate executives. Some are second-generation owners — there is even a third-generation owner in Montana — and the company is committed to an ongoing dialogue with them. The seven senior executives of the company made almost 500 restaurant visits in 1998, and plan to continue that pace in 1999.

The renaming of the corporate headquarters reflects the attitude toward franchisees: it is now the Taco John's Franchise Support Center. The building opened in 1985, a few hundred yards west of the old

Holmes Camper building in Cheyenne. It is a large, three-floor structure, designed to meet the future needs of the Taco John's system and to house the growing staff.

In 1987, Taco John's reached $100 million in systemwide sales. *Entrepreneur Magazine* named Taco John's the No. 1 Mexican fast food franchise in the country, and 83rd among the nation's Top 500 franchises generally.

Looking to position itself for the future, the company undertook a major research project in 1996, and a strategic plan was born. The research showed that the food is what keeps the chain alive. Specifically, people appreciated the quality, the quantity, and the fact that the taste is more Mexican than what the competitors offer. Consumers also thought the chain's Western heritage was an interesting and attractive point of difference. Those observations became the company's guiding lights.

Information from the research also translated into an award-winning ad campaign, launched in 1997: "A Whole Lot of Mexican." The television commercial begins with the phrase, "It started in Wyoming, or the story goes. Just a man making tacos. Now everybody knows." Subsequent increases in sales followed, and Taco John's plans to stick with the campaign for a long time to come. The slogan is not just words and music, but a philosophy of doing business.

Later in 1997, a new president and CEO, Paul Fisherkeller, brought together a new management team. It represents a wealth of experience. Paul came from 30 years in the restaurant industry, both quick-service and casual dining. The rest of the team brings experience with virtually all the other major food service companies.

A goal of the team is to have 500 restaurants by the end of 2000. In the beginning, the company's development plan focused on small town locations, with populations of less than 10,000, and part of its success derived from a willingness to enter markets where other quick-service restaurants were not operating. Although small town locations are still part of the plan, the company has entered large metropolitan areas, and has earmarked several new states as well. Upgraded travel centers are another targeted location.

In order to take advantage of developing technology, Taco John's has made a substantial investment in that arena. Its interactive Web site includes detailed information about food items and a job application that will arrive directly at the company headquarters. Still to come are Internet and CD-ROM-based training programs to allow franchisees to learn without leaving their homes and businesses.

The owners of Taco John's (from left): Harold Holmes, his wife Nona Holmes, Marian Woodson, her husband Jim Woodson

Taco John's is active in restaurant industry organizations, including the International Franchise Association and the National Restaurant Association.

While other restaurants may serve fast food, Mexican-style, Taco John's describes their products as great Mexican food that happens to be fast and convenient. The goal of the company is to become synonymous with high-quality Mexican food, and to stand out from the usual quick-service experience.

Taco John's today

Halladay Motors, Inc.

Tim Joannides purchased Halladay Motors, Inc. from Carl Halladay Jr. in 1993. Carl Jr.'s father, Carl Halladay Sr., opened the Cheyenne dealership in October 1944 as the Oldsmobile dealer and took on the Cadillac franchise shortly after auto production resumed after World War II, in 1945. He acquired the GMC Truck franchise in 1950.

Prior to settling in Cheyenne, Carl Sr. had spent 20 years with the General Motors Corporation. Initially, he worked as a test engineer at the General Motors Proving Ground in Milford, Michigan. He worked his way up there, eventually becoming a top executive in the sales division of that facility. The second half of his GM career was with the Oldsmobile Division working with dealers in several eastern and Midwestern cities. His last GM job was with the Oldsmobile gun school in Lansing, Michigan.

Carl Halladay Jr. joined his father full time in the dealership in 1964. That year they also took on the Datsun/Nissan franchise. In the years preceding Datsun, they tried several other imports, including Renault, Hilman and Land Rover. Carl Jr. worked side by side with his father until his death in 1982. Together they built one of the finest and most respected dealerships in the state. They both received the coveted *TIME* Magazine Quality Dealer Award.

Tim Joannides acquired a family business and, like Carl Halladay Sr., has included his son in the dealership operation. Chris Joannides recently graduated from the National Automobile Dealers Association's Dealer Academy in Washington, D.C., and is currently the vice president and general sales manager for the dealership.

Oldsmobile, Cadillac, Nissan, Suzuki cars and trucks, and GMC trucks are part of the Halladay Motors product line at its Westland Road facility today.

Joannides was instrumental in the 1992 acquisition of the Suzuki franchise and subsequent vehicle sales that placed Halladay Motors in the top ten Suzuki dealerships in the nation. He obtained a medium-duty truck franchise from GMC in 1995.

Joannides began his automotive career in Illinois where he also attended Bradley University. He gained excellent experience working for top dealers in that state and in Arizona prior to coming to Cheyenne in 1983. He believes strongly in employee enthusiasm as a means of delivering top-notch service. In the words of his philosophy statement, "Customers are never an interruption to work, but the purpose of it." Under Joannides' leadership of customer-friendly policies — such as extended customer service hours, overnight fleet vehicle maintenance and hassle-free vehicle purchases — the dealership received GMC Truck's Leaders of Distinction award in 1997 and 1998 and the Oldsmobile Elite Award for the same years. In 1999, Joannides also was nominated for the *TIME* Magazine Quality Dealer Award.

Joannides is very proud of his Greek heritage as indicated by the gold pin he wears daily. His father, who was a successful insurance businessman, emigrated from Cyprus in 1930 and married an American-born Greek. Jennie Joannides, Tim's mother, currently lives in Cheyenne.

The dealership moved to its modern 10-acre facility on Westland Road in 1978. Previously, it had operated at four downtown locations: Central Avenue in 1944, 18th Street and Capitol Avenue in 1945, and two East Lincolnway addresses, beginning in 1947 and 1955 respectively.

"Halladay Motors has always been a local, family-owned-and-operated business," Joannides says. "My son Chris and I are proud to be able to continue the tradition that the Halladay family established."

Oldsmobiles, Cadillacs and GMC trucks fill the Halladay Motors showroom on East Lincolnway in the late 1970s.

Spradley Motors, Inc.

Marvin Thompson, a young man from Michigan, rode the train out from Detroit to establish a Ford car dealership in the Wyoming capital in 1916. After unloading Model T's at the Union Pacific depot, Thompson drove them to his place of business on Central Avenue between 16th and 17th Streets. Built to be affordable, the cars sold for about $350 each. Thompson's low-key approach served him well for five years, but a Ford manager in Denver eventually pressed him to hire salesmen. He declined. "I don't think we need salesmen in Cheyenne," Thompson is reputed to have said. "People will just come in and buy."

When the manufacturer insisted on a sales staff, Thompson agreed to sell his business to J.H. Walton, a New York newsman who came west in 1903 to work at the *Cheyenne Leader*. By the time the dealership changed hands in 1921, Walton had left the newspaper and become a bank vice president. A highly regarded and community-conscious man, he moved the car business to Pioneer Avenue and 19th Street and added Ford tractors and hay balers to the product line. In time, Walton Motors became an authorized Ford parts rebuilder. Edward Krumm, who had started with the company as a 17-year-old "lube boy" in 1921, bought Walton Motors in 1961. He and his partner, Jim Foreman, discontinued farm equipment sales but maintained a thriving auto trade for 24 years. When Krumm died in 1975, Foreman sold the business to Oregon residents Jack Fassett and Nick Nickel. Walton Motors had served the Cheyenne economy for half a century.

With hard work, good management and thoughtful customer service over the next quarter century, Fassett-Nickel Ford became an outstanding franchise. It received Ford's North American Customer Excellence Award in 17 of its 23 years. The owners moved the business to Westland Road in 1977 and three years later were granted a Toyota dealership, which they operated under the same roof untll 1993. That business won the manufacturer's President's Award seven years in a row. Nickel eventually bought Fassett's share of the dealerships and in 1998 sold them to Dale Spradley and four other investors. Spradley, who had worked for Ford Motor Credit before opening a Ford store in Florence, Colorado in the early 1970s, owns four car dealerships in Colorado and the one in Cheyenne. The Wyoming dealership received the presidential citation from Toyota again in 1998.

As Spradley's managing partner Robert Womack points out, business principles have not changed since the Model T days, and the Spradley family, whose dealerships have also won awards, intends to carry on the tradition of their Wyoming predecessors. This includes civic involvement. Spradley Motors supports Cheyenne's Meals on Wheels and March of Dimes Walkathon, for example, and dealership volunteers help boost student motivation and attendance at Afflerbach Elementary School.

Womack has worked in car service and sales in his native Indiana, in Colorado and in Casper. He and his partners have a service-oriented mind-set. "We are strong believers in business ethics and in taking care of customers — not just giving lip service to those values," Womack says. In view of Cheyenne's increasingly diversified economy, he adds, business prospects are good.

Late 1930s cars are parked at 19th Avenue and Pioneer Street in Cheyenne, a long-standing location of Walton Motor Company. *Courtesy Jim Foreman*

New vehicles fill the lot at the Spradley Motors Ford facility on Westland Road. *Photo by Chuck Seniawski*

Webster Chevrolet

When Bud Webster talked his brother Owen into a partnership purchase of the faltering little Chevrolet dealership in Cody, Wyoming, he had no idea that 62 years later he would be running the longest continuously operated GM dealership in the nation on a square block of prime city real estate. In 1937 the 25-year-old Webster only knew that his job as a state auditor didn't satisfy his itch to be in business for himself.

The business — Bud's contribution was $600 cash and a year-old Ford — consisted of parts, accessories, furniture, fixtures and shop equipment, but not a single car. At the time, the freight-on-board price of a standard 4-door sedan was roughly $700. The Webster brothers wheeled and dealed, and the little business began to establish itself.

The recession of 1938 was the first twist that presented itself. Nationwide unemployment stood at 25 percent. Most of the personnel of the dealership, including the parts man, two salesmen and five mechanics, worked on commission, and their paychecks were very small, less than a living wage. Webster implemented a wage plan that is still in effect today, which is surely a factor in the extraordinarily low staff turnover of the business. He gave his employees a guaranteed salary, with bonuses for sales or production beyond the base. They came through the recession in the black.

On December 1, 1941, Webster bought his brother's interest in the dealership. Six days later, Pearl Harbor was bombed, and the United States was at war. Shortly there-

after, car production stopped and sales were frozen. Webster owned a car dealership that couldn't sell cars.

For a short time, however, he could buy cars. General Motors Chairman Alfred P. Sloan, in an effort to keep his dealerships alive, offered dealers who continued to buy cars until production ceased an equal number of new Chevrolets when production resumed. While dealerships around the country failed on a large scale, Webster bought and bought, not only from the factory but also from the closing dealerships, accumulating cars until the day he could sell again. He tightened his belt and held his breath and kept his staff on salary.

Webster Chevrolet survived, and even thrived, during the war on tires. Tire sales were frozen also, and frightened tire dealers were relieved and grateful to sell their entire inventories to Bud Webster. Regionwide, customers with rationing board-issued certificates knew where to go for tires, and a steady stream of tire traffic passed through the doors of Webster Chevrolet throughout the war.

When the factories fired up again after the war, Webster Chevrolet, because of its farsighted participation in the Sloan Plan, was in line to receive a great number of shiny, new Chevrolets. The dealership relocated and expanded several times, even acquiring the city alley in its square block. Customers came, and over the decades returned. Webster Chevrolet, with 86-year-old Webster still at the helm, has one of the highest percentages of repeat buyers in the nation. This may be due to Webster's guiding motto: "Give the best that's in you, because there's only one time around. There are no repeat performances brought back by popular demand."

RAG Coal West, Inc.

The future for RAG Coal West, Inc. (RAG) promises to be exciting and productive. The origins of RAG trace back to 1969 when AMAX, Inc. authorized the development of the Belle Ayr Mine, which started shipping coal in 1972, the first noncaptive coal mine in the Powder River Basin. AMAX merged with Cyprus Minerals in 1993, forming Cyprus Amax Coal. Cyprus Amax Coal was acquired in mid-1999 by RAG Coal International, a German mining consortium, with RAG Coal West as a subsidiary.

The 1970 Clean Air Act had created a Wyoming opportunity. Was there a market for the cleaner burning sub-bituminous coal found in the Powder River Basin? To date, Belle Ayr and its sister mine Eagle Butte, established in 1978, have shipped 640 million tons of coal and have 910 million tons under lease. Demand for this low-sulfur coal has grown throughout the 1980s and 1990s and shows no sign of slowing down. RAG has shipped coal to 18 states, fueling power plants that drive our economy, says Thomas J. Lien, president of RAG Coal West.

The mining industry is focused on technology and RAG mines set new standards. To meet the demands of around-the-clock train arrivals, the Belle Ayr Mine is operated from a central computerized nerve center. Real time information flows to haulage truck drivers, maintenance crews, crushing and load out operators, and management. Operators constantly monitor equipment performance and direct trucks to be loaded by specific shovels to maximize productivity. Global Positioning Systems are used to track equipment and optimize work.

RAG set a standard in 1990 when it instituted Participative Management and its Technician System. Extensive training programs have developed multi-skilled employees, who are compensated for their proficiency, not job titles. In 1995, RAG began promoting a "Team" environment. Today half of the work force are on self-directed work teams. "We believe in the talent, ingenuity and creativity that our employees bring to the job," says Lien. "We are all in this together."

The company has the same proactive philosophy in its business dealings. RAG regards the Wyoming Department of Environmental Quality as a partner, not an adversary. "Together we are returning the land to a higher and better use," says Lien. The history of recla-

mation in the basin has been extraordinary, serving as an example to other mining regions. The company has created a high public relations profile touring thousands each year through its operations to personally view coal mining.

Employing more than 120 directly, the mines also use the services of numerous local support industries spurring economic development opportunities. With coal supplying 57 percent of the nation's electricity, Lien believes this Wyoming industry has a solid future. "I am proud to be a part of this basic industry supplying a essential product used by millions each day."

Mining is a progressive industry. Lien says confidently, "I expect that you can return to Campbell County in 100 years, and there will still be coal mines here producing energy for our nation's economy."

Belle Ayr Mine — 72-foot-thick coal seam

Eagle Butte Mine — 85-ton shovel loading 240-ton haul truck with overburden

Solvay Minerals, Inc.

The gently rolling, sage-covered mounds that surround Solvay Minerals, Inc.'s mining facility outside Green River, Wyoming, offer few hints at the valuable treasure that lies beneath them.

A casual visitor would never guess that underneath this arid ground are the remains of an ancient lake that evaporated some 50 to 60 million years ago, leaving behind the ingredients that eventually formed trona ore. When processed, this undistinguished-looking, grayish-green mineral yields an alkali product known as soda ash, a prized chemical substance used in the manufacture of products ranging from glass containers and windows to household detergents and corn sweeteners, as well as other sodium-based products.

The mine site at Solvay Minerals, Inc.

As a world leader in the production of soda ash and related products, it is only fitting that a company like Solvay S.A., the parent company of Solvay Minerals, Inc., would have a stake in the mining of trona ore from Wyoming's Green River trona deposit.

The Belgium-based company was founded in 1863 by Ernest Solvay to implement his newly patented process for manufacturing synthetic soda ash. Over time, Solvay S.A. expanded its operations to include facilities in 41 countries and became the world's leader in soda ash, hydrogen peroxide and high density polyethylene production as well as the third largest producer of caustic soda and chlorine. Other products manufactured by this far-ranging company, which continues to devote significant resources to

Underground bore miner operation

research and development, are in the areas of plastics, plastic processing, and health.

As one of the most modern mining and production facilities in the world, the Solvay Minerals facility in Green River — in operation since 1982 — adds an important facet to the company's production base of soda ash plants located in continental Europe. By producing high-quality soda ash from the largest known trona deposit in the world, Solvay Minerals plays a key role in maintaining Solvay S.A.'s global role of industry leader.

From the Green River trona beds, which cover an area of about 1,300 square miles and are estimated to contain billions of tons of trona, Solvay Minerals produces soda ash and other chemicals, including sodium sulfite, sodium metabisulfite, and other trona products.

Mining from a bed located at an approximate depth of 1,500 feet under ground, Solvay Minerals employees use rotary boring continuous miners to extract the ore at a rate of between 10,000 to 11,000 tons per day, working in tunnels supported by steel rods that are bolted into the roof of the mined area.

Once the ore is cut, it is transported by shuttle car to belt conveyors, which discharge their loads into underground storage bins. From here, the ore is lifted to the surface in two alternating 20-ton skips, which come to the surface every few minutes.

A series of refining steps is then performed to extract soda ash from the trona ore. The raw ore is crushed, screened and heated, which causes it to

decompose and form crude soda ash. After this, the soda ash is dissolved in water, which allows separation from insoluble elements found in the ore.

Following treatment to remove any organic materials, soda ash in solution is refined to its final form, eventually creating a product with the look and feel of fine beach sand which is then shipped to key markets in North America and abroad.

Soda ash solution also is combined with sulfur dioxide to create sodium sulfite or sodium metabisulfite — two high-demand products used in the chemical, water treatment, textile, photochemical, and food and beverage industries.

With production facilities open for sodium sulfite since 1991, Solvay Minerals is today the leading producer of the chemical in North America, with an integrated plant operation that allows the company to maximize its facilities and produce a low-cost product.

Sodium metabisulfite has been produced at the Green River facility since early 1997, and will continue to play a key role in Solvay Minerals' operations at this facility in the years to come.

While concern for the environment is always tantamount for any company involved in mining and processing, it is of utmost importance in places like Wyoming, which makes up for its sparse human population with abundant wildlife and plant communities.

Preservation of the environment is a given. Solvay Minerals, while a relative newcomer to the Green River trona beds, has taken a leadership role in this area, employing the best available control technology for the particulates and gases created through its refining processes. In addition to controlling its emissions into

Surface rescue team in competition

the air, the company also has a total water containment program that captures rain runoff for use in manufacturing, and is an industry pioneer in underground tailings disposal. All emissions from the Solvay Minerals' facilities fall under Prevention of Significant Deterioration regulations — the most stringent in the industry.

Special effort is taken to protect the Solvay Minerals workforce as well. It takes roughly 430 employees to keep the 24-hour a day operation running smoothly, and ensuring the safety of these workers is top priority.

In addition to adhering to rigorous inspection and replacement schedules on all equipment, Solvay Minerals has three employee-managed rescue teams — two for underground and two for surface operations — trained in areas including rescue skills, firefighting, and hazardous materials response.

These teams, composed of between 30 to 40 people each, keep their skills honed to a top-notch level at rescue team competitions across the country, at which they frequently take top honors. In addition to these teams, the company keeps an ambulance on site in order to provide split-second response should an accident occur.

The goal, of course, is to prevent any problems before they happen, and Solvay Minerals prides itself on its stellar safety record that reflects a goal achieved. Couple this commitment to excellence with a highly motivated work force renowned for its exceptional innovation, productivity, and safe work performance, and it's no wonder the company's Green River operations have become an industry benchmark.

Working with these assets and the marketing arm of Solvay worldwide, Solvay Minerals is positioned to meet the needs and requirements of the industry, both now and in the future.

Solvay Minerals soda ash control room operation

Black Hills Bentonite

Bentonite, the "clay of a thousand uses," was utilized in Wyoming for cosmetics in the 1880s. Prior to that, American Indians used it as a soap for purging their buffalo robes. In the decades that followed, bentonite became one of Wyoming's invaluable natural resources.

During the 1920s, bentonite was found to be a superb binder of sand for foundry molding in the casting of steel. In the mid-1900s, it was used as a binder for the newly developed process of converting taconite, a combination silicate and low-grade iron ore, to iron ore.

Highwall in Tensleep bentonite pit

Increasingly, the bentonite industry in Wyoming flourished, reaching an all-time high between 1979-1982. It grew from less than 1 million annual tons in 1950 to more than 4 million tons annually by 1980.

In 1947, Harry T. Thorson molded a handful of the montmillonite clay, and with diligence and perseverance, gave birth to Wyoming's only home-based bentonite enterprise, Black Hills Bentonite.

Harry and Inga Thorson, conjointly with Al and Margaret Harding, structured the business subsequent to long, judicious hours of frugal thought and profuse trial and error, building their first bentonite plant in Moorcroft, Wyoming. Contemporary equipment was not an option, and it was necessary to find useable equipment wherever it could be found to construct the plant.

Black Hills Bentonite prospered with the industry. In 1964, the Casper plant was constructed, followed 10

Scrapers working at the bentonite pit in Kaycee, Wyoming

years later by a second processing plant in Worland. Today, the company has five plants; three in Casper, one of which is named the Harry Thorson plant in honor of the company's founder; one in Worland; and a lignite plant in Glenrock.

The Thorson family eventually acquired the Harding's interest and the company became primarily a family-owned operation. The Thorsons worked together under the flawless directives of their parents, striving to sustain their parents' professional principles and to consummate their plans for success.

In 1990, entrepreneurs from Texas came to Wyoming in search of a product that could be "mass marketed and produced in a low-tech environment." Bentonite filled the bill and Black Hills Bentonite was contracted to produce it.

The new product? Kitty litter, an ever-increasing market and one that services the needs of more than 66 million cats worldwide. Black Hills Bentonite can accommodate an international feline populace and a plethora of bentonite for other markets. Today, bentonite is used in everything from blood albumen to fertilizers, fruit juices, floor emulsions and spark plugs. It is also used extensively for drilling in the petroleum industry, and environmentally for plugging seismic drill holes, pit liners, landfill caps and other water containment barriers. The company sells 400,000-500,000 tons of bentonite annually and is a leading producer in the state.

The Thorson family credits the company's success to honest, dedicated employees, a long-standing relationship with Bethlehem Steel of Bethlehem, Pennsylvania, and the consistent hard work of their parents and the Hardings.

Looking forward to the future, the Thorson progeny stand stalwart against the rise and fall of the industry, beckoning opportunity and affecting the same determination and pride bequeathed to them by their parents — the progenitors of Black Hills Bentonite, Harry and Inga Thorson.

Wyodak Coal

From a distance, the Wyodak Mine rests on a quiet backdrop of sunlit plains and blue skies in Campbell County. On the outcroppings surrounding the mine, workers peel away tons of earth to reach the energy that will fuel power plants across the West for the next generation.

Back in 1921, the Homestake Mining Company had discovered a 102-foot-thick seam of sub-bituminous coal in what was to become one of the largest reserves of coal in the United States, the Powder River Basin. By 1923, low-sulfur Wyodak coal was in production to meet the rising customer demands of a still-new 20th century.

In the early years, mule teams hitched to slips removed overburden to unearth the rich, black and clean-burning coal. By 1925, more than 33,000 tons were mined annually and shipped by rail to supply steam-powered electricity-generating plants. What is thought to be the oldest continuing operating surface coal mine in the United States was in business.

Today, gigantic electric shovels move overburden in 27-yard increments in a high-tech, computerized operation. The coal is removed to crushers, transferred to conveyer belts, which then move it into storage silos

for three power plants. Coal is also shipped by trucks to additional customers further away.

The engineering department plots out the shortest distance between two points in order to move the smallest amount of topsoil possible. In this way, vital nutrients are preserved for cattle, sheep and wildlife to reap nutritious benefits.

Regulations are an important part of mining. Baseline data on soil, ground water, surface water and vegetation is kept to ensure that grasslands after reclamation blend in with the surrounding terrain. Engineers pay particular attention to restoring the rolling topography to preserve the integrity of the landscape for future generations.

The 43 employees at Wyodak go about their assigned tasks in a clean, safe, climate-controlled environment. Gone are the days of the miner's scourge, black lung. Safety is of the utmost priority. A team of experienced professionals pitch together, exploring new coal enhancement technologies, striving to meet an evergrowing demand.

One hundred nine years after Wyoming achieved statehood, the vitality of Gillette and the surrounding area is measured by the ton. For more than 77 years, the Wyodak Mine and its employees have forged progressive ties that immutably connect the mine and the citizens of Campbell County.

"We take pride in our people coming together for a common goal and our history is rich," says Safety Director Charlie Messenheimer. "When we go home at night, we know that the coal we mined that day contributes to the power supply for northeast Wyoming and the Black Hills."

Messenheimer points out that nearly 50 percent of the total cost of mining goes to taxes, purchasing amenities and infrastructure few cities the size of Gillette enjoy. Wyoming leads the nation in preferred low-sulfur coal production, and the Powder River Basin leads Wyoming. Under the present technology, Wyodak will have at least another 90 years of coal mining permitted.

For the men and women who work at Wyodak, the community of Gillette and the surrounding areas, that long-gone day in 1921 was the beginning of a century of growth and achievement.

Wyodak's Peerless pit with the power plants in the background
Creative direction by Hot Pink, Inc.; photo by Flash Box Studios

Hillcrest Spring Water

Hillcrest Spring Water plant

Hillcrest's Millennium — spring water for 2000 and beyond

In front of the Hillcrest Spring Water bottling plant in downtown Casper stands a spirit pole. The ornate wooden sculpture symbolizes the gift of life made possible by water, and also represents mankind's responsibility as a steward of that water. It is also a fitting symbol of the company's nearly one-century-old relationship with the people of Wyoming.

Hillcrest Spring Water was founded at the turn of the 20th century by Herbert C. Leavitt, who hauled spring water and ice to Casper in a wagon. In 1962, the company was purchased by James and Anne DeWitt, who continued to run it as a small but successful family business. After James DeWitt's death in 1971, the torch was passed to his daughter and son-in-law, Kathy and George Baker, who assumed ownership of the company along with Jay DeWitt, a partner until 1985. Capitalizing on the surge in popularity of bottled drinking water, the Bakers modernized their facilities and expanded their market, taking the company into a new era of growth.

Bottled water is the fastest growing segment of the beverage industry, and spring water accounts for more than 75 percent of the bottled water produced in the United States. Federal regulations define spring water as that derived from an underground formation that flows naturally to the earth's surface. Additionally, it must come from a spring that is protected from surface intrusion and other environmental influences. Hillcrest's spring water comes from such a protected spring at the base of Casper Mountain. From there, it is transported in stainless steel tankers to the Hillcrest plant where it is processed and bottled under strict sanitary conditions that insure its purity. Hillcrest Spring Water is a member of the International Bottled Water Association,

and has been awarded the prestigious Blue Ribbon Award by the Consumer Health Services Division of the Wyoming Department of Agriculture each year since 1994.

In addition to its famous mountain spring water, Hillcrest also provides distilled water, drinking water purified by reverse osmosis, a complete office coffee service and private labeling. It offers one, three and five-gallon containers, as well as a complete line of bottled water dispensers for homes and offices. In 1994, it successfully introduced a timely new brand called Millennium Premium Natural Spring Water that features new packaging and convenient half-liter and one-liter sport bottles. In keeping with its long tradition, the company still has a strong residential market, but aggressive marketing has expanded the commercial business to 60 percent of Hillcrest's revenues. The staff — once only three people — has grown to 22, a significant number of whom have been with the company for many years. And with the recent purchase of Rocky Mountain Bottled Water, the number of locations has grown to four: an office and bottling plant in Casper, and warehouses in Cody, Gillette and Rawlins. From its modest one-man, one-wagon beginnings, Hillcrest Spring Water now serves about 75 percent of Wyoming and a portion of Nebraska.

Because it is selling a product that is so easily available from other sources, Hillcrest knows that its success relies on two factors: the taste and quality of its water, and its relationship with its customers. "More than anything else, we are a service company," Kathy Baker observes. "And we have a lot of fun doing this. That's the key."

Questar Corporation

A discovery in southwestern Wyoming in 1922 led to the development of Questar Corp., one of the nation's leading integrated natural gas companies.

The Ohio Oil Co. had a problem.

While drilling for oil near Rock Springs, Wyoming, in 1922, a company rig hit a huge deposit of natural gas about 2,500 feet down. The flow was measured at about 36 million cubic feet a day.

But what could they do with it? These days, with a pipeline network in place, moving natural gas to market is no big deal. But in 1922, it wasn't so simple.

In those days, pipeline construction techniques were still very crude. So moving the natural gas to the nearest large market — 200 miles away in northern Utah — must have been a daunting prospect.

Fortunately, pipeline technology improved rapidly during the 1920s and, in 1928, The Ohio Oil Co. joined forces with two other companies to plan a network of main lines and gathering lines connecting gas fields in southwestern Wyoming to the cities of northern Utah.

To get natural gas to Utah for the winter of 1929-30, officials began construction in January 1929. Veterans of the pipeline project describe shoveling four or five feet of snow off the right-of-way and hacking through frozen ground to reach the softer soil underneath. In February, a convoy of trucks en route to the project was stranded for more than three days in a bitter snowstorm east of Rock Springs. As a crew from the state highway department worked with shovels to clear the road, the company arranged an airlift of food to the 55 besieged travelers.

When spring came and the snow melted, water filled the pipeline trenches and turned the soft ground to mud, trapping trucks, ditching machines and teams of horses, along with bulldozers sent to their rescue.

Nevertheless, work on the pipeline was finished by August. It was, in the words of one newspaper writer, a "construction project that has no western parallel." Before winter, natural gas service was available to many communities in northern Utah, and in Green River, Evanston and Lyman in southwestern Wyoming.

That winter, the company served about 18,000 natural gas customers. Today it serves more than two-

A construction crew lays pipe for Questar's Skull Creek line through the Mulligan Draw field in southern Wyoming. In the background, a drilling rig probes for new natural gas reserves.

thirds of a million. Now known as Questar Corp., the company has property in a dozen states and two Canadian provinces. The intervening years saw natural gas become the preferred fuel for space- and water-heating in the company's service area. As the cleanest-burning fossil fuel, it was also used to reduce emissions from factories and power plants.

That first gas well near Rock Springs stopped producing in the early 1970s. However, the prolific Moxa Arch, Green River and Vermillion basins of southwestern Wyoming and northwestern Colorado, bolstered by new field discoveries such as Church Buttes in 1946 and Brady in 1972, continue to provide much of the gas used by Questar's retail customers. Today the company holds leases on almost 400,000 acres in Wyoming and continues to explore the area for new gas reserves. Questar also has nearly 22,000 retail customers and about 290 employees in southwestern Wyoming.

As Americans grow more concerned about cleaner air, Questar sees a bright future for natural gas — and Wyoming — in the 21st century.

The Nightingale/Kanda/Coleman complex, six miles southwest of Rock Springs, provides compression for several major pipelines on the Questar system.

Cheyenne Light, Fuel and Power Company

Cheyenne Light, Fuel and Power Company's tradition of service and reliability goes back to the days of Thomas Alva Edison and the birthplace of the incandescent lamp. It was in Wyoming where Edison, whose many inventions led to the creation of modern electricity, first came up with the idea for his "light in a bottle." He was in Wyoming with a party of other scientists who had traveled across the rugged mountains and plains to see an eclipse. After returning home to his laboratory, Edison perfected the forerunner of today's incandescent electric lamp.

Cheyenne's venture into public utility began with the Brush Arc Lamp and its battery current. It was America's centennial year — 1876 — and a Centennial Exposition held in Philadelphia opened the door to progress in the field of electricity. As the electric era began, lighting for homes and streets came from burning coal or gas. But at the Centennial Exposition, people began murmuring about not only what had been but what was to be. A small, curious, man-made machine called the electric dynamo was able to supply a current to a single arc lamp. Although the unobtrusive electric dynamo was quickly forgotten amid the dazzle of other modern machinery at the exposition, the principle of electricity, harnessed for service, had been established in inventive minds.

That same year, a young man by the name of Charles Francis Brush began producing an electric dynamo that created illumination through arc lamps. A graduate of the University of Michigan, he was familiar with both the principles of electricity and the dynamo. Confident of his ability to improve upon its design, he remarked as such to George W. Stockly of the

Cleveland Telegraph Supply Company. Stockly, intrigued at the idea, offered Brush the telegraph company's facilities for its manufacture should the dynamo prove to be successful.

During the summer of 1883, Charles Brush and the Brush Electric Company became interested in obtaining the American rights of an incandescent lamp invented by Englishman Joseph W. Swan. Brush visualized an illuminating system that included both arc and incandescent lighting. He experimented with a storage battery of cast-lead plates and found that one horsepower would charge the battery sufficiently to operate 10 Swan lamps for an hour. Brush connected a number of these batteries to an arc light system, operated by a dynamo of large capacity. During the day he charged the batteries and at night he operated incandescent lamps from them. The lamps did not interfere with the arc light system as the batteries were equipped with an automatic "manipulator," which cut

Electric line truck and line employees are depicted here, circa 1928.

them into the circuit when they were to be recharged or cut them out as charging was completed.

The story of electric lighting in Cheyenne, Wyoming, began right around this time. Certification of the incorporation of the Brush-Swan Electric Light Company of Cheyenne was filed in what was

In 1942, Cheyenne Light, Fuel and Power moved its main office to this building on West 18th, shown here circa 1948.

then the Territory of Wyoming on August 2, 1882. Its mission was "to construct, establish, furnish and maintain a system of electric lighting in Laramie County, Wyoming Territory, and in the City of Cheyenne; provide electric lights for the City and County and inhabitants ther[e]of, and electric power for all purposes to which it may [be] applied or for which it may be used in said Laramie County, Wyoming Territory."

Electric lighting progress continued in Wyoming. One of the first commercial lighting plants in the West — certainly the first in Wyoming — was started by then-treasurer of Wyoming Territory, Francis E. Warren. Made up first of Brush-Swan lamps, machines and storage batteries, the Electric Light Company of Cheyenne delivered batteries to customers by wagon. The small company was frequently unable to meet the demand for electricity by residents who wanted to have their homes illuminated.

The story of electric lighting in the city of Cheyenne continued with a resolution in December 1883 that granted permission to the Brush-Swan Electric Light Company to erect poles and wires throughout the city's streets and alleys. The following year, in February, the company erected "arc lights" at the intersections of several streets in Cheyenne. The lights were to be kept burning from dark until dawn each day.

In late 1883, Cheyenne City Gas Company was incorporated "for the manufacture and sale of gas for illuminating, heating and other purposes by any and all processes...to supply gas to individuals, public or private corporations...." The absence of records to the contrary indicates that both gas and electric were delivered to Cheyenne residents on a satisfactory basis through the turn of the century. It was at that time that a corporation named Cheyenne Light, Fuel and Power Company was organized on April 19, 1900.

At the first meeting of the trustees of Cheyenne Light, Fuel and Power Company, held May 21, 1900, officers of the Cheyenne City Gas Company and the Brush-Swan Electric Light Company offered to sell to the new company all rights connected to the sale of light, heat and power. The offer was accepted and Cheyenne Light, Fuel and Power began providing services to residents throughout Cheyenne and Laramie County in what had become the state of Wyoming.

By 1918, improvements made by Cheyenne Light, Fuel and Power resulted in raising power efficiency by reducing coal consumption and eliminating gas and smoke irritation in the boiler room. Other additions included the installation of a higher pressure boiler over a modern chain grate stoker. Further expansion resulted in a highly efficient bench being added to increase the capacity and decrease the cost of gas generation.

Because of ever-increasing population growth in the city of Cheyenne, some other old engines were removed from the plant and improvements were made to the building where they had been located. Keeping buildings and equipment up-to-date technologically so that service is held to a high level has been a top priority of Cheyenne Light, Fuel and Power throughout the last several decades.

Circumstances in the early 1920s also led to the merger of Cheyenne Light, Fuel and Power with the Public Service Company of Colorado. Other changes included natural gas being piped into Cheyenne on July 7, 1926, from the Wellington Gas Field by the Colorado-Wyoming Gas Company. This event opened up a whole new era in gas service. In 1929, the Colorado-Wyoming Gas Company's pipeline was tied into the line of the Colorado Interstate Gas Company. This line was expanded into Cheyenne, which made natural gas from a field in Amarillo, Texas, available to Wyoming residents.

In July 28, 1938, Cheyenne Light, Fuel and Power began to purchase power from the Seminoe Dam, which had contracted with the U.S. Department of the Interior Bureau of Reclamation, Kendrick Project, Wyoming, a generating plant that would also be used for standby purposes.

Negotiations began in early 1941 for the construction of a new building to be used as headquarters for the company's offices. The continued growth of the city of Cheyenne made it necessary to expand services, thus making additions of gas mains and electric lines imperative to keeping up with demand. On January 31, 1942, Cheyenne Light, Fuel and Power moved into its current headquarters on 18th Street in downtown Cheyenne. The occasion was marked by a formal opening that was attended by more than 4,000 people.

Improvements have continued to be made throughout the 1960s and beyond. In 1962, an ultra-modern service center was opened and the company dedicated the first two of its six diesel-generation units. The following year, Cheyenne Light, Fuel and Power began to purchase electricity from Pacific Power and Light Company.

Statistics over the past century show that Cheyenne has emerged as one of the West's most progressive utility centers. Indeed, Cheyenne was perhaps the first city in the United States to have electric lights and it was certainly the place where many new lighting techniques were born. The company's service territory has expanded over the last hundred years to include the entire city of Cheyenne and a major portion of Laramie County, including the communities of Pine Bluffs, Burns and Carpenter. This expansive area combines to make up more than 1,200 square miles.

The latter years of the 20th century have continued to see improvements and extensions of existing facilities as well as the construction of new structures. Although the 1980s began with a shaky economy throughout the West, Cheyenne Light, Fuel and Power remained strong. Its employees even achieved national recognition for working a million productive hours — more than five years — without a disabling injury.

By 1989, the state's economy and that of Cheyenne had stabilized. Undergrounding and relocation, as well as drainage and street improvements, initiated by both the city of Cheyenne and the state of Wyoming, occurred in areas throughout the service territory. A strong economy fueled the addition of new residential and commercial construction. A large intermediate pressure line extension was begun in 1993 to tie the Union Pacific Resource's Silo Gathering field with Cheyenne Light, Fuel and Power's facilities in the Cheyenne Business Parkway. In 1998, the company initiated a new Service Guarantee Program. The program was designed to improve customer relations when the company fails to keep its commitment in providing certain expected levels of service. This program enables employees, through the issuance of a Service Guarantee Certificate with a monetary value, to recover good faith with the customer if a specific service level failure occurs.

The 1990s reflected continued growth and change as the company became a partner with New Century Energies, Inc. This was a significant milestone for the utility because, as part of a major corporation, flexibility and expertise in daily operations could be improved, ultimately benefiting customers in the form of lower utility costs. Other mergers are planned for the future as a way to improve reliability of service and decrease costs.

The company comprises an extensive system of electric transmission and distribution equipment and a far-reaching network of natural gas distribution facilities. The continued arrival of new businesses and industries to Cheyenne and Laramie County, and the continued construction of office buildings, shopping centers, hotels, restaurants and homes assure a promising economic future. These changes certainly present challenges for the utility industry, but the past has shown that seemingly insurmountable difficulties can be triumphed over again and again.

The scope of Cheyenne Light, Fuel and Power's operations is certainly much broader today than in those early days. Utilities today must operate in a constant state of transition. Economic concerns, government regulations, improving technology and growing needs of customers make the utility business anything but static. The company's commitment to serving a growing area of customers, however, remains steadfast.

Its commitment to the public is strong and deep as well. Cheyenne Light, Fuel and Power prides itself on taking a proactive approach when it comes to community involvement. It is actively involved with a number of local causes and provides support (both financial and volunteer) to numerous organizations.

The future of Cheyenne, Wyoming, is full of promise. There is an exciting potential for growth and Cheyenne Light, Fuel and Power looks forward to fulfilling the need for energy sufficiently and reliably. With the new century come changes in technology, such as wind-generated power, and new challenges. The strength of a utility will depend on its ability to remain economically strong, which means keeping prices competitive and service stable. One fact will remain: residents who have come to depend on the reliability of their power company will continue to do so. Their homes will remain warm and well lit.

The new millennium of utility service will emerge as one far different than any past era. Cheyenne has its own place in the history of electricity: Cheyenne Light, Fuel and Power has a place in the future.

This 250-kilowatt model wind-generation turbine west of Cheyenne underscores the growing importance of wind power in utilities today.

Bighorn Airways

Like many Americans, Bighorn Airways traces a 50-year lineage to the aftermath of World War II. Through decades of change in commercial air transport, the company has survived and prospered thanks to four families and five visionary men.

From the three decades the Yentzer brothers owned the company to the years Dan Hawkins and Gene Powers have shared control, and finally to father-son team Robert and Christopher Eisele, Bighorn Airways has enjoyed years of steady growth and stability.

Daring pilots dominated the end of the war, and in 1948, Dick Yentzer returned to Sheridan full of optimism and training as an aviator. The following years brought a surge in the economy, and the time was ripe to start a commercial operation from the tiny county airport. Sparsely populated, with great distances between cities, Wyoming was the perfect place for 20th-century agricultural aerial application and travel between cattle ranches. Although the industry was hardly in its infancy, commercial aviators were a small group in those days, and competition was scarce.

The Yentzer brothers began as a single airplane agricultural spraying operation at the Sheridan County Airport. Dick Yentzer performed the day-to-day operations from the cockpit of a Piper Super Cub at a sedate 90 miles per hour. Bighorn Airways prospered throughout the 50s, with Yentzer ferrying supplies and cattle barons to far-flung ranches and dusting crops.

By 1957, Robert Eisele was a senior in high school and had been bitten by the flying bug. The Yentzers had realized their ambition, and Bighorn Airways had expanded to become a full-fledged fixed-base operator, providing aircraft and lessons to Sunday pilots from its flight school. Eisele had his sights set on a license and a job.

Although never a big mining town, ethnic diversity and a cosmopolitan feel had arrived to Sheridan. Massive coal mines dotted the Powder River Basin, and the demand was growing from company executives for commercial air service.

By this time, Eisele had graduated to flying the new, single-engine Cessna 180. Although the core business remained spraying, the company was once again growing to accommodate the burgeoning charter business in the state. Eisele had assumed a major role in the company, flying wealthy business owners in several Cessna 340s recently added to the fleet.

The prosperity of the 70s had produced other aviation successes across the state. Greybull entrepreneurs Dan Hawkins and Gene Powers were looking in an easterly direction for new business opportunities to complement their successful firefighting and slurry bombing operation.

In 1971, Hawkins and Powers Aviation Incorporation purchased Bighorn Airways from the Yentzer family, and a new era began. Eisele stayed to manage the company for Hawkins and Powers, overseeing the construction of a new 20,000-square-foot facility.

The air taxi operation had continued to grow as Wyoming entered a boom in the oil industry. Additional hangar space was needed to service the proliferation of private and corporate aircraft, while the administrative needs of the company swelled to include accountants and office personnel.

By 1980, Eisele had worked and managed Bighorn Airways for both owners for 20 years. He was ready to invest some of his own

Bighorn's smoke-jumping aircraft used for firefighting

capital into the operation, and Hawkins and Powers knew he was the right choice to assume a full half of the company.

In the next decade, Bighorn was to become the dominant air charter operation in Wyoming with more than 20 aircraft, three divisions, and a satellite office in Casper. It boasts a maintenance staff of eight highly trained mechanics, bringing the total staff to 22 full-time employees.

Eisele says a lot has changed in the industry, and he is proud of the direction the company has taken under what he terms as a conservative leadership. Safety regulations, technical expertise and new maintenance requirements combine to make commercial aviation a capital-intense industry.

Many smaller operations in community airports have gone the way of the Sunday pilot during the 90s, but Bighorn has flourished. Eisele recently purchased four Dornier 228s to provide smoke-jumping support for government firefighting operations in Alaska. In addition, two Cassa 212s have been added to haul freight in addition to the pressurized twin-engine aircraft, bringing the fleet to more than 20.

Today the charter customers are companies, not individuals. Corporate aviation is dominated by businessmen who must get to meetings on time and in comfort. Eisele considers himself a curious combination of a risk taker and conservative. He is confident that the future will be filled with growth and opportunity. His son, Christopher, learned to fly at his father's side and is busy carrying on the family tradition, managing a portion of the operation and supervising a full staff of pilots. Chris is an accomplished and highly trained pilot, who has earned several aircraft type ratings well before others in his age group.

Eisele says that some might consider aviation to be a perilous occupation. He remarks that running a business today is a far more treacherous undertaking. "I wouldn't be in this business if I wasn't used to taking risks and wasn't willing to do that," he says matter of factly.

Knowing your market, knowing your company, and having a self-reliant style have enabled this family business to flourish while others have failed. Eisele readily admits he would find it difficult to work for anyone else. Looking back through more than 40 years in the industry, he says there is very little he would do differently.

Early summer mornings he most often can be found on the runway, preparing for takeoff in a single-engine crop-duster, something he still enjoys doing. He is a working owner and manager, demanding no less of himself than of others.

When he isn't performing delicate aerial work in the company helicopter, he is juggling crew schedules, checking weather conditions across the country and conferring with son Christopher while directing the multitude of workday tasks involved in any organization. Dan Hawkins and Gene Powers meanwhile enjoy a quiet retirement, knowing that the success of Bighorn Airways rests in the capable hands of the Eisele family.

The Sheridan community has been enriched by the company with annual payrolls of more than $1 million. Eisele says that in the coming years, he expects to be in Sheridan, right where he began. "I suppose I could do business anywhere, but this state is a fine state to live and work in. I'll stay here."

Wyoming Newspaper Group

Tracy S. McCraken sold newspapers when he was just a boy. At the age of 32, he began buying newspapers instead. Over the next 20 years, he established ownership in six of the state's nine dailies and formed the Wyoming Newspaper Group.

His is a story in the true Horatio Alger tradition. McCraken came west from Illinois to study journalism at the University of Wyoming in Laramie while working as a reporter for the *Laramie Boomerang*. After receiving his degree in 1917, he joined the Army, then returned in 1918 and set to work building his fortune. In 1926 he bought the struggling *Wyoming Eagle* with $3,000 — all of it borrowed.

From there he went on to acquire other papers, establish radio stations and pioneer television in Wyoming. He made himself a millionaire and a powerful presence in state politics, all the while insisting every one of his employees call him by his first name.

His legacy is alive today in the Wyoming Newspaper Group. From the beginning, the papers were locally managed and operated autonomously. This is still true today.

Wyoming Tribune-Eagle

The *Wyoming Tribune-Eagle* is the state's oldest newspaper. The *Wyoming State Tribune* began publication as the *Cheyenne Leader* in 1867, before Wyoming was even a territory. It recorded Indian massacres, vigilante justice and the fire of 1870, in which the paper's printing plant was destroyed. While undergoing various name and ownership changes, the paper played a part in achieving territory status and women's suffrage.

It also helped establish Cheyenne Frontier Days, started in 1897 and now the world's largest outdoor rodeo and Western celebration. One of the newspaper's owners, Edward Archibald Slack, considered to be the father of the event, used his paper to suggest and promote a celebration of the town's western heritage.

The *Wyoming Eagle* was a financially ailing weekly when McCraken bought it. By 1933, it was a daily and one of the state's leading papers. Four years later, McCraken and his associates bought another Cheyenne paper, the *Wyoming State Tribune*. Following Tracy's death in 1960, the newspapers were run by his son, Robert S. McCraken, and later his grandson, L. Michael McCraken, who is now president and publisher and who merged the newspapers into a single edition in 1994.

Rock Springs Daily Rocket-Miner

This newspaper began as the *Rock Springs Miner* in 1881, when Rock Springs was little more than a railroad work camp at the end of the tracks. In 1931, Tracy McCraken and his associates bought the competing *Rock Springs Rocket* and six years later, David G. Richardson began what was to be a 37-year tenure as publisher.

In 1941, Richardson brought the *Rocket* and *Miner* together under the same ownership, forming an alliance with the McCrakens that continues today. Richardson's son, Charles, stepped in as publisher with the 1974 death of his father. Holly P. Jackman became the first woman publisher of the combined publication in 1998, while Richardson remains as president of the company.

Richardson and the *Daily Rocket-Miner* are credited with helping establish Western Wyoming Community College in Rock Springs. Employees and owners have a long-standing tradition of contributing to the community, and that tradition continues today.

Laramie Daily Boomerang

When local Republicans backed the establishment of a newspaper in Laramie, they chose Edgar Wilson "Bill" Nye to head the enterprise. The first issue was printed in 1881.

A mule had walked up to Nye on a Laramie street, brayed in his ear, and would not be driven away. Consequently, Nye named the animal "Boomerang," then named his paper after his mule because "I never know where he is going to strike."

After Nye left because of health problems, the paper changed hands several times. It eventually became the *Republican-Boomerang* and Tracy McCraken, who had already acquired the competing *Laramie Daily Bulletin*, bought it in 1938.

R.R. "Russ" Allbaugh, who joined the company as general manager in 1945 and retired as publisher in 1992, oversaw the combination of the two papers into one in 1957, as well as computerization of the newsroom and offices and the introduction of daily color pages. Today Ronald A. Van Ekeren is publisher, continuing to maintain and improve the news coverage that has characterized the paper for more than half a century.

Northern Wyoming Daily News

The *Northern Wyoming Daily News* began as the *Worland Grit* in 1906. When Tracy McCraken bought the paper in 1939, he gave it its current name and hired Ted O'Melia as publisher. Together with circulation manager Elmer Downing (today the associate publisher) and news editor Robert Johnson (now on the board of directors), they soon had the paper up and running.

Hugh Knoefel continued as publisher when O'Melia left, and spent the next 38 years building up the paper. He oversaw its relocation to a new facility in 1955 and the conversion from hot lead to offset printing in 1973. Following Knoefel's 1984 retirement, Bill Frederick served as publisher until his death in 1988.

Bringing the paper into the new millennium under Lee Lockhart, the current publisher, is the staff: Deanna Blincow, Staci Brazell, Chuck Brazell, Mary Ann Brazell, Pat Crook, Bobbie Dorr, John Elliott, Dustin Fuller, Leonard Gentilini, Duane Groshart, Bonnie Sue Hall, Don Hall, Mary Lou Hanify, Al Haynes, Dennis Koch, Susan Lockhart, Richard Manning, Nash Mercado, Ellen Niles, Jeff Quintana, Diane Rideout, Dawn Rishel, Nyla Romero and Christine Weber.

Rawlins Daily Times

After launching the *Northern Wyoming Daily News*, Ted O'Melia moved back home to Rawlins and started publication of the *Rawlins Daily Times* in 1946. With the help of Tracy McCraken, he bought two weekly newspapers and made them into the daily. The paper, he wrote in its first editorial, "pledges its untiring efforts and such resources as it may command to aid other public-spirited institutions and individuals in a concerted effort to bring to fruition the great possibilities we know and you know are in store for Rawlins and the county."

O'Melia built the paper's current home in 1952, and had the foresight and faith in his paper to make it large enough to be still adequate today. After O'Melia retired, Russell Stout and then Ralph Geddes served as publisher, and since 1995 Dave Perry has held that job.

Wyoming Newspaper Group publishers photographed in February 1999 (from left): Lee Lockhart, *Northern Wyoming Daily News* (Worland); Dave Perry, *Rawlins Daily Times;* Holly Jackman, *Rock Springs Daily Rocket-Miner;* Ron Van Ekeren, *Laramie Daily Boomerang;* Mike McCraken, *Wyoming Tribune-Eagle* (Cheyenne)

The McCraken family continues its dedication to community journalism through its interests in these five newspapers to which Tracy first committed. His philosophy was that newspapers should be leaders in their communities. Today, a new generation of Wyoming publishers and journalists sees to it that they are.

Petroleum Association of Wyoming

Recognizing the importance of the petroleum industry, Wyoming Governor Brooks called the first meeting of what is now the Petroleum Association of Wyoming in 1910. Since its inception, the association's officers, members and staff have been dedicated to fostering the best interests of the public, the state and the ever-changing industry.

Oil was discovered in Wyoming by American Indians, who utilized it as liniment and paint. In 1851, explorers encountered black liquids bubbling in natural seeps near Casper. Mixing this oil with flour, they sold it as axle grease to westward bound wagon trains. Mike Murphy drilled Wyoming's first oil well in 1884, launching an industry that remains critical to the state today.

Soon after, Wyoming's great Salt Creek field was discovered. By 1925, 49 fields were located, many of which are still producing oil today. This era also saw construction of the state's first refinery and petroleum pipeline.

By the late 1920s, oil assumed a vital role in the national economy. Americans' love for automobiles assured oil a substantial position in the country's and state's futures. During the war years, Wyoming participated in several critical military supply contracts, almost doubling the state's oil production and reserves.

Within 40 years, Wyoming emerged as a significant petroleum producer, becoming the fifth-largest natural gas and the sixth-largest crude oil producing state. Reserves grew to fourth largest in natural gas and sixth largest in oil.

Wyoming's drilling levels reached epic proportions during the early 1980s; 14 refineries were in operation, extensive processing plants were constructed, the price of oil climbed to $32 a barrel and the industry directly accounted for 32,000 jobs. Shortly thereafter, prices for both oil and gas plummeted, drilling activity fell to a post-war low, refineries closed and, unfortunately, one-half of the industry jobs were lost.

At its peak, Wyoming's oil and gas industry accounted for 60 percent of the state's total taxable value. By 1998, it accounted for 39 percent. Nevertheless, 1998 taxes and royalties paid to state and local government tallied over $485 million, or about $1,000 for every man, woman and child in Wyoming. Payrolls and investments contribute hundreds of millions more.

The state and the petroleum industry have matured together in a partnership. The state has provided the place to conduct business, while the industry has furnished quality jobs and paid taxes that would have otherwise burdened residents.

The future of the industry is uncertain. Declining prices, higher costs, increased world oil supplies and weakened foreign economics have taxed the industry. Wells have been shut-in, projects abandoned and jobs eliminated. Wyoming's crude oil production and reserves peaked almost 30 and 40 years ago. Although natural gas production and reserves are rising, the rate of increase has slowed.

Much of the industry's future depends upon the decisions of the state's largest mineral owner, the federal government. As conflicts over expanded development and costs increase, investors will move elsewhere. Without investment capital, there can be no industry.

The petroleum industry has weathered many economic storms, thanks to dedicated, remarkable risk-takers who drilled just one more well, tested a dream or looked beyond the horizon. And, despite continual fluctuation, there remains considerable potential in Wyoming's oil patch. However, this potential can not be realized without commitments from the state, its residents and the industry.

(Right and far right) Petroleum Association of Wyoming yesterday and today
Right photo courtesy Wyoming State Archives

BP Amoco

BP Amoco has deep roots in Wyoming. It could be said that the company and the state grew up together. Since the early 1900s, the company has prospered through adversity, mergers and change.

The 1912 Wyoming Oil Mens Convention met in Casper to discuss a difficult problem-how to inform the public of the contributions from the oil industry. Weeks later, BP Amoco predecessor Standard Oil set in motion what was to become the core of Casper's future.

Breakthrough technology at Standard allowed refiners to double the yield of gasoline from a barrel of crude oil with a process called thermal cracking. Workmen traveled west from Indiana to build a vastly superior plant near the Salt Creek Oil Fields.

The refinery went on line in March of 1914, eventually processing 65 percent of the state's annual production. The 20s brought people and affluence to Casper. Paved sidewalks, new homes and steady work at the Standard refinery created continuity, becoming the center of social and workday life. The company prospered through the 20s, 30s and 40s by reacting quickly to market changes and continuing its dedication to lead technological advances.

Pipelines were constructed to carry crude oil to market, and in 1947 the company began a program of modernization that continues today. Standard and American Oil merged to become Amoco, while demand for petroleum products soared. Through the 80s, Amoco continued to serve its customers from the Casper refinery until the eventual closure in 1991. In 1998, the company and community signed an innovative agreement designed to return the property to productive use.

The merger between British Petroleum and Amoco in April of 1999 has allowed the company to reinvent itself. BP Amoco is the largest natural gas producer in the state, and although the name has changed, much remains the same. "We already were a multinational company as Amoco and are even more so now as BP Amoco," says Bill Stephens, community relations manager.

BP Amoco's goal is to play a leading role in meeting the world's need for energy and materials without harming people or damaging the environment. As the largest solar company in the world, with major holdings in petroleum, petrochemicals and natural gas, the company's environmental stewardship emphasizes production of low-sulfur gasoline and reduction of greenhouse gases.

Amoco Refinery was a leader for being environmentally sound, constructing a discharge pond that became the Soda Lake wildlife refuge. Amoco offered a full slate of lead-free products well before its competitors. "One of the things that has helped us survive is our drive to work safely and efficiently every day," says Site Supervisor Bob Brechtel.

There is the ability to respond rapidly to market changes, and the capital to jump into markets early. Management styles reflect accountability at all levels with room for creativity and the expectation that employees will find the best ways to achieve new goals.

BP Amoco is a strong player in natural gas exploration in the Jonah fields of southwest Wyoming. "This is one of the more exciting gas plays in the country," says Stephens. BP Amoco maintains a significant presence in the western United States as the largest natural gas producer in North America. As the demand increases, natural gas will continue to form a foundation for the company far into the next century.

Operations Specialist Randy Harvey of Baroil and countless other BP Amoco people of Wyoming share a proud tradition of helping meet the world's energy needs. Today's customers favor natural gas, and BP Amoco is a leading producer of this environmentally friendly fuel.

Exxon Company, U.S.A.

*O*ncorhynchus clarki pleuriticus.

Translated from Latin, it refers to the Colorado River cutthroat trout, a subspecies of the only trout native to Wyoming. With their vivid markings, including the orange throat slash that gives them their name, and their renowned ability for testing the skill of even the finest fishermen, the Colorado River cutthroat trout is a species in trouble.

Reported to inhabit about one percent of its historic range, and the trout's listing as a sensitive species, motivated Exxon's Black Canyon dehydration facility employees to take action.

The Sawmill Creek Trout Recovery Project in Sublette County was conceived by local Exxon employees and funded by a $75,000 pledge from Exxon U.S.A. in partnership with Trout Unlimited, the Wildlife Habitat Council and the Boy Scouts of America. Donations were received from local business and civic groups and many contractors and suppliers. Designed as a voluntary environmental project to help Wyoming's ongoing trout stabilization efforts, a location for the project was selected following a 1996 biological survey.

This 1.2-acre pond, which is the heart of the Sawmill Creek Trout Recovery Project, was conceived, designed and constructed by Exxon volunteers.

Built on a 40-acre site near Exxon's Sublette County well field, the project includes a one-acre pond to protect the fish by giving them a safe area in which to over-winter and spawn. Other enhancements include the renovation of a log cabin for use as a visitors center, the creation of picnic areas, and the installation of a wheelchair-accessible fishing dock for catch and release fishing. The pond and adjacent nature area will be used for educational field trips for local community groups and schools and will be home to about 300 Colorado River cutthroat trout.

Community efforts like the Sawmill Creek Trout Recovery Project underscore Exxon's ongoing commitment to protecting the environment. And, it reflects the company's desire to make a lasting contribution to the communities where its employees live and work.

Company oil operations are located 35 miles south of Gillette, Wyoming, at the Hartzog Draw Unit in the Powder River Basin, where Exxon operates approximately 160 wells, producing about 6,500 barrels of oil per day and 2 million cubic feet of gas per day. An active oil-drilling program will add even more wells in years to come. Employees at Hartzog Draw are proud to have recently doubled their contribution to the United Way of Campbell County, and employees support a variety of community events and organizations.

The LaBarge Operations, in southwest Wyoming, feature four major installations: the well field, comprising 17 producing wells in three federal units; the Black Canyon gas dehydration facility, where water is removed from produced gas; a feed gas pipeline, which carries dry gas south to Shute Creek; and the Shute Creek gas processing facility, where the gasses are separated for sale. Exxon began developing the LaBarge project in 1981 to produce gas from an enormous reserve located northwest of the town of LaBarge, Wyoming.

The gas reserves, originally discovered in 1956, contain a unique combination of carbon dioxide, methane, nitrogen, hydrogen sulfide and helium. Test wells drilled by Exxon in 1981 indicated significant amounts of these gases in a large underground reservoir.

Because of the gas field's location in the Bridger-Teton National Forest, Exxon had to develop methods for producing, treating and transporting the gas with the least amount of disruption to the area's wildlife and vegetation. And, due to air quality and other issues, production and manufacturing operations were divided over a large geographic area.

What resulted was an intricate gas gathering system that connects wells in three different areas to a centralized dehydration facility in Sublette County. More than 100 miles of gathering and utility lines are needed to move gas from individual wells to the gathering system. Here, the raw gas streams are combined into a single stream and routed to a separator, which removes most of the water.

The gases then flow to the dehydration facility to take out remaining water. The gas must be dried to allow it to be safely and economically transported for processing. The gas is transported via pipeline over 40 miles southeast to the Shute Creek gas processing facility in neighboring Lincoln County, where it is made ready for sale.

The importance of the LaBarge Operations to Wyoming and the United States would be difficult to overestimate. In addition to providing good jobs and tax revenues within Wyoming, LaBarge is an important player in product markets in Wyoming, across the country and around the world.

During construction of the LaBarge Operations, care was taken to preserve the area's natural and cultural resources, such as the tracks of the historic Oregon Trail that cross the well field. These efforts also included the restoration of the original homestead cabin near the Black Canyon dehydration site, completed with the assistance of the Sublette County Historical Society; and an archaeological excavation that uncovered the remnants of a society of prehistoric Native Americans near the Shute Creek processing facility. The recovered artifacts became the basis for an Exxon-sponsored exhibit at the Sweetwater County Historical Museum in Green River.

Exxon also showed concern for the impact that this $1.6 billion project would have on nearby communities. To help handle the temporary population increase caused by the influx of workers — at one point in 1985, some 6,000 people had jobs related to it — Exxon contributed $7.6 million to 44 different organizations in Sublette, Lincoln and Sweetwater counties. The funds were used to enhance schools, improve police and fire protection, pave streets, put in sidewalks, and support emergency, recreation and social service agencies.

In August 1986, after four years of planning, design and construction, Exxon's LaBarge project was completed. Gas production at the award-winning plant, named by the National Society of Professional Engineers as one of America's top engineering achievements in 1986, began at 480 million cubic feet a day. Through enhanced engineering and incremental investments, the production rate increased to 640 million cubic feet per day.

Today, Exxon's in-state operations employ approximately 140 Wyoming citizens and about 80 contract personnel. The Shute Creek gas-processing facility is one of the largest and most technologically sophisticated in the United States, with some of its climate controlled buildings covering an area greater in size than a football field.

From its LaBarge Operations, Exxon pays more than $10 million in production and ad valorem taxes to the U.S. government, the state of Wyoming, and to Sublette, Lincoln and Sweetwater counties. The company also spends about $48 million a year for goods and services related to operating and maintaining its

The Shute Creek gas processing facility in Lincoln County

Wyoming facilities, with two-thirds of this money remaining within the state.

Safety is a core value at Exxon. Employees strive to keep the workplace injury-free and to prevent accidents that might threaten public health or damage the environment. Employees and contractors receive ongoing safety training in accident prevention and emergency medical response procedures. Exxon's Wyoming safety statistics, as compared with that of other in-state companies, ranks among the best of the best. In 1997, for example, Exxon safety performance at its LaBarge Operations was about 30 percent better as compared with the oil and gas industry average. This accomplishment forms a record not only of Exxon's safety achievement, but also of its contributions to make Wyoming a cleaner, healthier and safer place for people to work.

While the LaBarge Operations and the company's other Wyoming-based facilities in Gillette and Kemmerer may be the more obvious examples of Exxon's contributions to the state, efforts like the Sawmill Creek Trout Recovery Project exemplify the company's commitment to making a positive and lasting impact on natural, cultural and educational resources as well. These are roles that Exxon plans well into the 21st century.

McMurry Oil

McMurry Oil is a Casper-based gas exploration and development company, one that, for most of its history, barely registered as a peer of the other Wyoming oil and

gas companies. By its own admission, it was a minor player — until a dogged vision, a willingness to take risks, and a dose of synchronicity changed its fortunes. Thanks to Jonah Field — a 33-square-mile gas field in southwest Wyoming — the company's simple motto, "We make gas," has taken on a much more dramatic meaning. The impact on the company has also been dramatic: under the leadership of founder W.N. (Neil) McMurry, President John W. Martin and Vice President Mick McMurry, the company quickly became the second largest gatherer of gas in Wyoming. The number of employees increased more than tenfold, from only six in 1992 to 70 in 1999. And the company's capabilities expanded to the level of a major player, overseeing exploration, development, production, transportation and marketing of its product.

The company's roots date back to 1970, when a friend of Neil McMurry convinced him to become a partner on a few oil wells. At the time, McMurry was part owner of a successful highway-construction firm, Rissler-McMurry Construction Company. The new venture proved successful on the first three wells drilled, and from that point on, McMurry kept his hand in the oil and gas business, using his construction income to finance the energy ventures. By 1983, he was the sole owner of the oil wells and needed someone to manage them for him. Laying the groundwork for what would later become a much larger enterprise, McMurry incorporated the business as McMurry Oil and hired John W. Martin — an experienced field engineer who had also served as Casper's airport manager — to run the company.

Bringing Martin on board eventually proved to be a positive move that helped the company's success, and he later became president and one of the shareholders, along with the McMurry family. For the first six months, he was the only employee. In the ensuing eight years, McMurry Oil remained small, but Martin was continually searching for the right property that would change its fortunes. In 1991, he found it in Sublette County's Jonah Field.

Like many oil fields in Wyoming, Jonah Field had been written off by the major oil companies as a non-commercial area. Unlike most of the others, however, it had never been seriously developed; its reserves were mostly untapped because the tight sand formations made it difficult and unprofitable to produce. Believing Jonah Field to have a large potential, and that the previous owners had used the wrong methods in attempting to drill the sites, McMurry purchased three natural-gas wells and leased 25,000 acres of land in Jonah Field in 1991. "It took a lot of guts to buy three old wells that had never produced and

constructing a pipeline to transport large volumes of gas to several markets. Before long, it was also transporting gas for other companies with a presence in Jonah Field, including Amoco, Ultra Petroleum and CNG. In 1999, the company operated more than 100 wells in Jonah Field, with a daily production of 249 million cubic feet of gas. Plans have been made for a new 45-mile, 20-inch pipeline and two compressor stations that will increase the field's production to 300 million cubic feet per day.

As a company with deep Wyoming roots, McMurry Oil has long been involved in the community, and is one of the largest benefactors of the University of Wyoming's Institute for Energy Research. Thanks to Jonah Field, it also has a dramatic economic impact on the state by making other contributions: creating a significant number of high-paying jobs; bringing new export sales into the state; and contributing additional tax revenues. With a final goal of 300 wells and an expected lifespan of 50 years for Jonah Field, that impact will continue for years to come.

McMurry Oil's meteoric rise has been hailed as a triumph of the little guys. And it is. Flying in the face of conventional wisdom, John Martin and the McMurrys believed in an opportunity that others thought nonexistent. Even in the absence of major financial backing, they went ahead with plans to develop the field. They struggled, kept on believing, and kept moving forward until Jonah Field became the success they always knew it would be. It seems likely that McMurry Oil's long history has only just begun.

McMurry's pipeline company, Jonah Gas Gathering Company, has put its construction equipment to work on building pipelines within the Jonah Field and to access major interstate pipeline hubs.

were 10 miles from a pipeline," Neil McMurry admits. Potential investors felt it was more a matter of sanity than guts, and all but two — Fort Collins Consolidated Royalties Inc. and Nerd Oil, a company owned by Neil McMurry's son Mick — declined to help develop the field. The company went forward without them.

In 1992, McMurry constructed a 10-mile pipeline, installed production equipment, and started producing natural gas and condensate. From the outset, the new enterprise exceeded expectations: instead of a yield of 1 million cubic feet of natural gas per day, the wells produced 2 million. With the company's belief in Jonah's potential justified, it quickly acquired an additional 100,000 acres and set about to develop the field. Such a large project required more financial resources than those of a small company like McMurry Oil, and Martin once again tried to raise capital by offering interests to major oil companies. Once again, they were skeptical and declined to become involved. Undaunted, the company kept on drilling. Finally, in 1994 — when it was clear that Jonah Field was a viable and rich source of natural gas — other investors joined the project and the development of the field began in earnest.

Within four years — after only partial development — Jonah Field became one of the top three most productive natural gas fields in Wyoming. As more wells were drilled, McMurry Oil grew quickly. McMurry's capabilities and vision grew as well. A small gas company's growth can be seriously hampered by having to rely on another — and usually larger — company's pipeline to transport its gas. As soon as state and federal environmental permitting allowed, McMurry began controlling its own destiny by

The Yellow Point #5-13 on the west edge of the Jonah Field demonstrates the ongoing fracturing and completion techniques that have made Jonah Field a success.

True Companies

Oil was first discovered in Wyoming by Native Americans who utilized the black tar from oil seeps as lubricants and paints. Captain Benjamen Bonneville, a French fur trader, located the "great tar spring" near present-day Lander in 1832, establishing Wyoming's first recorded history of petroleum.

The first oil well was drilled in Wyoming in 1884. Mike Murphy, a young entrepreneur, employed the use of a primitive rig and antiquated equipment to drill to a depth of 300 feet, giving birth to the state's oil and gas industry.

Wyoming's tremendous Salt Creek Field was discovered in 1889, and the first refinery in the state was built a few years thereafter. By the 1920s, oil assumed a momentous role in national economy, supporting war efforts in World War I and later, in World War II.

Wyoming Wildcatter H.A. (Dave) True, Jr.

It didn't take long for the major oil companies and smaller "wildcatters" or "independents" to see Wyoming as ripe for oil exploration. One of Wyoming's native wildcatters was H.A. (Dave) True, Jr.

As a young man, True dreamed of becoming an independent oil producer. After spending 11 years gaining field experience from The Texas Company, the aspiring 33-year-old received an offer to assume management of the Reserve Drilling Company. The "wildcatter" was ready to spring.

He sprang slowly, though — his equipment consisted of two broken-down rigs. However, True was resourceful. He combined pieces from one and components from the other until he had constructed one sturdy, fully operational rig.

True accepted a percentage of the net profits, and eventually the purchase of one-quarter interest in the company. The opportunity held uncertainty, but True was optimistic, persistent and indefatigable. By 1951, Reserve Drilling had expanded to five drilling rigs. When the then-current backers decided to sell their remaining interests, True "mortgaged everything to the hilt" in order to secure the buyout. Together with Douglas S. Brown, he formed an enterprise called the True and Brown Drilling Contractors. Soon thereafter, True acquired Brown's interest in the company. He and his wife, Jean Durland True, then formed the True Drilling Company and the True Oil Company.

The early years were rocky ones for the young True businesses. Financial uncertainties were the norm and meeting payrolls was often an effort.

True persevered, however, and continued to not only drill for others, but for True Oil Company. In addition to establishing production in the Clareton area (and after several dry holes), True made the first major Minnelusa discovery in the Powder River Basin at the Donkey Creek field. Soon followed other Minnelusa discoveries and the Coyote Creek field.

Unable to transport these new discoveries to market, True and several others formed Belle Fourche Pipeline Company to provide this service. As others also made major discoveries, Belle Fourche Pipeline Company expanded steadily. A decade after the inception of the Belle Fourche Pipeline, True purchased the remaining shares, then owning 100 percent of the pipeline's stock. The Trues later sold stock to each of their four children, Tamma, Hank, Diemer and David L., ensuring family ownership of the developing assets.

About the same time Belle Fourche Pipeline was being developed, the Trues expanded into the ranching business by acquiring the Double Four Ranch in 1957, which sits astride the North Laramie River on the

liquid hydrocarbons, and cattle. Today, Black Hills Trucking is one of the major heavy-haul trucking firms in the country.

The True's interests continued to expand, growing upward with each new venture. They recognized the need to get a better handle on their own financial picture and, in the process, acquired Midland Financial Corporation and its ownership of Hilltop National Bank in Casper, Wyoming. After that successful acquisition, the Trues stepped into the realm of geothermal activity, drilling in Hawaii and Nevada, and have since pursued several international oil and gas ventures. Dave True's business intellect and down-home demeanor led him and his businesses to prosper.

The True brothers have succeeded their father as entrepreneurs, involving themselves in every facet of the True companies. Tamma and her husband, Don Hatten, left the business to devote themselves, until recently, to their ranch in Thermopolis (the Kirby Creek Land and Cattle Co.).

Hank heads the pipeline as well as the crude oil and products purchasing and sales divisions of the True companies, while David L. directs the drilling and the agricultural aspects. Diemer manages the trucking business and the supply stores. All three partners take active roles in the operations of True Oil Company and Hilltop National Bank.

Wyoming's wildcatter, H.A. (Dave) True, Jr., said his wife Jean had been an excellent partner. They triumphed over challenges and controversy, making the term "independent wildcatter" a household word. Dave bequeathed a legacy to his family that has withstood the tests of time. He built it not of sticks and stones, but ingenuity, hard work and integrity.

southeast slope of Laramie Peak. The small start with a handful of cows and a single bull was the beginning of a new aspect of the True legacy, and laid the cornerstone for the True Ranches. Today, True Ranches consists of 11 operational units located in eastern Wyoming, South Dakota and Colorado. These operations constitute one of the larger agricultural operations in the Northern Rockies, and have included ranches, farms, feedlots, interest in packing plants, and retail marketing of "True Wyoming Beef."

The early 1960s brought a surge of growth for the True companies. They had succeeded with discovery wells at various sites and by 1963 had drilled their 1,000th well. The same year gave birth to what is now the Eighty-Eight Oil Company, a crude oil and refined products purchasing and sales operation stretching from the Northern Rockies to Oklahoma.

At this time, Toolpushers Supply Co. was formed to supply equipment to the affiliated companies; over time, Toolpushers Supply has grown to be one of the largest oil field equipment supply companies in the western United States.

True later decided to organize the trucking business that was so essential to all of his business ventures. Black Hills Trucking was born, thus enabling one entity to move heavy oil field equipment, crude oil and other

Jean and Dave True with part of their family

The Wold Companies

When asked for the name of an energy-producing state, the average person mentions Texas or Oklahoma. But the richest coal basin in the entire Western Hemisphere is located in the Powder River Basin of Wyoming and Montana. Wyoming is also rich in oil, gas, uranium and trona. At one time, major energy companies like Exxon or Amoco produced most of the energy — in the form of oil and gas — that came from the state's natural resources. By the 1990s, however, most of the exploration, development and production was being carried out by independent, Wyoming-based enterprises. The Wold Companies are among the leaders in that field. Headquartered in Casper, they are a family-owned group of companies with a reach and reputation that go beyond the state of Wyoming.

The Wold Companies were founded by John Wold, who became a well-known figure in Wyoming's mineral industry and has the distinction of being the first professional geologist to have served in the U.S. Congress. Coming to the Rocky Mountains after World War II, Wold started his career as an exploration and consulting geologist in the early 1950s. Laying the foundation for what would later become an energy dynasty, he used his expertise to evaluate and buy oil and gas leases, selling them to companies while retaining royalty interests. In the 1960s, he branched out into coal. When the federal government froze federal coal leasing in the early 1970s, he started Wold Nuclear Company, amassing extensive

Bob Wellborn (left), chief geologist for Wold Oil Properties, Inc. (WOPI) and Peter Wold review geophysical electric logs from the drilling operations at one of WOPI's central Wyoming oil fields.

On the job, John Wold well sitting, 1948

uranium holdings throughout the United States. The Wold Companies thus became active in all energy areas: oil, gas, coal and uranium, as well as trona.

Today, the Wold Companies' principle business remains oil and gas production. John Wold's sons Peter and Jack acquired full interest in Wold Oil Properties, Inc. (WOPI), in 1994. Peter handles the land and real estate operations of the company; Jack has followed in his father's footsteps as a professional geologist, and is a past president of the Wyoming Geological Association. With key employees Bob King and Mike Collodi, petroleum engineers; Bob Wellborn, geologist; Margaret Shearer and Travis Olsen, accounting; and Vi Pavkovich, office manager; the last half of the 1990s has seen significant changes in the Wold oil and gas activities.

An oil and gas production reserve base has been built in recent years primarily through careful acquisitions of properties that had become unprofitable for major energy companies. WOPI, however, can operate them at a profit because of its low overhead and expertise in finding missed production opportunities. Wold operates approximately 90 percent of the properties in which it has a working interest, with production split evenly between oil and gas. It drills wells, constructs pipelines, and handles all field production operations as well as product marketing. WOPI owns an interest in, and is operator of more than 230 wells in 20 fields throughout the state, with a presence in almost every Wyoming oil and gas basin. It also operates an NGL extraction plant and two sweetening plants to handle sour gas.

WOPI continues a long tradition of exploration and growth. It is constantly developing new ideas and ventures. The company is investigating a program to drill 200-300 coalbed methane gas wells in the Powder River Basin on Wold-owned leases in the first decade of the 21st century. A developmental drilling program for natural gas is also planned in its Muskrat and Riley Ridge fields.

The company has an exciting new venture in Southeast Asia. For years, exploration and production efforts have focused on Wyoming and neighboring states, but in the late 1990s, WOPI made a decision to pursue promising opportunities in Indonesia and Papua New Guinea, where energy demand is growing and the market is inviting for independent operators. As a result, WOPI is the owner and managing partner of Ramu International LLC, an overseas oil and gas exploration company. Ramu acquired three promising foreign concessions that cover 5.3 million acres — two in Papua New Guinea and one in Irian Jaya, Indonesia. In 1999, offices were established in Jakarta and seismic programs were conducted. Ramu accepted an agreement from Woodside Petroleum (affiliated with Shell Oil Australia) to partner on one of the Papua New Guinea licenses, and expects to negotiate similar arrangements with other industry partners on the other two concessions.

The Wold Companies' diversification strategy has also brought another important project to the point of fruition, the culmination of 30 years of careful planning. All U.S. glass contains a little bit of Wyoming — a white powder called soda ash, which is manufactured from the mineral trona (sodium sesqui-carbonate). Ninety percent of the world's supply of trona is found in the Green River Basin of Wyoming, and 90 percent of all soda ash produced in the United States is manufactured

John Wold standing at the base of Roland coal seam near Gillette, Wyoming

in Wyoming. With John Wold as president, Wold Trona Company has been developing the sixth trona mine and soda ash plant in the Green River Basin. Thanks to a revolutionary technology developed by Wold Trona Company at Hazen Research in Golden, Colorado, the company will produce Crystaltron™, a soda ash product with great purity and a manufacturing cost that is 40 percent less than competitors. "We are very excited about this new venture," Peter Wold explains. "Trona is one of the keys to our future."

For much of their history, the Wold Companies have been a step ahead of the industry because it anticipated future trends. As stewards of a broad spectrum of the world's natural resources, they have operated with the long-range future in mind. "We feel that our track record is one to be proud of. The company should continue to thrive and grow," Peter Wold predicts. "We are poised to be a major producer of low-cost energy and minerals for the United States and Southeast Asia in the next millennium. We look forward to meeting the challenge."

Peter Wold, Dr. H.L. Ong, John Wold, Bob King and Jack Wold gather following discussions on the Rombebai Production Sharing Contract in Irian Jaya, Indonesia, that the Wolds are developing with industry partners.

Fleischli Oil Company, Inc.

When Gus Fleischli bought a Cheyenne truck stop in 1955, Jerry Loghry was employed there as a fuel island attendant. The two men struck up a friendship, and later a partnership, and within a few years began to sell wholesale fuels and lubricants to area contractors. That enterprise grew into Fleischli Oil Company, Inc., providing petroleum products and related services to industrial end users, such as mining, construction, manufacturing and transportation companies.

Unloading fuel for one of the company's many mining customers

In the early 1960s, many of the contractors working for the Atlas Missile Program in Cheyenne fueled up and ate at the truck stop. Gus gathered, from conversations with the men, that they had a need for a fuel delivery service. Seeing an opportunity, he bought an old tank wagon and a 500-gallon tank.

When the missile project was finished, the era of interstate highway construction began, and Gus and Jerry delivered fuel for those contractors. A few years later, the uranium mining business boomed, and the mines bought fuel from Fleischli Oil. Coal and trona mining provided the next wave, and Fleischli Oil followed it into Colorado, Utah and Nevada. In Nevada, Barrick Goldstrike Mine became a customer and Fleischli Oil grew along with it and the rest of the Northern Nevada gold mining district.

Gus Fleischli

Gus and Jerry remained partners until 1997. That year, an employee buyout of Fleischli Oil was already underway when Meteor Industries, Inc., came in with an offer to purchase the company. Meteor, (NASDAQ: METR), led by Ed Names, is, through its subsidiaries, among the largest publicly traded petroleum products and services providers in the West. The offer was unanimously accepted by all employee owners.

Besides being a successful businessman, Gus Fleischli has also been a major figure in Wyoming politics. He was a legislator in the state house of representatives, a member of the highway commission, and a candidate for governor in 1976. In 1990, the Wyoming Mining Association named him one of the 25 Mining Men of the Century.

The company's goal, under the leadership of Bob Jensen, president since 1993, is to continue being the preferred supplier of fuels and lubricants to industrial customers in the Mountain West. High-quality maintenance programs and commitment to operator training, combined with excellent products and services from Fleischli Oil, all work together to reduce operating costs for those customers. Services offered include technical training for mine personnel on the complexities of fuel and lubricant formulation and application. In addition, Fleischli Fluids Management Group, LLC, offers on-site solutions to customers' varied fuel and lubrication staffing, inventory control, consumption and management needs. Fleischli Oil, through its affiliation with the ever-growing network of Meteor Industries distribution locations, is well-suited to handle the requirements of industrial customers into the future.

Fleischli Oil has always made a point of adapting its operations to the changing tide of economic conditions in the West, and now sells millions of gallons of fuel each year from warehouses and bulk storage facilities in Wyoming, Colorado, Utah, Nevada and New Mexico. The Fleischli|Meteor plan is to continue its success by exceeding the needs of customers, attracting more customers and acquiring more distributorships in the West.

Marathon Oil Company

Butch Cassidy and his Wild Bunch were still operating out of Hole-In-The-Wall. Masked gunmen like Bill Carlisle were still robbing trains. The year was 1912, and Wyoming was very much a raw frontier when Marathon Oil Company sent its first manager, John McFadyen to prospect for oil in the state.

This wild country had few roads, no navigable rivers, very few towns and hardly any people. Claim jumpers roamed the hills and had to be held off with guns while prospectors drilled for oil.

Marathon — then known as The Ohio Oil Company — persevered, however, and became a trailblazer in establishing a prosperous petroleum industry out of the Wyoming wilderness. In the more than three-quarters of a century that have passed, Marathon has emerged as the leading oil producer in the state, and a rising producer of natural gas as well. The company has used Wyoming's oil fields as a launching point for numerous advances in technology and production.

Marathon drilled its first Wyoming discovery at the Grass Creek Field in 1914. Grass Creek proved so prolific that the first million barrels were produced by the end of the year — selling for the handsome sum of 90 cents per barrel.

A string of successful discoveries followed over the next 20 years: Oregon Basin, Byron, Garland, Elk Basin, Lance Creek, Maverick Springs, Rock River and Big Medicine Bow.

Marathon entered Wyoming in 1912 to help pioneer the state's petroleum industry.

Those early operations were primitive. Established roads were few. Horses and mules hauled the drilling rigs, well service units and crude oil tanks. The appearance of rotary drilling tools, which replaced cable-tool drilling in the 1930s, and the advent of pipelines in the 40s were considered sizable advances.

A turning point came during World War II with a surge of new technology and cash flow to drive investments. By the end of 1991, Marathon had produced its one-billionth barrel of Wyoming oil.

Marathon continues to augment its Wyoming production through a diversity of advanced oil field techniques. They range from 3-D seismic analysis to infill drilling. A new focus on natural gas production has paid off with several successes in southwest Wyoming, as well as in the Oregon Basin Field of northwest Wyoming.

Recognizing Wyoming's pivotal role, Marathon has made Cody, Wyoming, the headquarters of the company's 13-state Rocky Mountain region, which stretches from California to North Dakota. Currently, Marathon has 270 employees in Wyoming, and a daily net production of 24,000 barrels of oil and 60 million cubic feet of natural gas. State and federal tax, and royalty payments generated by that production amounted to just over $21 million in 1998.

Marathon ranks as the largest oil producer in Wyoming.

As the industry has advanced, petroleum also has done much to bring about social progress in Wyoming. Marathon employees have helped numerous charities throughout the state, initiated youth programs for minority groups, and worked to develop museums, and cultural and environmental programs.

Marathon Oil is proud to have played a significant part in Wyoming's history and way of life since the pioneering days of oil production in the state. The company's exploration and production operations are sure to play an active part in Wyoming's future.

AIA Wyoming

A Chapter of the American Institute of Architects

For more than 137 years, the American Institute of Architects (AIA) has been the largest voice in the architecture community, working to advance the value of architects, architecture and the built environment. On June 15, 1946, 16 resident architects met in Cheyenne

On June 15, 1946, sixteen Wyoming architects convened to found AIA Wyoming. (See text for names of individuals.)

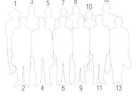

to form the Wyoming Chapter of the AIA. When the national AIA president signed a charter nine months later on March 15, 1947, the Wyoming Chapter became official.

As a component of the American Institute of Architects, AIA Wyoming is responsible for upholding the AIA mission, which is "to unite in fellowship the members of the architectural profession; to promote the aesthetic, scientific, and practical efficiency of the profession; to advance the science and art of planning and building by advancing the standards of architectural education, training, and practice; to coordinate the building industry and the profession of architecture to ensure the advancement of the living standards of people through their improved environment; and to make the profession of ever-increasing service to society."

Throughout its history, the Wyoming chapter has worked to further the mission by first establishing the Wyoming State Board of Architects in 1951, which tests and licenses all practicing architects to safeguard life, health and property of the citizens of Wyoming. William DuBois, commonly referred to as the "grandfather" of the profession in the state, was awarded Wyoming Architectural License Number 0001.

The 1960s brought an AIA focus on education and in the establishment of scholarships. Since the University of Wyoming has no nationally accredited curriculum in architecture, AIA Wyoming provided a leading thrust in the creation of the Wyoming Interstate Commission for Higher Education (WICHE) program. This has resulted in assistance being given to students in all types of accredited programs, from architecture to zymology. The AIA also helped the state of Wyoming adopt uniform building code regulations to safeguard life, safety, property and public welfare.

During the 1970s and 1980s, AIA Wyoming worked to advance public awareness in the importance of quality design in the built environment. To this end, statewide design award programs were established to recognize the best work in the state. The Wyoming Construction Industry Affairs Council was established to bring together architects, contractors, subcontractors, suppliers and major user-owners of building services to keep abreast of changes in the industry. It was also during the 1980s that then-AIA Wyoming President Christopher Robin Hard was recognized for his community service with the Volunteer of the Year Award, given by Governor Mike Sullivan.

AIA Wyoming has continued serving the people of Wyoming in the final decade of the century, first by publishing Conrad Schwiering's "High Country Meadows" painting, which later became the image on the state's centennial commemorative postage stamp and earned tens of thousands of dollars to benefit the Nicolaysen Art Museum in Casper. The Wyoming Chapter also established a scholarship fund. Endowments are awarded to worthy Wyoming students to study architecture in the name of Christopher Hard, who perished in a 1997 plane crash.

The complete chapter membership in the 20th century includes these Wyoming architects: Stephen Abel, Larry W. Abell, Delton Acker, Lavae Aldrich, William Allen, Louis Allen, Patrick Amend, Gerald

Anderson, Peter Anderson, Rod Armstrong, Earl Armstrong (4), Dennis Auker, Roger Baalman, Delmore Bailey, William Baker, Joseph Banner, James Barber, James Barlow, Timothy Belton, Robert Bence, Walter Bensman, Larry Berlin, Ira Blackwell, Mitchell Blake, James Boyle, Walter Bradley (5), James Brady, John Breternitz, Dale Buckingham, Kevin Burke, Richard Burnight, F. Byerly (10), Randy Byers, James Cappuccino, Dennis Carlson , John Carney , Nancy Carney , Elizabeth Carranza, Bonnie Chambers, Dick Cherry, Douglas Coates, John Conklin, Albert Cook, Harrison Cook, Robert Corbett, Larry Crane, Herbert Crowe, Claire Davis, Eugene Dehnert, Gerald Deines, Barry Dennis, Hal Dicks, Bruce Dilg, John Doerr, Edwin Dolence, James Donham, Kurt Dubbe, William Dubois, Margaret Duncker, Stephen Dynia, Daniel Eagan, Michael Eidem, Stephen Elliott, Dennis Emory, Jim Engelke, Harold Engstrom, Robert Fatovic, Richard Frazier, John Freed, Richard Frerichs, John Frullo, Glen Garrett, Roy Garrett, Ronald Goldberg, William Goodman, Leon Goodrich (1), James Goodwin, Ken Gorder, Paul Graves, Noel Griffith, Leon Hakkila, Forrest Hamilton, Peter Hanson, Chris Hard, George Harokopis, Fred Harrington, Merl Haworth, Bruce Hawtin, Randall Hein, Stephen Hines, Clinton Hitchcock (9), Elliot Hitchcock, Gustave Hollo (8), Bob Holzinger, Lisa Hubbard, Sam Hutchings (3), Fred Hynek, Ross Iverson, Chris Jensen, Morris Jones, Arne Jorgensen, Thomas Judson, Ravindra Kamat, Ed Kammerer, Armand Kellogg (11), Frederic Kellogg (6), Morris Kemper, Anthony Kimmi, Gary Kloefkorn, Roger Krebs, Karl Krusmark, Lee Krusmark, Mark Kucera, Michael Lascano, Alfred Lauber, W. Laviolette, Robert Liebsack, LeRoy Lowe, Richard MacConnell, A. Malone, Robert Marker, John McBride, Warren McCall, Kevin McDonald, Frank McFarland, Darrell McLain, Sallie Means, Linford Meese, Dill Morrison, Christopher Moulder, Richard Mumma, Thomas Muths, Robert Myrick, Albert Nelson, Kerry Norwalk, David Noyes, Ellis Nunn, Bradley Oberg, Daniel Odasz, James Outhier, David O'Malley, Stephen Pappas, Andrew Pappas, Jan Paul, Fredrick Petersen, James Pope, Frederic Porter Jr., Frederic Porter Sr. (2), Wade Porter, Robert Postin, Michael Potter, Rande Pouppirt, Kristoffer Prestrud, Keith Pryor, Michael Quinn, Charles Radich, Kenneth Richardson, Donald Richmond, Eugene Roberts, Richard Roche, James Rose, Arthur Roseblum, Larry Rosentreter, John Ruebel, Allen Saunders, John Sasama, Tim Schenk, Stanley Schoen, Bill Schropher, Keith Seebart, Douglas Selby, Dennis Sharp, Charles Shaver (7), Lynn Shoger, Edwin Shores, Everett Shores, Jim Silverthorn, Daniel Smith, Joe Sokal, Robert South, Pamela Spencer, Daniel Stalker, George Stein, Randy Stenson, William Stewart, Roger Strout, Lawrence Thal, Henry Therkildsen, James Thomas, Lori Tillemans, Kenneth Tobin, Stephen Tobler, John Toohey, Alan Torvie, George Tresler, Alan Tufford (13), Alan Turner, Charles Van Over, Joseph Vano, Jerry Voight, Robert Wallner, Thomas Ward, Richard Warvi, Robert Wehrli, Robert Weirdenaar, Clerence Whitney, Jan Wilking (12), Daniel Williams, Frank Witchey, and Oscar Woody.

AIA Wyoming looks toward the next century with renewed commitment to its mission with an emphasis on education, advancement of knowledge and an increasing scholarship fund. To better serve the profession and the public, the AIA looks forward to the creation of a permanent office in Wyoming with the associated employment. The architects of AIA Wyoming will continue to work with the public, the state and industry to build the great vision of Wyoming.

The architect-guided construction of the state capitol building in Cheyenne began in 1887 with continual additions in the 1920s and ongoing improvements throughout the 20th century.

Gorder|South Group Architects

As the turn of the century draws near, the professionals of Gorder|South Group look back with pride at their milestone accomplishments. Since the company's founding in 1970, Gorder|South Group has sought to give Wyoming and its fellow citizens useful, distinctive and enduring architectural designs. The firm is proud to have had the opportunity to work on so many fine projects and honored to have had so many distinguished clients. It is with eagerness and energy that the Gorder|South Group looks forward to the coming century, confident of its capacity to deliver the landmarks of the future.

Natrona County
High School Library/
Media Center —
Casper, Wyoming

Barrett Building
Addition and Remodel —
Cheyenne, Wyoming

Community First Bank
Remodel —
Casper, Wyoming

Nicolaysen Art
Museum —
Casper, Wyoming

Fox Theater —
Casper, Wyoming

Casper Surgical
Center —
Casper, Wyoming
(Consultant NBBJ)

Minerals Research
and Reclamation
Center, University of
Wyoming, Laramie
(Consultant NBBJ)
Photo by Bill Hook

Lathrop & Rutledge

Carlton Lathrop

Carl Lathrop

As a young man beginning legal practice in Green River, Wyoming, in 1928, Carlton Lathrop had assets. Intelligence was one, charm another. He was also a competitor. At a small Oregon college that played against major university teams, he excelled in basketball, baseball and tennis. A clergyman's son, he had a solid family background, and a Harvard degree and Rhodes Scholarship invitation to Oxford University highlighted his resume. The preponderance of evidence, therefore, was that he would succeed in law.

Lathrop's career was indeed exemplary. He compiled an impressive record of favorable court rulings, handled major estate and entity work, and was a fellow in the American College of Trial Lawyers. Highly regarded as a lawyer and Cheyenne community leader, he served as president of the chamber of commerce and the Rotary Club, and as director and general counsel for American National Bank. Musically talented, he enjoyed directing a church choir.

Lathrop's son, Carl, earned his law degree from the University of Colorado. He joined his father's firm in 1955 after having practiced law in Sundance, Wyoming, for three years. While practicing law with his father, Carl developed an impressive career of his own. He served as president of the Wyoming State Bar in 1980, was elected to fellowship in the prestigious American College of Trial Lawyers and American College of Trust and Estate Counsel, and has been listed in *Best Lawyers in America*. Carl has also found time for his community, serving on the school board, the chamber of commerce board and the Cheyenne Frontier Days Committee. As the senior member of the firm since his father's death in 1967, Carl has continued to lead by example both within and outside the firm.

Raised on a ranch, Kent Rutledge was inspired to go to law school because of both Carlton and Carl Lathrop, who were the lawyers for the Rutledge Ranch. The work ethic and principles Rutledge learned on the ranch coincided perfectly with those of the Lathrops, and he joined Carl Lathrop in the practice of law in 1974. Due in large part to the opportunities created by the Lathrops, Rutledge has enjoyed his own success as a lawyer, mainly in commercial and medical malpractice litigation. In 1999 he was elected to fellowship in the American College of Trial Lawyers. Rutledge has also been active in the community, having served on the board of the Cheyenne Chamber of Commerce, as chairman and as a board member of the Cheyenne Frontier Days Committee, and as a member of Rotary.

Lathrop & Rutledge continues to emphasize high ethical standards, hard work and quality representation in serving its clients. The firm's two other shareholders are Corey Rutledge, who joined the firm in 1989 and is involved primarily in medical malpractice litigation, and Jim Dinneen, a CPA and lawyer who joined the firm in 1994 and does mainly business and estate work. Sharing the values ingrained in the firm by Carlton Lathrop, they have contributed greatly to the firm's success. Corey has served as president of the Wyoming Association of Defense Trial Counsel. Lou Piccioni and Scott Meier joined the firm as associates in 1996 and 1998 respectively. Both provide support in litigation cases, and Scott, a CPA, also does real estate and business work.

American Heritage Center

The University of Wyoming's American Heritage Center is a major research facility and repository of manuscripts, rare books, the university archives, and materials related to the history of Wyoming, the West and American culture.

The American Heritage Center traces its origins to 1891 when Grace Raymond Hebard began serving as the university librarian. Hebard dedicated herself to studying, writing and teaching the people of Wyoming about their state's history. Among her major projects was the gathering of pioneer reminiscences, thus recording history that might have otherwise been lost. In the course of her 50-year career, Hebard amassed an impressive collection of Western history books, research notes and photographs.

After Dr. Hebard's death in 1936, the university used the materials she collected to form a small museum, housed in one room of the university library. In 1945, under the presidency of George Duke Humphrey, the room became the university archives and was named the Western History Research Center. The archives continued to expand, with the acquisition of 16 new collections, among them the Wyoming Stock Growers Association's records and the papers of the longtime U.S. senator from Wyoming, Francis E. Warren. By 1950 the center required two additional rooms to house its materials and its holdings continued to grow, eventually including 150 collections.

By 1958 the center occupied the south third floor of Coe Library. Under the directorship of Dr. Gene M. Gressley, the next three decades saw an aggressive acquisition program that greatly expanded the nature and volume of the center's collections. In 1977, to reflect these changes, the archives was renamed the American Heritage Center.

In 1991, as Dr. Michael J. Devine assumed the directorship of the center, construction began on the Centennial Complex, which houses both the American Heritage Center and the University of Wyoming Art Museum. Currently, the center maintains more than 7,000 manuscript collections related to Wyoming and the American West, the mining and petroleum industries, U.S. politics and world affairs, conservation, water resources, transportation, the history of books, and popular culture.

The center's largest collection, the Anaconda Geological Documents Collection, includes more than a million documents, maps and reports from the Anaconda Mining Company covering the United States and more than 10 foreign countries. The center is home to the Clara & Frederick Toppan Rare Book Library and also houses more than 500,000 historic photographs. Among the center's best-known photographic resources are the Charles H. Belden and Richard Throssell collections.

The American Heritage Center collects and preserves materials of enduring value and makes this material available to students, scholars from throughout the world and the general public. In 1998 the American Heritage Center's reference staff assisted more than 4,000 patrons. The center also continues to acquire and process new collections. Among the more significant recent acquisitions were the Wyoming Hereford Ranch Papers and the papers of Nellie Tayloe Ross, Wyoming's first woman governor. The center also serves the public by providing a wide range of scholarly and popular programs including symposia, lectures, concerts and exhibits.

The American Heritage Center supports the University of Wyoming's charge of teaching, research, public service and cultural outreach. Through each of these functions the center fulfills its mission of enabling and promoting the study and interpretation of our nation's history.

A mission of excellence — AHC is dedicated to meeting the informational demands of present and future generations by maintaining the highest professional standards in collecting, preserving, describing, researching, and allowing public access to historical resources.

Wyoming Business Alliance/
Wyoming Heritage Foundation

It is Wyoming's largest pro-business organization, having grown to nearly 1,200 members since its founding in 1979. Representing a broad cross section of business and industry, the Wyoming Business Alliance (formerly Wyoming Heritage Society) and Wyoming Heritage Foundation have achieved tremendous momentum in the last 20 years. Established by a group of businesspeople — Stan Hathaway, former governor of Wyoming, John Wold, a former congressman, Warren

Wyoming Heritage Foundation Annual Forum, November 19, 1998 (left to right) Phil Morrow, Dan McMullin, Keith Hay, Barbara Dilts

Morton, Mary Mead Steinhour and other leaders — the organization's goal is to promote Wyoming's economy.

The Wyoming Business Alliance is a private sector-funded, statewide advocacy group involved in public policy issues, legislative issues, economic research, regulatory efforts, and federal land problems facing the state. Based in Casper, it is Wyoming's only statewide association representing the interests of individuals and businesses of all sizes. Its partnership structure with state business trade associations is unique to Wyoming. No state chamber of commerce or business association anywhere in the country has the same kind of partnership arrangement.

The Wyoming Business Alliance membership reads like a who's who of Wyoming's economic forces. Banking, retail, manufacturing, business, ranching, mining, tourism, oil and gas, service organizations and individuals all participate in Wyoming Business Alliance efforts.

Harry Roberts, former state superintendent of instruction, was the group's original executive director.

When Roberts retired in 1987, Bill Schilling, former director of the Cody, Wyoming, Chamber of Commerce and Cody Economic Development Committee took the reins.

Now president of the organization, Schilling and his staff coordinate and organize Wyoming Business Alliance activities. The Wyoming Business Alliance relies on active volunteers. The organization's steering committee is comprised of 61 individuals. Forty-two of them are on staggered three-year terms. The other 19 are the presidents or a designee from state business trade associations, such as the Wyoming Stock Growers Association, Retail Merchants, Wyoming Contractors Association, Wyoming Association of Realtors, Petroleum Association of Wyoming and Wyoming Mining Association.

The Wyoming Business Alliance draws heavily on its members for their expertise. All of the association partnership members are encouraged to give reports on what's going on in their sectors. This represents a unique opportunity to share information and find common ground. They talk about their legislative agendas and business concerns.

One of those opportunities comes during the organization's annual public forum held in Casper each November. It has come to be known simply as The Wyoming Forum.

"We tackle some very tough issues," Schilling asserts. "We have the ability to orchestrate very objective, probing and thorough sessions with lots of viewpoints expressed. It's an extraordinary gathering of people and ideas. We bring in national talent. Those people invariably say that our forum is as good as any in the country."

Regularly attended by more than 700 people, the day-and-a-half forum is the largest of its kind in the Rocky Mountain region. The forums have taken on subjects like taxes and spending, the economy, economic diversification in Wyoming, education, and critical social issues, such as the proliferation of drugs in society.

The organization is involved in a host of ongoing public policy issues. For example, Wyoming is a state that gets the bulk of its tax revenues from the minerals industry. With commodity prices in the minerals sector depressed, the impact is really felt. The people of Wyoming have become accustomed to low-cost services, with the minerals industry paying most of the bill. Now other revenue sources must be identified or programs cut back. This is the kind of benchmark issue the Wyoming Business Alliance helps to resolve.

Direct impact by the Wyoming Business Alliance on the state's economy is evidenced by its role in the Kern River Pipeline Project. In the late 1980s, California was seeking a cost-efficient, reliable source of natural gas. Competing against pipeline proposals from Canada, New Mexico and Texas, Wyoming proposed a $1 billion pipeline from Wyoming to Southern California. The Wyoming Business Alliance led the legislative lobbying effort in Wyoming, as well as the marketing effort in California. The resultant 904-mile long pipeline, which carries 750 million cubic feet of Wyoming natural gas a day to California, has generated in excess of 500 jobs and more than $35 million annually in new state and local tax revenues.

The Wyoming Business Alliance also played the leading role in formation of, and legislative approval for, the Wyoming Business Council, a state-funded, governmental body whose charter is economic development in the state through job creation.

"We're the group that basically tries to make things happen," says Eli Bebout, current speaker of the house and chairman of the Wyoming Business Alliance.

Every other year the Wyoming Business Alliance holds an economic forum. The one in 1996 identified the need to move the state forward and to restructure economic efforts. The Wyoming Business Alliance raised $40,000 from the private sector for a feasibility study. Legislators were impressed enough that they allocated another $40,000. A state-appointed committee prepared a comprehensive study, which was released in November of 1997. Then in the 1998 legislative session, the Wyoming Business Alliance led the lobbying effort to get the Business Council legislation passed.

The Wyoming Business Council has been operational since May of 1998. Five of its 15 members are on the Wyoming Business Alliance Steering Committee.

The approach used by the Wyoming Business Alliance is an overarching one. It is interested in the economy and the overall quality of life in Wyoming. If it has the resources and the time to get involved, it will. That applies to any issue in any field. But it is important to be selective. "We try not to be all things to all people because it saps time, energy and resources," says Bebout.

Perhaps the most critical issue facing the state today is the importance of economic diversification. Over-reliance on just a few industries leaves the state's economy, and its tax base, vulnerable. The Wyoming Business Alliance plays an important role in ensuring that issues such as economic diversity are addressed in a manner that brings results. If the past is any indication, the degree to which the Wyoming Business Alliance is successful, the state of Wyoming also will succeed.

Mary Mead Steinhour Heritage Award recipients, Mike and Jane Sullivan, November 1998 (left to right) Bill Schilling, Sue Schilling, Jane Sullivan, Eli Bebout, Mike Sullivan (U.S. Ambassador to Ireland and former Wyoming governor), Lorraine Bebout

Blue Cross Blue Shield of Wyoming

In the late 1920s, an innovative approach to help individuals cover the cost of health care was developed, as Americans struggled with rising hospital and doctor bills during the Great Depression. It was an indemnity-type health insurance program that would shape the future of the health insurance industry. Following this revolutionary concept, Blue Cross Hospital Plans and Blue Shield Medical Plans organized throughout the United States. Next, the Blue Cross Blue Shield Association formed to set standards of business and cooperation between the independent plans. The Blue Cross Blue Shield brand was recognized as the leader in quality, service and dependability.

In Wyoming, the Blue Cross idea received help from the ladies of the Farm Bureau, who approached C.N. Bell, a Cheyenne insurance man and secretary of the Laramie County Farm Bureau, to find out how to get a Blue Cross operation started in Wyoming. After traveling to Chicago to visit with the national Blue Cross Association, and against the advice that Wyoming was too small to support a separate Blue Cross Plan, Bell and his associates in the Farm Bureau set out to establish such a plan in Wyoming. Wyoming Hospital Service was formed in 1945 and Arthur R. Abbey, from the Colorado Blue Cross Plan, was hired in 1946 to be the first director. In 1947, approval was received from the Blue Cross Commission for a separate Blue Cross Plan in Wyoming. That same year, Wyoming Medical Service (Wyoming Blue Shield) was formed to provide coverage for physician services. The two organizations consolidated in 1976 under the name Blue Cross Blue Shield of

Wyoming, and shortly thereafter Charles E. Chapman took over as president of the new organization. Blue Cross and Blue Shield of Wyoming has been guided over its 52-year history by a diverse 12-member board of directors that has included Wyoming health care professionals and businessmen and women who have remained committed to delivering quality health insurance programs to the residents of Wyoming.

Blue Cross Blue Shield of Wyoming is a major Wyoming employer with over 200 employees in its Cheyenne headquarters and 10 field offices throughout the state. The strength of the organization is dependent upon the talent and dedication of its employees. This strong employee base allows the company to continue offering the highest level of service to its customers and ensures the company meets its responsibilities as a good corporate citizen by involving itself and its employees in their communities. Blue Cross Blue Shield of Wyoming is the local presenting sponsor for the Komen Foundation's Race for the Cure® and has been involved since the race's inception in Wyoming. It is a statewide sponsor of the American Cancer Society's Relay for Life and supports many other runs, walks and blood drives, as well as the Special Olympics, the Senior Olympics and the Cowboy State Games. This community commitment holds true on an individual level as well. Many employees participate in their local civic organizations. It all comes from a belief in their responsibility to improve the quality of life and promote the activities available in Wyoming.

A corporate commitment to putting the customer first has led to the development of a team of knowledgeable, highly trained customer representatives.

Blue Cross Blue Shield of Wyoming President and CEO Tim Crilly meets with The Wyoming Caring Program Executive Director, Lynn Klockseim, and Caring Foundation Board Chairman, Dan Sullivan.

Blue Cross Blue Shield understand that there are those who cannot access the health care system as easily as others, and in 1989 it established the Caring Program Foundation to provide essential basic health and dental care for uninsured children. With the help of participating Wyoming hospitals, physicians and dentists, and the financial support from businesses, associations, churches, civic organizations and individual donors, the Caring program has provided primary, preventative and emergency health care to more than 2,000 Wyoming children. Blue Cross Blue Shield of Wyoming is the underwriter for the operational costs of the program and also donates funds to match the program's private donations.

Although Blue Cross Blue Shield of Wyoming operates statewide, it relies heavily on local marketing and service efforts, and local community involvement. In addition to the corporate headquarters in Cheyenne, offices in Casper, Cody, Gillette, Jackson, Laramie, Rawlins, Riverton, Rock Springs, Sheridan and Worland help meet the needs of Wyoming residents, preserving their access to health care. As the original founders of Blue Cross Blue Shield of Wyoming understood, the state of Wyoming, with its large geographical area and small population, is unique, and its health care environment is no exception. Insurance products that work elsewhere may not meet the needs of the people of Wyoming where, in a population of less than half a million people spread across a vast space, people may drive a hundred or more miles to the nearest health care professional or facility that can provide care for their particular needs.

Blue Cross Blue Shield of Wyoming also administers benefits for various public agencies including Medicare,

federal employees, and military dependents and retirees. The cost to individuals and employers is always a concern and must be balanced with the level of benefits offered, as the company seeks to provide the best benefits and service at an affordable price. Wyoming residents live and work under many different situations, but all share a desire for access to quality health care. In the Wyoming environment, a great deal of flexibility is necessary to deal with access and cost issues that are not always present in other states and geographical areas, resulting in some unique customization in the design and delivery of products and services.

One of the greatest strengths of Blue Cross Blue Shield of Wyoming is its affiliations with a vast network of health care providers. More than 1,500 Wyoming physicians, hospitals, dentists and other health professionals provide its members with easy access to the best medical care available. Blue Cross Blue Shield's Wyoming networks are also supported by a national network that includes over 5,100 hospitals and more than 482,000 physicians and medical providers throughout the United States.

Tim J. Crilly, president of Blue Cross Blue Shield of Wyoming, understands that as new technology evolves in the area of health care and new medicines and better treatments are found to cure diseases or relieve suffering, the issues of access to health care and the cost of health care will continue to play an important role in what consumers will demand from the health industry and their health insurance programs. According to Crilly, "as the needs for health care and health care coverage change, Blue Cross Blue Shield of Wyoming will continue its corporate mission to be a part of structuring an accessible and affordable health care environment for the people of Wyoming and to be an industry leader in meeting the health care needs of its residents."

The Church of Jesus Christ of Latter-day Saints

The man was just a tourist, really. Passing through. But his visit more than a century and a half ago would affect Wyoming history, lore and culture right into the 21st century.

A group of wagons climbs toward South Pass in July of 1997 as part of the Sesquicentennial (150 years) re-enactment of the crossing of the 1,100-mile Mormon Trail from Omaha to Salt Lake City.

On June 2, 1847, a stout New Englander stepped into the trader's store at remote Fort Laramie (about 90 miles northeast of today's town of that name). Perusing the shelves with only half-interest, he informed the sutler that he was seeking mostly information: distances, routes, weather. Asked about his intentions, the man said he was on his way over, and beyond, the Rockies, likely the basin of the Great Salt Lake. When the trader told him the mountain men reported that to be inhospitable country, home to practically no one, the New Englander assured him that that's exactly why he was going there. Camped down river about three miles were his colleagues — 141 men, three women and two children — well fit out and ready to keep moving. And on

Afton, Wyoming, in 1929 — one of more than a dozen Wyoming communities settled by Latter-day Saints

the trail behind them, strung out across Nebraska and Iowa, and coming this way were another 16,000-20,000 people, all recently forced from their comfortable homes in Illinois, and all seeking the refuge of a new homeland.

The trader stepped from behind the counter and offered his hand in greeting. "Ahh," he said quietly. "You must be Brigham Young."

Leading the Vanguard Company of a migration that would leave him noted in press reports of the day and historical records of the future as "the American Moses," Young's trek had really begun 16 months and 900 miles earlier in Nauvoo, Illinois. There, he and his fellow members of The Church of Jesus Christ of Latter-day Saints were routed from their own city by a surrounding populace that would no longer tolerate their growing political and economic strength, nor their unique Christian viewpoint.

Thus in Young's footsteps they would come for the next 22 years. Between 1847 and 1869, when the Transcontinental Railroad was completed, another 60,000 Latter-day Saints would follow this trail of hope across Wyoming, on their way to a land of promise 450 miles to the west. Most would exit the boundaries of the modern state just south and west of Evanston.

Some would later return. Some would never leave. But two occurrences in 1856 would render portions of the state sacred ground forever.

With Salt Lake City proving itself a true refuge, converts to the rapidly growing faith were encouraged to gather there from around the world. Many coming from Europe arrived with little in either cash or commodities, so a plan was devised in the mid-1850s that would enable them to travel lightly — pulling handcarts.

The first three companies of 1856, launching their 1,000-mile walk in spring, made good time and lost but few, mostly the aged and infirm. But two companies traveling late that year, against counsel, nearly lost everything. At Fort Laramie they found the provisioner mostly out of goods for the season, and daily rations were cut. Just before Casper they saw snow lying low on the mountains and just beyond Casper they met it, falling quickly and building fast. Young and old began to die. Wrote one diarist," Many a father pulled his cart, with his little children on it, until the day preceding his death."

The James G. Willie Company, 100 miles in the lead and breaking track through nearly 20 inches of snow, made it to an area of little shelter about 20 miles due west of today's Jeffrey City, Wyoming; the larger Edward Martin Company sought shelter in a horseshoe-shaped ravine in the granite hills just west of Devil's Gate on state Highway 220. In the next few days — frozen in place and starving — nearly 250 people died in the two companies before courageous rescuers arrived from Salt Lake City with a small caravan of supplies. Five more handcart companies would cross Wyoming in the next four years, and none would experience similar tragedy.

Throughout the decades of the 1900s, the state of Wyoming and The Church of Jesus Christ of Latter-day Saints would erect and expand memorials to the pioneers in places like Rock Creek Hollow (the Willie Company rescue site), Martin's Cove (Martin Company), Fort Caspar (where Brigham Young's Vanguard Company built the state's first commercial river ferry) and Fort Bridger (used in the mid 1850s as a supply station for the emigrants). Across Wyoming, visitors today can follow the trail experience at nearly three dozen historic sites. At the free visitor center and interpretive site near Martin's Cove, modern pioneers can even experience the rigors — minus the tragedy — of pulling an authentic handcart.

Latter-day Saints would return to Wyoming for permanent settlement over the next decades. In the late 1870s LDS colonizers discovered far western Wyoming's Salt River Valley, which one of their leader's soon renamed "Star Valley" because it was such "a star among valleys." Most of the communities between Jackson Hole, Wyoming, and Montpelier, Idaho — an area known as "Mormon Row" — descend from that colonization period.

In 1893 a few LDS families moved north from the Ashley Valley of eastern Utah to establish the community of Burlington in the Big Horn Basin. In 1900, Wyoming Governor DeForrest Richards made a formal request of church leaders to send more Latter-day Saints into the region to assist in colonizing northern Wyoming. That they did, establishing the communities of Lovell, Byron and Cowley. In Cowley the Big Horn Academy was founded in 1908, offering high school training to local students (of any faith) until other available options made it more economical to participate in the state system.

In the mid-1930s an attractive Institute of Religion was constructed on property adjacent to the University of Wyoming on Grand Avenue in Laramie. This facility continues to offer training in religious doctrine and history for young adults attending the university or living in Albany and surrounding counties. And for these students, a significant part of that history is local.

Due in large measure to the state's open spaces and clean air, and its own rugged heritage — Latter-day Saints today represent more than one-tenth of Wyoming's population. In 1999 there were 55,000 Latter-day Saints in nearly 145 congregations around the state, forging ahead on their own trail of hope.

Many sites along the Mormon Trail through Wyoming are considered sacred ground to millions of Latter-day Saints, but easily the best known is in Martin's Cove, where more than 160 pioneers died seeking shelter from early snows in 1856.

Throughout the late 1800s and early 1900s Latter-day Saints from Utah and Idaho re-settled in parts of northern and western Wyoming, as seen in this photo of one such "organizing company" camped in the vicinity of Kemmerer in 1900.

During the 1997 re-enactment of the crossing of the Mormon Trail, a group of about 50 hardy souls — ranging in age from three years to 65 — walked 1,100 miles from Omaha to Salt Lake City pulling their belongings in handcarts, just as some of their forebears had done.

Sheridan VA Medical Center

In 1898, after a concerted struggle by Wyoming congressmen and citizens of the Sheridan area, the U.S. Congress legislated funds for a Wyoming army post near Sheridan. The post, Fort Mackenzie, operated from 1902 through 1918, contributing significantly to the Sheridan economy through the purchase of goods and provisions and the employment of construction workers.

After the fort had outlived its purpose — protection against Native Americans — and was vanquished in the due course of army reorganization, the Sheridan community again mobilized to successfully lobby for a new use for the facility. In 1921, the grounds and buildings were transferred from the War Department and became part of the national health care system for veterans. Renamed "The United States Public Health Hospital at Fort Mackenzie," the establishment came into being as a 125-bed general hospital specializing in neuropsychiatry.

The new hospital began to expand immediately, quickly growing to accommodate 500 patients while simultaneously providing jobs and sales for Sheridan area residents. World War II saw a brief re-activation of the facility as a military presence in the form of a horse-breeding program for the War Department's Remount Program.

The post-war world included a new awareness of the importance of mental illness and new techniques and drugs for treating it. The Sheridan VA Medical Center has remained state-of-the-art in this arena, offering a number of specialty programs designed to meet individual mental health/emotional needs on modern inpatient units, facility outpatient clinics and at community-based outpatient clinics in Casper and Riverton.

These clinics, an outgrowth of today's increasing emphasis on outpatient programs, have followed the Sheridan VA Medical Center's lead in providing comprehensive primary care as well as mental health services. In accordance with a primary care model, patient health care is overseen by teams, which provide individualized care. A telephone consultation program permits patients to contact team members with questions about health care or eligibility.

Today the Sheridan Veterans Affairs Medical Center, the county's largest payroll and a member of the Rocky Mountain Veterans Integrated Services Network, is a modern neuropsychiatric and primary medical facility, offering services ranging from acute inpatient to supportive outpatient care and specialized programs for post traumatic stress disorder, substance abuse, geriatrics (a modern nursing home was established in 1994) and Alzheimer's. In 1999 the center's staff of approximately 400 will provide care to almost 7,000 veterans in 45,000 outpatient visits and 1,300 hospitalizations.

In 1998 Fort Mackenzie celebrated its centennial with glorious fanfare. Staff members appeared in period dress, and the Sheridan townspeople streamed up the hill to their former fort. Entertainment festivities peaked with a performance by descendants of the fort's most famous soldiers — two black cavalry regiments called "the Buffalo Soldiers" — who performed military drills on horseback in costume.

The sentinel on the hill above Sheridan looks much as it did in the early 1900s, its array of magnificent old buildings spread over the tree-dotted landscape. Now, as then, it offers protection to patients in need of intensive, acute or intermediate care benefits, through a competent staff of physicians, nurses and allied health care providers.

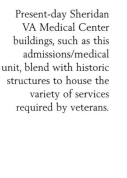

Present-day Sheridan VA Medical Center buildings, such as this admissions/medical unit, blend with historic structures to house the variety of services required by veterans.

Cheyenne VA Medical Center/
Cheyenne VA Regional Office

The Cheyenne VA Medical Center, established in 1934 as a facility capable of accommodating 100 patients, today provides inpatient services in medicine and surgery and outpatient services in medicine, surgery and psychiatry to veterans residing in Wyoming, Northern Colorado and western Nebraska. The medical center also supports a 50-bed nursing home care unit located within the main hospital building and community outpatient clinics in Fort Collins and Greeley, Colorado. The veteran population within the Cheyenne VA's service area is 51,000 veterans, an area of approximately 40,288 square miles.

The Cheyenne VA is affiliated with the University of Wyoming Family Practice Residency and the University of Colorado Medical School. The facility also has an active sharing agreement with the 90th medical group at F.E. Warren Air Force Base. Resources shared through this agreement include inpatient, outpatient and special medical services. Cheyenne is a TriCare health care provider for military retirees and their dependents and operates a national medication-by-mail program for ChampVA beneficiaries.

The VA's 50th birthday was marked in Cheyenne by a "Save the Shelterbelt" campaign to replace trees and shrubs lost over the years to severe winters. A crew of 40 planted thousands of evergreen and deciduous trees, many gathered from nearby hills, in the short span of a day-and-a-half, resulting in one of the finest shelterbelts in southeast Wyoming on the center grounds.

Cheyenne VA Regional Office

The Cheyenne VA Regional Office is part of the Veterans Benefits Administration, which is the VA department that provides nonmedical benefits to veterans. These benefits include home loans, education benefits, disability benefits for service-wounded veterans, and pension benefits for low-income wartime veterans. Veterans benefits were first handled by the Department of Veterans Benefits when the Veterans

Administration took over payments from the old War Bureau, which had processed the claims of Spanish-American War veterans.

In Wyoming, the Cheyenne VA Medical Center and the Regional Office have worked together since 1934 to

The Cheyenne VA Medical Center is housed in Spanish mission-style buildings, nestled on 51 acres of beautifully landscaped grounds. Visitors to the center find the environment both attractive and relaxing.

provide the total range of benefit services to veterans in Cheyenne and throughout Wyoming. The employees of the Cheyenne VA office are truly part of the Cheyenne community, serving veterans who are often their friends and neighbors.

In 1984, the year of its 50th anniversary, the Cheyenne VA Medical Center and Regional Office served 67,000 veterans. This number has since declined, but while the number of veterans served is decreasing, the dedication of the Cheyenne employees is not. In recent years, they have hosted town meetings for veterans across Wyoming, from Thermopolis to Casper to Gillette to Cody, and have initiated outreach programs for such specific groups of veterans as Native Americans, ex-POWs and women veterans. An extensive, successful search for Wyoming World War I veterans, who were awarded the National Order of the Legion of Honor by the French government in 1999, is an example of the service that the Regional Office and the Cheyenne VA jointly plan to continue in Wyoming during the next century as they remember their mission to serve and honor veterans who have served their country.

The Kemmerer Legacy

The late 1800s brought many entrepreneurs and business opportunities to the young state of Wyoming. One such pioneer was Mahlon S. Kemmerer, founder of the town of Kemmerer, Wyoming. Hailing from Cherry Valley, Pennsylvania, this Civil War veteran assembled an echelon of commercial enterprises throughout Wyoming, creating a legacy for his descendants, which is represented today by the Kemmerer family's proud ownership of the Jackson Hole Mountain Resort and the CM Ranch in Dubois.

It all began in 1895, when Mahlon met a man named Patrick J. Quealy Sr. on a train. Quealy, a cattle rancher and mine developer, was looking for a business partner to begin a coal mining operation in the Ham's Fork area. Ham's Fork was a logical place to begin an operation, as the area contained the only meaningful source of coal to support the coal-fired locomotives that ran through Ham's Fork on their way Northwest via the Oregon Short Line Railroad.

Rising above the splendor — Jackson Hole Mountain Resort

Mahlon joined Quealy as an investor in 1896 by executing the "Ham's Fork Land Proposition" in the Great Northern Hotel in Chicago. Shortly thereafter, Mahlon procured land north of Diamondville, Wyoming, for the development of coal properties. Within two years Mahlon and Quealy had created four organizations — the Frontier Supply Co., the Ham's Fork Cattle Co., the Unita Improvement Co., and The Kemmerer Coal Company. By the end of 1897, the town of Kemmerer had become a bustling mining town, having attracted 800 residents and its first hotel. Five years later, in 1902, retail merchant JCPenney began his national chain of department stores in Kemmerer, establishing a small mercantile known as The Golden Rule in the town. Although Mahlon made his home in Mauch Chuck, Pennsylvania, now called Jim Thorpe, the state of Wyoming retained a large portion of his heart, enticing even his descendants to savor a taste for the West.

Born in 1911, Mahlon's grandson, John L. Kemmerer Jr. continued a family tradition in the mining business that had started in the 1820s. After earning degrees in geology from Princeton and the University of Utah and meeting the necessary prerequisites, he joined the staff of the American Reinsurance Company as a mine inspector.

In 1939, John Jr. married Mary Elizabeth Halbach, a Short Hills, New Jersey, native and relocated to work for the West Virginia Coal and Coke Company until World War II called him off to duty in 1941. It was during the war that John Jr.'s father passed away. Upon his discharge at the rank

John L. Kemmerer Jr.

of major in 1946, John Jr. returned to run the family business, The Kemmerer Corporation, which then had holdings in Wyoming, Utah and Virginia. John Jr.'s entrepreneurial potential escorted him down the path of corporate success, making him a leader in his field.

Under John Jr.'s leadership, The Kemmerer Coal Company survived the transition from a railway and domestic coal producer to a major supplier to the utility and other general industrial markets. John Jr. attributes much of his success to the able leadership of business associates such as Glenn Sorensen, Company President; Orion Lorenzi, Treasurer; John Fagnant, Vice President and Chief Engineer; Jack Wanner, Consulting Petroleum Engineer; and Mike Zakotnik, General Superintendent, to name only a few. At the time of the sale of the Kemmerer Coal Company to Gulf Oil in 1981, the company had total estimated recoverable reserves of 1.8 billion tons of coal, producing 4.9 million tons per year. Unlike many of the leading coal producers in this country, the company was consistently profitable and possessed a remarkably strong financial position.

The Kemmerer Corporation was dissolved in 1982 after the sale of the Coal Company to Gulf Oil. However, the Kemmerer progeny continue to manage the family's assets through Kemmerer Resources Corp., a private, family investment company with many enterprises. Based in Chatham, New Jersey, Kemmerer Resources currently oversees stocks, bonds, private equities, the Jackson Hole Mountain Resort, and real estate development projects in five Western states.

Kemmerer Resources is now chaired and directed by John L. Kemmerer III, or Jay, as he is called. Jay is the son of John Jr., and the fourth generation of Kemmerers to adhere to the principles of his great-grandfather Mahlon. John Jr. still serves on the company's board.

A former director of Kemmerer Bottling Group, Inc., Penn Virginia Corporation, and the Seven Up Company, Jay currently serves as a trustee for the U.S. Ski and Snowboard Foundation, and the Jackson Hole-based Grand Teton Music Festival and Spring Gulch Preserve. Aside from directing the family's New Jersey enterprise, Jay is chairman of the Jackson Hole Mountain Resort (JHMR). JHMR is one of the last independently owned resorts, and is proud to be Wyoming's premier ski resort. Through the Kemmerers' support, JHMR is enjoying unprecedented growth, with current project plans tabulating tens of millions of dollars in capital improvements.

Jay works closely with his sisters, Connie Kemmerer and Betty Kemmerer Gray. Connie serves on the board of directors for JHMR and is in charge of special projects for the resort. Her attention and commitment to the resort's history has ensured its image as an authentic Wyoming landmark. Betty, a Sun Valley, Idaho, resident, remains a part owner of the resort while overseeing the family's other Wyoming asset, the CM Ranch, located in Dubois, Wyoming. A devoted conservationist, Betty currently serves on the board of the Idaho Nature Conservancy.

The Kemmerers' accomplishments do not end with the ski industry, however. The family's love for and devotion to wild, majestic Wyoming led to its procurement of the CM Ranch in 1997. The Kemmerers vacationed at the ranch for many years and developed affection for its rustic, alpine atmosphere. The guest ranch is located at the mouth of Jakey's Fork Canyon in the Wind River Mountains, six miles from the historic town of Dubois. It is one of the oldest guest ranches in Wyoming, and its sylvan charm complements the state's rugged, yet beautiful landscape.

Integrity and honesty are key principals that have guided the Kemmerer family in achieving success. Through cooperation, the family has sought fulfillment of a dream while securing a future for their offspring, honoring the memory of their forefathers whose faithfulness lay with those they trusted, and at the same time striving to maintain the family's commitment to Wyoming.

Hillside view of CM Ranch in historic Dubois

Kennedy-Western University

Students have been earning bachelor's, master's and doctorate degrees at Kennedy-Western University since 1984. With its high-quality curriculum and qualified, experienced instructors, there is just one difference between Kennedy-Western and other universities: students at Kennedy-Western attend school in "virtual" classrooms, earning their degrees via distance learning. With 15,000 students in the United States and abroad, Kennedy-Western is certainly succeeding in its goal to provide students with the tools they need to obtain their advanced degrees.

According to founder Paul Saltman, Kennedy-Western was established to meet the needs of mid-career adults who have neither the time nor the opportunity to attend a regular classroom university. Distance learning is fast becoming a cost-effective way for working professionals to obtain advanced degrees and move ahead in their careers. Many employers encourage their workforce to obtain career-related degrees even while they understand attending class is often not possible. Kennedy-Western provides an opportunity for students with travel, work or family commitments to obtain an advanced degree. Many companies even pay for all or a portion of their employees' tuition.

Although the university's main office is located in Cheyenne, administrative, back-office functions are located in California. Students are encouraged to make one trip there during the course of their studies to meet counselors and the student services department in person. In addition, the university believes it is important for students to have an actual physical visit to inspect the thesis and dissertation library and to review textbooks. The visits, described as "extremely rewarding," enable students to truly grasp that a state-of-the-art distance-learning program is there to assist them. Kennedy-Western will even reimburse enrolled students for airfare to California.

Programs are designed especially for students age 25 and older who are interested in a challenging and rewarding educational experience. The average student age is, in fact, 42 years. Not only do Kennedy-Western students draw from their career and life experiences in the classroom, they are often able to receive college credit for it. Degree programs are available in computer science, engineering, business administration, public administration, education, psychology and health administration. Requirements for graduation mirror those of any accredited university. Each program takes approximately 18 months to complete, although students are encouraged to work at their own pace.

The instructional process at Kennedy-Western is designed to acknowledge students' previous professional and academic accomplishments. Upon acceptance, students are sent a letter outlining program requirements. Students receive an interactive CD-ROM, which gives a virtual tour of the university. A catalog of course descriptions follows,

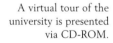

A virtual tour of the university is presented via CD-ROM.

from which students select courses and then speak with a faculty advisor about their choices.

After the students receive their course materials, which consist of a book list, course outline, practice exam and practice exam answers, they complete the work, contacting student services if tutorial assistance is needed. Upon completion of the course work, students request an exam, which is sent to a designated proctor. Students have 10 days to return the completed test, then are notified of their grades by mail. Many courses also have exams that can be completed online.

Once the majority of required course work has been completed, students receive guidelines on the final thesis or dissertation, which is required for graduation. The first three chapters of the final paper must be approved by faculty before students can proceed. Guidelines are quite stringent, with almost half of those submitted requiring more work before acceptance can take place. Upon completion and approval of the thesis or dissertation, one bound copy is placed in the Kennedy-Western library, one is given to the student and one is deposited in an alumni file. Students are then eligible for graduation.

Additional opportunities are available for students with Internet access. Once they are accepted as students, they receive an identification number that gives them access to online student services. Students can contact counselors or professors via e-mail. In addition to requests for tutorial assistance, tests and study materials, students can access the Kennedy-Western Electronic Library. There, the adult learner will have access to information for research and links to technical libraries all over the country. Students can also visit the student union and post messages to fellow students.

Although Kennedy-Western takes full advantage of technology, degree requirements can be met without the use of a computer if students desire. Mail, fax and telephone are still viable options for students who prefer a more traditional correspondence method.

Kennedy-Western's faculty of 300 experienced college professors are committed to providing a quality education to all students. From locations around the country, each professor currently teaches at an accredited university in addition to providing instruction for Kennedy-Western's distance-learning program. These academicians follow the same rigorous standards they use in their own classrooms. What this means for Kennedy-Western students is that they have the opportunity to work with professors from the best universities across the country without having to ever step foot in a classroom.

Graduates from Kennedy-Western University receive a diploma like those of traditional universities.

Faculty also play an active role in developing the curricula at Kennedy-Western. The university is reviewed each year by a visitation team of three educators who have no connection with Kennedy-Western to ensure that it is maintaining appropriate university standards. An on-site review demands proof of institutional objectives, administrative methods, curriculum, faculty qualifications, graduation requirements and financial stability.

The textbooks used by the university are reviewed regularly by the faculty to ensure the most current materials available are being used and comparable to what is being used at traditional schools. When demanded by the subject matter and breakthroughs in technology, textbooks are updated to remain current. Books are available to students from most university bookstores or by mail order.

Kennedy-Western University is committed to providing a high level of academic integrity while at the same time giving adult learners the opportunity to obtain a higher education that is accessible, flexible and convenient. Graduates of Kennedy-Western are provided with the analytical tools and accompanying skills to move into or continue successful careers in the business world.

Teton County and Town of Jackson

Jackson Hole, Wyoming, which encompasses most of Teton County including the Town of Jackson, is virtually irresistible. Though known for its harsh nine-month winters, glorious summers are worth the wait — evidently the fact of millennia. Artifacts found at Jackson Lake's north end attest to roughly 9,000 years of continuous seasonal inhabitation of this vast area. It is no wonder that some of last century's explorers stayed long enough that they called themselves guides instead of explorers.

F.M. Fryxell and Phil Smith pause at the summit of The Grand Teton, 1929. Courtesy American Heritage Center, University of Wyoming

The area's beauty, restlessness and resources attracted increasing attention in Washington, nearly from the time of its discovery in the early 1800s, but especially after the first settlers crossed Teton Pass into the valley in 1884. In 1897, the Teton Forest Reserve was created. As early as 1898, the U.S. Geological Survey recommended that Jackson Hole be either added to Yellowstone, or made a separate national park, though nothing came of that idea until much later. That same year, the Army built new roads for moving troops in case of uprisings known as "Indian trouble."

By 1900, cattle ranching nudged out hunting and guiding as the area's main enterprise. Still largely unsettled, and then actually part of Uinta County, the territory was only partially civilized. "Mountin' Law," as the vigilantes titled themselves, employed strategies from "bushwhacking" to murder as they fought to roust out Native Americans, horse thieves, cattle rustlers and sheep men. Called "Frontier" in 1907, summer rodeos continue to reflect Jackson's wilder days.

At that time, the townsite of Jackson consisted of a handful of buildings, including Foster's saloon, the post office and, the heart of the town, a little log store owned by one "Pap" Deloney. From horse collars to chocolates, the shop carried "everything." Perhaps it was his former status as head of the Teton Forest Reserve, or perhaps people found it natural to have faith in a man referred to as Pap; in any case, his store also served as a bank until Jackson State Bank was established in 1914. Cattlemen settled their accounts with Pap after selling their beef once a year, and guides trusted him with their cash. Isolated and left to their own resources, people worked together, an unforgotten legacy.

Ironically, although a large indigenous elk herd competed with ranchers' cattle for food and space, many residents sought to save it. Diminished rangelands, harsh winters and poachers, including "tuskers" who killed countless bull elk solely for their ivory canine teeth, threatened Jackson Hole's unique and priceless regional symbol with extinction.

One of Jackson's first settlers, Stephen Leek, and other concerned citizens called for government help. Leek's diaries, backed by graphic photographs, were some of the most influential data considered. In 1905 the Wyoming legislature created the Teton Game Preserve, almost 600,000 acres where no hunting was allowed, and in 1907, tusking became a felony. In 1912, the same year new counties were lined out and the area made part of Lincoln County, Congress founded the National Elk Refuge, a separate holding from the Teton Game Preserve, just northeast of the town of Jackson. Covering just under 24,000 acres, the refuge continues to provide winter shelter for an average of 7,500 elk.

About seven years before Jackson incorporated in 1914, the growing township recognized a need for organized education. A makeshift school was held near the square in the town's clubhouse, which housed a variety of social functions, until it moved to its own small log structure. In 1912, a two-story brick building supplanted the wood one, but burned down in 1915. Its replacement in 1916 housed younger children on the first floor and high school students on the upper story, until the high school was finished in 1929.

Once the town's educational needs were met, it was only natural to focus on its medical needs. Led by Reverend Royal Balcomb, yet another community effort manifested Saint John's Hospital in 1916, specifically to provide the well-loved Dr. Charles Huff a place to run his medical practice. Starting with four rooms, the log building was augmented in 1919, and again in 1925, when a water-pressurized piston elevator was installed. In 1960 the hospital moved to Broadway Street, where a new building was constructed. A new hospital and nursing home were built on the site in 1991.

Grace Miller's election as mayor in 1920 raised some eyebrows, due more to the fact that she led the country's first all-woman city government than that she was herself a female mayor. Wyoming had, after all, produced the nation's first female governor. Mae Deloney, Rose Crabtree, Faustina Haight and Genevieve Van Vleck rounded out the five-woman city council, sometimes fondly called "The Petticoat Rulers." Most of the ladies' pet projects during their one term in town office

centered on amenities like water and sewer service, and cleaning up the town square.

In 1921 Teton County was delineated. By 1923, settlers like Maude Noble already feared commercial exploitation of Teton County land and began to devise ways to protect it, as they had with the elk. Decades later, people continue to visit her historic cabin, the humble site of one of the first community meetings geared at land preservation options, attended by several prominent valley residents and then-Superintendent of Yellowstone National Park Horace M. Albright.

As the only incorporated town in 1921, Jackson was made the county seat, though the settlement of Kelly was larger and more the hub of activity for the next few years.

The deep melting snow and heavy spring rains of 1925 waterlogged the Gros Ventre Valley, creating small

earth slumps as mud and rock shifted on underlying shale. In the late afternoon of June 23, the sounds of a thundering stampede shook the area. Rancher Guil Huff curiously rode horseback toward the sound, only to turn and race for escape from an avalanche of rocks, mud and trees. Known as the Gros Ventre Slide, this massive rockslide effectively dumped a 225-foot-high, half-mile wide dam across the Gros Ventre River, backing its waters up the valley. Astonished witnesses quickly helped a frightened but uninjured Huff move his family and belongings to higher ground, to avoid the impending flood. Only a few cows near Kelly perished in the cataclysm, the river seeping benignly through the rock and returning to its normal flow after a couple of weeks.

Skiing has served the Jackson area as winter entertainment and transportation for nearly a century. *Courtesy American Heritage Center, University of Wyoming*

RUTH HANNA SIMMS SKI HILL

Two years later, Slide Lake overfilled with spring runoff and the natural dam gave way, sending a devastating wall of muddy water and debris violently down the Gros Ventre. This time, Kelly was not spared. The second calamity in two years claimed six lives, left 40 families homeless and caused $500,000 in damage. Many survivors moved to Jackson, firmly substantiating its significance.

Natural disasters notwithstanding, cattle ranching in the Tetons was always difficult, to say the least. Hay grown in this rocky, glaciated place was often insufficient to feed the many ungulates, domestic or wild. Some ranchers sold out or just walked away. Others used Yankee ingenuity or Eastern money, and eventually dude ranches were born, some of them quite fabulous.

Famous men, wealthy hunters and royalty were frequent visitors already. Some of the wealthiest established summer home ranches. One of the most

renowned, John D. Rockefeller Jr., came for repeated stays and eventually bought numerous parcels of land, though he never started a dude ranch of his own. Word of a paradise in the Grand Tetons spread back to the cities, and dude ranch reservations poured in. Still a viable part of the area's economy, the luxury dude ranch heyday lasted from 1915 through 1930. Rockefeller was allowed to donate about 35,000 of his acquired acres back to the federal government in 1943, after 10 years of angry politics and investigations into Rockefeller's intentions, and perhaps ultimately in response to a letter from Rockefeller to then-Secretary of the Interior Harold Ickes, giving the government one last chance before he divested his Teton County holdings. President Roosevelt immediately added another 165,000 acres from the Teton National Forest and other federal lands in the valley and, by proclamation, instituted the 200,000-acre Jackson Hole National Monument.

Visual artists have captured countless Teton County images in paintings, photographs and films. Famous names like Thomas Moran and Conrad Schwiering, as well as unknown amateurs, feel compelled to record its magnificence.

Hollywood started backdropping films with Jackson Hole in 1922. Money from movies like *The Big Trail*, John Wayne's 1930 film (his first as a star) eased some of the Great Depression's injury. During the summer of 1951, celluloid money flowed, as producers shot three blockbuster Westerns on locations across the valley. The Snake River hosted Kirk Douglas and the cast of *The Big Sky*, while Glenn Ford and Rod Steiger worked on *Jubal* at the Triangle-X Ranch, and Alan Ladd starred in *Shane* up against the Grand Tetons. The stars stayed in dude ranches and hotels right alongside regular tourists, making it a memorable summer for all.

Imported to Teton County in 1962, orchestral music began filling the summer air. Firmly established, and moved to the Teton Village Ski Resort in 1969, what became known as the Grand Teton Music Festival still draws locals and travelers alike to enjoy orchestral, spotlight and chamber music performances that rival the greatest in the world.

One significant institution of 20th-century Jackson Hole is the construction and development of the Teton

County Airport. In 1930, the year after Grand Teton National Park was established by President Coolidge, planes landed on an unpaved strip of the valley floor. In 1939 an airport site was selected, and a log terminal building was completed in 1946, the same year commercial flight service began. An act of Congress in 1950 incorporated the airport into Grand Teton National Park, making it the only commercial airport to operate within a national park. All normal airport issues remain complicated by this status and its resulting federal involvement, including land leases and special permits, construction and remodeling decisions, plane upgrades, facility uses, and noise and air pollution matters.

Born in Laramie in 1899, beloved town and area historian Cecil "Slim" Lawrence began saving artifacts as a young boy. By 1927, he was a Jackson resident. Slim's fascination with relics that sang of the Old West soon resulted in a mounting collection. By 1940, his friend Homer Richards suggested he start his own museum. Eighteen years later, Lawrence and co-founder Richards opened the Jackson Hole Museum. Since 1958, the museum has housed the best single record of Jackson Hole's pioneer history.

In 1963, retired California advertiser Paul McCollister formed the Jackson Hole Ski Corporation, putting winter tourism on the menu. He opened the Jackson Hole Mountain Resort in 1965 and started seriously campaigning for skiers, with some success, though its inaccessibility dampened the northwestern Wyoming corner's appeal. More than 20 years later, McCollister's efforts involved compensating American Airlines to start direct flights from Chicago and Dallas, encouraging other airlines to compete for business, and introducing more skiers to Wyoming's snow. Jackson High School's Alpine and Nordic ski teams are highly competitive, due in no small part to their easy access to world-class runs.

One of the biggest cultural additions to Jackson occurred in 1987, when wildlife art collector Bill Kerr and his wife, Joffa, herself a sculptor, opened the Wildlife of the American West Art Museum. Specifically choosing Jackson for the convergence of art and wildlife there, the Kerrs learned quickly the power and energy of community support and response to the success of their project. Housed in a new building since 1994, the

Jackson Lake Lodge, c. 1930
Courtesy American Heritage Center, University of Wyoming

collection which started with more than 250 pieces by 33 artists has been renamed the National Museum of Wildlife Art.

Government protection of land and other resources restricts Teton County's commercial and housing development to just under 3 percent of its entirety, a space comparable to that of Manhattan. Some development includes private nonconstruction, as individuals and special interest groups choose to buy land for the specific purpose of saving it from another's bulldozer for scenic easements or protecting wildlife.

Jackson Hole's natural assets and its preservation have long distinguished the area from any other. Today, chiefly due to the numerous and encompassing constraints placed on human activity of all sorts, this area remains part of the largest intact ecosystem in the earth's temperate zone. The surrounding national parks simultaneously create the conditions protecting the environment, as well as those filling it with outdoor activities. Maude Noble would be proud.

Intermingled ecological and commercial success necessitates intense land-use planning by city and county officials, in conjunction with state and federal contingencies, an ongoing process since the 1970s and comprehensively updated in 1994. The delicate balance among diverse entities takes patience, unique plans and well-thought regulations. Though neither designed nor expected to control occurring changes, planning does steer and manage change. Local planners involve the community as much as possible, both in preparation for the future and out of respect for its initial activists who, seeing the splendor of Jackson Hole more than 100 years ago, started its legacy of preservation.

University of Wyoming

Founded in 1886, four years before statehood, the University of Wyoming has served the state and its people as a land-grant institution dedicated to providing quality undergraduate and graduate education, research and service for more than a century .

The University of Wyoming opened on September 6, 1887, with one building, five professors, two tutors, and 42 students. Programs of study available to those first students included philosophy, literature and science. By 1891, the university graduated its first class of two students. That same year, UW established an agricultural school and an experiment station. By 1893 the university boasted a second building, and the following year the colleges of liberal arts and engineering were formed. In 1897, the campus underwent a major transformation, when more than 150 trees were planted on Arbor Day.

Throughout the 20th century, the university continued to grow and expand. The Wyoming Union was built in the 1930s as a Works Progress Administration project. Construction of the original phases of War Memorial Stadium and the Fieldhouse was completed in 1949. The University of Wyoming awarded its first doctor of philosophy degree through the geology program in 1953.

By the end of the 1950s, the university's campus doubled in size and enrollments increased fivefold. To meet the demands of its growing student body, the first residence halls and the Classroom Building were built during the 1960s. The 1970s saw the completion of the Fine Arts Center. Today, UW offers some 85 undergraduate and a like number of graduate and professional degree programs within the colleges of agriculture, arts and sciences, business, education, engineering, health sciences, and law, as well as the Graduate School.

Professors have come to teach at UW from among the world's most respected colleges and universities. Recognized nationally and internationally as experts in their fields, they are deeply committed to the success of people who depend on the University of Wyoming. This commitment is evident in their dedication to excellence in teaching, especially for undergraduate students.

Students at the University of Wyoming benefit from the fact that their professors' primary responsibility is the education of undergraduate students. Regular faculty teach more than 90 percent of all credit hours, and the University of Wyoming maintains a low student-faculty ratio that allows for individualized instruction and attention, providing professors the opportunity to really get to know their students. This relationship transcends teaching to include academic advising and inclusion of undergraduates in cutting-edge research projects.

Education at UW is not confined to the buildings that comprise the main campus in Laramie. Bringing educational opportunity to students in all 23 Wyoming counties continues to be a top priority. Almost since the university's inception, courses have been taught throughout the state using the leading technologies of the day. Today, courses are taught through video technology, allowing professors in Laramie and students in communities throughout Wyoming to hear and see each other in classrooms hundreds of miles apart. Selected undergraduate and graduate programs are also extended to Wyoming communities through traditional independent-study

A campus landmark — Old Main has been the centerpiece of the University of Wyoming campus since its founding.

A clear mission — Quality teaching is a priority at the university and the low student-teacher ratio allows unique opportunities for one-on-one interaction.

approaches, face-to-face instruction, audio telecommunications, the Internet and correspondence.

While UW's faculty, staff and students are what make the university truly exceptional, the main campus and its modern facilities support their efforts. The Laramie campus encompasses 785 acres, including some 80 major buildings. There is a pleasant mix of modern and traditional structures; many constructed of native Wyoming sandstone.

The William Robertson Coe Library houses general reference, humanities, social science, and education and medical materials, as well as government documents and maps. In all, the university libraries, which include the Science Library, the Brinkerhoff Earth Resources Information Center, the Film Library and Audio Visual Services, the Learning Resources Center, and the George W. Hopper Law Library, have collections numbering more than 1.2 million volumes.

Several outstanding museums offer a look at the natural and cultural history of Wyoming and the world. The UW Art Museum has more than 6,000 holdings in its permanent collection, including drawings, paintings and sculpture. The American Heritage Center houses more than 7,000 collections on Western history, transportation, livestock, literature and economic geology. The Rocky Mountain Herbarium, with more than 540,000 dried plant specimens, is the largest and most representative collection of indigenous plants from the central Rocky Mountain region. The Geological Museum features one of the world's five mounted *Apatosaurus* (Brontosaurus) skeletons and one of the most complete *Allosaurus* skeletons ever found.

The environment and development of natural resources provide a special focus for many current UW research efforts. The establishment of the School of Environment and Natural Resources demonstrates the university's commitment to environmental and natural resource research and curriculum. UW has environmental research units located throughout Wyoming, including the Red Buttes Environmental Biology Laboratory, the Red Buttes Observatory and the Elk Mountain Atmospheric Science. The Atmospheric Science Flight Facility at Laramie is the only university-owned, balloon-launch facility in the world. The university also operates the UW-National Park Service Research Center in Grand Teton National Park and four regional Agricultural Research and Extension Centers. UW has several natural resource research centers including the Enhanced Oil Recovery Institute, the Minerals Research and Reclamation Center, the

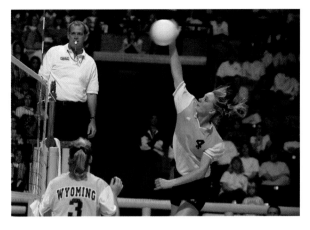

A proud tradition — As members of the new Mountain West Conference, the Cowboys and Cowgirls will continue to draw fans from across the state.

Composite Materials Research Group, and the Environmental Simulation Laboratory.

Athletics have a long and proud tradition at the university. UW's student-athletes compete in a variety of Division I-A sports as part of the new Mountain West Conference. Fans from throughout the state and the region enthusiastically support the teams, often driving for many hours across the state to cheer "their" Cowboys and Cowgirls.

The university's influence on the state extends beyond sports, where nine of the 10 finalists for Wyoming's Citizen of the Century have some affiliation with the institution. In fact almost half of the nominees, in every category, have some connection to the university, either as a graduate, an employee, a trustee or major supporter.

Today the University of Wyoming remains committed to fulfilling and expanding its grand vision begun in 1886. The university's mission continues to be serving the educational needs of students, through teaching, research, service and outreach, while preserving the state's rich Western heritage. With limitless new developments and innovations on the horizon, past successes are but a small measure of what the university is poised to accomplish as the 21st century approaches.

Preserving its cultural heritage — The UW Art Museum, which boasts an impressive permanent collection, is one of several museums located at the university's main campus.

Wyoming Medical Center

Centrally located in Casper, Wyoming Medical Center has served the health care needs of its community and state for almost 90 years. Opening in 1911 as a small county hospital, Wyoming Medical Center has grown into a sophisticated multimillion-dollar, regional medical facility with the latest medical expertise and equipment available for its patients who come from around the state.

Memorial Hospital of Natrona County — 1930s

Expanding and building to meet the region's increasing health care needs have been the goals of the hospital since it first opened. Funded by state monies, the original $22,000 was used to build and equip the branch of the Wyoming General Hospital System. Politics and power struggles delayed the initial construction and the official opening of the building — originally set to be completed in August 1910. These hurdles postponed the opening until the following year. The facility operated as a branch of the state system until 1922 when Natrona County purchased the hospital for a single dollar. The county operated "Memorial Hospital of Natrona County" until 1986 when the hospital underwent a major corporate restructuring and became Wyoming Medical Center, a private, not-for-profit charitable organization.

Providing the physical facilities to handle increases in population and meeting the varied health care needs of the community have been ongoing priorities since the first addition was built to the original hospital in the 1920s. Following World War II, Casper's population increased by 5,000 residents in two years, creating a critical need for additional medical facilities. Voters approved a $1 million bond issue for construction of the north wing, completed in 1956. The last section of the original 1910 building was torn down to make room for the present six-story center building, opened in 1967.

Remodeling and updating of hospital facilities, services and equipment have continued with the parking structure, completed in 1981; the Central Services building, finished in 1990; and the Wyoming Cancer Center addition, opened in 1992. The latest addition to Wyoming Medical Center is the Casper Surgical Center, an outpatient center that opened in May 1999. The $48 million east wing expansion, which includes a new emergency medicine department,

Early health care professionals — 1912

a new intensive care unit, a new surgical suite with six operating rooms, and 24 private patient rooms, should be ready for patients by early 2000.

Financing for the new addition was accomplished without tax dollars; instead the hospital used a revenue bond issue in 1995. As a corporation, Wyoming Medical Center maintains a BBB+ rating. In addition, the hospital has budgeted $9 million for upgrading capital equipment for the coming year. Wyoming Medical Center's commitment to caring for all of Wyoming's citizens enables the hospital to provide $3.5 million of charity care annually to the communities it serves.

Patients were originally transported to the hospital by horse-drawn carriages through the dusty streets of Casper. Today, modern ambulances provide transportation within the area, and Wyoming Life Flight, the state's only emergency air ambulance provider, transports patients from all over the state. A helicopter and a fixed-wing plane comprise the fleet of air ambulances that transport trauma patients to the most appropriate medical facility available, whether it is the local hospital or Wyoming Medical Center. Back-up

The five-story addition to the hospital's east wing will have Wyoming Medical Center ready for the new millennium.

helicopters and planes are available when Wyoming Life Flight is busy.

Expanding and building to meet the region's increasing health care needs have been the goals of the hospital since it first opened.

When the planes are not used to transport patients, they carry doctors and nurses to outlying Wyoming communities for clinics. Patients needing to see a cardiologist, urologist, medical oncologist or infectious disease specialist don't have to leave their hometowns thanks to Wyoming Medical Center's outreach programs.

But Wyoming Medical Center is more than buildings and technology. At the center of the hospital's mission to provide the highest quality of health care are its 1,000 highly skilled and trained employees. On-call and part-time personnel swell this number even further, making Wyoming Medical Center the second-largest employer in Natrona County as well as a leader in economic impact and development.

As Wyoming Medical Center enters the new millennium, its mission, as it was almost 90 years ago, will be to serve its patients, its community and the state in providing the best possible health care.

Wyoming Medical Center today

Buffalo Bill Historical Center

The town of Cody, Wyoming, keenly felt the 1917 death of its founder, Buffalo Bill Cody. Within a few weeks townspeople had formed the Buffalo Bill Memorial Association (BBMA) to commemorate Cody's life and the Western way of life that he symbolized.

Eventually, the BBMA decided to commission a monumental-size sculpture of Buffalo Bill. Well-known American artist and socialite Gertrude Vanderbilt Whitney rendered the piece, attended by considerable national press attention, and later bought and donated the adjacent land, which is today the site of the Buffalo Bill Historical Center.

In 1927 the first Buffalo Bill Museum came into being, largely through the efforts of Cody's niece, Mary Jester Allen, who organized such various local fund-raisers as bake sales. The resulting small log museum was a stopping place for tourists for the next 40 years, including tourist Calvin Coolidge.

The first of the modern buildings within the historical center complex was the Whitney Gallery of Western Art, built in 1958. Its director, art expert Harold McCracken, helped establish the museum as a notable Western art museum. The Whitney Gallery launched a period of phenomenal growth and development for the museum complex which continues to the present day.

In 1968 the Buffalo Bill museum obtained a new home, a new name, and a new purpose. The Whitney Gallery was expanded to include an admissions area and a second wing for the Buffalo Bill collection. The Buffalo Bill Historical Center was no longer just a museum or gallery, but a complex, connected physically and also connected by its collections. The two wings together were and are more than just a testimony to the life and career of Buffalo Bill. They established an entity that began to use its collections to advance knowledge of the American West.

Eleven years later, the Plains Indian Museum was dedicated. This museum, featuring the art and culture of the most important tribes of the Northern Plains, houses one of the richest collections of American Indian artifacts in the world. More recently, in 1991, the Cody Firearms Museum was added. This museum contains the world's largest collection of American-made firearms, as well as European arms dating back to the 1500s.

Together, these four museums form today's Buffalo Bill Historical Center, along with the McCracken Research Library, an extensive, highly regarded special library visited by scholars around the United States.

Today the tiny collection originally established through grassroots fund-raisers has a $6 million operating budget and occupies a stunning 237,000 square feet. Its permanent staff of 70 has tripled since 1976. In the summers, 135 part-time personnel swell its employee ranks. A quarter of a million people each year enjoy the permanent collections; special exhibitions; educational programs that include films, gallery demonstrations and tours; and such popular annual events as the Patrons Ball, the Cowboy Songs and Range Ballads program, the Frontier Festival, the Plains Indian Powwow, a Western Film Series and various seminars.

The Buffalo Bill Historical Center, with its long and rich history, grew up with the state of Wyoming in the 20th century and today forms a bridge between the 19th and 20th centuries. James Michener, perhaps, described this collection-rich center best. He called it "the Smithsonian of the West."

Buffalo Bill Historical Center

Martin-Harris Gallery

In a town known for its galleries, the Martin-Harris Gallery is one of Jackson's largest and most important exhibitors of fine contemporary American Western art. Opened in 1990 by Martin Kruzich and Ron Harris, it achieved that status in only 10 years by offering a different focus than what is usually seen in American galleries. For many years, legitimate American Western art was considered to be only the works of representational artists like Charles Russell and Frederick Remington who explored the romance of the cowboy legend. Thanks to new artists with a different vision, and because of innovative exhibitors like Martin-Harris, the scope and focus of American Western art has changed and gained a new legitimacy, freeing the genre from a narrow definition that was as old as the genre itself. The gallery's slogan, "It took hundreds of years to bring the West this far," is not much of an exaggeration.

"Contemporary American Western art is more abstract and less iconographic than traditional, representational art," Martin Kruzich explains. "It has a modern point of view and explores the essence — the spirit — of the subject, instead of merely reproducing the form. The art that we show expresses the passion of the West." In the Martin-Harris Gallery, the expression of that passion takes many forms — paintings, dimensional watercolor, sculpture, baskets, fine American crafts, hand-pulled lithographs, serigraphs and etchings. The materials used by many of the artists are nontraditional, or are used in nontraditional ways, like the art of Jan Lindsay, who transforms watercolor paper to look like Native American garments. Nearly 40 well-known, contemporary American Western artists are represented, including Nelson Boren, D.G. Hines, Donna Howell-Sickles, Richard Murray, Native American artists John Nieto and Kevin Redstar, Charles Ringer, Bill Schenck, Susan Stone, Russell Chatham, and Gene and Rebecca Tobey. The collection is eclectic, because pieces are chosen by the gallery's selection committee instead of being judged by only one eye.

Recognizing that furniture can also be art, the gallery represents 14 artists who make beautiful, one-of-a-kind, hand-crafted furniture. Martin Kruzich muses, "The craftsman has to apply the same concepts to a furniture piece as a painting or sculpture: assembling raw materials in a manner that is pleasant to the eye — and, in this case, functional — and doing it by hand instead of using machines." Exhibiting beautiful, quality furniture has been such a successful addition to the gallery's collection that Martin-Harris' "Art as Furniture" show kicks off the summer season in Jackson. Having become a very popular event in a short period of time, it draws furniture collectors from around the country.

One of the keys to the gallery's success is its central location in Jackson — on the square, next to one of the town's finest and best-known restaurants, the Snake River Grill. But more important to its success are the warmth and elegance of the gallery and its staff — and the unique presentation of the collection. Ironically — but perhaps not so surprisingly — this unassuming gallery in the Wyoming wilderness has quietly built a large clientele that includes government officials, actors, celebrities and collectors from around the world. In the process, the Martin-Harris Gallery has become not just an incidental stop for Jackson Hole tourists, but a primary reason to go to Wyoming.

Martin-Harris Gallery

National Museum of Wildlife Art

The Grand Teton and Yellowstone National Parks are two of the few remaining areas of the United States where an abundant and diverse native wildlife population roams free. It is only fitting that the National Museum of Wildlife Art is positioned at their gateway in Jackson Hole, Wyoming. One of the premier institutions that celebrates and preserves fine wildlife art, NMWA is home to one of the most prestigious collections in the country.

The museum opened in 1987 as a showcase for the wildlife art collection of Joffa and Bill Kerr. After outgrowing its first facility, a larger museum was built on a butte overlooking the 20,000-acre National Elk Refuge. With a unique architectural motif designed to blend in with the natural landscape, the museum is a 51,000-square-foot facility with 15,000 square feet of exhibit space, 12 galleries, a 200-seat auditorium, two full-sized classrooms, a conference room, a gift ship and a cafe.

Some of the most prestigious collections of fine wildlife art have been brought together at NMWA. The JKM Collection, with works by many of the genre's most respected artists, forms the core of the museum's holdings. NMWA also has the second largest Carl Rungius collection in the world. Another gallery contains the John Clymer Studio Collection, which re-creates the famous artist's studio by using his personal effects and approximately 200 artifacts collected by Clymer. The museum is also proud to have the unique American Bison Collection, which serves not only as a commentary of the legendary beast's relationship to nature and man, but also as a chronicle of the cultural and perceptual changes that occurred in the West since the 18th century.

Currently, nearly 2,300 wildlife paintings, sculptures and works on paper are displayed or archived at NMWA. An impressive list of American and European artists are represented, including many masters of the genre: John J. Audubon, Robert Bateman, Albert Bierstadt, Karl Bodmer, Eugene Delacroix, Albrecht Dürer, Richard Friese, Théodore Géricault, Bob Kuhn, Carl Rungius and Charles Russell. The works — some dating back to the 15th century — represent a broad spectrum of wildlife art. The early 19th-century explorer artists, through whose eyes much of the country first saw the West, are included, as are the sporting artists who followed them. Landscape artists are also represented by many stunning pieces, as well as the illustrator artists of the late 19th and early 20th centuries, who captured the romance of the West in photographs and travelogues. The galleries also include many beautiful and thought-provoking works by contemporary artists. In addition to its own collections, NMWA regularly hosts major exhibitions by other renowned artists and brings fascinating traveling collections of Native American and Western historical material to Jackson Hole.

Under its stated goal of "bringing people, wildlife and fine art together," the National Museum of Wildlife Art strives to create fun, educational experiences for the 120,000 children and adults who pass through its doors each year and for the thousands more who visit its Web site. Bill Kerr, one of the museum's co-founders, explains, "Our mission is to teach people about this genre in all of the ways that we possibly can, to enrich and inspire people to appreciate fine art and, at the same time, examine humankind's evolving relationship to nature."

The National Museum of Wildlife Art is home to one of the premier collections of fine wildlife art in the United States.

National Outdoor Leadership School

Unprepared and irreverent, 16-year-old Paul Petzoldt made a dangerous ascent of Wyoming's Grand Teton ("The Grand") in jeans and cowboy boots. Instead of an early demise, he met the underlying force of his life: to live to be an old mountaineer. That was 1924.

Memories of three harrowing days at the mercy of The Grand provided a continual source of inspiration for Petzoldt over the years. In the mid-1930s, he explored Europe, including an impressive double-traverse of the Matterhorn, then joined the first American expedition to K2 in India in 1938. During World War II, he served in the famous 10th Mountain Division. In the late 1950s, the mountains pulled him "home" to Dubois, Wyoming.

Early in the 1960s, Petzoldt read a magazine article about a new Outward Bound School in Marble, Colorado, which employed his ski trooper acquaintance, Tap Tapley. Tugged by destiny, Petzoldt went to see about a job and was quickly hired, though meagerly paid.

Within a couple of years, Petzoldt and Tapley agreed that Outward Bound's goal was incomplete, that building students' confidence and physical endurance should be only a part of outdoor instruction. They also felt that a rigorous training program for outdoor instructors was necessary to generate the acceptance an outdoor educational model would need in order to flourish. Creating a new program became their answer.

When Petzoldt founded the National Outdoor Leadership School (NOLS) in Lander, Wyoming, in 1965, he united a dream, the fates and his lifelong love of mountaineering. The revolutionary concept concentrated on outdoor skills and leadership development, and emphasized environmental responsibility. Petzoldt immediately appointed Tapley his co-director.

Over the years, NOLS has expanded to include eight branch schools worldwide: Rocky Mountains (Wyoming); Southwest (Arizona); Northwest (Washington); and Alaska round out the U.S. sites. Internationally, NOLS operates in Kenya, East Africa; Patagonia, Chile; the Yukon of Western Canada; and the Baja Peninsula of Mexico, its charter expansion in 1971. In addition, the school runs programs in Australia and India.

Subjects are diverse and exciting in the outdoor classroom.

Today, each class differs slightly, depending upon weather conditions, personalities of group members, and instructors' styles, yet the same lifeblood of the Petzoldt-Tapley legacy courses through all of NOLS.

Though most people still discover what NOLS has to offer by word-of-mouth, the school educates about 3,000 students per year. The nonprofit organization grows steadily, an average of about five percent per year over the last 20 years. Many instructors are NOLS alumni. All instructor applicants are closely screened for previous experience, education and skills. NOLS accepts only about 50 percent of instructor applicants for training.

The original Lander, Wyoming, headquarters now employs 100 people full time, year-round — a large employer by Lander's standards. Housed in the historic Noble Hotel and several other buildings downtown, NOLS continues to expand. In addition to its field-based courses, the school's Wilderness Medicine Institute (WMI) offers wilderness medicine training in locations around the world.

Whether using outdoor skills for recreational camping, or leading an IMAX film crew on location at Mount Everest, alumni categorically agree that the NOLS experience is one of the most powerful educational experiences of a lifetime.

A NOLS student practices lead climbing in the Wind River mountains near Lander.

Wyoming Business Council

From offices in a restored historic hotel in downtown Cheyenne, the Wyoming Business Council has a great view of the old Union Pacific train depot. More than a century ago, the railroad brought commerce and industry to Wyoming. But today, Wyoming must work harder to assure job opportunities for its youth. The Business Council works to make job scarcity another part of Wyoming's past.

Wyoming business leaders have long recognized that the state must diversify its economic base beyond the extraction industries to create jobs and to provide revenue. They were concerned that if the state did not diversify into areas such as technology and tourism, the brain drain of its bright young people in search of jobs would continue.

As a result of these realizations, in 1998 the state legislature formed the Wyoming Business Council. The Business Council is a partnership between state dollars and private sector manpower. The organization is led by a chief executive officer and a board of directors, sharing the organizational structure of a business rather than a cumbersome state agency. For the first time, the Department of Commerce's Division of Tourism and Division of Economic and Community Development; the Department of Agriculture's Division of Marketing and Promotion; the Energy Office; and the Science, Technology and Energy Authority are managed as private businesses.

The mission of the Business Council is to create more and better paying jobs in Wyoming. The Business Council will help existing businesses expand, bring in new businesses and help create a trained work force to meet the demands of these enterprises. The Business Council works with local communities to achieve their economic goals.

The Business Council has launched five programs to help it meet its goals. The Existing Business Program nurtures businesses and encourages new product development and diversification, and helps small businesses develop technology-related projects. The New Business Program works with local economic development organizations to recruit new businesses, especially in the fields of communication and information management, e-commerce and tele-industry and customer/product processing and distribution center firms.

The Business Council's aim is to have Wyoming be known as a place that encourages young entrepreneurs. The Business Council's Youth and Business Program helps youth-oriented companies succeed so that they will be able to encourage a strong next generation of entrepreneurs.

The Investment Ready Communities Program administers the Community Development Block Grant for community, economic and infrastructure development. If the Business Council is to help Wyoming be open for business — as the state's slogan goes — communities need to have a consensus on the type of industry each would like to attract, and to be prepared when those businesses show interest in them.

The Business Council believes that partnerships are critical to the success of enterprise in Wyoming. The Business Council's Strategic Alliances Program creates partnerships between the Business Council and local economic development associations, chambers of commerce, the seven community colleges and the University of Wyoming, Laramie.

The Business Council's biggest obstacle to overcome is the economic development inertia the state experienced in the 1980s and 1990s. The Business Council believes one way to overcome that obstacle is to assist at the local level. The Business Council sees itself as a facilitator — not an instigator — of local development. The Business Council has opened six regional offices in order to make economic development a goal to which all Wyoming citizens can contribute.

Echostar Communications is the type of technology-based business the Wyoming Business Council works to see flourish in the state. These satellite dishes sit near Echostar's facilities in Cheyenne.
Photo by Randy Wagner

Ucross Foundation

One day near the end of the 1970s, Raymond Plank — WWII bomber pilot, maverick visionary, founder and chairman of Apache Corporation, an independent oil and gas exploration company — stood amongst the falling plaster, bats and beehives of a second-story room in an abandoned ranch house in Ucross, Wyoming. The company had recently purchased the ranch where the house stood. Razing the buildings appeared inevitable, but looking out on grounds flanked by a big red barn, bunkhouse and a ring of 100-year-old cottonwoods, Plank felt the pull of history.

Built a century earlier, the complex was known as Big Red, and had served as the headquarters for the Pratt & Ferris Cattle Company which comprised four ranches: Big Red and Big Corrals in Wyoming's Powder River basin, and the PF and the Upper PF in Goshen County near the Nebraska line. Big Red was an imposing visual landmark on the prairie, a former Pony Express stop and on the stagecoach route that serviced Buffalo to Clearmont (1891-1911). Tepee rings on the hills testified to an earlier history as Indian hunting grounds.

Plank challenged friends and associates to reinvent Big Red in the 20th century, and a vision formed: the restoration of these historic buildings could render this site as relevant to people in the future as it had been to those of the past. The Ucross Foundation was incorporated as a nonprofit organization, and the 22,000-acre property continued as a working cattle ranch. The Foundation's mission was threefold: (1) A residency program providing uninterrupted time and space in which to nurture the creative spirit for selected artists and writers; (2) meeting facilities for community and regional consensus-building;

and (3) a model of land stewardship integrated with ranching in the open spaces of northeast Wyoming.

The foundation accepted its first residents in 1983 and today is an internationally known working retreat for over 60 artists and writers annually, hosting painters, poets, sculptors, writers, photographers, filmmakers and others from across the United States

Built in 1882 and one of the oldest standing houses in the area, the Big Red Ranch House serves today as the main office of the Ucross Foundation.
© *Rhona Bitner*

and around the world. Applications are reviewed by an independent committee and selected individuals are awarded residencies of two to eight weeks at Big Red, which include meals, private studios, and the experience of the High Plains landscape. Many participating artists choose to present their work publicly, providing a significant cultural resource for local communities. Conference facilities and the Big Red Art Gallery draw many visitors year-round.

The Ucross Ranch is a developing model for ecologically sound, holistic ranching practices. In 1999 the foundation will protect its historic landscape in perpetuity with a conservation easement. As part of this initiative, the residency program is expanding to include fellowships for those working in the natural sciences.

Today, the ranch house where Raymond Plank contemplated yesterdays and dreamed of tomorrows is home to the Ucross Foundation, is listed on the National Historic Register and rings with the energy of commitment to the historic and cultural community of the West.

Cowpokes in 1898 in front of the Big Red Barn, which today houses visual studios for selected artists as well as a conference facility in the spacious loft
Courtesy American Heritage Center, University of Wyoming

Wyoming Game and Fish Department

The story of the Wyoming Game and Fish Department begins in one of the richest areas in abundance and variety of wildlife in the contiguous United States. From the days when magnificent big game roamed freely across mountains and plains, and fish swam in countless rivers and streams, to the present day, wildlife has been and likely always will be a crucial part of the Wyoming experience.

In the late 19th century, wildlife conservation was in its infancy. The people of that era witnessed the collapse of wildlife populations throughout the West — the question was how to respond. The need to conserve the continent's natural resources was only slowly coming to light.

Delegates to the Wyoming territorial legislature in 1869 passed a law to protect fish and game, but it was ineffective. In 1879, the first territorial fish commissioner was appointed and in 1899, just nine years after Wyoming became a state, the legislature expanded the authority of the state fish commissioner by creating the office of state game warden. The first warden, Albert Nelson, was given the task of enforcing game laws, which at the time were a radical departure from those the emerging state had been operating under. The job was a challenge, since many Wyomingites saw unrestricted hunting as a fundamental right.

The restrictions proved, however, to be not only morally right but also a good financial investment for the state. Wyoming slowly began hammering out a wildlife management policy that would become a model for the country. The Game and Fish Commission was created in 1921, and in 1937, the state legislature gave

Elk drink from the Gibbon River at Yellowstone National Park. Photo by LuRay Parker

the Game and Fish Department a set of state-of-the-art wildlife laws and control over its own license revenue.

The passage of the Federal Aid in Wildlife Restoration Act (Pittman-Robertson) in 1937 heightened the professionalism of wildlife management by helping fund wildlife research and habitat purchases and ensuring that state license money was appropriated for wildlife conservation.

The success of the Game and Fish Department's management over the decades was clear as, during the 1950s, wildlife numbers and big game populations continued to rise. In 1952, construction began on the Sybille Big Game Research Unit, furthering the progression of wildlife management in Wyoming. This, coupled with the concerted effort that began during the 1960s to educate the public on the philosophy behind natural resource protection, has underscored the commitment behind the department's existence.

In the past 20 years, the Wyoming Game and Fish Department has broadened its scope and now concerns itself with the entire spectrum of game and nongame animals. The recent reintroduction of the near-extinct, black-footed ferret, for instance, has been a resounding success. In an aggressive approach to recognize interests in wildlife other than hunting, Wyoming's Wildlife Worth Watching program was successfully established.

Indeed, as it has for the past hundred years, the Wyoming Game and Fish Department will continue for the next century and beyond to ensure that this rugged state preserves its priceless wild heritage.

The sage grouse is perhaps the most distinctive of Wyoming grouse. Photo by LuRay Parker

United Medical Center

Their first names have faded from memory in Cheyenne, but two enterprising physicians who came west with the railroad established a community service legacy. Beginning in a tent colony set up by the Union Pacific Railroad near Crow Creek, a Dr. Irwin and a Dr.

Graham treated illness and injury in men who worked on the nation's first transcontinental rail link. As the track builders moved west, toiling in the sun and wind, Graham and Irwin stayed to care for a fast-growing population of settlers who created a city government in July 1867.

With sweat and $2,500, Irwin and Graham erected a two-story structure next to a modest office they moved into on Ferguson Street. The *Cheyenne Leader* praised the result. "A stroll through the entire building," a writer for the newspaper declared, "will convince one that the hospital is gotten up with good judgment, and with a view of the comfort and convenience of patients." The doctors reserved some of their 40 beds for the "indigent sick " — people of limited means the town founders cared for under contract.

As the descendant of the Irwin-Graham operation, United Medical Center (UMC) is one of the oldest hospitals in continuous service west of the Mississippi River. It has been moved, expanded and renamed several times. When the wife and children of World War I Gen. John J. Pershing perished in a San Francisco fire in 1915, Cheyenne residents mourned. Francis Warren Pershing

had grown up in their city and was so well-regarded that county officials, who had become the hospital's directors, named a new building in her honor. The present structure at 23rd Street and Evans Avenue was modernized in 1986, and UMC's greatest organizational change occurred in 1992 when county commissioners authorized the purchase of DePaul Hospital across kltown. hospital. United Medical now has three locations: an east and west campus and UMC Health & Fitness.

Today UMC is a model care facility, combining professional skill, up-to-date technology and an instinctive feeling for people. "Members of our staff are wonderfully compassionate," says hospital representative Dave Hall. "We at times run errands for patients; and for outpatients and family members who live far from Cheyenne, we provide housing in a volunteer-run section of the hospital called 'Home Away from Home.' It is very nice — just like a hotel."

A United Way Pacesetter and longtime supporter of local performing arts groups, United Medical Center is also a creative partner in education. For a sense of what surgeons do, young children on school tours can "operate" on dolls. To maintain its high level of care in the new millennium, hospital officials intend to keep a superb staff, stay abreast of technical advances and continue to put people first. These goals place them squarely in their founders' footsteps — providing quality medical services and doing so "with good judgment, and with a view of the comfort and convenience of patients."

"County Hospital" was built in 1882 at 23rd and Evans — a corner that is still the location of Wyoming's oldest hospital, United Medical Center.

Second-grade students in surgical masks and caps tour an operating room at UMC today. Such experiences help alleviate children's fears of surgery and give them information about health care careers.

Wyoming State Historical Society

For nearly half a century, the Wyoming State Historical Society (WSHS), an independent, nonprofit organization, and its many members have been promoting the collection and preservation of Wyoming's history. Since its beginnings in 1953, the society has also served as a strong advocate for Wyoming's historical resources.

A number of historical organizations preceded the WSHS. In 1895 the state legislature approved a bill establishing the Wyoming Historical Society, although with an annual budget of only $250 the society could not fulfill its duties. In 1921 the state again authorized the formation of a state historical society. State historian Frances B. Beard headed the society, which encouraged membership (annual dues were $1), and in 1924 began publishing what is today *Annals of Wyoming: The Wyoming History Journal*. However, by 1932, Wyoming again was without a state society.

Several county historical societies remained active at this time, but it was not until the early 1950s that another statewide society came into being. In 1953 Wyoming had an archives and historical department, although it lacked adequate staffing and funding to collect and preserve the state's history. Chapter 143 of the 1953 Session Laws of Wyoming charged the director of the department to "promote the founding and development of a state historical society and of county historical societies, and to do all in his power to create and maintain locally and statewide an interest in the history of the State and region."

Lola Homsher, the department's director, took this charge seriously. She traveled the state discussing the importance of a society and encouraged people to participate in an organizational effort. Her work resulted in a meeting held at the Woman's Club House in Casper on October 18, 1953, attended by more than 70 people from all areas of Wyoming. The attendees selected Frank Bowron of Casper as president of the new Wyoming State Historical Society, adopted a constitution and bylaws and determined that its purpose shall be "to collect and preserve all possible data and materials including historical relics, relating to the history of Wyoming and illustrative of the progress and development of the state; to promote the study and preservation of such data and materials and to

encourage in every way possible interest in Wyoming history." Shortly thereafter county chapters began to form, with the Fremont County Historical Society being the first.

The new society formed a unique partnership with state government. The Wyoming Archives and Historical Department served as the headquarters for the society and the department director was the society's executive secretary. For dues of $3.50 per year, WSHS members received copies of Annals of Wyoming and the society's newsletter, "History News," both published by the department.

In 1995 the WSHS separated from state government, and today it is a completely independent organization. The society has formed partnerships with a number of institutions. The WSHS publishes *Annals of Wyoming: The Wyoming History Journal* in cooperation with the history department and the American Heritage Center at the University of Wyoming and the Department of State Parks and Cultural Resources. The WSHS encourages quality teaching of Wyoming history in all schools and since the early 1980s has been a supporter of Wyoming History Day which is administered by the American Heritage Center. The society continues its popular annual trek, which is one of the best ways to get to know Wyoming, supports historical preservation efforts in Wyoming, and recognizes individuals and organizations for contributions to Wyoming history. Membership in the WSHS is open to all persons who support and enjoy the history of Wyoming.

Sinclair Oil Corporation/
Holding's Little America

R. Earl Holding is a self-made man who excels in the field of business as a result of his own hard work and vision.

Earl Holding
© 1999 Busath
Photography

Holding was born and raised in Salt Lake City, Utah, where he learned the value of a day's labor as a youth during the Depression working several jobs for the Covey family. Upon graduation from the University of Utah with an engineering degree, Holding was offered the opportunity to invest in the Covey's Little America service station and motel on the western prairie of Wyoming. In October 1952, Holding and his wife Carol moved to Sweetwater County and began a lifelong career in the lodging and oil business. Though the

Sinclair Oil Refinery
in Wyoming

property was losing money at the time, the Holdings' tireless and creative efforts turned it into the highest-volume service station in the country within just two years. During the 1960s, they installed 55 new gas pumps, built 100 new rooms and dedicated themselves to giving excellent 24-hour service on every front.

After his success at the first Little America, Holding's vision of expansion led him to build a new property in Cheyenne, Wyoming, in 1965. The new facility was soon selling more than 1 million gallons of fuel per month. It now features 189 guestrooms, two restaurants, a 9-hole golf course, and many other first-class amenities. The Cheyenne Little America is known nationwide by truckers and other travelers due to its reputation for excellent services and quality.

In 1967, Holding seized the opportunity to purchase the closed refinery in Casper, Wyoming, from Mobil Oil Corporation and reopen it with nearly 100 Wyoming workers. This refinery then supplied his truck stop and motel business across Wyoming, providing the already thriving businesses with a steady supply of petroleum products. It also developed new marketing areas for wholesale petroleum distribution in Colorado, Idaho, western South Dakota and Utah. Holding pursued each project with the careful attention to detail that has become his trademark.

Although many people assume that Holding's Little America was eventually acquired by the large petroleum giant, Sinclair Oil Corporation, it was actually the other way around. Holding's hard work put him in a position to buy the Sinclair company in 1976, when it was being divested as part of the Sinclair/Atlantic Richfield merger. This bold move changed Holding's business from a regional chain of truck stops and motels to a large oil company covering much of the territory west of the Mississippi River. But Holding's heart remained in Wyoming, where the Sinclair Oil Corporation has owned and operated its Wyoming oil refinery since the 1920s.

The Sinclair Refinery is the largest oil refinery in the Mountain West, with a 60,000-barrel-per-day capacity and a hydrocracker expansion project in the works. It is connected to an extensive Sinclair pipeline and trucking system that ships Sinclair petroleum products throughout the western United States. Sinclair gas stations dot the continent from Oklahoma and Missouri to Utah and

Idaho. Holding pursues an active exploration, drilling and production program with oil/gas wells in Wyoming, Texas, Colorado and North Dakota.

A third refinery in Tulsa, Oklahoma, was purchased in 1983, reopening another closed plant and putting more people back to work. Holding personally oversees most facets of the day-to-day operations, ranging from purchasing and monitoring crude oil supplies to setting retail marketing strategies and building a new modern convenience store. "You get what you inspect, not what you expect," is a favorite Holding motto. Holding is scrupulously honest and requires nothing less from his employees.

Also during the 1970s, the Holdings constructed a new Little America in Flagstaff, Arizona, and expanded the Little America Hotel in Salt Lake City, where guests know and enjoy the famous Holding hospitality on a grand scale. The addition of a high-rise tower brought the total number of guestrooms to 850, with spacious banquet and convention facilities. The family acquired the graceful European-style Westgate Hotel in San Diego in 1976, and it carries on its tradition of elegance today, hosting many prominent social and political events in Southern California. Earl and Carol Holding are constantly updating the ambience of these properties with the finest in marble and granite materials, luxurious hand-woven fabrics and beautiful wool carpets. Their family's wonderful attention to detail in each room is well-known among their employees, who are not surprised to see a member of the Holding family stepping in to help serve a particularly busy Sunday brunch or help make up a room for a guest.

The Holding family's decision to acquire Sun Valley Ski Resort in Idaho in 1977 set the stage for their continued involvement and support of Alpine sports and Winter Olympic events. Holding bought the resort and invested millions in state-of-the-art snowmaking systems, lift equipment, and stunning new day lodges and restaurants. He personally oversaw the design of the new lodges with special attention to their breathtaking mountain views. Holding's love of the western outdoors marks many of his endeavors.

The Snowbasin ski area in northern Utah was purchased by the Holdings in the mid-1980s and will soon host the major ski events of the 2002 Winter Olympics. The family has spent years planning and designing the development of the once-tiny day area to maximize its year-round use. Snowbasin boasts one of the best world-class men's downhill courses in the world, and Holding plans to create amenities second-to-none at the expanding resort.

Now under construction in Salt Lake City, Holding's latest project is a 776-unit luxury hotel that covers an entire city block with beautiful granite buildings, plazas and terraces. The hotel will include 400 deluxe suites, plenty of convention and ballroom seating, and fine restaurants and lounges.

Despite his diverse and challenging business interests, Earl Holding continues to devote much of his time and interest to the Wyoming landscape where he began his business and has lived for more than 40 years. (The family has a lovely home in the Sunlight Basin near Yellowstone.) He has acquired 400,000 acres of ranch land in northern Wyoming and southern Montana. This property is a working 50,000-head cattle ranch, and the Holding family — including three grown children and eight grandchildren — spend many summer months enjoying the wide-open spaces of the state.

Holding's commitment to his family is evidenced by the fact that his children have all been active in his business ventures. His son, Stephen, resides in Cheyenne with his wife and children, overseeing the operations of the three Little America truck stops. "My parents believe in giving their customer good value for their dollar, and they have been rewarded by loyal customers," Stephen notes. "We are proud of the fact that most of our customers are repeat visitors who have had a pleasant experience at a Little America property."

Even today, Earl Holding is still putting in long workdays, usually starting at 5 a.m. and wearing out many of his employees before he is ready to stop. His wife Carol is seen often at his side, and together they continue to build and manage one of the most successful family-owned businesses in the country. He is a leading citizen and entrepreneur of whom Wyoming can be proud.

Holding's Little America in Cheyenne, Wyoming

Cheyenne Frontier Days

What began back in the 1890s as a one-day rodeo show to bring people to Cheyenne, Frontier Days has grown to a 10-day event that truly is a community effort. Now in its 104th year, Cheyenne Frontier Days™ takes place annually the last full week of July.

Myriad events and activities — many of them free — make up this outdoor celebration, including concerts, an art show, parades, pancake breakfasts and authentic Old West fun, but the focal point has always been the rodeo. It's officially called the "Daddy of 'em All"® and

The 103rd Annual Cheyenne Frontier Days General Committee: (back row) John Steil (Contestants); Dale Von Krosigk (Grounds); Col. Joe Mulcahy (Military); Col. Bob Rodekohr (Indians); (standing) Jim Ward (Parades); Rick Keslar (Tickets); Wayne Korhonen (Public Relations); Dave Johansen (Executive Director); Joe Prunty (Concessions); Bill Lloyd (Security); Randy Calhoon (Contract Acts); (kneeling, front) Jim Johnson (General Chairman)

Cheyenne Frontier Days hosts the world's largest outdoor rodeo.

with good reason. Cheyenne Frontier Days is host of the largest outdoor rodeo in the world, with more than 1,250 contestants. It also boasts the third-largest purse in rodeo for its winners.

Offering a true glimpse of the Old West, each of the four annual Cheyenne Frontier Days Parades features one of the world's largest collections of horse-drawn, antique carriages and classic automobiles complete with riders in turn-of-the-century dress. The three free Pancake Breakfasts held in downtown Cheyenne feed approximately 10,000 people each in two hours and are a favorite of visitors every year. Displaying the restless spirit of the cowboy and the history of Cheyenne Frontier Days through the exhibit "Dust and Glory: The Daddy of 'em All"®, the Cheyenne Frontier Days Old West Museum provides a year-round cultural and educational resource for Wyoming residents and the thousands of tourists who visit annually.

Ever since the Shoshone tribe of central Wyoming was invited to participate in the second Cheyenne Frontier Days in 1898, Native Americans have played an important role in the festivities. The ever-popular Indian Village is set up each year and includes booths featuring Indian jewelry and crafts, as well as native foods, storytellers and musicians. The Wind River Dance Group, made up of Arapahoe, Shoshone and Sioux tribe members from Wyoming and South Dakota, performs regularly.

One of the primary reasons this great rodeo and Western heritage celebration is able to take place each year is because of its volunteers. The General Committee comprises 12 volunteers who head up a group of more than 2,500 people who donate their time throughout the year to make this "Mardi Gras in Rawhide" a resounding success. With just 14 full-time, year-round staff members, celebration organizers extol the virtues of what the volunteers accomplish. No job is too big or small for the volunteers, who handle everything from working in the rodeo arena and cooking food to taking tickets and laying fiber-optic cable.

The Cheyenne-based F.E. Warren Air Force Base has been an important part of Frontier Days from the start. Then known as cavalry post Fort D.A. Russell, it provided security as well as fired the cannon that announced the beginning of this unique event. Today the U.S. military tradition continues with tours of military homes, the F.E. Warren Military Museum, and a performance by the U.S. Air Force Thunderbirds Aerial Demonstration Team.

With attendance that continues to grow from year to year — and boasting visitors from no less than 22 countries in 1999 — Cheyenne Frontier Days seems assured of its place in Wyoming culture for the next 104 years and beyond.

Elk Country Motels, Inc.

Amidst Jackson's unique blend of the Old West and modern attractions, the Elk Country Motels are among the best places to experience authentic Western charm. Antler Inn, 49er Inn & Suites, and Elk Country Inn are family-owned-and-operated by longtime local residents with more than 35 years in the hospitality business. Each inn is within easy walking distance of Jackson's shops, restaurants, nightspots and galleries — and situated at the gateway to the magnificent Grand Teton and Yellowstone National parks.

offers more than 100 rooms that are decorated in traditional Western style, many of which are quaint cedar log rooms, and rooms featuring wood-burning fireplaces as well as modern amenities. Antler Inn also has conference facilities to accommodate 100 people, and offers a 20-person hot tub, sauna and fitness room.

The Laws bought the site for 49er Inn & Suites in the late 1970s, and then expanded and improved the facility five times over the next 20 years. Located at the downtown corner of Pearl and Jackson, 49er has 148

Just one block south of Town Square, Antler Inn is one of the best places in Jackson to experience authentic Western charm and service.

The success and charm of the Elk Country Motels is the legacy of one of Wyoming's most notable women, Chairman and CEO Clarene Law. After careers as a newspaper reporter and court clerk in Utah, she moved to Jackson in 1959 and worked for the Wort Hotel. In 1962, when the hard-working young mother learned that Antler Inn was for sale, she seized the opportunity — and the challenge — by buying the business. From that point on, Law's work ethic, personal strength and timing turned a fledgling enterprise into a thriving business that gave her opportunities to expand professionally — and in public service, as a member of Wyoming's House of Representatives. Her family — husband Creed Law, daughter and son-in-law Charisse and Curt Haws, son and daughter-in-law Steve and Wendy Meadows, and daughter and son-in-law Teresa and Orion Jillson — have also played crucial roles as stockholders and managers of the company properties.

The Antler Inn was originally a small, 12-cabin operation, but now covers an entire block after three expansions. Only one block south of Town Square, it

rooms and suites, including 30 luxury suites with fireplaces and kitchens. It has two conference rooms, large indoor and outdoor hot tubs, a fitness room, and offers fine dining nearby.

The newest property is the eclectic Elk Country Inn, acquired in 1991. With the addition of new cabins, the motel offers 43 units, including 15 two-room log cabins with extended kitchenettes, 10 family units with three queen beds, double queen units and economy rooms. A perfect place for visitors at any season, it is on the shuttle line to ski resorts, offers a ski wax room, winter car plug-ins, and a large barbecue and picnic area.

Few businesses reflect their owners as much as the Elk Country Motels. To enter one of the properties is to immediately feel the spirit of the Old West — which is also the spirit of Clarene Law. It is the spirit of hard work, congeniality and of giving back to people in important ways. Tourists seeking to experience the true flavor of Jackson should not only consider the Elk Country Motels, but they might also consider a visit with the owner before their stay is over.

Hitching Post Inn

The main streets of Wyoming are lined with stories of partnerships, but few as successful as the one between Mildred and Harry P. Smith. History placed these two newlyweds, each a child of immigrants, at the crossroads of burgeoning growth in Cheyenne. Through hard work, a little chutzpah and Mildred Smith's indelible sense of style and Harry's sense of business, the Hitching Post Inn grew from a small hotel called Lincoln Court into one of the finest hotels in the West.

Building on his parent's commitment to renovate and update, Paul A. Smith, now owner and president, added to the hotel his signature stamp — to innovate to reach more people and serve more guests in full style. Smith recently said it best, "My parents started with something, an idea, and turned it into a family." Frequently, the Hitching Post Inn registers would be the Who's Who of state politics.

Harry married Mildred in 1941. At the time Harry was in his 20s, and the enterprise was a small motel handed to him following his father Pete's death in 1938. Then called the Lincoln Court, Harry invested in improvements, knowing the potential to make it a true center for Wyoming's tourism industry was high. Located at the intersection of two interstate highways, the Lincoln Court offered a place for folks to call home during their stay. With the start of those 40 rooms, Mildred and Harry designed dreams to offer folks more.

The first swimming pool in Wyoming was built by these newlyweds. And families flocked. They added more rooms and enlarged others. It was a formula for success. The Smiths then built a restaurant just down the street from the Lincoln Court. They named it The Hitching Post, and it caught on quickly. Lines formed down the street on opening day, Mother's Day 1946. With that kind of success, Harry and Mildred knew they had something.

Harry and Mildred's Hitching Post restaurant focused on what people wanted — good service, great food and warm hospitality. Duncan Hines recommended it and, again, families flocked. The popularity of the restaurant grew so much in fact that "The Hitch" became the name folks used.

Through those years, there were other additions. The Smiths were starting a family of their own. Evelynn and Paul were born into hotel history and grew up with a wide family network, raised not only by their parents, but by the housekeepers and waitresses, some of whom are still working there today.

Harry passed away in 1983. In 1982, Paul purchased the complex from his father and began to lead the enterprise in significant changes and new directions. Mildred continued with the strong, new partnership of her son until her own passing in 1996.

In the course of 33 years, Paul not only built upon the family traditions, but also directed landmark innovations — The Carriage Court, the lobby relocation and the Cheyenne Cattle Company. On the theory of excellence in multileveled service, Paul gave Cheyenne new restaurants, enhanced dining, and premier convention facilities for serious economic development well into the next millennium.

The history of the Hitching Post is a story emblematic of Wyoming: family, risk, change and lives touched by the best of the West.

Hitching Post Inn, 1999

Hotel Wolf

The doors of the Hotel Wolf opened on New Year's Eve, 1893, with a masquerade ball that was talked about for years. Soon after, the *Saratoga Sun* reported, "Wolf's new brick hotel presents a very handsome and substantial appearance, and will add greatly to the beauty and solidity of the town." It still does so today.

Frederick G. Wolf had built the three-story, red brick building — the tallest building in town — for only $6,000. He announced his enterprise with an advertisement stating, "The Hotel Wolf is now open. The best is always the cheapest. Give it a try." Wolf, a German native, was a popular man and his hotel soon became the hub of the community. Back then, the town of Saratoga was a tiny stop on the stage line that traveled between Encampment

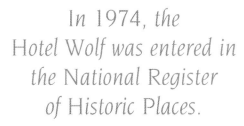

In 1974, the Hotel Wolf was entered in the National Register of Historic Places.

and the main line of the U.P. Railroad at Walcott. Travelers leaving either Walcott or Encampment on the 7:30 a.m. stage could arrive at the Wolf in time for lunch.

In 1913, Wolf's widow sold the hotel for $10,000 to George W. Sisson. He changed the name to Hotel Sisson in 1920. Two years after Sisson's death in 1935, his widow sold the hotel to J. Earle Moore. He died in 1947, but his widow Mary, who had brought the first professional beauty shop to Saratoga, Wyoming, ran the hotel for another 30 years.

Changes were made along the way. During World War II, the restaurant was closed because of food rationing. The bar moved into the dining room and a barbershop moved into the bar.

Doug Campbell and Mike Self bought the hotel in 1977 and it once again became the Hotel Wolf. Doug

and his wife, Kathleen, bought out Self in 1982 and have owned it ever since.

They have worked to return the building to its original state, moving the bar and restaurant back to where they had been and reopening the restaurant. In the early days of the hotel, its food was highly praised. Mrs. Wolf, who had been a cook's apprentice in Germany, did much of the cooking. Today, that tradition of excellence continues.

The Campbells have tried to preserve the hotel's history, while making it a nice, but not a fancy, hotel — because that is the kind of place it always was. Several rooms are furnished with original dressers and iron beds. Swinging doors open into the bar, where mounted heads of moose and antelope and elk antlers hang on the walls alongside old photos of the hotel and its people. The Campbells have worked to improve the building, putting money into the structure. They recently finished removing four coats of paint from the outside, in order to bring it back to the original brick and mortar. The 100-year anniversary party on New Year's Eve 1993, with a masquerade ball and dinner just as Frederick Wolf held, was another great milestone in the history of the hotel and of Saratoga.

In 1974, the Hotel Wolf was entered in the National Register of Historic Places. Back in 1893, a local paper wrote, "Long live the Hotel Wolf!" — words that seem now not merely a wish but a prophesy.

Lost Creek Ranch & Spa

Not many places can boast incredible scenery, indigenous wildlife, real cowgirls and cowboys, and luxurious accommodations all in one location. One that can is the world-class resort, Lost Creek Ranch & Spa. Just north of Jackson, Lost Creek is situated in one of the world's most scenic locations. It overlooks the Jackson Hole valley and the magnificent Grand Teton Mountains and is surrounded by 10 million acres of national forests and parks. At an elevation of 7,000 feet, bordered by stunning mountains on all sides, it draws visitors from all over the world, not only for the incomparable views but for the incomparable service as well.

The Jackson Hole valley was originally a fertile hunting ground for Native Americans. In the 1800s, settlers carved out 100 homesteads, most of which were later acquired by John D. Rockefeller Jr. in 1929. Lost Creek Ranch is one of only a handful of the original homesteads that have continued to be privately owned. In 1968, its 120 acres were purchased by Jerry Halpin, and have since remained in the family. Mike and Beverly Halpin, the proprietors of Lost Creek Ranch since 1987, have taken great care to preserve the unique melding of Western ambiance and wilderness wonders.

Lost Creek Ranch has succeeded in creating accommodations that are at the same time rustic and luxurious. Each of the 10 cabins has distinctive, comfortable furnishings, an authentic Western decor and luxurious amenities. The ranch's centerpiece is a 6,000-square-foot lodge with a spacious living room that features a large, stone fireplace and offers breathtaking views of the Tetons. Among the lodge's other amenities are a billiard room, card room and a large dining room. The Lost Creek experience also includes elegant meals that are served family-style in the dining room, as well as traditional outdoor barbecues. Weekly packages include meals, lodging and a comprehensive array of leisure pastimes.

The perfect place to experience the outdoors in a near-virginal setting, Lost Creek offers guests virtually every conceivable outdoor activity. Foremost among them is horseback riding. With excellent facilities and more than 100 quality horses, the ranch's riding program draws many novices as well as experienced riders. Lost Creek also offers hiking trips into the mountains, fly-fishing, rafting on Snake River, skeet, water aerobics in the outdoor swimming pool and tennis; and it is only an hour away from Yellowstone National Park. It also affords ample opportunities for solitude in a quiet, inspiring setting.

Lost Creek's definition of luxury also includes a state-of-the-art spa that opened in 1998. Guests can choose from a wide variety of services that are designed to rejuvenate the body and calm the mind, including natural body treatments; four types of massage; mineral baths; an outdoor heated swimming pool and whirlpool; Yoga classes; and a fitness center featuring personal trainers. The spa also has a tea room, lounge and full salon. Programs can be tailored to individual needs, and all treatments are performed by certified staff.

Lost Creek Ranch & Spa strives to provide "a touch of luxury off the beaten path." With its dedication to service, wondrous natural setting and Western hospitality, it does indeed offer the best of two worlds. And the range of programs and services offered make it uniquely qualified to cater to the whole person — meeting physical, mental and spiritual needs.

Lost Creek Ranch is a world-class resort that overlooks the spectacular Jackson Hole Valley and Grand Teton Mountains.

The appearance of a lush, green oasis in the midst of the rocky ground and sagebrush of southern Wyoming is something of a surprise, but the Old Baldy Club, a private membership club in Saratoga, has provided that sight for more than 35 years. Named after nearby Bald Mountain, Old Baldy Club affords golfers strolling its fairways views of the Sierra Madre and Snowy Range Mountains, as well as the North Platte River.

The man behind the club was George Butler Storer. He was an Easterner, living with his parents in Toledo, Ohio, until his mother won a newspaper puzzle contest in 1907. The prize was a trip to Estes Park, Colorado. Seven-year-old Storer and his family were enchanted by the Western landscape, with trips to the west an annual event and the West a life-long attachment.

But Storer continued to live in the East, running the Standard Tube Company. He later branched out with a string of service stations, which he tried to advertise on the radio. When he discovered how hard it was for newcomers to buy advertising, he bought his own radio station. After purchasing several other radio and television stations, he created the Storer Broadcasting Company.

In the 1950s, he began holding company business meetings at the Saratoga Inn. A few years later, he bought the Oral Tikkaner Ranch east of Saratoga, eventually adding the E.L. Gould Ranch, the Blom Ranch, the Shay Ranch and the Good Ranch west of Saratoga.

He used most of that land to develop his ranch and build his home, but he also had an idea of creating a haven for sportsmen. In 1959, plans for a golf course were a reality, and the following summer saw the start of construction. The sagebrush was stripped and 7,000 trees were planted. Before long, a 7,108-yard, championship 18-hole golf course appeared. By 1964, the

clubhouse, the pro shop and the locker rooms were up — and Old Baldy was in business.

In both his public and private lives, Storer was known as a philanthropist and an extremely tough businessman with a kind heart. He was interested in contributing to the welfare of Saratoga — the Old Baldy Club is one of his lasting legacies. The Old Baldy Club has continued in that tradition and has stayed involved in the community, assisting in numerous community projects over the years, including the recent Corbett Medical Facility.

Today, membership holds steady at 250, the maximum allowed by the club. Besides golf and fishing, Old Baldy offers its members a full resort facility with hotel suites and guest cottages, a swimming pool, two tennis courts, a skeet and trap range, Lake George and picnic grounds on the banks of the North Platte River.

After his death, several members formed a corporation and purchased the club from his estate in October of 1976. A five-member board of directors governs the club.

Old Baldy was said to be one of Storer's favorite accomplishments, in a lifetime with many from which to choose. Today he would find it just as he left it — a place of beauty and a sportsman's paradise.

Parkway Plaza Hotel

For years, "We'll meet you at the Ramada" was one of the most oft-heard phrases in Casper. People met there for dining out, for special events — and especially for business. All of that ended in the late 1980s when a statewide recession caused the hotel to fall on hard times, but after a brief reversal of fortune, the Ramada was resurrected as the Parkway Plaza Hotel. It is now well on the way to recapturing its former position of prominence in the community.

The property alongside the Platte River parkway has a rich and colorful history. Opened in May of 1966 as a franchised Ramada Inn, the hotel was operated by Ralph Schauss for 20 years. The very best of everything went into its construction, design and decor; the result was Casper's most elegant hotel. It offered 325 sleeping rooms, fine banquet facilities, a 24-hour coffee shop and a gourmet restaurant that boasted outstanding chefs. From the start, it was a rousing success, achieving 100 percent occupancy for the first four years. Once reportedly the world's largest Ramada, it was also one of the largest employers in the state, employing as many as 360 people. During the oil boom of the late 70s and early 80s, it was the premier business hub of central Wyoming. "If there was a deal to be done," Ralph Schauss recalls, "most of the time it was done here." Celebrities who visited the state to check out potential oil investments also stayed at the Ramada Inn, including such famous actors as John Wayne, Robert Taylor and Lee Marvin.

In May of 1994, the hotel was purchased by a group of Wyoming investors, the Hospitality Development Corporation. They renamed it the Parkway Plaza Hotel, and with Patrick Sweeney serving as the new general manager, set about to restore its former reputation and business. Adopting the motto, "The Tradition Returns," the new owners launched an extensive renovation to recapture the style, convenience and Western hospitality for which the hotel had once been known. The sleeping rooms were remodeled — some of which were being expanded and converted to upscale extended-stay suites — and the ballrooms were remodeled to recapture their former elegance. The restaurants and bar were also given a new look: the old coffeehouse was replaced by the Parkway Cafe, the award-winning Poor Boy's Steak House continued the tradition of fine dining, and the former Bourbon House bar was remade as All That Jazz, a club offering a little taste of New Orleans.

By the late 90s, the old motto of "The Tradition Returns" was replaced by one that more aptly describes the position the hotel has carved out for itself: "Wyoming's Meeting Place." With 275 sleeping rooms and 25,000 square feet of multiuse meeting space, the Parkway Plaza Hotel is now Wyoming's largest full-service hotel and convention center under one roof. An aggressive marketing campaign continues to increase the convention and meeting business, targeting government and corporate clients for state, regional and national meetings. The opening of the new National Historic Trail Center is expected to bring in tourists as well. "It's tough to lure people away from the chains," Patrick Sweeney admits. "We took a chance by staying independent, but it's paying off. Once people stay here, they tend to come back."

The Powder Horn Ranch and Golf Club, L.L.C.

The site of The Powder Horn Ranch and Golf Club is steeped in early Wyoming history. It was settled by German immigrants who came to the Little Goose Valley in 1879. Edith Gerdel was born at The Powder Horn in February of 1880, the first white child born in Sheridan County.

Within just a few miles of The Powder Horn are the sites of the Wagon Box Fight, the Fetterman Massacre and Fort Phil Kearny. The Bozeman Trail traverses the base of the Big Horn Mountains a stone's throw away, and the oldest bar in Wyoming sits just down the road in Big Horn.

It was in this valley that Homer Scott Jr. was inspired to develop The Powder Horn Ranch and Golf Club. Realizing that such a site required the ultimate in planning and land usage, Scott saw in The Powder Horn's setting a way to satisfy the demands of today's populace. The meadows, rolling hills, and mountain vistas would transition into an environmentally friendly, western golf community. Its focal points would be Little Goose Creek with its massive cottonwoods and the ranch's old red barn.

The championship golf course, designed by Dick Bailey, opened in 1997 to rave reviews. It features four sets of tees and is just over 7,000 yards in length, with ample sand and water challenges. It sports two distinctively different nine holes of golf and, in only its third year, has been ranked the No. 2 course in the state.

Residents of The Powder Horn enjoy this gorgeous setting for their custom home sites. Just six miles from downtown Sheridan, The Powder Horn offers paved roads, central water and sewer systems, underground utilities, and cable television. Residents can build their dream home, purchase an existing home, or choose a maintenance-free patio home. Strong covenants preserve the integrity of the total development while encouraging a variety of building styles, giving The Powder Horn the feel of a mature country club rather than a cookie-cutter suburb. While early buyers were primarily local, the national market has also discovered that The Powder Horn offers affordability, value and beauty in a state with very friendly people and an equally friendly tax rate.

The Powder Horn and its surrounding area are rich in recreational and cultural opportunities. The Bighorn National Forest, just a few miles away, offers fishing, camping, hiking, hunting, skiing, snowmobiling and mountain biking. Polo is a popular area summer diversion, continuing the equestrian legacy of Sheridan's 19th-century English settlers. For a more Western take, Sheridan's three-day rodeo celebration is one of the top events on the Professional Rodeo Cowboy Association circuit.

The Powder Horn remains a family operation. Homer's daughter Sandy Scott handles sales, while his son Jim runs the golf operations. Brimming with pride, Sandy notes, "Dad's lifelong dream was to build a golf course to enhance the quality of life for those who live and play there. In doing so, he's created a modern playground where they can bring friends and family, and where newcomers, too, can gain everything they've ever wanted in a new residence or a second home."

A former cattle ranch, The Powder Horn has preserved environmental and cultural amenities such as the old red barn along Little Goose Creek.

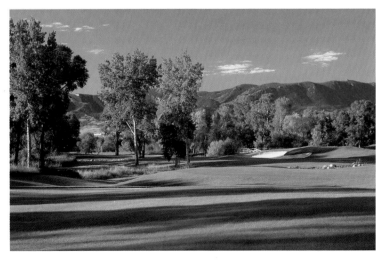

The Powder Horn offers championship golf beneath stunning vistas of the Big Horn Mountains.

Saratoga Inn Resort and Hot Springs Spa

Since 1884, the Saratoga Inn has been enticing guests with the promise of the best of two worlds — luxury in the rugged heart of Wyoming.

The trophy room provides a cozy gathering place.

One of the 56 tastefully appointed rooms available

The town was originally called Warm Springs, but because the springs were a major attraction, it was renamed Saratoga in 1884 in the hope of spawning a smaller version of the Saratoga Springs spa in New York. That same year, Saratoga Inn was built by William H. Caldwell and Judge M.E. Hocker. A local newspaper claimed it was being constructed "of the finest materials." That proved important in 1902, when a fire tore through the hotel. Today the original rock wall in the lobby and Whitney's Western Wear Boutique, as well as the barn wood throughout the main lodge (which came from the old rodeo grounds) still remain.

Before the fire, people had been coming to the hotel in droves to "take the waters," so afterward the state of Wyoming built a bathhouse to allow them to continue. But it was not until 1949 that Bill Walker created the new Saratoga Inn Resort.

Today the entire inn reflects its Western heritage, and there is no mistaking that this is Wyoming. Guests are met everywhere by the sight and smell of wood and leather — there are overstuffed leather chairs and couches, Indian blankets and rawhide lampshades. On the wall, old rodeo posters and photos of Saratoga hang. Each room continues the Western theme, with hats on the wall and boots next to the feather beds. Cowhides cover the floors and the chandeliers are made of antlers. Branding irons and oil lamps hang outside the bathrooms.

Amenities include daily wine and beer tasting, featuring beer from the inn's own award-winning brewery. The Baron's Restaurant offers innovative Western cuisine. A professional spa operates on site, offering massages, facials, body wraps and other pampering. Smaller touches are not overlooked at the Saratoga Inn. For example, warm chocolate chip cookies are delivered to rooms each evening, and fresh-popped popcorn is available to accompany the extensive selection of free videos.

With the inn as a starting point, recreational possibilities abound. A private 9-hole golf course features a cliff-top tee box and three over-river shots. Some fishing spots are reserved just for guests. A variety of adventures on the river are available, including scenic tours and a twilight float for two, champagne included. Working with the Sierra Madre Guest Ranch, the inn offers horseback rides, one with an overnight trip and a Western cookout. Winter brings the opportunity for cross-country skiing and snowshoeing. There are hundreds of miles of snowmobile trails in the nearby Medicine Bow National Forest, and the inn can arrange for rentals, transportation and guide service.

And of course, there are the famous hot springs. A hot springs swimming pool is adjacent to several smaller soaking tubs, including private ones covered by tepees. Guests enjoy unlimited access to their soothing waters.

No matter what brings them to Saratoga Inn, guests are sure to find more than they imagined, and many reasons to return.

Spring Creek Ranch

Nestled atop a butte that overlooks a magical and inspirational place, Spring Creek Ranch is Jackson Hole's premier property. It is also the area's premier luxury mountain resort, a planned community that is known not only for having the best unobstructed view of the majestic Tetons but also for the excellence of its service. It is little wonder that *Condé Nast* has named the ranch as one of the top 500 places to stay in the entire world.

Opened in 1981, Spring Creek Ranch is surrounded by two of the most popular vacation and leisure destinations in the United States — the Grand Teton and Yellowstone National Parks. Its 1,000 acres are home to a wide array of native wildlife: moose, deer, bald eagles, Red-tailed Hawks, and are also on a migratory corridor for mule deer and elk. The coexistence of wildlife and resort development is made possible by a design that preserves the wide open feel of the West and provides for significant space between the ranch's 140 guest units. Spring Creek offers three types of exceptional accommodations: 36 luxury inn rooms; 93 spacious condominiums that have from one to three bedrooms; and 11 executive homes that provide up to 6,000 square feet of elegant living space. Each is constructed with natural materials and beautifully outfitted with traditional lodgepole furniture and other comfortable, Western amenities. Most of the accommodations include stone fireplaces, balconies with breathtaking views, refrigerators and/or full kitchens, and daily maid service. Spring Creek's restaurant, The Granary — recognized by *Wine Spectator* and the Distinguished Restaurants of North America for its excellence every year since

Guests at Spring Creek Ranch enjoy horseback riding against the magnificent backdrop of the Grand Teton Mountains.

1997 — provides fine American and Continental dining with a spectacular view. For conferences, the ranch offers an efficiently designed, full-service facility that is perfect for meetings of 50-60 people and includes 1,400 square feet of meeting space. The combination of Spring Creek's reputation and the area's natural wonders draws the conferences of Fortune 500 companies every year.

In an area that lends itself naturally to a variety of pastimes, the ranch has developed a wide array of distinctive recreational activities for its guests. In the summer, it offers Western riding (in the "dude ranch" tradition), world-renowned fly fishing, swimming, tennis, golf, whitewater rafting and authentic Western barbecues. It also boasts hiking or running trails that afford unparalleled solitude and natural beauty. Winter activities include cross-country skiing, snowshoe tours and horse-drawn sleigh rides. And since the town of Jackson is only a few minutes away, guests also have a wide variety of shopping, eating and entertainment options from which to choose.

Spring Creek Ranch offers another "activity" that is potentially priceless: the opportunity and place to get away from it all — far away from city life, demanding careers, and everyday worries. For high-profile guests seeking refuge in anonymity and seclusion, the ranch is as committed to protecting privacy as it is to providing service. And for every guest, regardless of celebrity, the incomparable panorama of mountains reaching skyward above the Jackson Hole valley is simply an experience they will never forget.

Spring Creek Ranch — the premier luxury resort in Jackson Hole

The Wort Hotel

It could be argued that the Wort Hotel is the heart of Jackson Hole, the embodiment of what makes the region a special place. Certainly it has been a fixture in the life of the town. An elegant and charming hotel that was recently designated a National Historic building, it enjoys a well-earned reputation that has drawn people for more than 50 years.

The warm and elegant lobby of Jackson's famous Wort Hotel

When the Wort brothers — John and Jess — announced plans to build Jackson's first luxury hotel in 1940, the residents of the town scoffed. But one year (and only $90,000) later, the hotel was not only a reality but one of the town's favorite meeting places. By the time a fire destroyed it in 1980, the Wort had become a beloved part of Jackson, as well as the hotel of choice for travelers to the region. Its Silver Dollar Bar and Grille was especially popular and remains so today.

There was no question of rebuilding, and the Wort was reopened in 1981. Recapturing its former status was not an easy task after the disaster, and eventually, in 1994, the owners brought Lee Riley and his wife Jacquie into the partnership, giving them the mission of restoring the Wort to its former glory. Lee became the managing partner, and Jacquie assumed the duties of director of sales and marketing. Together, they helped usher in a new era for the Wort — already a AAA Four-Diamond hotel every year since 1982, it was named one of the Great American Inns by *National Geographic Traveler* in 1999, one of only four inns named in the Rocky Mountain states.

Service is the Wort's first priority. "All of the staff members have that wonderful, service-oriented mindset. We offer good, old-fashioned Western hospitality," Lee Riley explains. "If a guest needs or wants something, we figure out a way to make it happen." Specializing in small conferences and individual travelers, the hotel plays host not only to thousands of tourists, but to the CEOs and staffs of major U.S. companies, celebrities, politicians and even heads of state.

Part of the Wort's charm is its uniqueness. None of the 60 rooms and suites are the same size or have the same configuration, and the hotel employs five different authentic motifs. The decor is New West — comfortable and natural, with Molesworth-style furniture, lodgepole pine beds, Western and Indian fabrics, linens from Scandia Down, oversized pillows and even teddy bears on the beds. Above all, the Wort's amenities are designed for comfort. "When guests walk into one of our rooms," Lee Riley says, "we want them to feel as if they're walking into a bedroom at home."

Because of its reputation as an elegant but affordable meeting place, the Wort continues to enjoy a special

> *"All of the staff members have that wonderful, service-oriented mindset. We offer good, old-fashioned Western hospitality."*

relationship with the town of Jackson and the thousands of travelers who come there. According to Jacquie Riley, that is not likely to change: "The goal of the ownership is that a legacy be left to the town of Jackson, that the Wort Hotel be kept as beautiful as it is, and that no matter who walks through the door — whether they be king, president or a ranch hand — they are treated the same, with gracious Western hospitality."

Advanced Computers

In a way, Bruce Brackley "returned to his roots," when he made Wyoming his home. His father, born and raised in Laramie, attended the University of Wyoming before being commissioned into the Army Air Corps.

Born in 1955, Brackley spent his childhood in various military installations. When he was 9, his father was a full colonel in the Air Force, and the family was stationed in Wiesbaden, Germany. Three years there introduced Bruce to his first loves: mountains and electronics. He remembers sneaking out of bed to spy on his father and a visiting OCI agent as they discussed a "fascinating silver box with flashing lights." Peering through the cracked basement door, Bruce had no idea he was actually looking at a top-secret, Cold War radar jamming device. At age 11, it really didn't matter what it was. His attention and curiosity were ensnared.

Certainly, electronics and the first computers gained the attention of a generation of youngsters in the late 1960s. After returning to the United States and relocating to Houston, Brackley's aptitude led him on a hungry search for technology. By 1970, his hobbies included tinkering with Radio Shack's 101 Projects, Heathkit ham radios, test equipment and other gear. He also enjoyed tearing apart salvage yard gadgets to see how they worked and rebuilding them.

As teen-agers, he and some friends rebuilt old tele-type machines and, for fun, wired their houses with telephone-switching equipment to communicate. In essence, they created a current-loop version of a wide-area network (WAN). His junior and senior years of high school were dominated by college-level electrical engineering classes.

By his graduation in 1973, he spent his spare time assembling some of the first computer processor kits available, including those by Altair, Imsai and Processor Technology. With their scant 256 bytes of memory, programs performed simple operations.

Building these primitive processors on his own represented more lab work and experimentation than most colleges could then offer. Even the biggest companies, like Texas Instruments and Xerox, didn't seem to know completely what to do with this explosion of new technology — much of it their own developments. Those who could see the future of personal computers became "Triumphant Nerds," emerging gurus who began to envision the bits falling into place.

In 1976, a neighbor who shared Brackley's love of computers, Dr. Richard Sugden, asked the 19-year-old to help move his family to Jackson, Wyoming. The moment Brackley descended into that high mountain valley, he knew his Texas days were numbered.

After he, too, moved to Jackson, Brackley worked with Sugden in a computer service bureau called Teton Data Systems. His troubleshooting and reverse troubleshooting expertise served as touchstones. Wholeheartedly believing that success in this high-tech industry requires embracing continual change, Brackley opened Advanced Computers in 1981.

Discerning celebrities and "lone eagles" in Jackson and the surrounding region continue to depend on Bruce to provide a technology lifeline. Many work in every corner of the nation and the world, making corporate consulting one of Advanced Computers' fastest-growing services.

Today Advanced Computers specializes in engineering and consulting; local- and wide-area network design; productivity and efficiency solutions; Internet e-commerce; and systems integration. The staff at Advanced Computers takes pride in giving its clientele a variety of solutions and options, allowing them to make educated decisions concerning their data processing needs.

Bruce Brackley, president of Advanced Computers, amidst the mountains he loves
Photo by Jim Evans

UniLink Software

Jackson Hole is an unusual location for the headquarters of a software company. But then UniLink Software is an unusual company. The brainchild of a dynamic and progressive entrepreneur, Roger Amadon, UniLink is a young but already successful business. Its history is one of steadily accelerating growth made possible by a unique approach to the market, the workplace and the concept of service.

Roger Amadon, founder and president of UniLink Software

When personal computers became available in the early 1980s, Roger Amadon was working as a programmer at Teton Data Systems. Experienced in the development of accounting software, he realized that as PC use inevitably grew among business professionals, there also would be a burgeoning demand for software applications — particularly in accounting. To meet that demand, he founded UniLink Software in 1983. With only one other employee — Bob Kratz, now senior programmer — Amadon operated UniLink from his home in Wilson, Wyoming, spending the first year in research and development. The company sold its first software, General Ledger and Payroll, in the fall of 1984, but because the PC market was still in its infancy, growth came slowly.

Initially, UniLink's products were developed primarily for professional accountants and their clients.

Designed to provide flexibility while helping the client increase productivity and cash flow, the software was also written to be user-friendly. Once the company was established in the accounting software field, it decided to branch out into practice management software in 1985. The result was TB-Link, a time and billing package that allowed CPAs and other professionals to record and bill the time spent on a client. Its release proved to be a turning point in the young company's history, and by the end of that year, UniLink had 50 clients and had grown from two to six employees.

The second half of the 1980s saw even more growth as UniLink met the increased demand for PC products. But it was not merely the PC boom that fueled the company's expansion. Its powerful products and unparalleled support were also strengthening its reputation as an emerging major software company, earning UniLink a deeper as well as broader place in the market. That reputation also captured the attention of the business community. In 1988, the company received the first annual Governor's Quality Award, and in 1990, the magazine *Inc.* listed UniLink as one of the top 500 fastest-growing privately held companies in the United States.

The 1990s saw UniLink's potential become realized in a major way. In 1991, having outgrown its old facility, the company moved to a new, 11,000-square-foot building designed specifically for its needs and growing work force. In 1993, UniLink took another major step forward by releasing TB*Plus Version 2. The program's newly designed interface and other features solidified the company's position as one of the leading producers of time and billing software. That same year marked the company's 10th anniversary, as well as other important milestones. Several new products, including Due Date*Plus (a project management aid) and TimeLink (an electronic time sheet that links with TB*Plus) were successfully launched. Even more importantly, UniLink entered the Windows-compatible software market with the release of TimeLink for Windows. As a result, the company had the most successful year in its history and made a firm commitment to become a full Windows-based software supplier.

Because many of the people who use computers in a professional setting are not technically minded, service and support is crucial. Clients expect calls to be returned in a timely fashion and technical advice to be given in a clear, understandable manner. One of the keys to UniLink's success is its outstanding support of the products it sells. The company is genuinely willing to go the extra step to build and maintain its relationship with clients. That means helping a client with a problem — even if it turns out not to be related to UniLink's software — and exceeding industry standards by returning calls within two hours. The company's reputation is so strong that the word-of-mouth advertising it generates is constantly bringing in new customers. Whereas most companies charge per incident call, UniLink provides six months of free software support. It also offers an annual maintenance agreement that essentially offers unlimited calls. And because it has a genuine commitment to customer satisfaction, the company also extends a 60-day, money-back guarantee. UniLink's definition of client support also includes comprehensive documentation and tutorials, and user training in Jackson and other sites around the country.

One of the things that sets UniLink apart from the average American company is Roger Amadon's progressive management philosophy. The company was started at a time when IBM — then the model in the computer industry — was a very structured, bureaucratic entity. Amadon deliberately chose to build a corporate structure that was as unstructured as possible. His vision of UniLink was a unified whole, not an organization that was fragmented into rigidly defined departments and functions. Toward that end, he created a flat-structured framework that was short on regulations and designed to facilitate open communication and the free flow of ideas. Most of all, it was designed to foster creativity, the lifeblood of software development. "Technically, some of our departments have department heads," General Manager Jared Kail explains. "But, in reality, they are essentially communications facilitators. Our philosophy is to give people the resources they need to be as creative as possible, and then let them do their jobs the best way they see fit. If you need a boss, you can't work at UniLink." Amadon believes people should enjoy their work. With that in mind, the work atmosphere at UniLink is casual while at the same time productive. The company is also genuinely family-friendly, and was so long before it became fashionable.

Because of its committed, responsive approach to the market, and its enlightened management philosophy, UniLink is now national and international in scope. The number of software products offered has grown to 16, and more than 30,000 versions are installed in 10,000 client locations. The number of employees has grown to 60, and the company has once again purchased a new building to accommodate continuing expansion. Roger Amadon's unusual approach to crafting a company has succeeded — and done so in the unlikely setting of Jackson Hole. Situated in a picturesque valley that naturally promotes harmony and reaching for greatness, perhaps UniLink Software is headquartered in an appropriate setting after all.

Screen shot of a transaction entry in UniLink's soon-to-be-released TB*32 — Time & Billing for Windows

The UniLink Software family

Union Telephone Company

The stories of the West typically depict hardship, hard work and overcoming a multitude of obstacles. The story of Union Telephone Company fits right into the historical mosaic of the West. John D. Woody incorporated Union Telephone Company under Wyoming law on January 28, 1914 — only 38 years after Alexander Graham Bell famously bellowed, "Mr. Watson, come here. I want you!" on the first telephone.

John Woody's vision of uniting separate communication systems was inspired by area ranchers who needed a more expedient form of communication. The ranches were remotely situated and Woody imagined that if the individual phone companies were united, calls would take less time to connect, saving time and money for all parties.

The name Union Telephone was created by the joining of the Smith's Fork Mutual Line, the Black's Fork Telephone Line and the Lonetree/Linwood Telephone Company. Operations began serving grounded rural lines on a homemade switchboard that used 30/40 and 30/30 Winchester rifle cartridges as plugs and jacks. Operation of the company required the efforts of each of the family members. Woody's only son, Howard, joined his father in the family business upon returning from World War II. Woody's wife, Mary, his three daughters, Verla, Lottie and Bonnie, along with Howard's wife, Esther, all took turns manning the switchboard during Union Telephone's inception. Esther Woody recalls the military men from World War II lining up to use the one telephone available.

All ran smoothly for a time and in 1946, the Fort Bridger Telephone Company merged with Union Telephone. However, in 1956, Woody had grown well past retirement age and found the company struggling to sustain itself along with his family. He had no choice but to close the operator board due to the lack of financial stability and the invention of the dial system. The Union Telephone board of directors then agreed to offer the whole company to AT&T for the sum of $1. AT&T refused the offer.

As a result, Union sought and received financing from the Rural Electrification Association (REA) to upgrade to a dial system. Simultaneously, the Lyman Telephone Company merged with Union for this upgraded service. As part of the REA loan paperwork, Union sought and received certificates of Public Convenience and Necessity in both Wyoming and Utah. Howard and Esther Woody had five children who are vested in the company. They were determined to ensure Union Telephone's longevity.

Union Telephone bases its successful history on its dedication to being family-owned-and-operated and prides itself on family values and supporting the communities it serves. Howard and Esther Woody remain active in the daily operation of the company. Their dedication effected the cellular division in June 1990. Union Cellular began its business with eight cell sites. Its cellular territory has grown to cover more than 58,000 square miles with a network of more than 50 cell sites. Union Telephone has further expanded with the purchase of additional telephone exchanges and with forays into Internet and cable TV service.

Union Telephone and Union Cellular currently serve communities in Wyoming, Colorado and Utah. John D. Woody's vision, coupled with technology, has produced a successful operation. The history of Union Telephone reflects a dream followed through with action, persistence and dedication to making it a reality.

Howard Woody (left) and Esther Woody (right), son and daughter-in-law of John Woody, Union Telephone Company founder

293

BIBLIOGRAPHY

CHAPTER ONE

Burroughs, John Rolfe. *Guardian of the Grasslands: The First 100 Years of the Wyoming Stock Growers Association.* Cheyenne: Pioneer Print & Stationery Co., 1971.

Chamblin, Thomas, ed. *The Historical Encyclopedia of Wyoming.* Cheyenne: Wyoming Historical Institute, 1970.

Edgar, Bob and Jack Turnell. *Brand of a Legend.* Cody, Wyoming: Stockade Publishing, 1978.

Edgar, Bob and Jack Turnell. *Lady of a Legend.* Cody, Wyoming: Stockade Publishing, 1979.

Georgen, Cynde. *One Cowboy's Dream: John B. Kendrick: His Family, Home & Ranching Empire.* Sheridan: Trail End Guilds, 1995.

Hale, Marge. "A Tall Man of Many Hats." *The Record Stockman.* 1977.

Kirkbride, Dan. "Saddle Soap." *Wyoming Stockman Farmer,* Volume 97. November, 1990.

Kirkbride, Peggy. *From These Roots.* Cheyenne: Pioneer Printing & Stationary Company, 1972.

Krings, Marcia. "Prosser Lives to Serve Others." *Western Livestock Reporter Breeder Edition.* October 6, 1983.

Larson, T.A. *History of Wyoming.* Lincoln: University of Nebraska Press, 1965.

Love, Louise. "Wyoming Pioneers." *Cow Country.* Vol. 80. September, 1952.

"Manville Kendrick," *Casper Star-Tribune.* September 16, 1992.

Manville Kendrick Biographical File. *American Heritage Center,* The University of Wyoming.

"Meeteetse Rancher Wins Conservation Award." *Casper Star Tribune.* July 15, 1987.

James Mickelson Biographical File. *American Heritage Center,* The University of Wyoming.

Mohatt, Mary. "Cattleman: Years in the Saddle Create Memories." *Sunday Magazine, Wyoming Tribune-Eagle.* August 9, 1992.

"Mr. & Mrs. Manville Kendrick." *Sheridan Journal.* January 4, 1929.

Repanshek, Kurt J. "Wyoming Rancher Wins Award from Cattlemen's Association." *Laramie Daily Boomerang.* 8 November 8, 1991.

Jack Tracy Turnell Biographical File. *American Heritage Center,* The University of Wyoming.

Wakefield, Virginia. "The Connection: Harding-Kirkbride Families," *Wyoming Livestock Roundup,* January 4, 1997.

Walter, Terri. "Les Maxfield Keeps Livestock Industry Rolling Along for 40 Years." *Torrington Telegram.* September 27, 1989.

Winter Cattleman's Edition. *Wyoming Livestock Roundup.* January, 1997.

CHAPTER TWO

Chamblin, Thomas, ed. (1970). *The Historical Encyclopedia of Wyoming.* Cheyenne: Wyoming Historical Institute.

"Webster Named Buick Dealer for Cody Country," *The Cody Enterprise.* December 18, 1958.

"Glenn E. Nielson." *Casper Star-Tribune.* October 24, 1998.

Glenn Nielson Biography File. American Heritage Center, University of Wyoming.

Jackson, Hugh. "H.A. Dave True Leaves Vast Legacy." *Casper Star-Tribune.* June 7, 1994.

Clarene Law Citizen of the Century Nomination. American Heritage Center, University of Wyoming

McKennon, Anne. "H.A. "Dave" True Jr. Dies." *Casper Star-Tribune,* June 5, 1994.

Patrick Quealy Biography File. American Heritage Center, University of Wyoming.

"Patrick Quealy III." *Casper Star-Tribune,* July 15, 1997.

Newell Sargent Citizen of the Century Nomination. American Heritage Center, University of Wyoming

Scott, John David. *Wyoming Wildcatter.* Private Profile Publishing: Palm Beach, 1985.

Homer Scott Citizen of the Century Nomination. American Heritage Center, University of Wyoming

H.A. "Dave" True Biographical File. American Heritage Center, The University of Wyoming.

C.E. "Bud" Webster Citizen of the Century Nomination. American Heritage Center, University of Wyoming.

Velocci, Tony . "A True Westerner." Nations Business. December, 1979.

CHAPTER THREE

Mabel Brown Biographical File. American Heritage Center, University of Wyoming.

Mabel Brown Citizen of the Century Nomination. American Heritage Center, University of Wyoming.

Bonnar, Penny (1984, July 29). "History Still an Obsession for Retired Historian." *Casper Star-Tribune.*

George C. Frison Biographical File. American Heritage Center, University of Wyoming.

George C. Frison Citizen of the Century Nomination. American Heritage Center, University of Wyoming.

George Duke Humphrey Biographical File. American Heritage Center, University of Wyoming.

T.A. Larson Biographical File. American Heritage Center, University of Wyoming.

"Ralph MacWhinnie." *Laramie Daily Boomerang.* February 15, 1998.

Larson, T.A. *History of Wyoming.* Lincoln: University of Nebraska Press, 1965.

Velma Linford Biographical File. American Heritage Center, University of Wyoming.

Velma Linford Citizen of the Century Nomination. American Heritage Center, University of Wyoming.

Verda James Citizen of the Century Nomination. American Heritage Center, University of Wyoming.

Ralph McWhinnie Biographical File. American Heritage Center, University of Wyoming.

Mary Odde Citizen of the Century Nomination. American Heritage Center, University of Wyoming.

Susan Stanton. "38-Year Dean Morgan Science Teacher Retires." *Casper Star-Tribune.* May 20, 1995.

"T.A Larson." Laramie Daily Boomerang. October 11, 1985.

Tom Rea. "Teachers Lead Colleagues, Students Through 30 Summers of Field Science." *Casper Star-Tribune.* July 6, 1993.

Dana Van Burgh Citizen of the Century Nomination. American Heritage Center, University of Wyoming.

CHAPTER FOUR

Bama, James. *Western Paintings.* New York: Coe Kerr Gallery, 1977.

James Bama Biographical File. American Heritage Center, University of Wyoming.

Boyle, James M. Boyle/Forrest. Laramie: University of Wyoming Art Museum, 1985.

James M. Boyle Biographical File. American Heritage Center, University of Wyoming.

Peggy Simson Curry Biographical File. American Heritage Center, University of Wyoming.

William Dubois Biographical File. American Heritage Center, University of Wyoming.

Edgar, Bob and Jack Turnell. *Brand of a Legend.* Cody, Wyoming: Stockade Publishing, 1978.

Forrest, James Taylor Bill Gollings: *Ranahan Artist,* 2nd ed. Big Horn: Branford Brinton Memorial, 1986.

Forrest, James Taylor *Bill Gollings: The Man and His Art.* Flagstaff: Northland Press, 1979.

Fowden, Vanita Van Fleet. *The West of Charles Josiah Belden.* M.A. Thesis, University of Wyoming, 1984.

Gollings, William Elling. *The Cowboys Alphabet.* Cheyenne: Wyoming State Press, 1987.

William Gollings Biographical File. American Heritage Center, University of Wyoming.

Headlee, Richard. *Architectural History of Southern Wyoming.* M.A. Thesis, University of Wyoming, 1979.

Hedgepath, Don. *Spurs Were A Jingling: A Brief Look at the Wyoming Range Country.* Flagstaff: Northland Press, 1975.

Junge, Mark. J.E. Stimson, *Photographer of the West.* Lincoln: University of Nebraska Press, 1986.

Kelton, Elmer. *The Art of James Bama.* New York: Bantam Books, 1993.

Krakel, Dean Fenton. *Conrad Schwiering, Painting on the Square.* Oklahoma City: Powder River Book Co., 1981.

Mary O'Hara Biographical File. American Heritage Center, University of Wyoming.

O'Hara, Mary. *Flicka's Friend: The Autobiography of Mary O'Hara.* New York, Putnam, 1982.

Jerry Palen Biographical File. American Heritage Center, University of Wyoming.

Roberts, Phil and Roberts, David and Roberts, Steven. *Wyoming Almanac,* 4th ed. Laramie: Skyline Press, 1996.

Russin, Robert. *Robert I.* Russin Exhibition, February 28-March 31, 1978. San Francisco: Maxwell Galleries, 1978.

Russin, Robert. *Robert I. Russin: Wyoming Master.* Laramie: University of Wyoming Art Museum, 1991.

Robert Russin Biographical File. American Heritage Center, University of Wyoming.

Roripaugh, Robert. "Literature in the Cowboy State." *Wyoming News* 3 (1978): 29-30.

Conrad Schwiering Biographical File. American Heritage Center, University of Wyoming.

Starr, Eileen. *Architecture in the Cowboy State, 1849-1940.* Glendo: High Plains Press,

Stimson, J.E. *Treasures of Wyoming: J.E. Stimson, 1870-1952.* Cheyenne, Wyoming State Museum, 1995.

J.E. Stimson Biographical File. American Heritage Center, University of Wyoming.

University of Wyoming Art Museum. *Towards Diversity: Exhibition of Work By the Faculty of the Art Department, University of Wyoming.* Laramie: Spring, 1980.

Vinson, James, ed. *Twentieth Century Writers.* Detroit: Gale Research, 1982.

Wakefield, Robert. *Schwiering and the West.* Aberdeen, South Dakota: High Plains Press, 1973.

Whitehill, Sharon. *The Life and Work of Mary O'Hara, Author of My Friend Flicka.* Lewiston, NY: Edwin Millen Press, 1995.

CHAPTER FIVE

Thurman Arnold Biographical File. American Heritage Center, University of Wyoming.

Thurman Arnold *Citizen of the Century Nomination.* American Heritage Center, University of Wyoming.

Thurman Arnold Papers. American Heritage Center, University of Wyoming.

Debra Baker Beck. "Law Prepared Sullivan Well For Political Service." *University of Wyoming AlumNews.* September, 1998.

Glen Barrett Collection. American Heritage Center, University of Wyoming.

Tom Bell Biographical File. American Heritage Center, University of Wyoming.

Tom Bell Citizen of the Century Nomination. American Heritage Center, University of Wyoming.

Fred Blume Biographical File. American Heritage Center, University of Wyoming.

Fred Blume Citizen of the Century Nomination. American Heritage Center, University of Wyoming.

Chamblin, Thomas, ed. *The Historical Encyclopedia of Wyoming.* Cheyenne: Wyoming Historical Institute, 1970.

Dick Cheney Biographical File. American Heritage Center, University of Wyoming.

Dick Cheney Citizen of the Century Nomination. American Heritage Center, University of Wyoming.

Loretta Fowler. *Arapahoe Politics: Symbols in Crises of Authority.* Lincoln: University of Nebraska Press, 1982.

Georgen, Cynde. *One Cowboy's Dream: John B. Kendrick: His Family, Home & Ranching Empire.* Sheridan: Trail End Guilds, 1995.

"The Hallmark of Wyoming Politics." *Wyoming State Tribune.* April 28, 1960.

Cliff Hansen Biographical File. American Heritage Center, University of Wyoming.

Cliff Hansen Citizen of the Century Nomination. American Heritage Center, University of Wyoming.

Ed Herschler Biographical File. American Heritage Center, University of Wyoming.

Ed Herschler Citizen of the Century Nomination. American Heritage Center, University of Wyoming.

John Kendrick Biographical File. American Heritage Center, University of Wyoming.

John Benjamin Kendrick Collection. American Heritage Center, University of Wyoming.

Larson, T.A. *History of Wyoming.* Lincoln: University of Nebraska Press, 1965.

Louise Love. Wyoming Pioneers. *Cow Country.* Vol 80. 15 September 1952.

"Mrs. Susan Quealy." *Casper Tribune Herald.* 18 May 1945.

Carl Moore. "Joseph Christopher O'Mahoney: A Brief Biography." *Annals of Wyoming.* October, 1969.

Murie, Margaret E. *Two in the Far North.* Anchorage: Alaska Northwest Publishing Co., 1978.

Margaret Murie Biographical File. American Heritage Center, University of Wyoming.

Olaus & Margaret Murie Papers. American Heritage Center, University of Wyoming

Joseph O'Mahoney Biographical File. American Heritage Center, University of Wyoming.

"Output Kemmerer Coal Company to High." *Wyoming Eagle.* July 30, 1943.

Susan Jane Quealy Citizen of the Century Nomination. American Heritage Center, University of Wyoming.

Teno Roncalio. "The Century Old Grouch." *Wyoming Blue Book.* Volume IV.

Nellie Tayloe Ross Biographical File. American Heritage Center, University of Wyoming.

Nellie Tayloe Ross Papers. American Heritage Center, University of Wyoming.

Alan Simpson Biographical File. American Heritage Center, University of Wyoming.

Alan Simpson Citizen of the Century Nomination. American Heritage Center, University of Wyoming.

Thomas Stroock Biographical File. American Heritage Center, University of Wyoming.

Thomas Stroock Citizen of the Century Nomination. American Heritage Center, University of Wyoming.

Michael Sullivan Biographical File. American Heritage Center, University of Wyoming.

Michael Sullivan Citizen of the Century Nomination. American Heritage Center, University of Wyoming.

F.E. Warren Biographical File. American Heritage Center, University of Wyoming.

Joe Watt Biographical File. American Heritage Center, University of Wyoming.

Joe Watt Citizen of the Century Nomination. American Heritage Center, University of Wyoming.

CHAPTER SIX

Barker, William. "Skinned Alive Every Year." *Rocky Mountain Empire Magazine,* July 30, 1950: 41-44.

Francis Barrett Citizen of the Century Nomination. American Heritage Center, University of Wyoming.

O.A. Beath Biographical File. American Heritage Center, University of Wyoming.

O.A. Beath Collection. American Heritage Center, University of Wyoming.

Chamblin, Thomas, ed. (1970). *The Historical Encyclopedia of Wyoming.* Cheyenne: Wyoming Historical Institute.

June Etta Downey Biographical File. American Heritage Center, University of Wyoming.

George P. Johnston Biographical File. American Heritage Center, University of Wyoming.

George P. Johnston File. Wyoming State Archives, Cheyenne.

John David Love Biographical File. American Heritage Center, University of Wyoming.

Samuel Howell Knight Biographical File. American Heritage Center, University of Wyoming.

Samuel Howell Knight Citizen of the Century Nomination. American Heritage Center, University of Wyoming. Submitted by Frederick W. & JoAnn B. Reckling.

Aven Nelson Biographical File. American Heritage Center, University of Wyoming.

Walter E. Reckling Biographical File. American Heritage Center, University of Wyoming.

Walter E. Reckling Citizen of the Century Nomination. American Heritage Center, University of Wyoming.

Sara Jane Rhoads Biographical File. American Heritage Center, University of Wyoming.

Sara Jane Rhoads Collection. University of Wyoming Archives, American Heritage Center, University of Wyoming.

Roberts, Phil and Roberts, David and Roberts, Steven. (1996). Wyoming Almanac. (4th ed.) Laramie: Skyline Press.

Williams, Roger Lawrence. *Aven Nelson of Wyoming.* Boulder, Colorado Associated University Press, 1984.

Wheeler, Marilyn Margaret. *The Rocky Mountain Herbarium and Its Founder.* Laramie: 1949.

CHAPTER SEVEN

Vernon Joseph Baker Citizen of the Century Nomination. American Heritage Center, University of Wyoming.

Roy E. Cooper Citizen of the Century Nomination. American Heritage Center, University of Wyoming.

"General R.L. Esmay Dies at 67" *Wyoming State Tribune,* November 13, 1965, p. 1.

Gould, Lewis L. *Wyoming: From Territory to Statehood.* Worland, High Plains Publishing Company, 1989.

"Guard Armory Dedicated to an Exceptional Soldier" *Sheridan Press,* August 20, 1990, p. 1.

Emory Scott Land Biography File. American Heritage Center. University of Wyoming.

Larson, T.A. *History of Wyoming.* Lincoln: University of Nebraska Press, 1965.

Francis X. McInerney Citizen of the Century Nomination. American Heritage Center, University of Wyoming.

George Oliver Pearson Citizen of the Century Nomination. American Heritage Center, University of Wyoming.

"Quiet General George Pearson Made Big Noise in His Day" *Sheridan Press,* August 19, 1990, p. 1, 11.

Samuel C. Phillips Biography File. American Heritage Center. University of Wyoming.

Peter Jan Schoomaker Citizen of the Century Nomination. American Heritage Center, University of Wyoming.

Francis E. Warren Biography File. American Heritage Center. University of Wyoming.

CHAPTER EIGHT

Brown, Mabel. Inga and Harry. Casper: Black Hills Bentonite, 1995.

Chamblin, Thomas, ed. (1970). *The Historical Encyclopedia of Wyoming.* Cheyenne: Wyoming Historical Institute.

Fred Goodstein Biography File. American Heritage Center, University of Wyoming.

Larson, T.A. *History of Wyoming.* Lincoln: University of Nebraska Press, 1965.

Robert Peck Citizen of the Century Nomination. American Heritage Center, University of Wyoming.

Roy Peck Biography File. American Heritage Center, University of Wyoming.

C.B. Richardson Biography File. American Heritage Center, University of Wyoming.

Paul Stock Biography File. American Heritage Center, University of Wyoming.

Harry Thorson Biography File. American Heritage Center, University of Wyoming.

John Wold Biography File. American Heritage Center, University of Wyoming.

John Wold Citizen of the Century Nomination. American Heritage Center, University of Wyoming.

CHAPTER NINE

Sister Clementina Citizen of the Century Nomination. American Heritage Center, University of Wyoming.

O.R. Delmar Citizen of the Century Nomination. American Heritage Center, University of Wyoming.

James Hartmann Citizen of the Century Nomination. American Heritage Center, University of Wyoming.

Pius Moss Citizen of the Century Nomination. American Heritage Center, University of Wyoming.

Hubert Newell Citizen of the Century Nomination. American Heritage Center, University of Wyoming.

John Roberts Biography File. American Heritage Center.

John Roberts Collection. American Heritage Center.

Ernest Sun Rhodes Citizen of the Century Nomination. American Heritage Center, University of Wyoming.

The Wind River Rendevouz. Volume XIV, July/August/September, 1984. No. 3.

The Wind River Rendevouz. Volume XXI, July/August/September, 1991. No. 3.

The Wind River Rendevouz. Volume XXVIII, July/August/September, 1998. No. 3.

Father Jerome Zummach Citizen of the Century Nomination. American Heritage Center, University of Wyoming

CHAPTER TEN

Larry Birleffi Biography File. American Heritage Center, University of Wyoming.

Larry Birleffi Citizen of the Century Nomination. American Heritage Center, University of Wyoming.

Keith Bloom Citizen of the Century Nomination. American Heritage Center, University of Wyoming.

John Corbett Citizen of the Century Nomination. American Heritage Center, University of Wyoming.

Curt Gowdy Biography File. American Heritage Center, University of Wyoming.

Glen Jacoby Biography File. American Heritage Center, University of Wyoming.

Lew Roney Citizen of the Century Nomination. American Heritage Center, University of Wyoming.

Kenny Sailors Citizen of the Century Nomination. American Heritage Center, University of Wyoming.

Ev Shelton Biography File. American Heritage Center, University of Wyoming.

Milward Simpson Biography File. American Heritage Center, University of Wyoming.

Bill Strannigan Citizen of the Century Nomination. American Heritage Center, University of Wyoming.

CITIZEN OF THE CENTURY NOMINEES

The Wyoming Citizen of the Century Council acknowledges all nominees for Citizen of the Century:

AGRICULTURE
Mr. S.M. Covey
Ms. Katherine
  Louise Edwards
Mr. Duncan Grant
Ms. Annie Mary
  McKenzie Hines
Mr. Manville Kendrick
Mr. Ken Kirkbride
Mr. Lester Maxfield
Hon. James Mickelson
Hon. Dean Prosser Jr.
Mrs. Susan Jane Quealy
Mr. H.A. "Dave" True, Jr.
Mr. Jack Tracy Turnell

BUSINESS
Hon. Joseph M. Carey
Mr. S.M. Covey
Mr. C. Edwards Deming
Mr. Fred Goodstein
Mr. Manville Kendrick
Hon. Clarene Law
Mr. Glenn Nielson
Mr. Frank Norris Jr.
Mr. J.C. Penney
Hon. Pat Quealy II
Mrs. Susan Jane Quealy
Lt. Col. Hardy V. Ratcliff
Mr. Newell Brush Sargent
Mr. Homer Scott Sr.
Mr. Harry Sinclair
Hon. Thomas F. Stroock
Ms. Clara Toppan
Mr. H.A. "Dave" True, Jr.
Hon. Francis E. Warren
Mr. Bud Webster

EDUCATION
Dr. Francis A. Barrett
Mr. Thomas Bell
Donald L. Blackstone, Jr., Ph.D.
Mrs. Mabel Brown
Dr. George C. Frison
Mr. Harold William Garrett
Grace Raymond Hebard, Ph.D.
George Duke Humphrey, Ph.D.
Hon. Verda James
Samuel Howell "Doc"
  Knight, Ph.D.
Hon. T.A. Larson
Ms. Charlotte Levandosky
Hon. Velma Linford
Mr. Ralph McWhinnie
Ms. Agnes Milstead
Aven Nelson, Ph.D.
Mr. Paul Novak
Hon. Mary McBeath Odde
Ms. Nancy Thomas Pajak
Mrs. Susan Jane Quealy
Ms. E. Jeanette Teller Smith
Mr. Dana Van Burgh

Laura White, Ph.D.
Mr. Karl Frederick Winchell

FINE & PERFORMING ARTS
Mr. James Bama
Mr. Charles Josiah Belden
Mr. James Boyle
Ms. Katherine Burt
Col. William Frederick Cody
Mrs. Peggy Simson Curry
Mr. William Robert Dubois
Mr. Nick Eggenhoffer
Mr. Bill Gollings
Mr. Wilbur Hitchcock
Mr. William H. Jackson
Samuel Howell "Doc"
  Knight, Ph.D.
Ms. Caroline Lockhart
Ms. Mary O'Hara Alsop
Mr. Jerry Joseph Palen
Ms. Lucille Nichols Patrick
Mr. Jackson Pollack
Mrs. Susan Jane Quealy
Mr. Robert Russin
Mr. Conrad Schwiering
Ms. Elinore Pruitt Stewart
Mr. Joseph Elam Stimson
Ms. Mae Urbanek

GOVERNMENT & COMMUNITY SERVICE
Hon. Thurman Arnold
Mrs. Helen Louise Bardo
Mr. Dale Marine Bardo
Mr. Tom Bell
Mr. Loren Clark Bishop
Hon. Freidrich Heinrich
  Blume
Mrs. Mabel Brown
Lt. Col. Henry Burgess
Hon. Elizabeth Byrd
Mr. James Byrd
Hon. Joseph M. Carey
Hon. Robert Carey
Dr. Oliver Chambers
Hon. Richard Cheney
Mr. Winfield Collins
Mr. William Chapin Deming
Hon. Frank Emerson
Mr. Leon Graffen Flannery
Ms. Johanna Gostas
Hon. Harry Scott Harnsberger
Hon. Clifford Hansen
Hon. Stanley Knapp Hathaway
Hon. Edgar Herschler
Hon. Joseph Hickey
Hon. Lester Hunt
Hon. John Benjamin Kendrick
Hon. Gale McGee
Mr. Elwood Mead
Hon. Leslie Miller

Hon. Frank W. Mondell
Ms. Margaret Murie
Mr. Olaus Murie
Mr. Frank Norris, Jr.
Hon. Joseph O'Mahoney
Hon. Glenn Sherrow Parker
Hon. Robert Peck
Mrs. Susan Jane Quealy
Dr. Walter Ervin Reckling
Hon. John Riner
Hon. Teno Roncalio
Hon. Nellie Tayloe Ross
Mr. Newell Brush Sargent
Ms. Sandy Gail Higgins
  Shuptrine
Hon. Alan K. Simpson
Hon. Milward L. Simpson
Hon. Thomas F. Stroock
Hon. Michael John Sullivan
Mr. Tosh Suyematsu
Hon. Keith Thomson
Hon. Thyra Thomson
Hon. Willis Van Devanter
Hon. Malcolm Wallop
Hon. Francis E. Warren
Mr. Joe H. Watt
Chief Yellow Calf

HEALTHCARE, SCIENCE & TECHNOLOGY
Dr. Francis A. Barrett
Orville A. Beath, Ph.D.
Dr. C. Dana Carter
Dr. Oliver Chambers
June Etta Downey, Ph.D.
George C. Frison, Ph.D.
Dr. George P. Johnston
Samuel Howell "Doc"
  Knight, Ph.D.
John David Love, Ph.D.
Dr. Don MacLeod
Aven Nelson, Ph.D.
Ms. Nancy Thomas Pajak
Dr. Frederick Wood Phifer
Rebecca Raulins, Ph.D.
Dr. Walter Ervin Reckling Sr.
Sara Jane Rhoads, Ph.D.
Ms. Lucile Wright

MILITARY
Maj. William Edward Adams
Lieutenant Vernon Joseph
  Baker
Lt. Col. Henry Burgess
Sgt. Charles Frances Carey, Jr.
Brig. Gen. Roy E. Cooper
Capt. Walter Edward Doyle
Adj. Gen. Rhodolph L. Esmay
Hon. Stanley Knapp
  Hathaway
Hon. Edgar Herschler
Vice Adm. Emory Land

Vice Adm. Francis Xavier
  McInerney
Major General George Pearson
Gen. Samuel C. Phillips
Gen. Peter Schoomaker
Brig. Gen. Robert Reed Scott
Hon. Francis Emory Warren

MINERALS, OIL & GAS
Mr. Fred Goodstein
Mr. Cy Iba
Samuel Howell "Doc"
  Knight, Ph.D.
Mr. Glenn Nielson
Hon. Robert Peck
Hon. Roy Peck
Hon. Pat Quealy II
Mrs. Susan Jane Quealy
Mr. C.B. Richardson
Mr. Paul Stock
Mr. Harry Thorson
Mr. H.A. "Dave" True, Jr.
Hon. John S. Wold

RELIGION
Rev. Sherman Coolidge
Brother Benny Delmar
Mr. Scott Dewey
Mr. Ben Friday
Rev. W.B.D. Gray
Msgr. James Hartmann
Mr. Paul Hoffer
Mr. Pius Moss
Bishop Hubert Michael Newell
Rev. John McClure Pattison
Ms. Margaret Prine
Mr. Ernest Sun Rhodes
Rev. John Roberts
Ms. Nelly Scott
Sister Clementina
Mr. Anthony Sitting Eagle
Rev. Eugene Todd
Chief Yellow Calf
Father Jerome Zumach

SPORTS
Mr. Larry Birleffi
Mr. Keith Bloom
Mr. John "Coach" Corbett
Mr. Lloyd Eaton
Mr. Curt Gowdy
Mr. Glenn "Red" Jacoby
Mr. Layne Kopischka
Mr. Everett Lantz
Mr. H.T. "Ted" Neuman
Mr. Jay Novacek
Mr. Lew Roney
Mr. Kenny Sailors
Mr. Everett Shelton
Hon. Milward Simpson
Mr. Bill Strannigan

PARTNERS INDEX

Advanced Computers..289

AIA Wyoming, A Chapter of the American Institute of
Architects...240

American Heritage Center.......................................245

American National Bank..179

Big Horn Federal...186

Bighorn Airways..224

Black Hills Bentonite..216

Blue Cross Blue Shield of Wyoming.........................248

BP Amoco...229

Buffalo Bill Historical Center...................................266

Cheyenne Frontier Days..278

Cheyenne Light, Fuel and Power Company.................220

Cheyenne VA Medical Center/Cheyenne VA Regional
Office..253

Church of Jesus Christ of Latter-day Saints, The........250

Coliseum Motors & Big Wyoming.............................202

Crum Electric Supply Co...195

Eastridge Autoplex..205

Ed Murray & Sons..188

Elk Country Motels, Inc...279

Exxon Company, U.S.A..230

First Interstate Bank..183

Fleischli Oil Company, Inc.......................................238

Fowler & Peth...177

Gorder|South Group Architects................................242

Halladay Motors, Inc..210

Hillcrest Spring Water..218

Hilltop National Bank...190

Hitching Post Inn...280

Holly Sugar...170

Hotel Wolf..281

Kemmerer Legacy, The...254

Kennedy-Western University....................................256

Lathrop & Rutledge..244

Lost Creek Ranch & Spa...282

Marathon Oil Company...239

Martin-Harris Gallery...267

McMurry Oil..232

National Museum of Wildlife Art..............................268

National Outdoor Leadership School.........................269

Natrona County School Employees Federal Credit
Union..194

Norwest Bank...192

Old Baldy Club..283

Parkway Plaza Hotel..284

Petroleum Association of Wyoming..........................228

Powder Horn Ranch and Golf Club, L.L.C., The...........285

Questar Corporation..219

RAG Coal West, Inc..213

Reiman Corp...178

SafeCard..193

Saratoga Inn Resort and Hot Springs Spa.................286

Sheridan VA Medical Center....................................252

Sierra Trading Post..206

Sinclair Oil Corporation/Holding's Little America........276

Solvay Minerals, Inc...214

Spradley Motors, Inc..211

Spring Creek Ranch..287

Taco John's International, Inc...................................208

Teton County and Town of Jackson..........................258

True Companies...234

Ucross Foundation...271

Unicover Corporation...196

UniLink Software...290

Union Telephone Company......................................292

United Bancorporation of Wyoming, Inc....................180

United Medical Center..273

University of Wyoming..262

Vision Graphics, Inc...199

Warren Live Stock Company....................................172

Waterworks Industries Inc......................................200

Webster Chevrolet...212

Westech/Wotco..201

Willow Creek Ranch At The Hole-In-The-Wall, The......174

Wold Companies, The...236

Wort Hotel, The...288

Wyodak Coal...217

Wyoming Business Alliance/Wyoming Heritage
Foundation...246

Wyoming Business Council......................................270

Wyoming Game and Fish Department.......................272

Wyoming Machinery Company.................................198

Wyoming Medical Center..264

Wyoming Newspaper Group....................................226

Wyoming State Historical Society.............................274

Wyoming Stock Growers Association.........................176

Wyoming: A 20th Century History of its Citizens, Businesses and Institutions

303